de HAVILLAND

IN CANADA

de HAVILLAND
IN CANADA

FRED W. HOTSON

CANAV Books

Front endpaper: Views of the latest version of the world famous Dash 8 regional airliner series, the Q400. The first examples were delivered in 1999. (Bombardier)

Back endpaper: A Gordon Bain portrait of a de Havilland classic — the D.H.83C Fox Moth. Watt Martin built this example from various original components and ones that he manufactured in his shop. Here CF-DJB was being flown by George Neal. Today it may be seen in Canada's National Aviation Museum in Ottawa.

Half title page: RCAF Chipmunk 18060 at a 1960s Goderich, Ontario, fly-in. Its UM code letters show that it was based nearby at RCAF Station

Centralia. Later this Chipmunk became CF-BKN, then was sold in the U.S. (Jack McNulty)

Title page: The D.H.60 Moth, first flown in 1925 by Geoffrey de Havilland, became the backbone of Canada's flying club organization, RCAF pilot training, and bush operations. In 1962 DHC test pilot George A. Neal purchased this D.H.60G Moth in the UK, registering it in Canada in honour of Canada's original (1929) CF-AAA. After flying his Moth for several years, George sold it to Watt T. Martin, who kept it airworthy into the 21st Century. Gordon Bain of England took this photo of CF-AAA, flown by Watt, near Milton, Ontario in the 1990s.

The RCAF takes over the first production run of DHC-5 Buffalo aircraft in 1967. (DHC28856)

Canadian Cataloguing in Publication Data

Hotson, Fred W., 1913–
    De Havilland in Canada

Includes bibliographical references and index.
ISBN 0-921022-10-7

1. De Havilland Aircraft of Canada, Limited – History. I. Title.

HD9711.C34D45 1998   338.7'62913334'0971   C98-931001-9

Design: Robin Brass Studio, Toronto
Cover art: Tom Bjarnason, Port Hope, Ontario
Photo retouching: Stephen Ng/ML Studio, Toronto
Proofreading: Ralph Clint, Colin Fisher, Robert G. Halford, Julie
    Hanson, Larry Milberry, Bill Perry

Printed and bound in Canada by Friesen Printers Ltd., Altona, Manitoba

Published by
CANAV Books
Larry Milberry, publisher
51 Balsam Avenue
Toronto, Ontario M4E 3B6
Canada

CONTENTS

Global Express serial No. 9004 makes its first flight from Downsview on September 8, 1997. Soon it was at the Bombardier Flight Test Center in Wichita, where it joined the first three aircraft in certification flying. For this program, No. 9004 was designated the function and reliability test aircraft. Transport Canada type approval was obtained on July 31, 1998, with the FAA and JAA certification by the end of the year. (DH)

Six LAN-Chile Twin Otters in a pre-delivery photo session over southern Ontario in February 1974. (Bombardier Aerospace 39607)

FOREWORD

Beginning with the famous Vedette flying boat of 1924, Canada is renowned for its indigenous aircraft. Of all its historic aviation companies, however, one stands out for its reputation, not just at home, but around the world – de Havilland Canada. With this book we are proud to present its full story.

Only a qualified author can produce a worthy book. In this case, there could not have been a better man to do the job. After all, Fred Hotson has been following the de Havilland Canada story since he was a boy in the 1920s. He attended airshows, built model airplanes, took pictures and clipped every newspaper report he spotted about de Havilland. In 1928 he took his first flight, fittingly, in a D.H. Cirrus Moth. The association didn't stop there, for he went to work at DHC, where he had the chance to associate with all the key people.

Fred begins his story with the British parent company's decision to launch its line of Moths in Canada. He explains how DHC evolved, surviving the worst of economic calamities, then booming through the Second World War. More difficulties lay ahead, but DHC surmounted them and from time to time could revel in a new triumph. Once you start turning the pages, you will be engrossed in all the details.

Ultimately, the book is about creative people dedicated to the art of aircraft design and production. Illustrating this, Fred describes how the Beaver and Otter put DHC on the postwar map. Any operator needing a light, rugged transport knew where to turn. Beavers and Otters spread quickly around the world, followed, in due course, by their successors.

The proof of DHC's success lies not just in archival reports but in the proven value of its products. After a half century, hundreds of Beavers and Otters are still flying. Whether doing agricultural work in Australia, supplying mines or forestry camps in Canada, or serving fishing resorts in Alaska, these superb bushplanes seem to fly on forever.

Then, there are the latest products. Today the company flies under the banner of Canada's leading aircraft manufacturer, Bombardier Aerospace. The future is bright. The famous plant, from where Tiger Moths and Beavers once flew, now produces the world-class Dash 8 commuter airliner and the advanced Global Express business jet. Yet, historic DHC is not forgotten. Although its famous logo no longer flies over head office at Downsview, its accomplishments have long since become an indelible part of Canada's flying heritage.

LARRY MILBERRY, PUBLISHER

RCAF No. 3673, the 28th Otter, was delivered in January 1954. It served in search and rescue, and transport with units in Nova Scotia, Manitoba and Ontario until retiring. In 1998 it was C-FSVP of Northern Lights Air Service in Goose Bay. Here it's shown on amphibious floats. (Rodger Chapman)

INTRODUCTION

The story of this book dates to 1978, when I was asked to join the committee for de Havilland Canada's 50th anniversary year. As a committee member, I prepared a booklet covering the company's history. Ten years later I became involved again, this time with DHC's 60th anniversary, working with *Canadian Aviation* magazine on a special issue that went to all employees. In the meantime, *The de Havilland Canada Story* was published by CANAV Books for the rollout of the Dash 8. Early in 1997, Bombardier asked that our earlier material be updated to coincide with de Havilland's 70th anniversary.

My own connection with the company goes back to 1932 when I wrote as a schoolboy asking for employment. I received a letter explaining that there were no jobs – those were depression years. My next contact was in December 1935, when I was chosen from the graduating class of Central Technical School to join the work force at Downsview. The wages were 25 cents an hour, which looked wonderful at the time.

The next five years were exhilarating, as we worked on everything from the small Moths to twin-engine Rapides, learning our trade through discipline and long hours. Lee Murray was a combination of managing director, chief engineer and chief pilot. W.R. "Bill" Calder held the reins as works manager on the shop floor. The man in the upper office guiding company finances was secretary-treasurer George Mickleborough. Bruce Douglas and Don Long comprised the engineering team.

George Blanchard, John Slaughter, Harry Proctor, Ab and Frank Warren, Russ Borrett, Harry Beffort, John Neal and Walter Rinaldo were the senior work force at the time. In the fabric shop were Hilda Currell, the McNichol sisters (Betty and Rhoda), Lou Thorpe and Ethyl Almond. This era was not noted for big paycheques, but what we lacked financially was made up for by the knowledge that we were part of the growing aviation scene.

At the outbreak of war, I moved to active flying, which took me far from the time clock at de Havilland. I left with the blessing of manager Phil Garratt, but by the time I rejoined the company in 1967, he had retired. I was not returning as a stranger, however, for I had always kept in touch with my friends at de Havilland. My return to Flight Test provided new associations that continued until my retirement from the sales engineering department.

These events provided the background for the 50th anniversary publication, which happened to coincide with my retirement year. It set the scene for a talk months later with our new president, John Sandford. He encouraged me to continue my research, working towards a larger edition. There was co-operation from all quarters, for everyone agreed that the history of de Havilland Canada should be told in greater depth.

No effort has been made here to duplicate existing good works covering the de Havilland England years. Such writers as Martin Sharp, A.J. Jackson, K.M. Molson, H.A. Taylor and Sir Geoffrey de Havilland himself have covered that topic. This book is about the thousands of Canadians who carried the original de Havilland tradition of excellence and made it grow over 70 years. I have also tried to relate the impact of company products on world transport, and to give fair coverage to each de Havilland Canada design.

Everyone will agree that there is so much more to be told. We couldn't possibly squeeze it all into one book – the people stories behind each major project, the worldwide aspect of the job, the travels, the good times and the bad. It is fortunate that we have Bert Ellis' compilation of personal recollections in *de Havilland You STOL My Heart Away* to fill that gap.

As this is my third such history, the number of people assisting has grown. I have had help from many sources and would like to acknowledge them here, from John Sandford and his original request to the continued interest in our his-

The prototype Turbo Beaver during float trials in Toronto Harbour. After a long career as a DHC demonstrator, it was donated to the Canadian Bushplane Heritage Centre in Sault Ste. Marie. (DH)

tory by Bombardier Aerospace. The research goes back to the years when I collaborated with the late Don Long in gathering de Havilland Canada historical material. He left his writings and photographs in my custody and I have used them here to advantage.

It is a new world within the company since the last book was written, and a new generation is carrying the torch. My thanks go out to all who fielded my questions and, as before, to the photographic department, which came through with prompt co-operation. A special thanks goes to my former colleague, John Shaw, who took the time to read manuscript and discuss the highs and lows of our company history. A sincere acknowledgement to the Bombardier side of our team, Colin Fisher, Julie Hanson and Bill Perry, who not only supplied information, but kept the project on track.

Of special interest in this edition are the photographs and detailed captions put together by CANAV Books publisher Larry Milberry. Once again, tight deadlines, particularly

with design and assembly under Robin Brass, tested our abilities. Larry and Robin worked miracles in getting the book to the printer. Others to thank include:

Peter Adams, Gary Aldred, Len Appleyard, Blake Arnold, Bob Arnold, Jean-Marie Arseneault, Chris Austin, Ernest Ball, Lenn Bayliss, Richard Beaudet, Russ Bannock, Dick Becker, Harry Beffort, Sheldon Benner, Bruce Best, Philip Birtles, George Blanchard, Bill Boggs, Lou Thorpe Borrett, Russ Borrett, Bill Bozanin, Bob Bradford, Mackenzie Brown, Charles Bryant, Buck Buchanan, Fred Buller, Bill Burlison, Alan Butler, Jack Charleson, Andy Clancy, Andrew H. Cline, Ralph Clint, Reg Corlett, Maurice Crawford, George Cull, John Cunningham, Waclaw Czerwinski, Mike Davy, Norm Davis, Bill de Creeft, Fred de Jersey, Ray Decorby, Punch Dickins, Alex Downey, Bill Duck, Ed Dukes, Bill Etherington, Betty Ewens, Ewan Fallow, Robert Fear, Dennis Field, Pat Fillingham, Colin Fisher, Mich Found, Bob Fowler, Joe Fugere, Paddy Gardiner, Jessie

Garratt, Phil Garratt, John Garratt, André Gaudet, George Georgas, Ian Gilchrist, Paul Giles, Dick Gleasure, R. Gobalian, Bruce Goddard, Geoff Goodall, Bartlett Gould, Andy Graham, John Griffin, Bob Halford, Phil Halsey, George W. Hamlin, Fred Hamm, Jack Hayes, Bill Heaslip, Anton Heumann, Dick Hiscocks, Tony Honeywood, Marg Hotson, Bill Hotson, Bill Houston, Richard Hulina, George Hurren, Ruben Husberg, Kenji Ikegami, Ron Jackson, Ted Johnson, Terry Judge, Peter Keating, Tim Kelly, John Kimberley, Ben Knowles, Enid Koyle, Howard Levy, Z. Lewis Leigh, Guy Levesque, John Loader, George Lucas, George Luesby, David C. MacKenzie, Jim Maitre, Al Martin, Peter Martin, Watt Martin, Shirley Matthews, Bill Matthews, Bob McIntyre, Jack McNulty, Pierre Meagher, Norm Merrin, George Mickleborough, Dick Moffett, Ken

New Zealand's original Antarctic Beaver, NZ6001, shown on p.160, served on the frozen continent in the 1950s. There it crashed and remains to this day. To commemorate this famous Beaver, the RNZAF obtained ZK-CMU, a former crop duster, painted it to represent NZ6001, and displayed it at Airforce World in Christchurch. Later, some warbird enthusiasts repainted ZK-CKH as NZ6001. Lenn Bayliss photographed it in its splendour at RNZAF Ohakea on North Island in March 1998.

A classic Richard Hulina photo showing Beaver C-GMGD getting away on skis from Sioux Lookout, Ontario. Bernie Cox, owner of Pickle Lake-based North Star Air, was at the controls.

Molson, Sab Morita, John Morrison, T. Mowatt, Don Murray, Kay Neal, John Neal, George Neal, Tom Nettleton, Ron Nunney, Anita Paalanen, Cathy Parsons, Joël Paul, George Phillips, Harry Proctor, Bob Prout, Rick Radell, Mark A. Rattiner, George Robinson, Robbie Robinson, Donna Rodrigues, Frank Russell, Terry Rawlins, Mick Saunders, Gordon Schwartz, Terry Schwetz, John Scott, Martin Sharp, John Shaw, Bill Shaylor, Fred Shortt, John Slaughter, Richard K. Smith, Charlie Smith, Walter Smook, Fred Smye, Steve Snider, Bill Somerville, Frank Stanley, Jan Stroomenbergh, Kenneth I. Swartz, John W.R. Taylor, Henry Tenby, Bill Terwissen, Dave Thompson, Arthur Toplis, Len Trotter, Harry Umphrey, Mike and Tony Valenti, Georges Van Belleghem, Pierre Verhelst, Tony Verrico, Gary Vincent, Terry Waddington, Brent Wallace, Max Ward, Ab Warren, Frank Warren, Don Whittley, Gordon S. Williams, Gerry Wooll.

FRED W. HOTSON

Dash 8-100 LN-ILS (serial No. 396) of Luftfartsverket, the Norwegian government's airways calibration unit, has been based in Oslo since 1995. (DH 95-0281B7)

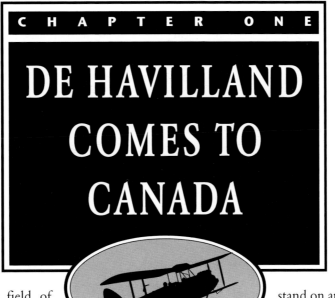

CHAPTER ONE

DE HAVILLAND COMES TO CANADA

The enthusiast who seeks to walk the hallowed ground of Toronto history need go no farther than Trethewey Drive in the suburb of Weston. No monument marks this level plot of ground, once known as the Trethewey farm, but the present housing development forms an historic link with the city's aviation past. A quiet walk around Hearst Circle will cover the centre field of Toronto's earliest flying display, the first ever held in Ontario.

A group of touring aviators with Wright and Bleriot machines arrived at the farm on July 8, 1910, under the auspices of the Ontario Motor League to stage a nine-day show. Count Jacques de Lesseps from France was the star performer in Bleriot XI monoplanes, while the Wright Company team of Ralph Johnstone, D. Chapelle and F.T. Coffyn flew a Wright biplane. Not every flight was a success. On July 12 de Lesseps made only one flight and John Stratton crashed attempting to fly a Bleriot owned by William Carruthers of Montreal.

The highlight of the week-long event came on July 13 when Count de Lesseps took off in his special Bleriot XI*bis* monoplane *Le Scarabée* for the first flight of a heavier-than-air machine over the heart of Toronto. Everyone realized the

historical importance of his flight and he returned to re-sounding cheers from the crowd in the special grand-stand erected for the show. The meet also provided the first occasion when two aircraft were in the air at once over Toronto.

Another walk in the same neighbourhood, down the present Westchester Street (where it meets Parkchester), will enable the visitor to stand on another site of historic interest. Admittedly it was only a wooden hangar during the years 1928-1929, but it provided employment for 30 of the local inhabitants and launched the industry that would be known for the next half century as The de Havilland Aircraft of Canada Limited. The name of de Havilland was well known in Canada long before the company established a branch in the Toronto area. Canadian pilots returning from the air battles of WWI had a deep respect for the sturdy line of de Havilland war-planes they flew in France, particularly the D.H.4 which was produced in great quantity. The D.H.4 was built under licence in the United States and was to play a part in early Canadian aviation history.

As early as 1917 a sample D.H.4 was imported to Canada for use by the University of Toronto in the ground school training of mechanics.

(Above) Count Jacques de Lesseps about to take off from Trethewey farm during the 1910 Toronto air meet. This was the first aircraft to fly over the city. (Dr. Jewell)

(Right) Ralph Johnstone flies his Wright biplane over the crowd at Mount Dennis. (James Collection, City of Toronto Archives)

(Right) The first de Havilland aircraft in Canada, a D.H.4 imported in 1917, is shown on the grounds of the University of Toronto. It was used for ground school training during WWI. (Below) The first British-designed aircraft manufactured under licence in Canada was this lone D.H.6. It was built in Toronto in 1917 by Canadian Aeroplanes Limited. (NAM, K.M. Molson Col.)

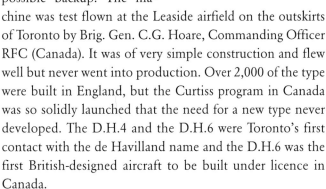

In July of that year Canadian Aeroplanes Limited, Toronto, built an all-Canadian version of a D.H.6 trainer at their plant on Strachan Avenue. Canadian Aeroplanes were in the midst of producing a huge order of Curtiss JN-4 Canucks for training purposes and built this one for the RFC (Canada) as a possible backup. The machine was test flown at the Leaside airfield on the outskirts of Toronto by Brig. Gen. C.G. Hoare, Commanding Officer RFC (Canada). It was of very simple construction and flew well but never went into production. Over 2,000 of the type were built in England, but the Curtiss program in Canada was so solidly launched that the need for a new type never developed. The D.H.4 and the D.H.6 were Toronto's first contact with the de Havilland name and the D.H.6 was the first British-designed aircraft to be built under licence in Canada.

Like many prominent designers of WWI aircraft, Major Geoffrey de Havilland spent the postwar years trying to stay in business by modifying military planes for civil use. During this difficult period, in a world still talking of war, the 37-year-old de Havilland directed his thoughts along peaceful lines. Gone were the ministry orders for weapons of destruction; it was time to turn his ambitions and those of his associates along new paths. This small group, who had continued to work under the name of Aircraft Manufacturing Co. (Airco) since the end of hostilities, banded together on September 25, 1920, to form The de Havilland Aircraft Company Limited. They established an "aerodrome and sheds" in Stag Lane in the quiet little London suburb of Edgware, Middlesex.

The early exploits of Geoffrey de Havilland and his close associate, Frank T. Hearle, show foresight mixed with practical application and determination. Hearle became manager, and those who joined the two pioneers in the formation of the DH company, displayed similar qualities of character and drive. The financial planning of the firm was securely in the hands of secretary W.E. Nixon, while C.C. Walker, as chief engineer, directed his genius for science toward aeronautics. A businessman turned salesman, F.E.N. St. Barbe, rounded out one of the most talented aviation teams of any era. Another wartime associate, A.E. Hagg, joined the group as assistant designer. No task seemed too difficult for the men of Stag Lane in the 1920s as they turned mainly to the production of single-engined planes. Their method of construction and design style became as distinctive a trademark as the company logo itself: wire-braced biplanes with a tail section as graceful as a butterfly's wing. One contract they undertook in 1924 to build a private touring aircraft proved highly beneficial for it brought Alan S. Butler into the organization.

Alan Butler

The story of Alan Butler and how he came to join de Havilland is a company legend. His contact with Canada is also important in view of his later role as the first president of de Havilland in Canada. Butler was the son of a wealthy British family and had learned to fly at the end of WWI. He bought a surplus Bristol Fighter which he had converted to civil use. The experience he gained as one of the first air tourists in Europe fired his spirit of adventure. In 1920-21 he joined with V.S. Bennett and Sydney Cotton to open the first air service in Newfoundland, using Martinsyde biplanes. On his return to England in 1921 he sought a sturdy touring aircraft and was referred to Geoffrey de Havilland through C.G. Grey, editor of *The Aeroplane*. The people at Stag Lane were pleased to discuss such a project with Butler but were a little sceptical that he would want to pay the cost involved. Their new customer not only signed the contract, but, as he was leaving that day, offered to invest in the company. The coincidence was heaven-sent because the directors were being forced to buy their aerodrome property at the time and were desperately in need of financing. The loan was accepted, the new aircraft started and Alan Butler became a member of the board of directors. He was made chairman in 1924 and served with distinction and wisdom through 28 years.

Working on Butler's machine, the D.H.37, rekindled Geoffrey de Havilland's own interest in planes for air touring. Most of the available aircraft were too big or too complex for the sport pilot. He designed the D.H.51, which was in the private owner class, but it was handicapped by a heavy war-surplus engine. It did clear up many design points for de Havilland but the lack of a proper engine in the 60 hp class was proving to be a major handicap. The next two designs were at the other end of the scale, a glider (the D.H.52) and a truly light airplane (the D.H.53 Humming Bird). They were both built for competitions and did much to provide the catalyst for the ultimate sportplane.

The next two designs involved a 12-passenger airliner and a military two-seater but these never went into production. Meanwhile de Havilland had come to a decision on his engine problem and sought the advice of his long-time colleague Major Frank B. Halford. Their careers had run parallel as far back as the D.H.3 and

Halford was now one of Britain's leading aircraft engine designers. He had joined the Aircraft Disposal Company following the war and, although still associated with the company, had been out on his own in a design capacity since 1923.

The ADC specialty was upgrading a large stock of war-surplus engines for the struggling civil market. In one typical case they had boosted an old Renault engine of 80 hp to 140 hp with such improvements as aluminum heads and overhead valves. They called it the Airdisco. The eight-cylinder, V-type, air-cooled engine was giving reliable service and provided Geoffrey de Havilland with the answer he was seeking for a small powerplant of reasonable weight.

"Why don't you take half an Airdisco," asked de Havilland, "mount it on a new crankcase and give me an engine of about 60 hp?" Halford agreed to take on the task while de Havilland went back to work designing a new airplane around this novel engine concept. With the D.H.60 design, the magic combination was achieved. The company called the new creation the Moth because of his long interest in entomology. The ADC engine that Halford produced from the Airdisco was called the Cirrus I, was rated at 60 hp, and weighed 290 lb. (132 kg).

The Moth

The D.H.60 was a scaled-down D.H.51, still with two seats, but combining all the things Geoffrey de Havilland had been planning for years: low fuel consumption, folding wings for economical storage, simple construction and moderate price. Even the name "Moth" caught on in the unexpected sales rush that followed. As with his other models, de

S/L Thomas A. Lawrence on the float of the first Cirrus Moth in Canada, *Spirit of the Valley of the Moon,* during the Hudson Strait Expedition in 1927. (NAC)

The Cirrus Moth, one of which is shown on the left, replaced the Curtiss HS-2L flying boat (right) in forestry service with the OPAS. (NAM/K.M. Molson Col.)

Havilland tested it himself on February 22, 1925. His new Moth performed flawlessly and was an instant commercial success. One of Britain's aviation visionaries, Sir Sefton Branker, saw it as the answer to Britain's sagging air strength and came up with a national flying club program. His efforts resulted in the formation of five Air Ministry-subsidized, Moth-equipped flying clubs.

As in many a success story, when the product is just right for the market, the development of the Moth turned the tide for the de Havilland organization. Not only did the little airplane catch the public imagination, but it started the flying club movement throughout the world. Additional interest was sparked by the generosity of Sir Charles Wakefield, CBE, head of the huge Castrol empire, who extended his philanthropy to a number of clubs by donating Moth trainers. The Moth began to gain world recognition on May 29, 1925, when Sir Alan J. Cobham flew from Croydon to Zurich and back in one day. Its transition to seaplane status was also simple, for Short Brothers had a set of floats designed for their Mussel which tested perfectly on the Moth in November 1926.

Australians had long been involved with de Havilland designs: the Moth looked like the answer to their great distances. Private flyers in the United States became interested enough to talk of manufacturing the Moth in that country – and then there was the growing need in Canada.

The honour of being the first of the Moth line in Canada fell to aircraft G-CAHK, which arrived in Halifax in 1927, crated, on board a ship from England. It had been purchased by the Canadian Department of Marine Fisheries and was intended as a reconnaissance seaplane for the upcoming Hudson Strait Expedition. The purpose was to study ice patterns in the shipping lanes between the proposed grain port of Churchill, on the western shore of Hudson Bay, and Europe. The high-sounding name of the Moth, *Spirit of the Valley of the Moon*, was not in keeping with the inhospitable north, but it left Halifax on July 27 on the icebreaker *Stanley*, ready for work. It served well but had a rather short career, which was recounted 44 years later to a meeting of the Canadian Aviation Historical Society by the pilot, A/V/M/ Thomas A. Lawrence, who flew it during that period:

OPAS Moths and crews on the ramp at Sault Ste. Marie. This base was ideally located on the waterfront and had one of the best overhaul and repair shops in the business. (MNR)

By the time the expedition reached Wakeham Bay on August 22, 1927, the Moth had made five survey flights in four different areas along the Hudson Strait. In 14 hours of flying, we had three base sites selected, which would have taken weeks if done by land or water. The Moth could not be taken ashore until a strip of beach was cleared of stones, which would only have been a matter of a day's work. Despite my protests, the captain of the icebreaker ordered the Moth removed from his vessel. It had to be placed at a mooring already set out for the ship's boats.

In a few hours a wind storm of gale force blew up, making all traffic between the ship, the Moth or the shore impossible. 'HK weathered the storm for some time, up to the point where it was literally flying at the mooring, when one wing went down into the water and the craft turned upside down. In a few minutes only the floats and a mass of twisted wreckage remained. The storm lasted for about four hours. Instead of being able to take a serviceable seaplane ashore by nightfall, we salvaged only the floats and engine – all because of a non-cooperative ship's captain.

Another pilot who had a good reason to investigate the Moth was Captain Roy Maxwell, colourful head of the Ontario Provincial Air Service. Maxwell's prestige in Canadian aviation stemmed from his role in protecting Ontario's valuable forest wealth. He had pioneered in forestry flying with the Laurentide Pulp and Paper Company of Grand'Mère, Quebec, and moved to Ontario as head of the new OPAS. The aircraft being used at the time for water operations were war-surplus Curtiss HS-2L flying boats, long past their prime. The aging equipment and the complexity of even getting them into the air brought about a complicated organization which Maxwell managed with all the flair of a circus ringmaster – in everything from high boots and leather jacket to a blue Cadillac roadster. He saw the Moth as a new way to patrol Ontario's forests and travelled to England to investigate its potential first-hand. His visit resulted in the purchase of four Moths on float undercarriages, which did much to whet de Havilland's appetite for export markets and convince Francis St. Barbe of the potential in Canada. This first sizeable shipment of Moths to Canada arrived at Sault Ste. Marie in crates during July 1927 and they were put into service immediately as G-CAOU, 'OV, 'OW, and 'OX. With their ability to dart from base to base carrying fire spotters and even pumps when needed, they proved a pleasant change from the big boats. The Moths flew 700 hours during their first four months of operation to the satisfaction of all concerned. Another six were ordered for delivery in 1928.

An interesting Moth arrived in Canada during 1927 as the result of a demonstration flight by Sir Alan Cobham, the famous British pilot. Cobham had done considerable testing and delivery work in England and was chosen to demonstrate the Moth in the United States. Arrangements were even then under way with a group in New York for the manufacturing rights in the U.S., so it was to be a demonstration of considerable importance. Serial number 273, which had been used in the original float tests at Shorts, was delivered by ship to New York.

In an appropriate display of showmanship, Cobham had the Moth offloaded at Sandy Hook and flew the remaining miles to New York. The sight of the tiny Moth cruising along the Hudson River waterfront and landing gracefully in the harbour caused plenty of excitement. It was later fitted with wheels for a demonstration to members of Congress before it went on tour. When number 273 finished its demonstration in the U.S. it became Canadian. J.H. Holley picked it up at Buffalo, New York, and flew it to Winnipeg, where he had it registered as G-CAIL.

Two examples of the Cirrus II Moth, designated the D.H.60X (with a split axle instead of the single crossbar), were shipped directly to Dominion Airways, Vancouver, and Western Canada Airways, Winnipeg. By the end of 1927 the number of Moths registered in Canada had grown to eight and the Canadian government was taking an active interest.

Back in 1920

Aircraft manufactured by the de Havilland Company first appeared in Canadian government records in 1920. The British government sought to promote a strong air force within the Commonwealth and sent 12 D.H.9As to Canada as Imperial Gifts. They even allocated a block of registrations from their own civil listing, starting with G-CY-. Eleven of these sturdy 9As were registered and, in a decision of great merit, one machine was reserved for spare parts. Three aircraft, G-CYAN, G-CYAJ and G-CYBF, took part in the first trans-Canada flight in 1920 from Halifax, Nova Scotia, to Vancouver, British Columbia. During the same year four U.S. Army D.H.4s built in the U.S., with American Liberty engines, flew from New York through Canada to Alaska.

In 1921 another batch of 12 aircraft arrived in Canada under the Imperial Gifts Act; this time they were D.H.4s, which were converted into D.H.4Bs and used for transport duties and forestry patrol at High River, Alberta. They were also given the G-CY- series of registrations and were not phased out of service until 1928. It has often been noted that, from the beginning of aircraft records in Canada to the present, there has never been a day without a de Havilland aircraft of one type or another in the Canadian military.

A D.H.4 with a Rolls-Royce Eagle VII engine at High River, Alberta. It shows the British style of registration adopted for use in Canada. The lettering was applied according to Air Regulations 1920.
(NAM, K.M. Molson Col.)

This ski-equipped D.H.9A was used during the last leg of the 1920 trans-Canada flight.
(NAM, K.M. Molson Col.)

The first de Havilland machine on the Canadian civil register was a D.H.9. It was bought from the Royal Air Force by a Major W.T. Blake, who registered it G-EBDF, for an ambitious round-the-world trip in 1922. He planned to fly it from Vancouver to Montreal but, when the first stage of the flight, using another D.H.9, came to grief in Calcutta, the project was cancelled and the aircraft became surplus. It was sold to Laurentide Air Service of Montreal in 1925 and based at Larder Lake. It was given the Canadian registration G-CAEU and converted to a modified '9C but had a very short life as a bushplane. It was written off on a flight from Larder Lake to Rouyn, Quebec, only 12 days after it joined the company. The pilot, C.S. Caldwell, was unhurt.

The first contact between The de Havilland Aircraft Limited in England and Canada's Department of National Defence began August 5, 1927, when a telegram was sent to England asking for information on the D.H.60 Moth. Cables went back and forth that summer on the merits of the ADC Cirrus engine and one of slightly less horsepower, the Armstrong Siddeley Genet. The correspondence was typical of government mail order shopping from 3,000 miles (4,800 km) away and quotes were asked on quantities of three, five and seven.

On November 10, 1927, J.A. Wilson, Controller of Civil Aviation in Canada, announced the purchase of the first 10 Moths for the flying clubs and wrote de Havilland in England for their policy on spare parts and service. R.A. "Bob" Loader, assistant business manager at Stag Lane, wrote back promptly that the company was "fully alive to the need for after-purchase service on these machines," and stated that, "F.E.N. St. Barbe is on his way to Canada at the time of writing, to make the necessary arrangements."

Francis St. Barbe had a busy time in Canada during December 1927, visiting all those interested in the Moth. He held a series of meetings with J.A. Wilson and various technical officers in Ottawa, where a number of decisions were finalized. The de Havilland company would establish a Canadian branch in Toronto as soon as possible.

A great deal of correspondence developed with de Havilland in England on the technical side, particularly the choice of engine. Most of the questions came from G/C J.S. Scott, W/C E.W. Stedman, W/C A. Ferrier and F/L A.E. Godfrey, indicating that the Department of National Defence was giving the Moth a critical eye for RCAF requirements. Forest conservation groups across Canada were closely watching the patrol operations in northern Ontario and evaluation in High River, Alberta, of the Dominion Airways Moth.

St. Barbe's return to England started a new round of activity at Stag Lane, where the expanding factory was trying to keep up with the mounting orders. He wrote glowingly of Canada in the *de Havilland Gazette*, describing his observations during the whirlwind tour he had just completed:

After WWI the main aircraft available for commercial, private or club flying were from war surplus stock. Especially popular was the JN-4 Canuck, built in Toronto under licence from Curtiss of the U.S. The JN-4 had equipped RFC (Canada) training schools in southern Ontario. Hundreds were available after the war at rock bottom prices. After a few years, such planes were fading fast, victims of accidents and old age. The appearance of new types like the D.H. Moth was well-timed. JN-4 G-CAEQ, seen here, was bought after the war by A.D. Goodwin of Toronto. (Thompson Col.)

In Canada you will find a set of geographical, climatic, economic and social conditions providing aviation with an ideal breeding ground. An indication of the way Canada is forging ahead comes in a report of 1926. That year was a record one for construction, for industrial development, newsprint production, mining output, agricultural produce and railway earnings. It has also come up with the largest favourable trade balance yet achieved.

Splendid openings for the speed of air transportation are everywhere and one of the most encouraging factors in the situation is the Canadian character. Coupled with a measure of good old British caution, you find a people with a big outlook, with imagination and courage. When a Canadian steps, he will step quickly with all the broad-minded enthusiasm of his enterprising nature. After the war, instead of leaving commercial concerns to influence civil aviation, the RCAF tackled the job by breaking the ground for subsequent private enterprise. The Civil Operations Branch of the RCAF is the organization breaking this new ground and is commanded by Col. J.S. Gordon. They support law enforcement, assist the native population and have done an enormous amount of aerial survey. It also has a number of machines patrolling the forest lands of Alberta, Saskatchewan and Manitoba, engaged in fire detection and suppression.

The Controller of Civil Aviation is Mr. J.A. Wilson, assisted by F/L Tom Cowley and S/L J.H. Tudhope. The year 1928 is going to show a big stride forward because of these men. One rejoices to find that Mr. Wilson is as air-minded as our own Sir Sefton Branker – that is saying a good deal – and, like Sir Sefton, he has the gift of conveying his enthusiasm to others.

One of the most important developments, which have far-reaching results, will be the establishment of flying clubs on the lines of those running so successfully here in England. Five clubs are to be started first in Toronto, Montreal, Hamilton, Winnipeg and Vancouver. These are to be followed by a further ten as soon as their constitutional arrangements have been made. The first five clubs are each being given two Moths free by the government, and for every additional machine provided by the club, the government will add a further gift one, subject to certain reasonable conditions.

Having met some of the enthusiastic ex-military pilots promoting the clubs in Montreal and Toronto, I have no doubt about the success of the club movement in any of these localities. I attach a great deal of importance to the club movement because, up to the present, there have been no facilities in Canada for cheap flying tuition. It is fairly obvious that there is a great potential for private owners.

The Flying Clubs in Canada

One of the largest orders returning to England in St. Barbe's briefcase came about as the result of a new flying club movement that was to spread across Canada. It was almost a copy of the British system, which was proving highly successful, and was described by St. Barbe in his report on Canada:

The Royal Canadian Flying Clubs Association planned to increase flying training in all the provinces. It was promoted by J.A. Wilson and backed by the Canadian government.

The Founding Year – 1928

The Canadian orders received prompt attention in England because St. Barbe realized the importance of this foothold in North America. He appointed his assistant, R.A. Loader, as general manager of the new Canadian company with instructions that it be established as soon as possible in the New Year. Bob Loader had started his aviation career as the business manager for Lep Air Services, a passenger flying group with an office in the Piccadilly section of London. When the Lep organization moved to Stag Lane in early 1920 during the formation of the de Havilland Company, Francis St. Barbe asked Loader to become his personal assistant. In this new capacity Loader became heavily involved with Moth sales outside England, including early correspondence with the Canadian government. He spent a busy January of 1928 preparing for his new assignment and set sail at the end of the month with a packet of travellers cheques in his pocket and a crate carrying two Cirrus Moths in the hold. One was G-CAJU, a gift to the newly formed Toronto Flying Club from the British enthusiast Sir Charles Wakefield, and the other was destined for the first private customer, Toronto businessman Leigh Sheppard. The ship's hold was full of products from other enterprising British firms, including boxes of billiard tables stored alongside the Moths.

Loader arrived in Toronto during the first week in February, probably the worst time of the year to go searching for a flying field. He knew that Count Jacques de Lesseps had used a field in the suburb of Mount Dennis for the first flight in the city. It had been given the unofficial name of de Lesseps Field from that day on and in 1928 was still owned by the Trethewey family. Loader found Frank L. Trethewey's office in downtown Toronto and the meeting that followed proved historic as well as fortunate for all parties. Frank Trethewey was a member of the newly-formed Toronto Flying Club and was reorganizing the family's prosperous mining business after the death of his father. On that particular day his brother-in-law, George J. Mickleborough, was in from British Columbia assisting as business manager.

Mickleborough had grown up in British Columbia and had a background in banking. Both men liked the thought of an aircraft plant on their property and drove Loader out to look over the farm. It was during their discussions on the preparation of a lease that another fortunate coincidence arose. An old produce shed, also on the Trethewey property,

The old canning shed that was de Havilland's first assembly and storage building in Canada. Part of the Trethewey property, it was across the tracks from Cobalt Street in Mount Dennis. In the interior view Cirrus Moths from England are assembled by Ernie Hedger, Arthur Robins and Frank Warren. The last alive was Frank Warren, who passed away on April 1, 1998. (Left) Robins and Warren are in the doorway. The CPR and CNR mainline tracks went by the door. (DH10708, Hotson Col.)

would shortly become available. It had a spur line off the Canadian National Railway and was only a short distance from the flying field. The meeting was successful from everyone's point of view. Trethewey saw the new Moth as a useful part of his company's prospecting business and put in his own order for an airplane. During the tour George Mickleborough became air-minded and suggested to Loader that de Havilland might soon require a business manager. Loader agreed on the spot and it was now up to Mickleborough to find someone who could take over his recently acquired title of business manager with Brett-Trethewey Mines.

Bob Loader must have been very pleased with the day's work. After sorting things out, he had acquired not only a flying field but a works shed, a business manager and an order for another Moth. What he didn't know was that the name Trethewey would play a prominent part in company activities for many years to come. Frank L. Trethewey was a native of Vancouver, a graduate of Ridley College and was attending Cambridge University in England at the outbreak of WWI. After a distinguished career as a motorcycle dispatch rider and an officer in the Royal Naval Air Service, he returned to Canada to the family mining company. Brett-Trethewey Mines was highly successful in the twenties and Trethewey senior had bought considerable property surrounding his farm on Holmsted Drive in Weston. The present Nickle and Cobalt Streets in Weston reflect the company's influence on the district. Holmsted Drive later became Trethewey Drive.

From that eventful meeting at the Trethewey farm on a cold February day, events moved quickly because more crated Moths (shipped two to a crate) were already on their way to Canada. Loader leased a small office on the 17th

TORONTO DAILY STAR
MARCH 6, 1928

WESTON

WILL MAKE 'THE MOTH' AT WORKS IN WESTON

Plant is Expected To Be Ready for Operation in Month

Special to The Star

Weston, March 6 – The de Havilland Aircraft of Canada Limited has now completed arrangements for an assembly plant and service station for their light airplane, "The Moth," at Weston. A contract has been placed for the erection of a small plant capable of expansion and it is expected that it will be completed within three or four weeks. Machines will arrive from England to be assembled at Weston, whence they will be flown to their purchasers in all parts of the dominion.

Among the first machines to be built will be the Moth which is being presented to the Toronto Flying Club by Sir Charles Wakefield, the late lord mayor of London. It is interesting to note that the airdrome at Weston, which is part of the Trethewey estate has historic associations, for it was from here that the pioneer flier, the late Count de Lesseps, made the first flight in Ontario in 1910. It was later used by the Wright brothers.

"The Moth" is a little two-seater light airplane with an engine no bigger than that of many automobiles on the streets of Toronto. It is the standard equipment of practically all the flying clubs of the world of which there are about 15 in Great Britain and by April at least half a dozen will commence operations in Canada. It is used by many private owners as they would use a motor car and also by the Ontario government air service for patrol fire protection.

floor of the Stirling Tower at 372 Bay Street in downtown Toronto, and while he was busy arranging lease documents with the Trethewey family and construction plans for a temporary hangar, lawyer William Zimmerman was engaged to formalize a corporate structure. By March 1 two leases for the building and flying field were signed. A short time later the contract was let for a temporary wooden hangar to be constructed on the southeast corner of the field.

Arthur C. Robins, a seasoned factory man, came out from Stag Lane to act as works superintendent. He took part in the preparations and was joined by a young man, Ernie Hedger, whom he had met on the boat. Together they cleaned up the old produce shed, a narrow two-storey frame building, 40 by 100 ft. (12 by 30 m), with corrugated siding. It had been used for vegetable storage in the days when Mount Dennis was a thriving agricultural area but was a most unlikely aircraft "works." One of the first moves was to have the company name placed in bold letters on the building with an even bolder advertisement for "Moth Aeroplanes." There must have been a certain amount of haste or perhaps the sign writer had a bad day, as the name on the canning shed had only one 'l' in de Havilland.

The paint on the sign was hardly dry before it brought results – the company's first Canadian employee. Frank Warren lived across the tracks from the shed and on March 31 had spent the morning in a fruitless search for work in Weston. When he arrived home to tell his mother of the disappointing news she pointed to the new sign and suggested he go over and see if there was any work to be done. He went over immediately and his timing could not have been better. The crate of Moths that had travelled across the Atlantic with Loader had just arrived on the railway siding and Warren pitched in to help with the unloading. He showed up

Aviation artist R.W. "Bob" Bradford produced many Beaver, Otter and Caribou paintings during his years with de Havilland Canada. Here is his impression of Leigh Capreol's historic flight over the company's first building. (DH46765)

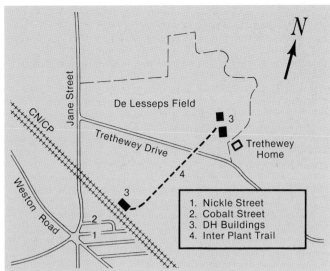

This map shows the location of the cannery shed (near the railway tracks) and the buildings put up later in 1928 (north of Trethewey Drive).

People who had much to do with de Havilland's start in Canada. At left is R.A. Loader, first general manager, who came from England to start the operation. Preparing for a trial flight is Hon. W. Finlayson, Minister of Lands and Forests for Ontario, who approved the purchase of the first four Moths for the Ontario Provincial Air Service. Beside him is the man who brought them together, Roy Maxwell, head of the OPAS. In the cockpit of Cirrus Moth G-CAPH is Leigh Capreol, the first DH Canada test pilot. (DH9649)

again the next morning to continue helping, and before the day was through, Robins had offered him a job starting the following Monday.

The company was formally incorporated under the name The de Havilland Aircraft of Canada Limited, on March 5, 1928, as a branch of the English company. A *Toronto Star* article a day later announced that construction was under way on a new hangar at Mount Dennis. The first two Moths arrived at the old canning shed on March 30 and were assembled for flight. By then, the hangar was near completion so they were moved to the airfield and flight tested on April 18. Two more Moths arrived on the 16th, which rather deflates the legend that the hangar was made of Moth crates.

Good Ontario lumber was used to build the 50 by 50-ft. (15 by 15 m) structure with a sloping roof and a set of sliding doors, just big enough to take a Moth with the wings extended. The simple frame structure was set on cement pillars and had a wooden ramp to move the planes in and out. Like the works shed it had the company name (spelled correctly) along the side and once again "Moth Aeroplanes." Two more Moths arrived on the railway siding on April 16; it was time to start the flying.

To handle the flying duties, Loader had hired an RCAF flying instructor, F/L Erskine Leigh Capreol. Leigh Capreol was born and educated in Ottawa, where he joined the Canadian Army after graduation. He served in France with the 77th, 73rd and 85th Battalions of the Canadian Expedition-

One of the first two Moths assembled by the company (G-CAJU) was the *Sir Charles Wakefield* for the Toronto Flying Club. It is shown at the club's first quarters, Leaside, Ontario, with instructor Carter Guest (left) and president Earl Hand. (NAC)

Leigh Capreol did the first flying for DHC when he tested G-CAJU and 'JW on April 18, 1928. 'JW was the first in the air and required three flights, 'JU only one. (Via Alex Downey)

ary Force until seconded to the Royal Flying Corps in 1917. He joined the Central Flying School at Upavon Downs as a flight lieutenant and while there was seriously injured in a training accident. He spent the rest of the war in hospital and did not return to Canada until 1920. He spent six years with the American Bank Note Company in Ottawa but by 1927 was back with the RCAF at Camp Borden, Ontario. He served 14 months as a flying instructor before joining de Havilland. The historic first flight from the new hangar occurred on April 18 when Capreol flew G-CAJU, the *Sir Charles Wakefield*, destined for the Toronto Flying Club. Within the hour he tested G-CAJW and followed with the new company demonstrator, G-CAJV, two days later. On another historic date, April 27, the Toronto Flying Club and Leigh Sheppard received the first two flyaway deliveries from the new Canadian company.

During the spring months George Mickleborough was busy organizing his responsibilities at the mining office so he could take over his promised job with de Havilland. He had his eye on a capable young man in the bank below the Brett-Trethewey office and, when the time was right, asked Len Appleyard if he would consider leaving the bank. Appleyard took over the business management of Trethewey's mining interests on July 26, which allowed Mickleborough to join Loader in his crowded Bay Street office. The office had room for only one large table and three chairs, enough for the two men and Mrs. E. Coates, who handled the correspondence duties. Whenever a guest arrived to discuss Moth airplanes, someone had to move into the hall.

As business grew, one door on the works shed had to be enlarged to accommodate loading from the flatcars, but there was still a problem. The long crates had to be turned at right angles on the flatcars and inched into the building with crowbars and rollers. Accurate timing was required and a certain amount of speed so that half the crate was not projecting over the active set of tracks when a train went by. Moths began arriving on the siding in ever-increasing numbers during May and June and were built up as quickly as possible to avoid congestion in the small work area. The fuselages were assembled on their undercarriages then towed, without wings, across a prepared path to the airfield. The wings followed by truck to the hangar where they were assembled and rigged for flight.

Three 1928 Cirrus Moths: G-CAKO, Saskatoon Aero Club; G-CANA, F.W. Trethewey; and G-CAJV, DHC demonstrator. The gentlemen in the photo are, left to right, L.E. Maynard, Jack Sanderson, J.H. Reid, Frank Trethewey, Leigh Sheppard, P.C. Garratt, R.A. Loader, Leigh Capreol, A.C. Robins and Frank Warren. This view also shows the temporary wooden hangar completed on April 20, 1928. It served de Havilland until September 1929. It was taken over by Frank Trethewey after the company moved to Downsview and was later destroyed by fire. (DH9642)

(Above) Deliveries from the temporary quarters at Mount Dennis included G-CAKX for the Halifax Aero Club, which used it for training on floats. A year later it was destroyed in a glassy water landing. (C.D. Long)

(Right) The second wooden hangar at Mount Dennis was designed in sections by Mathers & Haldenby. It was moved to the plant at Downsview in 1929. It was moved again during WWII and was still a part of the north complex at the time of writing. (Via G. Mickleborough)

On May 2 the first commercial Moth, G-CANS, was delivered by rail to Dominion Airways in Vancouver. Early in the month a second shipment of Moths was delivered to the Ontario Provincial Air Service at Sault Ste. Marie for assembly and they were officially entered in the Canadian register on the 11th. The first flying club Moth allotted by the government was registered to the Montreal Light Aeroplane Club on May 12. Only a small proportion of the first flood of orders went through the newly established shops at Mount Dennis. Since the Moths from England had already been test flown there, most were shipped directly to the clubs and companies outside the Toronto area.

As the number of Moths grew, so did the repair business. The small assembly hangar, which was always crowded with stored aircraft, was inadequate for the doping of fabric and when a crisis arose in the overcrowded workshop, repaired components were hauled to the unfinished Trethewey billiard room for doping operations. Larger components, such as fuselages, had to be carried in and out of the window, somewhat like coffins. This became a regular procedure until the eventual move to new quarters.

June was exceptionally busy. Seven Moths were received on the 4th, including one allotted to Frank Trethewey. Four days later his G-CANA was tested and delivered to him the same afternoon. He began taking instruction immediately, including a few "circuits and bumps" with his friend Philip C. Garratt of Allerdice & Garratt Chemicals Limited. The list of clubs, firms and private operators grew throughout the year at an even pace; by August 3 the RCAF had their first D.H.60X (with a Cirrus II engine) delivered to Camp

Borden. It did not hurt the company's financial position that first year when they received $2,000 for a flying display by Leigh Capreol at the annual Canadian National Exhibition.

The first fatality connected with company operations occurred during the first year on the tracks that ran by the assembly shed. Ed Lediard, who had only been with the company for two weeks to do moving between the two buildings, died as the result of a crossing accident when a train demolished the company truck.

As the output of Moths grew steadily through 1928, so did the need for working space. Even the Trethewey farm, which looked adequate during the early months, was becoming overcrowded. With Freddie Shaylor's Skyways Limited training school occupying the west end of the field, DHC's management realized that a new hangar and airfield would soon be needed.

The staff had grown from three to 30, sales were over the 50 mark and a substantial backlog of orders was on hand. Frank Hearle was over from England discussing the situation with Loader and they found an answer to the first of these problems. They ordered a new wooden hangar designed by Mathers & Haldenby, and had it built facing the first on the southeast corner of the Trethewey field. Their specifications showed considerable foresight: a temporary building designed in sections for easy moving.

Metal Moths

When the system of combining wood in alternate glued layers was introduced, Europeans quickly adapted this new technique to aircraft construction. The de Havilland company had always made wide use of plywood in their fuselages and used this accumulated experience to produce the Moth. Its fuselage was a plywood box, built around spruce longerons and supporting cross members. Casein glue and brass wood screws were used throughout to produce a sturdy, light-weight frame. It was protected on the inside with varnish and on the outside by a layer of tightly doped fabric. The wings were of standard construction, spruce spars and built-up ribs, securely covered with fabric and doped.

With the export of the Moth to the world at large, these plywood box fuselages were subjected to a wide variety of temperatures and climates. Under most circumstances they proved quite adequate but in particularly damp areas suffered from what one American designer of metal aircraft referred to as "veneerial" disease. The American method of fuselage construction, by comparison, was usually of welded steel tubing, suitably faired with wooden stringers, and a fabric cover doped to drumhead tightness.

As early as October 1927 the use of wooden Moths in Canada was being questioned. The Ontario government aircraft experienced shrinking in the wooden engine bearers, while the varying western climate of High River, Alberta, played havoc with the rigging of the wings. On October 3, a letter to Stag Lane was the opening shot in a strictly Canadian campaign for the use of metal fuselages. The Canadian

Early Cirrus Moths: G-CATJ of General Airways, a bush operator from Rouyn, Quebec, and G-CAUD of National Air Transport of Toronto, a flying school, barnstorming and charter operation. AUD is seen at Leaside aerodrome on the northeast outskirts of Toronto in 1929. (NAM/ K.M. Molson Col., A.E. Barton)

The Trethewey farm (de Lesseps Field) in Mount Dennis as it appeared in 1931 (the top of the photo is north). The hangars of Skyways Limited are on the left, close to Trethewey Drive. The Trethewey home can be seen in the ravine at the lower right. The original square hangar built by DH Canada is at the southeastern corner of the field. (Via W.F. Shaylor)

A typical Gipsy Moth assembled at Mount Dennis sits in front of the first hangar. It is a wooden-fuselage D.H.60G with a split-type axle and a Gipsy I engine. Gipsys had a cooling cowl, in contrast to the exposed cylinders of the Cirrus. (Via L.B. Best)

(Right) The Halford-designed 100 hp Gipsy was the first in a long line of light aircraft engines manufactured by de Havilland in England. (Via Mrs. Mickleborough)

company continued the pressure, with considerable opposition from some in the British company, until a new type 60M or metal-fuselage Moth was introduced.

The Canadians won their battle for metal fuselages at the end of 1928 when the first D.H.60M, G-CAVX, was sent to Canada for evaluation by the RCAF on wheels, skis and floats. Rigorous trials were conducted at London, Ontario, and the results were a major incentive for the next series of orders by the RCAF and the OPAS. Many of the original wooden Moths were later converted to the 60M, particularly in the forestry hangar at Sault Ste. Marie, where they had excellent shop facilities. As time went by it became common practice to upgrade Moths with higher-powered engines, a metal fuselage or a split-type undercarriage. These changes were all covered within the licensing regulations and many a damaged Moth rose again with the use of borrowed components. The price of a metal Moth at the time was given as $4,450 for the landplane and $6,250 for the seaplane version.

The RCAF received 17 Moth 60X aircraft which went early to High River, Alberta, for fire patrol. Two Armstrong Siddeley Genet Moths were evaluated at Camp Borden but the remaining 72 Moths on the RCAF

The historic Trethewey farm area at it appeared in the 1960s, bounded by Trethewey Drive on the south and Jane Street on the west. The Black Creek ravine remained relatively unchanged to the east. (Ontario Government)

inventory over the years were Gipsy-powered with metal fuselages.

The growing worldwide sales of Moths in 1927-28 made de Havilland uncomfortably dependent on Cirrus engines from the Aircraft Disposal Company, which also had other customers to supply. Major Frank Halford was once again called in for consultation and was invited to design a completely new engine of 100 hp. Halford relinquished his connection with ADC in 1927 and was soon busy developing an engine that Geoffrey de Havilland named the Gipsy. The Series 1 achieved the magic 100 hp at a weight of 285 lb. (129 kg) and was the forerunner of a long line of Halford engines produced under the de Havilland banner.

Mount Dennis

Life was never dull around Mount Dennis flying field in 1928-29 with DH Canada and Freddie Shaylor's Skyways Limited sharing the action. Skyways did a lot of flight training, so there was always some activity to enliven the average day. On one occasion an instructor and student took off into a hazy sky for some air work in the Toronto area. One of the de Havilland ground crew noticed a wheel fall off the Moth as it disappeared in the haze and immediately alerted the Skyways officials. According to the stories that have been written about such events, someone runs around holding a wheel in the air hoping the pilot will get the message and avert a crash. And that is just what was done this time. Every

available wheel from the Moth stores was taken onto the field. When the instructor returned to the circuit, he found a row of people across his landing path, each holding a wheel. Needless to say he circled again and completed a successful precautionary landing with no damage.

For those who joined the de Havilland staff early, the training was direct and thorough, as recalled by Harry Proctor. Proctor joined in the fall of 1928 with no previous aircraft experience but with plenty of ability and determination. He recalled:

Arthur Robins was a good boss, and we learned fast. I remember him giving me instructions on the hours of work when I joined the company. "As long as you are here before I get here and leave after I do, that's all you have to remember." That is the way he operated and if there was a special job where he worked into the night, we worked too.

An aeronautical engineer, M. R. Waters, from England, was with us for a while and looked after things like designing skis. The first ski pedestals for the Moths were of welded steel tubing – that is, until one noon hour, after we had been skating on an ice patch behind the hangar. Mr. Waters picked up one of my skates and studied the construction where the metal cone met the boot. "I think I'll build a ski pedestal that shape," he said, and from then on all de Havilland skis had welded cone-shaped pedestals. Waters left to take a job in California before we moved to Downsview.

Most of us had our first flight with Leigh Capreol and we were always pleased to be asked to go along on a flight. I got one of these calls during the first winter while we were developing Moth skis. It wasn't until we got up in the air that Cap told me what he wanted. Through the "Gosport" tube that connected both cockpits, he asked me to crawl out on the lower wing and see if the skis were at the proper angle. Now, I'm the kind of guy who can get dizzy on a tall ladder and here I was about to do my first wing-walking. One look over the leading edge confirmed that the skis were perfect and I hurried back into the cockpit to break the news to Cap.

Talk about learning in a hurry! We were all given amazing jobs at one time or another. I remember one metal Moth seaplane which was in for repair after sinking. Robins' approach was that if one person took it apart and rebuilt it, there would be a minimum of supervision and less chance of error. I was given the job and, as we had no drawings, I went at it piece by piece. By the time I was finished, I knew quite a lot about a metal Moth.

Incorporation

For the first six months DH Canada, which began under the laws of the Province of Ontario, operated as a branch of the British parent with provisional directors. It was always hoped that a Canadian company with its own identity could be formed when the business climate was right. The favourable showing of the first six months allowed a confident reorganization and a public stock offer with the English company holding majority control. The board of directors reflected a balance of British/Canadian participation. Alan S. Butler was named president, with Geoffrey

de Havilland, C.C. Walker and F.E.N. St. Barbe, as the English directors. Canadians on the board were W.R.P. Parker, chairman, J. Homer Black and Frank L. Trethewey, all from Toronto. Bob Loader remained as general manager of the Canadian company with William Zimmerman as secretary.

During October 1928 a new site was chosen for future operations in open farmland in Downsview, north of the city. The area north of Wilson Avenue at the corner of Sheppard Avenue and Dufferin Street provided a level field, clear of all obstructions, alongside the mainline CNR tracks. A 70-acre (28 hectare) lot was purchased in April 1929 and architects Mathers & Haldenby were chosen to plan a new brick and steel building.

Everyone connected with the Canadian operation must have been elated with the sales results of 1928. A total of 62 Moths had been delivered as well as two of the new D.H.61 Giant Moths assembled by Canadian Vickers, one of which went to Western Canada Airways as G-CAJT and the other to the OPAS. The WCA machine was lost in a non-fatal accident two months later but the big eight-passenger G-CAPG of the OPAS had a long and eventful career (it was retired in 1941). A third Giant Moth was imported that year for London Air Transport Limited but the company never took delivery (it was later re-engined and ended up as CF-OAK).

The small downtown office was bursting with activity. Not only did the company have a new corporate identity and a new factory under way, but also a backlog of Moth sales that would keep them busy well into 1929. Thirty-four of these aircraft were to go to the RCAF training establishment and five to the Civil Aviation Branch as additional aircraft for the flying clubs.

Even though DH Canada had no connection with the Moth sales in the United States, it was encouraging to note that the Moth Aircraft Corporation had formed in New York, with a factory at Lowell, Mass. The U.S. model was advertised as "the light car of the air." Minton M. Warren was president with Earl L. House and Frank M. Smith as

Several Moths lined up behind the de Havilland hangar. The company shared de Lesseps Field with Aircraft Limited, the predecessor of Skyways Limited. (DH7312)

The OPAS D.H.61 Giant Moth G-CAPG came to Sault Ste. Marie with a Bristol Jupiter engine. It was re-engined later with a P&W Hornet as shown here and enjoyed a memorable career until 1941 when it was withdrawn from service. (DH10342)

(Below) Western Canada Airways' six-passenger Giant Moth G-CAJT at Calgary while flying an experimental mail route. It was lost after takeoff near Calgary on October 23, 1928. (Western Canada Aviation Museum)

The front of the new building in 1929. It faced Sheppard Avenue. Of solid brick and steel, it was still standing in 1998. (Pringle & Booth)

(Below) The view from the flying field during the Tip Top Derby air rally of 1931. (F.W. Hotson)

(Right) The DHC complex on Sheppard Avenue, looking west. The wooden storage hangar, nearest, was brought from Mount Dennis. Note the circular concrete pad used for compass swinging. Beside the wooden hangar are the new assembly shop, offices, engine test house, stores and paint shop, and heating plant. The CNR siding runs along the far side of the plant. (Via British Aerospace)

vice-presidents. At the annual general meeting of de Havilland England for the year 1929, Alan Butler reported that the Wright Aeronautical Corporation had begun building the Gipsy engine under licence in the U.S.A. He also added that the Moth Aircraft Corporation had joined with the powerful Curtiss-Wright group, production was in progress and royalties had been received.

The year 1929 is always regarded as the beginning of the Great Depression but it started out well for de Havilland Canada. The RCAF Moths began to flow in a steady stream along with the first model of the new D.H.75 Hawk Moth for RCAF evaluation. The Hawk Moth was a promising-looking, high-wing monoplane of 3,650-lb. (1,660 kg) gross weight, with an Armstrong Siddeley Lynx engine, and carried four people. It had a lot of the Fairchild FC-2 look and hopes ran high that it would experience a similar success in Canada on skis and floats. The total of 78 de Havilland airplanes was delivered in 1929, more than in the previous year; similar successes would continue for another year.

A New Home

It took little work on the new field at Downsview to make it suitable for flying. The steel for the new factory was up by mid-July. Excitement built among the 35 employees at the thought of new quarters. The entire operation moved over from Mount Dennis during the first week in September, including Loader's portable wooden hangar with the curved roof, which was to prove extremely useful in the years ahead. The new building of 20,000 sq. ft. (1,860 sq. m) was well laid out for the state of the company's growth at the time. It faced north onto Sheppard Avenue with the Canadian National tracks along the west side. A railway spur line was connected to a loading ramp outside the stores department, paint shop and heating plant. The erection shop had 7,500 sq. ft. (700 sq. m) of unrestricted floor space and a set of typical sliding hangar doors facing the flying field. Two shops were on the ground floor at the front entrance to the building, one for machining and metal work and the other for engine overhaul. The engineering and business offices were upstairs above the shops and were reached by a set of stairs inside the hangar.

The wooden hangar from Mount Dennis was placed about 50 yards (45 m) to the east with its main door and entrance ramp facing the open field. Two additional items rounded out the new quarters, a cement compass rose to the east of the wooden hangar and a small test house for engine runs beside the heating plant. Once again, signs played an important part because the district then was quite rural and isolated. There was nothing for miles but open fields and farm houses. An attractive sign was installed at the corner of Sheppard and Dufferin with an arrow pointing to the plant and a host of other information: address, telephone number, cable address, the company logo and that it was "The Home of the Moth." To assist aerial visitors, the word Moth was painted in large letters on the round hangar roof with an arrow indicating north.

One of the first problems encountered at the new site was the establishment of a water supply. In the isolated Downsview farm area a water main was out of the question. The only alternative was to drill a well. An old-timer was found in the area who had some antique drilling equipment and boundless optimism. He did a survey near the factory and estimated he would find water after about 40 feet of drilling at a cost of something like $100.

At the end of the first week, the hole reached a depth of 50 feet without any sign of water. To make matters worse, the drill struck a layer of hard rock. The expert was still optimistic and authority was given to extend the drilling to a depth of 100 ft. (30 m). At that depth there was still nothing but rock to report and the situation was becoming serious. Costs were going up and the only one to remain

unmoved was the well-borer himself, who held steadfast in his optimism. In growing desperation, successive increases were authorized. At 250 ft. (75 m) the so-called well was a dry as ever and a board meeting was called.

With not much alternative, the board authorized another limit, even though the thump-thump of the equipment was beginning to get on everyone's nerves. As the digging got lower, so did the spirits of all concerned; even the aged expert began to show signs of strain. At exactly 298 ft. (91 m) water gushed forth to resounding cheers, but the drama of the well was not over.

It should have ended as a shining example of man's conquest of adversity, but it was not to be. The water was so brackish that it was completely useless for drinking – or even washing. In the end it could only be used for the factory boiler and it probably didn't do that any good either. For years the drinking water for the staff had to be brought in and dispensed in paper cups from a cooler.

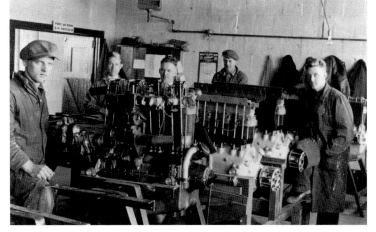

Alf Rinaldo, Peter Loveday, Walter Rinaldo, Ed Lambie and Bill Etherington were in the engine shop for this early DHC photo. A Cirrus engine (foreground) and two Gipsys were being overhauled. Below is the metalworking and machine shop, with Bill Etherington at the bench, Russ Borrett at the buffer and Alex Lamont at the drillpress. (Pringle & Booth via W. Etherington)

(Above) Six RCAF Gipsy Moths (and one civil) shortly after the move to Sheppard Avenue. (Via W. Etherington)

The D.H.75 Hawk Moth demonstrator at Downsview, still in British markings. Three of these aircraft came to Canada, but had only short careers with the RCAF. One is shown below after a mishap. (NAC, Hotson Col.)

(Left) Bill Calder who served as inspector, works manager and service manager through his 30 years with de Havilland Canada. (Hotson Col.)

The Economy Slips

The de Havilland organization fared well during 1929 but the world trade depression, signalled by the collapse of the U.S. stock market, was not long in making its presence felt in both Canada and the U.K. British export trade suffered somewhat in 1929 and by 1930 the corporate profits of de Havilland in England had declined to the point where five per cent dividends replaced the 10 per cent of the year before.

The comfortable new quarters at Downsview proved efficient in spite of their distance from a residential area. Not everyone had a car and there was no bus service that far from the city. Car pools were the only answer and the street corner pick-ups provided a circuitous route for many a driver. By the time the last pick-up was made in the morning

the cars would be rather crowded and the girls, being lighter, would usually end up sitting on some lucky fellow's knee. The reorganization at Sheppard Avenue also brought about staff changes.

On the flying side, S/L Geoffrey S. O'Brian, a distinguished RCAF officer, joined as sales manager. Arthur Robins, the original works manager, returned to England, and M.R. Waters, the aeronautical engineer, moved to California. Vernon O. Levick came out from England to fill both positions as he was also an aeronautical engineer. William A.R. "Bill" Calder joined at that time as inspector.

Bill Calder became something of an institution at DHC in the years that followed. He had come originally from Scotland and was the brother of Sir Ritchie Calder, noted mathematician and author. He had gone to the same school

Frank Warren (far left) rigs Moth CF-AGJ with Bill Calder in the cockpit. Walter Rinaldo and Pete Loveday install an engine. (Via W. Etherington)

The Kingston Flying Club's Gipsy Moth G-CAVX in 1932. It lasted until April 4, 1937, when it was badly damaged landing on Wolfe Island, near Kingston. (A.E. Barton)

as Elizabeth Bowes-Lyons, the Queen Mother, and had served his apprenticeship in shipbuilding. He worked on Rolls-Royce engines as well as the airships R-33 and R-34, which provided his entry into aviation. When the first flying club was formed in Scotland – the Scottish Flying Club, Glasgow – he became its first air engineer. Calder came to Canada in 1928 and after a year in the Maritimes moved to Toronto and de Havilland.

Three D.H.75 Hawk Moths went to the RCAF in the spring of 1930, two new ones and the company demonstrator which had arrived the year before. It had the registration

CF-CCA and was allotted to civil aviation inspector D.G. Joy. The two Air Force machines, slightly heavier at 3,870 lb. (1,757 kg) gross, started as floatplanes, but all three began to show structural deficiencies. Landing accidents due to a nose-heavy condition provided work for the shops but did nothing to enhance the aircraft's reputation. The undercarriage proved inadequate for the pounding it took on skis; it required additional centre-section bracing and wing-spar modifications.

The employees began to look upon the Hawks as a source of perpetual employment, and when one was seen to overrun the airport boundary and nose over in a neighbouring field, a loud cheer went up in anticipation of more work. Despite its sturdy appearance, the Hawk Moth was a disappointment to the British company and a complete failure in

The demonstrator D.H.80A Puss Moth CF-AGO shortly after arriving in Canada in July 1930. (Via Larry Milberry)

George Mickleborough (left) and DHC pilot Geoff O'Brian, with Puss Moth CF-AGO, which they flew from Toronto to Vancouver. (DH)

A Puss Moth advertisement in the *Canadian Air Review* of August 1930. (Hotson Col.)

Canada. Eight were built and the three in Canada only totalled 183 hours before they were declared unserviceable. The final indignity came October 8, 1935, when a request to cut up the airframes to provide experience for RCAF welding classes won unanimous approval.

The Puss Moth

In July 1930 the era of the D.H.80A Puss Moth began in Canada. Nine of these arrived as complete aircraft from England and were assembled and tested during 1930. (Later serial numbers were built up from basic components and given a DHC series of numbers from C201 to C225). The eye-pleasing cabin monoplane showed such improved comfort over the open-cockpit Gipsy Moth that it held promise of duplicating the Gipsy's profitable sales record. The production model with its metal fuselage and inverted Gipsy III engine of 120 hp was an immediate success on both sides of the Atlantic, accomplishing many flight records during its career.

Canada received serial No. 4 from the British production line as its demonstrator aircraft. It needed only to be assembled and was given the registration of CF-AGO on July 8, 1930. Two days later the cream-coloured Puss Moth began a cross-Canada tour which was probably the largest such sales promotion in Canada to that time. The new pilot,

Geoff O'Brian, flew the trip and George Mickleborough, who now held the position of secretary/treasurer, was along to navigate, pay the bills and talk to customers. Similar trips became routine in the years that followed but this was a major adventure in 1930.

Leaving Toronto on July 12, the pair touched down at Detroit, Chicago, Madison, St. Paul, Fargo and Grand Forks, landing at Winnipeg that evening after 14 hours flying time. At Winnipeg, the Puss Moth participated in the Manitoba Jubilee Air Meet and dozens of demonstration flights were made before the tour continued to Brandon, Regina, Moose Jaw, Medicine Hat, Calgary and High River – with more demonstrations en route.

Crossing the Rockies by way of the Crow's Nest and Coquihalla Passes, the tourists saw Cranbrook and Grand Forks before stopping at Vancouver, their western terminus. After five days of demonstrations for British Columbia aviation enthusiasts, the Puss Moth headed homeward, crossing the Rockies at 6,000 to 12,000 ft. (1,830 to 3,660 m). On the return trip their route was planned to touch down at Lethbridge, Milk River, Edmonton, North Battleford, Saskatoon and South Bend. The last leg of the journey from Winnipeg to Toronto added another 12 hours to the flight log.

The trip covered 6,050 miles (9,730 km) in 57 hours flying time, with an average cruising speed of 104 mph (167 km/h), which was no mean achievement considering the lack of anything resembling air routes or servicing facilities. The flight received much publicity and resulted in several sales, including 17 machines to the Canadian government.

Many years later it was suggested to George Mickleborough, long after Geoffrey O'Brian had died, that there must have been a story

Geoff O'Brian (left) who combined purchasing, sales and assistant test pilot duties, with Phil Garratt, who was a regular visitor to de Havilland in 1930. (DH 5954)

somewhere during those thousands of miles. Mickleborough recalled:

Yes, there was, and although it wasn't exciting, it sticks out in my memory. We were in Alberta and were headed for the Ross Ranch, near Lethbridge, late in the day. All ranches out there look alike in the setting sun and we couldn't find it. Geoff decided we had better get down while we could still see. He picked a nice field but it was all wheat and we cut quite a swath in landing. By the time we had tied up to a fence, the farmer came out. He was quite pleasant but we

The only D.H.60T Tiger Moth in Canada, CF-APL had swept-back wings, an inverted Gipsy III engine and a special deep door for the front cockpit. (F.W. Hotson)

hastened to ask how much it would cost for the damage to his crop. We settled for $20 and he drove us into town for the night.

The next day, when we arrived back at the Puss Moth, we could hardly see it for people. They had trampled even more wheat and we settled with the farmer for another $20. We soon found the Ross Ranch – after taking off through our trail of the day before – and it is interesting to note that we sold a Puss Moth, CF-AGY, to George G. Ross, who formed Ranchers Air Line Limited two years later. (It is also interesting historically that Ross' son Stubb later built an airline, Time Air, using both the de Havilland Twin Otter and the Dash 7.)

When we left for a much longer flight across the Rockies, we wondered what the funny smell was in the cabin. It got worse and had the aroma of burnt coffee. It wasn't until we landed at Vancouver that we realized it was all the wheat we had taken into the heater at

(Facing) R.W. Bradford's painting of the O'Brian-Mickleborough flight through the Rockies. It was presented as a retirement gift to secretary-treasurer George Mickleborough and his wife, Doris. George had spent 37 years with DH Canada. (Via G. Mickleborough)

Lethbridge. We had to have the whole system cleaned before we took up any passengers. Here I was, back in my home town, and I couldn't let it be said I brought a bad smell to Vancouver.

DH Canada showed a net profit in 1930 of $18,020.54 with substantial assets on the books: land $29,000, buildings $90,468 and an $18,700 investment in road improvement. Eight Puss Moths were assembled and tested that year along with 50 Moths (and the two Hawks). The market for new airplanes declined, but a welcome order for 10 Puss Moths arrived at the end of the year as the result of the cross-Canada demonstration flight. DH Australia suffered a loss during 1930 and the ambitious manufacturing program in the United States faded completely in spite of the fact that 200 American Moths had been built.

Business was still strong in 1931 but the boom was beginning to taper off. The total of planes sold that year was only 23, compared to 67 in 1930. Twenty-two of these were Puss Moths with one new type, the D.H.60T, forerunner of the Tiger Moth. Demand for the Gipsy Moth had dried up suddenly although improvements to satisfy the Canadian requirement were developing all the time. The main complaint with the instructors was the difficulty of dragging a clumsy parachute in and out of the restricted front cockpit.

Only eight pre-production Tigers were made. It was a "rearrangement" of the Gipsy Moth, rather than a new model. It had a Gipsy III inverted engine similar to the Puss Moth and an enlarged entrance to the front cockpit. The centre section and fuel tank were placed a whole bay forward to give the desired access to the front via the walkway on the lower wing. The rigging of the wings was simply adjusted until everything worked right and the Tiger Moth was born. The pre-production model shipped to Canada was registered CF-APL and the "Apple," as it was called in the Toronto area, proved extremely popular. (CF-APL remained as the DHC demonstrator until 1934 when it went to the Austin brothers in Toronto as their first airplane. Walter Deisher of Ottawa had it for two years but most of its active life was spent at the Toronto Flying Club to 1942. Even after it was retired from active flying it went as a training airframe to Central Technical School in Toronto.)

By now the shop in the new plant was equipped with basic machine tools and a reputation for skilled workmanship prevailed. Overhaul and repair work was encouraged to offset the drop-off in Gipsy Moth sales and prepare for the new models expected from England. The Moths had been in operation long enough to result in a small but steady flow of overhaul and reconditioning work. Modifications were always taking place to "Canadianize" them for the cold winter or add a new convenience. Vernon Levick took on the design of a blind flying kit for the rear seat of the Puss Moth at the request of the RCAF. He even went to the point of having the device patented.

Capreol's Accident

The first serious accident at Downsview, which occurred in January 1930, resulted in injury to test pilot Leigh Capreol. The fact that he was flying a competitor's aircraft, a Curtiss-Reid Rambler, made the circumstances all the more ironic. Like many accidents it resulted from a series of little things, but primarily the fact that the aircraft was a stranger at Downsview. It was a Rambler II registered CF-ABS in the name of Curtiss-Reid as their demonstrator; "Cap" had been invited to fly it during a Toronto stopover. The Rambler had folding wings, somewhat like the Moth, but the locking mechanism was of different design and the early models lacked an inspection hole.

It was always policy for the pilot to supervise the folding and locking of the wings, which was naturally a two-man job. When Capreol was ready to fly he called on a passing workman to give him a hand, not realizing the man was the shipper, not a mechanic. The combination of an unfamiliar locking system and a non-aviation helper resulted in the misalignment of a locking bolt (it had happened before in a Rambler). Capreol took off and had only reached 1,000 ft. (305 m) when one wing folded over his head and the aircraft started to spin earthward. "The ship started to swing wildly," reported Capreol later from hospital, "and the worst was I couldn't see. The lower part of the loose wing blocked my view so that I was helpless. By instinct I opened and shut the throttle to keep the nose up and break the fall."

His flying skill had kept him alive but it took nearly an hour to saw him from the wreckage. Harry Proctor was the first from the plant to reach the downed aircraft, moments after a Bell Telephone crew who had been working nearby. He noticed that a huge snowdrift had absorbed much of the fall and helped deflect the nose of the aircraft. Capreol was still conscious but jammed down almost underneath the engine. Harry made him as comfortable as possible while

tools were brought to untangle the wreckage. By this time Dr. Scott, the company physician, had arrived and a Bell telephone ladder was used to carry Capreol to the parking lot and a waiting ambulance. His worst injuries were to his right leg and ankle and it was six months before he was back in the air testing again. He walked with a limp the rest of his life and needed a special boot, but completed an illustrious career of test flying. He was nominated to Canada's Aviation Hall of Fame in 1981.

Bert Hinkler

It was on a cold February morning in 1931 that a short, well-dressed man visited the company's office in downtown Toronto. He introduced himself as Bert Hinkler and General Manager Loader recognized him immediately as one of the world's most successful long-distance flyers. His full name was Herbert John Louis Hinkler and he was an Australian who only a year before had established a fantastic record of 15 1/2 days, London to Darwin, in a Cirrus-powered Avro Avian. Hinkler was called "Little Bert" because of his 5 foot 4 inch (162 cm) height, but he had a reputation for dogged persistence and an instinctive mechanical ability. He was admired for his competence as a navigator and had twice won the Britannia Trophy for his outstanding flights.

He had been in the United States since September 1930 looking over the light aircraft market there and contemplating starting charter flying in that country. He had come to Toronto to purchase a Puss Moth and part of any arrangement was that he be allowed to prepare it himself for long-distance flying. Puss Moth number 2049 was one of nine shipped and ready to fly. It was assigned to Hinkler and given the Canadian registration of CF-APK on April 29. From then on, Hinkler was to be seen almost daily, dressed in overalls, working along with the men in the shop. After the test flight, the Puss Moth was moved to the wooden hangar with the round roof, where Hinkler worked day in and day out on his own designs, doing his own modifications.

Everyone helped him at one stage or another and, although he kept his intentions to himself, all developed a liking for this quiet, solitary man. Ab Warren was in charge of stores at the time and recalled seeing a lot of him during his eight months at de Havilland: "He was always very polite but never said very much. He got to know where things were kept in the tool stores and would slip back and forth borrowing what he needed." Frank Warren had similar recollections: "I remember him as a very fine gentleman, going about his business and never bothering anyone. He tried

Bert Hinkler (centre) poses in front of a Puss Moth with V.O. Levick, DHC works manager; R.A. Loader, general manager; Charles D. Browne, manager of C.C. Wakefield & Company Limited, sponsor of the flight; and S/L Geoffrey S. O'Brian, DHC sales manager. (DH31630)

everything possible to save weight and even removed the navigation lights from the aircraft."

CF-APK was painted silver with the struts and registration letters in red. Fabric replaced the rear windows and all upholstery was removed to install the long-range fuel tank. The tank, which Hinkler had had manufactured in Long Island, was apparently a tight fit, taking up the rear of the cabin. He also imported a set of streamline bracing wires to modify the undercarriage. He was anxious to dispense with the weight of the standard rubber blocks in the undercarriage legs and rigged the struts into a solid unit, leaving only the tires to absorb compression. The idea didn't work. He blew both tires on his first overload test flight and had to settle for a compromise arrangement.

Harry Proctor and Frank Russell assisted Hinkler from time to time and Proctor recalled helping solve the problem of replenishing the oil from inside the cabin. "Bert wanted to keep a minimum of used oil in the engine system and regulate the flow so as to get maximum use of the fresh oil. We were discussing this on a warm day in June and Bill Calder, Bert and I went into the shop for a drink at the cooler. I poured a cup for each of us and watched as a bubble went up in the water jug along with a resounding gurgle. 'There is your answer,' I said. 'We'll make it work like the cooler.' We built him a system to feed in new oil and all he had to do was keep a jar within easy reach, full of oil. It fed automatically, the same as the water cooler. To overcome the fact that he had to carry so many big cans in his small cockpit, we provided a pair of tin snips so he could cut the light metal into small pieces and pass them out the window."

John Slaughter was another of the employees who helped the Australian aviator, by replacing the original tail skid with a wheel. After 60 years, he always remembered the caution of Hinkler's every move. "Whenever he took the aircraft for a flight, he would taxi very slowly and check the engine a long time before he took off."

All the employees who encountered Hinkler at de Havilland stressed the quiet, capable efficiency that went into his preparations. George Mickleborough recalled that once the business of purchasing the aircraft was through, he was in the plant all the time: "He told us vaguely of his plans to fly down the east coast of South America but nothing more."

Three things stood out in Frank Russell's mind in recalling Bert Hinkler – his high-heeled boots, the fact that he chewed gum all the time, and his liking for the ginger beer he used to bring in from the United States. George Blanchard helped Hinkler install the big cabin tank and modify the seat. "When you worked for Bert, you were the helper – he was the boss. I did what I was told and we got along fine. I remember he was a good workman."

When other pilots of note stayed in Toronto they were

The D.H.80A Puss Moth in which Bert Hinkler was lost in the Alps in January 1933. (Hotson Col.)

For years the author wondered what occasioned the cheering pose in this photo. Some research into the Bert Hinkler story provided the answer and the search for names was renewed. Many de Havilland employees worked with Hinkler to prepare his Puss Moth and they were thrilled with his crossing of the South Atlantic in 1931. Shortly after the news was received that Hinkler had reached England, Bob Loader orga-

nized this staff photograph. Vernon Levick stands at the right giving the signal to cheer. The resulting photo is not only a historic record, but a study in human reactions. After much research, here are the names of most of those present. Bob Loader, George Mickleborough and Geoff O'Brian are missing from the picture.

1. Bill Calder
2. Stan Dibble
3. Tom Glasson
4. Harry Proctor
5. Bill Matthews
6. Scotty ?
7. Roy Shermerhorn
8. Bill Etherington
9. Russ Borrett
10. Ab Warren

11. Pete Loveday
12. John Neal
13. Walter Rinaldo
14. Jack Jones
15. Lou Thorpe
16. Harry Beffort
17. Hilda Currell
18. Dorothy Kirkman
19. Eric Tetsull
20. Kate Nixon

21. Esther ?
22. Jack Macintosh
23. Bert Witham
24. Edith Mitchell
25. Joe Banigan
26, 27, 28. Three women from the downtown office.
29. Unknown
30. Leigh Capreol
31. Vernon Levick

32. Bill McMillan
33. Vick Tetsull
34. George Blanchard
35. Ethel Almond
36. Frank Warren
37. Jack Dawson
38. Frank Russell
39. Bob Sheppard

invited to take part in the social life of the city and were well entertained. Hinkler on the other hand was no social lion and spent every weekend possible in New York. It wasn't until his life story was published in 1992, *The Last Flight of Bert Hinkler* by Edward Wixted, Vantage Press, New York, that we learned that Bert had courted and wed a lady there named Katherine while still married to Nancy in England. The later complications can be imagined.

Bert Hinkler left Toronto quietly on October 20 with no advance publicity. He took off from Jamaica, New York, on October 26 at 2:00 p.m. with the same secrecy and headed south over the Atlantic. Because he had removed the navigation lights he was not allowed to fly the overland airways of the United States. He planned his flight so that he would spend the hours of darkness over the Atlantic coast. That night bad weather and headwinds forced him slightly off course and at 8 o'clock on the morning of the 27th he landed in Kingston, Jamaica, a distance of 1,850 miles (2,975 km), after 18 hours in the air.

He worked his way to Natal in Brazil in easy stages and left on November 25 for a stormy crossing of the South Atlantic. He landed at Bathurst in British Gambia, a flight of 2,600 miles (4,160 km) in 22 hours. (A false report was published of his arrival at Dakar, then nothing for the waiting press for 48 hours. There was considerable concern back at Downsview until his arrival was confirmed, and it wasn't until Bill Calder received a letter a month later from Hinkler that they knew the reason. He had taken time at the tiny Bathurst airport to do a top overhaul of the Gipsy engine while the reporters were looking for him in Dakar and St. Louis.) A further two hours took him to St. Louis, Senegal, in French West Africa, where he landed at 2:00 p.m. on November 27. The next day he continued his flight to Casablanca in Morocco and he completed his final leg of the flight to England via Paris. He landed finally at Hanworth Airport in London to a hero's welcome.

For this outstanding flight from Canada to London, he received the Seagrave Memorial Trophy, presented by the British Royal Aeronautical Society for the most daring flying feat of 1931. Other awards he received at that time were the Britannia Challenge Trophy for the third time, the Oswald Watt Gold Plaque and the Johnston Memorial Prize.

A Canadian Moth Abroad

The Moths in Canada took on a variety of roles as had been expected. Fire spotting by air was a particularly Canadian task and some early Moths were used commercially in remote areas as bushplanes. Most were used for training pur-

A typical Cirrus Moth, G-CAUA started its career in 1928 with International Airways in Hamilton. Later it belonged to Carl Burke, founder of Maritime Central Airways, who donated it in 1962 to Canada's National Aeronautical Collection. (DH 15749)

poses and a few saw service as private aircraft for pleasure flying. In the sport of air touring few can match the record of serial number 783, a metal Moth, that started in Montreal and ended its career in Australia.

CF-ADC was delivered to Dougall Cushing of Montreal on floats in 1929 and was sold in the summer of 1932 to a Montreal businessman, Jacques R. Hébert. He had been a co-founder of the Montreal Light Aeroplane Club, learned to fly there and had built up 100 hours of flight experience. His purpose in buying ADC was to make a sightseeing trip around the world combining boat and plane. He planned to ship the Moth to England, fly to Australia, return to Vancouver by boat and fly the rest of the way to Montreal.

In England Hébert had de Havilland modify CF-ADC for long-range flying and departed on his pleasure trip on October 12, 1932. He reached Cairo on October 23 where he met Tony Spooner, the former instructor of the Montreal Club. Spooner showed him around the area during the next three days, then it was off again for Amman and Baghdad. He made his way over deserts and mountains and by December 6 was ready for the dangerous over-water stretch of the Timor Sea. He took off from Koepang and reached Darwin, Australia, after eight hours in the air.

It was four days later, while making his way to Sydney, that he damaged his undercarriage substantially trying to avoid some errant goats in a field at Cloncurry. When he found out how much time it would take to make the necessary repairs, he sold the aircraft to Qantas Airlines and returned to Canada by boat. The Moth was repaired and, as VH-UQV, spent an interesting career of instruction, joy riding and private flying.

CHAPTER TWO

HARD TIMES

In spite of the decline in sales during 1931, de Havilland Canada showed a satisfactory "liquid position" in cash and government bonds, even though a net loss of $29,555 was reported. The sudden slump was enough to bring chairman Alan Butler and director of finance W.E. Nixon out from England for the annual meeting on January 16, 1932. The report read that day stressed the need for "large economies" in the year ahead and it was not long before a series of furloughs was introduced. These became the norm, but there was an understanding among the workers of the economic conditions and a promise of a call-back when things got better. The situation worsened with the report in April that the Canadian government had cut its budget for aircraft purchases from $5 million to $1.7 million.

One incident to brighten the lives of the remaining workers during February 1932 was a visit by their friend Bert Hinkler. He had returned to Canada by boat after his triumphant reception in England and was making the rounds of the Toronto aviation fraternity. He went through the plant thanking everyone who had helped him and chatted with them at lunchtime about his South Atlantic trip. One story involved a small monkey he was given in Brazil as a good luck mascot before taking off for Africa. During the long night the monkey roamed through the Puss Moth unrestricted and unnoticed until the going got rough. At one stage Hinkler had to navigate through one of the worst storms in his career, with bolts of lightning which he described as "looking like telephone poles." During the height of the lightning the monkey climbed on his shoulder and remained there, shivering and drinking the rainwater that leaked through the cabin roof.

(Right) Leigh Capreol with the first Fox Moth demonstrator in Canada. The location was the Toronto Flying Club on Wilson Avenue, where a TTC subway station now stands. (C.D. Long)

(Below) The product lineup in 1932: the DH demonstrator Giant Moth CF-OAK; a Fox Moth, with the original British registration G-ABUO (later CF-API); Puss Moth CF-AGO; Tiger Moth CF-APL and two D.H.60M Moths, CF-AGX and CF-AAA. (DH)

Jim Mollison

The next Puss Moth in the growing sport of Atlantic hopping was Jim Mollison's *The Heart's Content*. Mollison left Port Marnock, Ireland, on August 18, 1932, with his declared destination New York City. His unscheduled landing at Pennfield Ridge, New Brunswick, provided a topic of conversation at DH Canada on the morning of the 19th. Mollison flew to New York the next day and was met by Bill Calder and Walter Rinaldo, who arrived from Toronto to check the Puss Moth and its Gipsy engine. Mollison's original intention was to make a round-trip crossing and the two DH Canada representatives completely overhauled the engine for the return flight. The west-to-east journey got as far as New Brunswick, where it was terminated, and the Puss returned to England by boat.

The de Havilland organization felt the backlash of the Depression in 1932. The yearly dividend was down in England to 2$\frac{1}{2}$ per cent with salary cuts and shorter working hours in the shops. Canadian sales dropped to three: one Puss Moth and two of the new D.H.83 Fox Moths. The Giant Moth that had come over in 1928 was re-engined with a Pratt & Whitney Hornet and leased to the Ontario Provincial Air Service as CF-OAK. Another trading loss was recorded in the annual report but the Canadian company retained its satisfactory position.

The year 1933 started badly with the news in January that Bert Hinkler was lost on a flight to Australia. He had set out from England on the 7th in his Canadian-registered Puss Moth and was reported passing over the Italian Alps. Nothing was heard for months, then one morning in May the following year, high up in the Pratomagno Mountains of the Appenine range, the wreckage was found. Bert Hinkler had died in much the same way as he had lived: quietly and alone.

The mystery of Hinkler's disappearance persisted throughout a troubled year for DH Canada. The company received considerable publicity in 1935 but it was not the kind that influenced bank managers. The Mollison name was in the news again, but even this episode was not a complete success. Jim Mollison had married the equally famous pilot Amy Johnson, and they were planning an Atlantic flight as a husband and wife team. They chose a DH twin-engined Dragon I, G-ACCV, and had it christened the *Seafarer*. Their first attempt to leave London Airport for New York ended in a damaged undercarriage. They finally got away at midnight on June 22 from the beach at Pendine Sands and battled the usual headwinds associated with a westward crossing of the Atlantic. They were six hours behind time when they reached Newfoundland and, instead of

(Above) Trans-Atlantic flyer Jim Mollison and his Puss Moth *The Heart's Content*. In August 1932, he flew it solo from England to New Brunswick. (NAM)

Early DHC employees Frank and Ab Warren in front of the Mollison *Seafarer II* after assembly at Downsview in September 1933. (DH47048)

Jim Mollison makes a final inspection of *Seafarer II* before his attempted takeoff from Wasaga Beach. (Below) Bob Loader and Jim and Amy Mollison walk the beach. (Via D. Williams, Hotson Col.)

of the damaged wood and fabric, ran a gigantic sale, decorated the store with the debris and gave away a sample piece with each purchase. It proved an advantage to de Havilland, as they didn't have to do all the cleaning up.

Sir Charles Wakefield came to the Mollisons' aid in early September and shipped a new Dragon to Canada, named *Seafarer II* this time, combining their initials in the registration G-ACJM. The publicity spotlight shifted to Dufferin Street and Sheppard Avenue, Toronto, when reporters heard the famous pair were preparing their new plane for a Canada-Baghdad flight. The hangar staff pitched in with overtime and soon the Dragon was ready for test by Leigh Capreol. George Blanchard went along on the test flight to crawl back and forth in the narrow crawl space to test the centre of gravity. The Mollisons had taken off from a beach in England and chose the level sands of Wasaga Beach on the shores of Georgian Bay for their Canadian departure.

While preparations were in progress, Jim and Amy were royally entertained by Toronto Flying Club members and had free use of the company demonstrator Puss Moth. Capreol acted as advisor and tested the sand conditions at the beach with the new demonstrator Fox Moth. By the morning of October 3, 1933, the *Seafarer II* was fuelled for the attempted takeoff, but the fates frowned for the third time on the flying twosome. The winds, which blow predominantly across the beach at Wasaga, severely complicated the takeoff. On the third attempt to become airborne, one wheel of the 3½-ton machine buckled under the load.

Russ Borrett rushed the strut to Toronto for an overnight repair but conditions the next day discouraged the intrepid aviators. *Seafarer II* was flown to Downsview for shipment back to England. The newspaper headlines of the Mollisons' activities were not hiding the fact from the directors that it was a bad financial year. Only six new aircraft were sold during the twelve-month period: five Fox Moths and the first Dragon 4 (similar to the *Seafarer II*) to Canadian Airways.

landing at New York in daylight, were faced with an emergency night landing at Bridgeport, Connecticut, when fuel ran out.

The poor wooden Dragon was severely damaged in an over-run accident at the unfamiliar airport. The newlyweds were hospitalized in Bridgeport and reached New York on July 25 with mixed emotions as to their trans-Atlantic accomplishments. Their original plan was a long-distance record flight to Baghdad, but *Seafarer* would never rise again. An enterprising department store in Bridgeport collected all

The excellent start of the first four years coupled with

Experience with the Giant Moth favoured the Pratt & Whitney R1690 Hornet engine over the original Bristol Jupiter XI. CF-OAK was fitted with a Hornet at DHC and leased to the OPAS in June 1932. It is shown with Leigh Capreol in the cockpit. OAK was destroyed in an accident at Gander Lake, Ontario, on May 23, 1935. (Via Larry Milberry)

current assets of $198,813 and $82,677 in cash and bonds, meant that the situation was not desperate, but the net loss of $19,952 at the end of 1933 called for drastic "further economies." This time they were to go right to the top and involve senior personnel. The parent company sent out L.C. Lee Murray to fill the multiple role of manager, aeronautical engineer and test pilot. This allowed Loader and Levick to return to England and Bill Calder to move up from inspector to works manager. Leigh Capreol left to form a charter flying company at the Toronto waterfront with Chuck and Jack Austin.

Lee Murray was a pleasant, soft-spoken Australian who had studied engineering in his native country and turned his attention to aviation. He began flying at Point Cook, Victoria, in 1924 when he joined the Royal Australian Air Force and went on to a colourful flying career in India. In later years he owned a Desoutter II monoplane in Australia. When he accepted a job with de Havilland England in 1932, he chose a novel way of getting there. He had the plane shipped with him to Vancouver, then flew it across Canada to Montreal. He left it to be sold there and made the rest of the trip to England by boat. Murray arrived in Toronto on December 1, 1933, during deteriorating economic times to try to keep the company alive. Only a skeleton staff remained at Sheppard Avenue and even their work hours were drastically reduced.

The Puss Moth Mysteries

In spite of the lovely flying qualities of the Puss Moth and its thousands of record-breaking miles, the aircraft developed a Jekyll-and-Hyde tendency and a reputation for mystery that was never shaken. An accident on October 13, 1930, in Western Australia brought the first indication of an elusive structural problem which recurred in an unfortunate series of similar events. All accidents took on the same pattern in which one or both wings would come off in flight. Most were associated with turbulent weather and high speed; nine such accidents were recorded by the end of 1933.

DH Canada's test pilot, Leigh Capreol, had occasion to complain of rudder flutter at high speeds and a great deal of correspondence resulted in view of the growing concern. Testing was done at Downsview and the Canadian report provided considerable input into the investigations. The only wing separation accident in which anyone survived occurred in Ottawa on March 21, 1932, to F/O Arthur L. James (later A/V/M/ James). He made an important contribution with his detailed report about the accident.

Dougall Cushing's ill-fated Puss Moth, rebuilt after an emergency landing in the water reservoir off Yonge Street, Toronto. Bought by Leavens Brothers Air Services on June 20, 1937, it was involved in a fatal crash a month later. (F.W. Hotson)

Puss Moths were used by Canadian Government regional offices. These aircraft had the main structural member painted white for easy regular inspection. Stuart Graham of the Montreal branch was investigating the death of Stanley Siscoe at Lake Matchi-Manitou which required several ski landings on hard packed-snow. On one flight he was sketching the area and noticed chips of white paint falling on his clipboard. He could see nothing obvious but immediately made a cautious landing for further investigation. As the aircraft came to a stop the wing tips slowly sank to the snow – the true definition of a close call. All Puss Moths in Canada were recalled for mandatory strengthening modifications.

On January 7, 1933 a second Canadian-registered Puss Moth was lost, Bert Hinkler's CF-APK, which everyone at Downsview knew so well. Details of the investigation were scarce for the wreckage was only found months after the event. The pattern was familiar: turbulence of the Italian mountains had evidently caused the wing to break away in the air. All modifications had been applied to Hinkler's machine in England, where it had been re-engined with a Gipsy Major and given a thorough check before his last flight. That the wing had broken away in the air was demonstrated by the lack of splitting at the wing joint and the fact that the wing was found 270 yards from the fuselage. The Italian authorities gave their opinion that the wing broke off as a whole in the air.

The company and airworthiness officials were continually alert to the situation for the next few years, but one more case arose involving a Canadian Puss Moth. It had originally been sold to Dougall Cushing of Westmount, Quebec, and at the time of the crash was owned by Leavens Brothers Air Services, Toronto. Arthur Leavens was flying CF-AGQ from Toronto to Detroit on May 20 with two passengers when he encountered thunderstorm turbulence near St. Marys, Ontario. Eyewitness accounts told the unfortunate story: "The airplane appeared to lose a wing while still in the air." In spite of its acceptance in Canada and around the world, the wing failures of the Puss Moth were a blot on its history.

The Len Reid Story

Any conversation with DHC veterans of the 1933-34 era will sooner or later turn to the story of Len Reid. Most of the tales were told with a chuckle, for Len was one of those likeable characters who never took life seriously. He was sent out from the English company, yet he was not an Englishman. He had family prestige but he shunned high office. Captain Leonard Gillespie Reid was born in Montreal, the grandson of Sir Robert Reid, who had made his fortune building railway bridges in the time of John A. Macdonald. He was the third son of Sir William Duff Reid of Hockcliffe, Bedfordshire, England, who had been instrumental in building Newfoundland's railway. Another attribute to which he laid no claim was that he was the brother-in-law of Alan S. Butler, chairman of the board of de Havilland in England.

In 1929 Len Reid joined the group at Mount Dennis in a role that Bill Calder used to refer to as "remittance man." He

Richard Ayling (left) and Len Reid pose for a PR shot with the *Trail of the Caribou*, while preparing for their record attempt in 1934. Then, Mrs. Murray talks over the food supplies for the trip with the two airmen, while Bill Calder stuffs rags into the engine intakes to keep out blowing sand. (Via Larry Milberry, Hotson Col,)

was made stores manager, married a Toronto girl, Phyllis Austin, and flew as a private pilot at the Toronto Flying Club. He left Toronto in 1931 but a year after the Mollison failure at Wasaga he returned as an aspiring trans-Atlantic pilot. He came with a well-known Britisher, Captain James Richard Ayling, intending to try for the distance record the Mollisons had abandoned. He had spent all his money on the long-range Dragon that had been sitting idle in England and which was shipped again to Canada, this time as the *Trail of the Caribou.*

Reid said the renaming was just a matter of sentiment, resulting from his many pleasant years in Newfoundland and his service with the Newfoundland Regiment during World War I. The attempt was to be sponsored by Alan Butler and the Mollison's flight plan was to be duplicated – including the takeoff at Wasaga Beach. During assembly and testing at Downsview, Len Reid had some innovations of his own to add, involving an idea to overcome carburetor icing in the Gipsy Major engines.

The regular Gipsy drew warm air from the crankcase automatically at low throttle settings to overcome the icing problem in a glide, but took cold air at full throttle. Reid reasoned that with a special control to the valve he could get crankcase heat whenever he wanted it and look after the dreaded icing. He bought two automotive push-pull controls and connected the long cables from the engines to the cock-

pit. (It is not known what authority or approval he got for this modification.) He also learned that the Mollisons had kept the tail of the Dragon too low on their takeoff attempt; he was determined it would not happen to him.

There was considerable delay awaiting suitable weather for the flight. One early-morning attempt with reporters and photographers in attendance had to be called off due to strong crosswinds on the beach. Lee Murray was an advisor for this flight and tested the winds with a circuit in a Gipsy Moth. On August 8 they tried again. John Neal of de Havilland described the activity that morning:

We worked from two o'clock in the morning, filling the huge tanks with 400 gallons of special fuel imported in drums from Holland. When the sun came up the gasoline overflowed and got into the spar caps and crevices. We had to work our way into these areas on our stomachs and mop up the excess gasoline with rags. We had to have someone standing by to pull us out by the feet in case we passed out with the fumes. Reid and Ayling got away as early in the morning as possible and, although there was a bit of crosswind, they ran the whole length of Wasaga before they inched into the air and disappeared over the treetops.

Observers noted that the tail of the aircraft rose higher than in the Mollison attempt – one of Len Reid's ideas had worked. Five hours later they were sighted over Quebec City, but during the rest of the day and night speculation ran high at Downsview. Atlantic crossings were still dangerous and Baghdad was a rather ambitious destination. The guessing game ended suddenly at noon Greenwich time, August 9, with a news flash that the *Trail of the Caribou* had landed at Heston Airport, near London, after 30 hours and 50 minutes in the air. The pilots had abandoned their long-distance attempt for lack of fuel, but had completed 3,700 miles (5,920 km) and the first non-stop flight from the Canadian mainland to England.

The story of that historic flight might have been lost in the shuffle of unconfirmed reports if Len Reid had not returned to a job at Downsview. He rejoined his friends, in the shops this time, and bit by bit the story of that long Atlantic flight came out. Icing had indeed played a major part in the crossing and provided their greatest concern. "But what of the heater controls?" The answer was apparently, "Nothing," for they stuck when needed and forced the engines to take in unheated air at all times. When the conditions were right for carburetor ice, the engines simply lost power until the aircraft descended into warmer air, often with the waves only feet away. Bumping the throttles to clear the ice only resulted in bending one of the controls, further complicating their situation. And so it went, up/down, ice/de-ice, throughout the long night with a considerable waste of fuel. They still had 200 gallons (900 litres) when they reached London, but decided not to press on to Baghdad.

Once the story of the flight satisfied the boys in the shop, the next question was, "What happened to the *Trail of the Caribou*?" In keeping with the bad luck story, Reid explained that, once the flight was over, he had spent all his money and there was not much coming in. He tried taking the aircraft around the British Isles, selling rides, but ended writing it off in a field at Hamble where he clipped a hedge on landing. "Even that didn't go off well," explained Reid. "I had a lady on board at the time and her husband was quite prominent in the neighbourhood."

Len Reid was killed some years later in an automobile accident in London, England, but his name and that of his companion, Jim Ayling, live on. The Historic Sites and Monuments Board of Canada erected a cairn in memory of the flight near the spot where they took off at Wasaga Beach. It was fittingly unveiled on August 24, 1954, in front of a crowd that included some who recalled those early flights of daring.

A Taste of the Headlines

During the excitement of preparing the *Trail of the Caribou* for its Atlantic flight, a new era was descending on Ontario. The election that year had unseated the long-standing Conservative government of George S. Henry and replaced it with a Liberal regime under Mitchell Frederick Hepburn. The mercurial onion farmer from the Elgin West Riding won the greatest Liberal victory in the province's history on the promise of cutting costs, and he went at the task with vigour. He began by cutting his own salary and those of his ministers the moment he was sworn in on July 10, 1934. He closed the Lieutenant Governor's official residence, and followed up with mass firings at Ontario Hydro and the Liquor Board. Every warden in the provincial Department of Game and Fisheries was summarily fired.

With the newspapers warming to the story, he chose the extensive government automobile fleet for his most spectacular showmanship. He spurned the chauffeur-driven government car of his predecessor, George Henry, and bought his own in a well-publicized stunt. He organized a ceremony in which he was to present his cheque and receive the keys. He was a master of quips and when asked to smile for the assembled photographers, his retort was, "How can you smile when you hand over a cheque for $1,700?"

His next grandstand manoeuvre was to gather 47 automobiles used by the former government into Varsity Stadium in Toronto and auction them off to the tune of $34,000. By July 27 he had started six inquiries, including one into the affairs and operations of the Ontario Provincial Air Service.

Meetings were convened in Sault Ste. Marie and Toronto under Commissioner D.W. Lang, K.C. Questions were asked about everything from the original purchase of flying boats in 1924 to the making of non-aircraft andirons in the shops. The cost and supervision of an $1,100 pigeon loft was also severely questioned. It wasn't long until the purchase of DH Moths came up and it was noted that American Edo floats had been ordered to replace those made by the British Short Bros. These evidently added 30 pounds extra weight so that new, higher power Gipsy II engines had been installed. As in all such inquiries, there were shop specialists who disagreed with Roy Maxwell's flamboyance and were pleased to inform the judge that they had also arranged for

The de Havilland employees of 1935 gather for a photo at the annual picnic in Port Dalhousie on August 16. Left to right, front row: G. Blanchard, G. Otter, J. McNamee. Second row: B. McNichol, H. Currell, G. Mickleborough, L. Thorpe, Lee Murray, L. Granger, W. Calder, E. Almond, M. Currell. Third row: D. Long, B. Witham, J. Slaughter, T. Glasson, M. Borczak, R. Barber, W. Rinaldo, H. Proctor, R. Borrett, A. Nixon, F. Warren. Back row: H. Beffort, G. Gilmour, P. Loveday, J. Neal, R. Ruse, A. Warren, D. Murray. (Via C.D. Long)

one of the mechanics to work on the superintendent's big blue Cadillac.

Things were going badly for Maxwell, whose own unorthodox way of developing an air service did not sit well with either the legal mind or the accountant's fine pencil. Ontario's taxpayers were treated to a first rate sideshow with daily reports in the newspapers. The headlines flamed anew when it was revealed that Maxwell held shares in de Havilland Canada, which during 10 years had sold the OPAS $197,924.42 of aircraft and equipment (including the disputed Gipsy II engines). Needless to say, by the time Commissioner Lang published the report of his findings, Roy Maxwell had resigned from the OPAS. It might not have been coincidence that he was replaced by a pilot friend of Hepburn's, George Ponsford, who had been his personal driver at election time.

Bruce West, in his book on the Ontario firefighting services, *The Firebirds*, covers the subject in detail and puts an

accurate appraisal on the de Havilland purchases in his summary of the event:

In the matter of Maxwell holding some shares in de Havilland Aircraft of Canada, this was clearly a case of creating a direct conflict of interest. Nevertheless, there seems to be no question whatever about the fact that – as events later proved beyond doubt – the DH Moth was one of the most useful and economical pieces of flying equipment ever acquired and operated by the OPAS. There was nothing to indicate that Roy Maxwell allowed his stock in de Havilland to influence him in the purchase of machines inferior to others of the same type which might have then been available on the market.

The Low Point

The parent company in England had weathered the storm of 1934 but the Canadian plant came closer to closing than at any other time. It was definitely the worst year so far, with a total net loss of $41,000. Some progress was made developing a set of floats for the Dragon in conjunction with Fairchild Aircraft Limited, but at this point there was only one Dragon in the country. The only bright spot during the year was the introduction of the D.H.89 Dragon Rapide and a sale to the leading operator of the day, Canadian Airways. Two Puss Moths were the only other aircraft sold during 1934. The board of directors was bolstered that year with three proven businessmen: A.H.K. Russell, W.M. Archibald and R.A. Laidlaw.

The pattern of furloughs that had been introduced in

A 1936 advertisement for the Canadianized Hornet Moth on Fairchild floats. (Hotson Col.)

1933 became even more prevalent as time went on because there was a great need to keep the well-trained staff. "We all took turns sharing duties with the regular watchman," recalls John Neal, "and it was arranged around the type of work to be done. I remember getting a call to be watchman one day because there was a Bellanca rudder to repair. I had the place all to myself and before I was finished, I had done metal work, woodwork, fabric work, doping and painting. When it was all finished I even crated it up ready for shipping. We had to be able to do a lot of things in those days."

Frank and Ab Warren, who had been on the staff since Mount Dennis days, also shared in watchman duties, coming and going whenever there was a job to be done. Ab Warren, as head of the stores department, probably experienced more employment than most throughout the crisis. "I had to go in on the weekends," he said, "look after any parts orders and keep heat on in the boilers. The boiler wasn't a difficult job. I only had to keep it at 15 pounds pressure."

About mid-summer overhaul work improved considerably and the year ended on a happy note. A steady trend continued through 1935 with RCAF Moths to overhaul and an influx of new machines from England. Overhaul work resulted in a small financial comeback in 1935 and accounted for a net profit of $4,077 at year's end. Sales were up to seven, the highest they had been in four years. The first D.H.87A Hornet Moth arrived that year, along with the first D.H.82A Tiger Moth. There were one each of the Puss, the Fox and the Rapide and two twin-engine Dragons sold.

Hornet Moth CF-BBE came to DHC from the U.K. in March 1937. It quickly was sold to Consolidated Mining and Smelting, which used aircraft for speedy communications between head office in Trail, B.C., and remote mining and exploration areas. BBE left CM&S in 1946 to serve other operators from Yellowknife to Vancouver. It faded from the scene after 1958. (F.W. Hotson)

The Dragon Line

If ever there was an aircraft that proved the point of designing to economic conditions, it was the D.H.84 Dragon, the poor man's airliner. A.E. Hagg and his British design staff had done well with Moth development as far as the Fox Moth with its 17 ton-miles per gallon. With the advent of difficult times, DH England came up with the Dragon 4 that gave 19 ton-miles per gallon. It became known as the first multi-engine transport that could pay its way without subsidy. It flew like a big kite and, although the payload was not great on Canadian Fairchild floats, it did get into the air and the economy was right. It had folding wings outboard of the engines and could accommodate six people or be modified for eight on short hops. Only three Dragons came to Canada: CF-APJ and CF-AVD served with Canadian Airways from 1933 to 1944; CF-AVI started out with Consolidated Mining and Smelting but ended up with Howard Watt and North Shore Airways Limited competing in winter on the St. Lawrence with Quebec Airways and their Rapides.

The Dragon was the first twin-engine aircraft used by Canadian Airways and set

Canadian Airways' CF-AVD, a Dragon II with Gipsy Major engines, came to Canada in January 1935. The fuselage was the plywood box type and the outer wing panels were standard Moth wings which could be folded. Canadian models had the extended dorsal fin shown here. This aircraft served in many parts of Canada on wheels, skis and floats until May 26, 1944, when it was destroyed in a takeoff accident at Baie Comeau, Quebec. (Gordon S. Williams)

the scene for the D.H.89 Dragon Rapide, which followed in fair numbers. In appearance the Rapide closely resembled the Dragon as it used the same fuselage shape. It had finely tapered mainplanes and sleek engine nacelles combined with faired wheel pants. The larger 200 hp Gipsy Six engines gave it a much more lively performance and improved payload. It also carried six to eight people, and although its fuselage was made of plywood like the Dragon, the wood stringers and fabric cover gave it a sleek streamlined appearance. Sixteen eventually came to Canada. Three were in ac-

Dragon CF-APJ is serviced on the de Havilland ramp in 1933. It was with Canadian Airways until 1942 when it was used for parts to keep AVD flying. (C.D. Long)

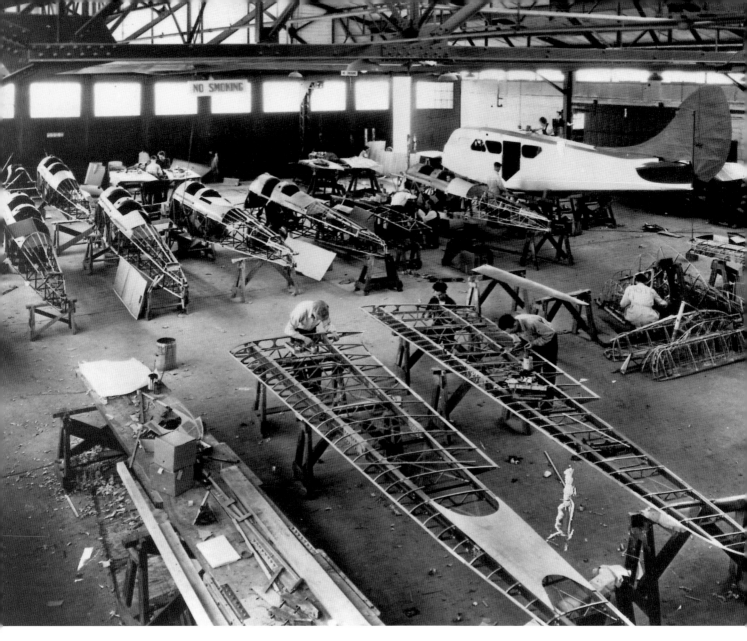

The plant interior during 1934-35. In the middle are RCAF Moths for overhaul, while Rapide wings are assembled in the foreground. At the south end, by the hangar doors, engine mounts are being assembled in the stub wings for the same Rapide. A fuselage sits covered and ready, while ladies from the fabric shop rib-stitch Moth wings. (DH)

tive use from 1936 to 1951, while seven were used regularly from 1939 to 1946.

In retrospect it can be said that the Rapide was a success in Canada, for it not only carried the budding airline industry from the single-engine to the twin-engine stage but proved to be one of the first real money-making aircraft in the business. Its size and economy proved just right for the period and, although it was never designed with tough Canadian flying in mind, it converted well to skis and floats. Canadian Airways Limited made wide use of Rapides on the west coast, but it was with their affiliate, Quebec Airways, that the Rapide was best known.

The entire North Shore of the Lower St. Lawrence River became ice-bound and isolated during winter. Quebec Airways and a number of private operators had always spent busy winters keeping communications open and the mail flowing. Quebec pilot Romeo Vachon had pioneered the air mail to Sept-Îles while chief pilot for Canadian Transcontinental Airways. With the arrival of the Rapide he was the logical person to inaugurate an improved winter service along the North Shore.

The added seat capacity of the Rapides, compared to the earlier single-engine ski-planes, made them popular. The distances involved were short and winter landing strips were prepared by the local communities to improve service. The success of the operation was reflected in 1939 with the presentation of the Trans Canada (McKee) Trophy that year to Romeo Vachon. He left Quebec Airways in 1938 but Rapides continued the winter runs into the postwar period when Canadian Pacific Airlines and, later, Quebecair modernized the air service.

A typical winter scene along the St. Lawrence, with a Quebec Airways Rapide dropping the daily mail bag for a North Shore community. (Hotson Col.)

(Below) Engineering for the Dragonfly's Elliot Brothers skis was done by DHC. The skis, mounted on DHC pedestals, required torque struts, check cables and bungee cords. (C.D. Long)

The streamline skis built by DHC for the National Research Council in 1938. They were only flown once. (F.W. Hotson)

Skis and Floats

In January 1936 de Havilland Canada were asked by the National Research Council to build a set of experimental skis for a Rapide. They were to have a number of novel features and be self-aligning in the air due to their streamlined shape. The objective was to do away with the complex fore and aft cables associated with standard skis and eliminate much of the drag. Engineer J. Bruce Douglas was responsible for overseeing the NRC directives while George Blanchard and the author were assigned to build the skis. They were to be 15 ft. (4.6 m) long with spruce planking over a series of bulkheads to produce the streamlined form.

A similar ski attachment, used for the Rapide, included a specialized lower cowling. The system is shown on a Quebec Airways Rapide. (W.D. Murray)

The D.H.89 Rapide was a popular Canadian airliner and bushplane in the late 1930s and through WWII. (Hotson Col.)

CF-AYE on the 18th. It was heavy, wet snow, and although the skis looked perfect in their shining silver, they creaked and groaned as Lee Murray taxied out. Professor Tom Loudon of the University of Toronto was on the flight along with DHC engineer Peter Loveday. They headed for Camp Borden, where there was more snow, and completed a number of landings there. When it started to rain they headed back, knowing that the little snow at Downsview would soon disappear. There were open patches but the skis rode over the slippery grass as easily as snow. The skis performed well aerodynamically but were too weak structurally to have been placed in regular service.

Canadian modifications to British de Havilland types proved a challenge for the small DHC staff. Through the critical years, from the Fox Moths to the Rapides, the design work was shared by J. Bruce Douglas and C. Don Long, graduates of the University of Toronto. Most of the designs during that period involved improvements for winter conditions. Keeping the engines and pilots at operating temperatures had a high priority, but the design of ski undercarriages was the real specialty.

From the days of the Cirrus Moth, DHC had built their own ski pedestals and the art had improved through the period of the Fox, Hornet and Tiger. Laminated wooden skis with copper rivets and brass bottoms, made by Elliot Brothers of Sioux Lookout, proved the most suitable. They were installed with a standard set of rubber bungee cords and check cables to hold the skis in proper flying position. The bigger Rapide and Dragonfly presented additional torque problems due to the greater track and the use

After the spruce structure was built, it was varnished on the inside and covered with doped fabric on the outside. The snow bottoms were ash planks rivetted to the shell and protected with metal sheathing. A standard streamlined ski pedestal was used and the only check cables used were almost entirely contained within the cowling.

The skis were ready by the middle of March. A spring snowfall, however, permitted a test flight with Rapide

of differential power, but these were overcome with struts and braces.

The streamlined wheel pants on the Rapide were not practical for skis and floats, so a new, lower cowl, looking like half a bathtub, was devised to replace the original. It allowed for the torque strut positioning on skis and for the float struts, with all their bracing wires, in the summer configuration. Seaplane installations were handled by Fairchild of Longueil near Montreal, first with floats of their own design and later with the American Edos.

Before Toronto Island Airport existed, this crane at the air harbour was used for launchings. Here Fox Moth API is readied for delivery to General Airways of Rouyn/Noranda. (C.D. Long)

Another feature of the winter Rapide was the quick-drain facility for removing hot oil. It protruded below the cowling for easy access and was covered with a quick-release fairing. Another modification was installation of an additional door on the starboard side for seaplane use. Probably the most distinctive feature of the Canadian Rapide was the extended dorsal fin tapering down the back of the fuselage. It provided the lateral control needed to offset the forward bulk of the seaplane floats.

Quebec Airways' Rapides had a chute built into the floor in the rear of the cabin for dropping mail bags. The mechanic on the flight opened a trap door at the appropriate time and threw out the bags as quickly as possible when the pilot signalled with a buzzer.

DHC air engineer Don Murray spent a winter with Quebec Airways in 1937 and participated in the mail drop. "I learned in a hurry not to let the mail bag get into the slipstream before the buzzer went," said Don. "On my first drop, the wind began taking the bag, making it more and more difficult to hold. By the time the pilot signalled to drop, I was starting to slide out of the hole!"

During the summer float season in the 1930s there was always a lot of traffic between Downsview and the Toronto Air Harbour at the foot of Yonge Street. Repair and modifi-

Rapides on floats were a common sight on the West Coast. Here AYE sits at a Vancouver dock in the colours of Canadian Airways – deep blue fuselage with orange wings and tail (Gordon S. Williams)

cation was always in progress and sometimes the workers would be down there for weeks on end. At changeover time there was always the task of moving the aircraft through city traffic; nobody liked the assignment. The bigger machines required a motorcycle policeman in front and a car behind for safety. Most of the difficult towing was planned for the early hours of the morning.

Harry Beffort's first such trip took place in Moth days when he was in charge of the company truck. It was fall and a Moth had been removed from floats at the waterfront. The early Moths were designed for towing behind a car with their biplane wings folded and locked. Even though he was alone, Beffort regarded it as an easy assignment as he headed for the centre of the city.

He had just entered University Avenue, northbound, when a policeman stopped him with, "Where do you think you are going?" Beffort explained his mission and got the reply, "Not with that thing, you're not!" It was the day of the Santa Claus Parade and by now he was in no position either to back up or to turn around. The police helpfully ushered him up a narrow lane and he sat through the parade wondering how he would get the Moth back onto the street again. Fortunately there were plenty of police, once the parade was over, who enjoyed solving their first aircraft traffic problem.

Then there was the story of George Otter and the Hornet Moth oil tank. George was a young engineering student who, because he had a motorcycle, was assigned the job of taking a repaired oil tank down to the waterfront. He padded it up, tied it securely and set off from Sheppard Avenue about mid-afternoon. He made the trip down in good time, but on arrival could find nothing but some rope and bits of packing tied to his carrier. It must have been a traumatic moment as he visualized the expensive aluminum tank lying on the road somewhere, flattened beyond recognition.

Slowly he retraced his route, looking back and forth at every curb. He passed the other employees leaving work and arrived at last back at the de Havilland parking lot, wondering what excuse he would use first. Most of the cars were gone but he was pleased to note that Russ Borrett was still there. At that moment Russ came out with a parcel under his arm and said, "Looking for this, George?" Evidently the tank had been found beside the road, half a mile from the plant, returned to have a few scuff marks removed, and repainted ready for a second trip to the lake – this time successfully.

Drama at Moose River

A news drama of some impact broke in Nova Scotia during the early months of 1936. The Moose River gold mine, near Halifax, suffered a collapse in its lower levels, trapping a prominent Toronto doctor and his two companions, who were down on an inspection trip. The event affected DH Canada and emphasized dramatically the value of aircraft in emergencies. The affair took a serious turn when one of the men died and the Toronto medical profession made an all-out effort to assist in the rescue of Dr. D.E. Robertson and Alfred Scadding. At the mine site a hole had been drilled into the area where the men were trapped and contact established. Back in Toronto it was decided that help could be administered through that hole and two projects got under way involving de Havilland machines.

Veteran forestry pilot George Phillips of the Ontario Provincial Air Service was detailed by Ontario Premier Mitchell F. Hepburn to fly bales of woollen strips to the mine head on the theory that they could be forced through the hole and would provide warmth for the trapped men. Phillips used the Giant Moth and, in keeping with the news value of the trip, carried reporters Ken McTaggart of the *Mail and Empire* and Ron Williams of the *Globe*.

The second project involved DH Rapide demonstrator CF-AYE and DH general manager Lee Murray. The radiology department of the Toronto General Hospital reasoned that if a radium capsule was lowered to the men, it could give the rescue crews better direction in the digging operations. The plan received immediate approval at Queen's Park and they contracted with de Havilland for their new Rapide. Excitement grew at Sheppard Avenue as government officials and reporters phoned back and forth. The Rapide was still receiving its finishing touches as it was pushed from the hangar on April 21 to load the radium container and board the experts who were to accompany the flight. Pete Loveday and Lee Murray climbed on board, but AYE had only taxied about 100 yards (91 m) when it became stuck in the mud. Everyone on the field joined in a great pushing exercise and, with the engines running full blast, managed to get the aircraft to higher ground. At 2:00 p.m. the plane took off and made a successful trip to Halifax, with a stop at St. Hubert Airport near Montreal. The trapped men were eventually rescued, but there were never any reports of them wrapping themselves in wool strips.

The Tiger Moth

Through the hiatus of the 1930s the Tiger Moth made its faltering start in Canada. When the first D.H.82A Tiger, CF-AVG, was approved on August 24, 1935, the RCAF was in a state of hold. Although training officers loved the Tiger Moth's improved flying features, there was no budget for a

British-built Tiger Moth CF-AVG with an early design of coupe top. AVG became DHC's model for production jigs and fixtures. It was later rebuilt, modified and delivered to the RCAF as No. 238. (C.D. Long)

purchase. CF-AVG was fitted with a coupe top, inverted flying equipment and everything the RCAF thought important. Lee Murray took it to Ottawa, Camp Borden and every flying club within a reasonable distance of Toronto. The effort resulted in four sales to the flying clubs but the aircraft spent most of its time as a hack for local flying around Downsview.

The overhaul of RCAF Moths continued into 1936 but was sporadic. Lee Murray applied his diplomacy with two tactful letters to Ottawa. On January 2 he wrote: "We have completed the RCAF aircraft allotted and there is very little work from other sources. If it is convenient for you to issue two or three aircraft requiring overhaul, it would be most appreciated." When nothing happened, he wrote again on February 14 inquiring if the RCAF was likely to have any overhaul work in the next few months. "This particular part of the year is always rather slack," wrote Murray, "and any government work would be most helpful."

His letters brought results but the staff had hardly begun reconditioning Moth 60s than a rush of civil work plus the arrival of four Tiger Moths from England cut into RCAF contracts. As so often happens in this cyclical industry, Murray had to write again to Ottawa, but this time with apologies for delays. He explained the situation, saying that his staff were working overtime "to within the limits of Provincial labour laws" and that they were trying desperately to "apportion the work."

Philip Clarke Garratt

On May 8, 1936, an event occurred in the DH Canada family atmosphere when manager Lee Murray brought a tall, smiling man around and introduced him to each employee. Some on the shop floor did not know Philip Clarke Garratt,

but he had been part of the de Havilland scene since the days of the first Moth tests. He was manager of his own chemical company in Toronto but had been indulging his great love of flying by helping with the testing duties in his spare time. He became a director of de Havilland Canada in 1935 and on May 8 was preparing to take over from Murray as general Manager. (The official "signing in" took place May 10.) A farewell party was held at the St. Regis Hotel later in the month for Mr. and Mrs. Murray, who were returning to life in England where he was to become DH general manager. They were to see Canada again during the war years.

P.C Garratt was born in Toronto and educated at Jarvis Collegiate and University of Toronto Schools. He was studying medicine at the University of Toronto when WWI broke out, and began taking flying lessons at the Curtiss Aviation School at Toronto in 1915 as a means of getting into the Royal Flying Corps. He joined the RFC the following year

Senior DHC men: Bob Loader, who opened the first operation at Mount Dennis and supervised the move to Downsview; Phil Garratt, who was manager from 1936 to 1965; and Lee Murray, whose term began in December 1933 and ended in 1936 when he handed the reins to Garratt. (DH)

Anne O'Neil was Mr. Garratt's first secretary. According to letters in the National Archives she was kept busy when the company was trying to sell Tiger Moth CF-AVG to the Canadian government. They said "No." (Hotson Col.)

as a second lieutenant, saw service as a fighter pilot in France and was posted as captain to flying instruction in England. In 1920 he became associated with Bishop-Barker Aeroplanes and he served for a while as instructor in the RCAF at Camp Borden. He settled into the chemical business in 1928 and later managed his own company. He kept close to aviation by assisting with test flying at Mount Dennis and Downview.

One incident on Phil Garratt's arrival as manager was typical of his direct approach to all problems. He never did like the sign at Sheppard and Dufferin. It was an awkward corner and the ditches were high. More than one car had come to grief and he reasoned that the sign, with all its information, was a bit of a distraction. In a matter of days the sign was painted black, with large letters reading only "De Havilland Aircraft."

When Phil Garatt took over at DH Canada, he was faced with "What to do with the demonstrator Tiger Moth?" The four club machines were being picked up by Moose Jaw, Hamilton, Kingston and Calgary and it was time to try a new tack with W/C E.W. Stedman and the men who made the decisions in Ottawa. An interesting series of letters followed which indicated the possibilities. Either the air force training budget was extremely small, or the thinking of the decision-makers was even smaller.

Garratt opened the correspondence on July 25, 1936, offering the demonstrator Tiger, CF-AVG, at $5,000 (plus tax). He stressed that the aircraft was imported to interest the department, adding that an expenditure of over $6,000 had already been made and "that it wasn't being used to advantage." W/C Stedman agreed that it would provide an opportunity for the RCAF to test the type, particularly as they had a spare Puss Moth engine in stock. He evidently did not comprehend that the Tiger had the new Gipsy Major for he

requested a quote on the machine less engine. The general manager wrote back that he would greatly regret selling the airframe alone as the Gipsy III, of less horsepower, would not show the aircraft to its best advantage. Another letter from George Mickleborough repeated the point, adding that all the inverted flying gear would have to be removed in such a case and emphasizing the extra work involved.

During the summer, the correspondence went back and forth. Garratt offered to take the Gipsy III in exchange for $300 and revised his quote to $4,700. W/C Alan Ferrier then got into the act, asking about their policy on spares and the exchange of Gipsy IIIs. In his next letter Garratt regretted that the issue was not clear, explained the difference in engines and repeated his offer. When the fact that the Major was an upgraded Gipsy III finally sank in, Stedman replied that they would be dealing with "a lone engine of a new type" and suggested that the idea of the sale be dropped. Finally, with the arrival of fall, a letter was received on September 24 from the director of contracts that "His Majesty's Government has decided not to take up de Havilland's offer for one Tiger Moth."

The All-Canadian Tiger Moth

As suppliers of elementary trainers to the RCAF, de Havilland's supremacy came to an abrupt end in 1930 when Gipsy Moth orders ceased. Thirteen Puss Moths were delivered in 1931, but they were intended for advanced instruction and instrument training in Ottawa and Camp Borden. Fleet Aircraft of Canada under Jack Sanderson had done an excellent job of promoting the robust Fleet Fawn and sold 20 to the RCAF in 1931. Even while Phil Garratt was trying to sell the lone Tiger demonstrator in 1936, 10 more Fleet Fawn IIs went to the air force.

These facts did not deter Garratt, who continued to prepare for a made-in-Canada Tiger Moth incorporating all the improvements the RCAF kept requesting. By 1937 there were 35 Fleets on RCAF strength and a strong case was developing for a second primary trainer in the service. Early in March a load of assorted angle iron was dropped off at Sheppard Avenue and the "buzz" on the shop floor was that it was for Tiger Moth jigs. On the 12th the speculation was over; an order was confirmed for 26 machines (the much discussed demonstrator and 25 others). These were to be the basic British "A" model with designed-in-Canada modifications: wide walkways on the lower wings, mass-balanced ailerons, metal interplane struts, a new Perspex canopy, heavier axles, single hinged cowlings and a host of smaller things based on eight years of experience with the Moths.

(Left) The first all-Canadian Tiger Moth (RCAF No. 239) in the final stages before test flight. The senior workmen are John Neal (left) and Frank Warren. (C.D. Long)

(Below) The noon-hour turnout of employees to assist with and witness the first flight of Tiger Moth 239. Phil Garratt is strapped in and ready to do his part. (C.D. Long)

From the moment the order was confirmed, things moved quickly. CF-AVG was dismantled and stripped to bare components for use in building jigs and fixtures. Two new "tin hangars" were built, backing onto the spur line, beside the heating plant. The closest was fitted as a paint shop, while the other was for aircraft storage. The much-used wooden hangar was transformed into a woodworking shop and an experienced specialist, W. "Bill" Houston, joined to take on the manufacture of ribs and formers. "Marm" Borczak checked out on the new router to

This December 21, 1936, photograph by the author shows P.C. Garratt taxiing out to fly the first DH aircraft wholly manufactured in Canada since WWI.

59

Once production was under way, the sight of Tigers being tested became common at Downsview – including this "low-and-over." (Hotson Col.)

become the expert on wing spars. New people were hired to round out the existing departments and the Tiger work soon blended with the comings and goings of the Rapides, Dragonflies and Hornet Moths. The year 1937 was busy: by fall, Tiger production was in full swing – enough to have serial number C301 (RCAF 239) ready for testing a few days before Christmas.

Phil Garratt came down from his office on the cold noon-hour of December 21, 1937, climbed into 239 and took it for its first test flight. A few workers braved the cold to watch the proceedings, while those inside jockeyed for position and ate their lunch beside the nearest windowsill. It was rather an historic occasion since it was the first Canadian-made de Havilland airplane since the WWI D.H.6 and the first completely manufactured in Toronto since Canadian Aeroplanes Limited closed in 1918. It tested perfectly and was delivered to the RCAF 28 days later, starting a pattern that continued at regular intervals throughout the rest of the year.

The first D.H.82A (Can) Tiger Moth had been delivered in 10 months from receipt of order, and throughout this period a trickle of RCAF Moth 60Ms had been in for overhaul. There had always been a cry of not enough equipment in the RCAF so it was rather a surprise when a letter arrived from Ottawa dated February 10, 1938, announcing headquarters' decision that there would be no more Moth 60 aircraft rebuilt, nor would any more Gipsy I and II engines be overhauled when they were "time expired." Now that the Tigers had been ordered, the policy was to slowly withdraw the Moths from service.

The D.H.90 Dragonfly

Years after the era of the Dragon and Rapide, Don Long prepared an article for the Canadian Aviation Historical Society *Journal* describing the D.H.90 Dragonfly. He called it a milestone in the career of de Havilland Canada and the end of a decade as importers and modifiers of British airplanes:

The builders of fifteen thousand biplanes made their last contribution to this configuration with the most beautiful of all, the D.H.90 Dragonfly. The final stage in the evolution of the de Havilland biplanes started in 1932 with the D.H.84 Dragon. It proved that an ugly airplane could be effective, but its immediate descendants, the D.H.86 Express Airliner and the D.H.89 Dragon Rapide, put style back with the functional high aspect ratio wing.

By this time the men at Hatfield realized that future airliners would have to be monoplanes with monocoque structures, but in 1935 they distilled all of their biplane experience into one last fling, a twin-engined airplane too small for an airline, but suited to the well-heeled private owner and the business executive.

One could say that they went too far in quest of beauty, but with the materials used it wasn't that expensive, and it was worth it! The wings were long and tapered, with unequal spans and unequal chords, and with less exposed bracing than any biplane since the Fokker D VII.

The lower centre section was a cantilever, running through the fuselage from one landing gear to the other, carrying the engine nacelles and two 30-gallon fuel tanks; this provided bending and torsional stiffness without external bracing, and a platform on each side of the cabin that you could walk all over without fear of breaking through or of scalping yourself with wires. All the controls and services to the nacelles were carried through the leading edges of the wings which were hinged at the front spar. The main gear was assisted by side stays and torque linkages when skis were used.

The fuselage was plywood-skinned, nearly elliptical in section, with flat sides tapering to nothing at the nose and tail: a true

Phil Garratt welcomes fellow director William Archibald, who was taking delivery of Consolidated Mining and Smelting's Dragonfly CF-AYF. (Right) AYF landing at Vancouver. (C.D. Long, Gordon S. Williams)

Three of the women from the fabric shop in 1936, following the compass swing of Dragonfly CF-AYF. Left to right: Ethyl Almond, Betty McNichol (forelady) and Hilda Currell. (C.D. Long)

The compact cockpit of a Rapide. The Dragonfly had a similar layout. (C.D. Long)

monocoque construction. A cabin door on the left side led to the wide rear seat, to a single seat on the right side, or forward through a wide space to the pilots' seats and dual controls. There was a large luggage space in a compartment behind the cabin.

The powerplants were Gipsy Majors with Schwarz-finished wooden propellers, in cowlings which were split and hinged on their centrelines so that they could be very easily opened. There was electric engine starting plus navigation and landing lights, directional gyro, artificial horizon, and airlog, as well as the customary instruments of the time.

The performance was quite snappy, with a cruising speed of 125 mph on 12 gallons of fuel per hour and an ultimate range of 625 miles. The takeoff ground roll was 900 feet in a five mph wind and the landing distance from 50 feet was 1,020 feet. Nowadays this would be regarded as nearly STOL! Two short split trailing-edge

flaps on the lower centre section steepened the glide about 25 per cent. The early price tag was $8,000. The first Canadian Dragonfly went to Consolidated Mining and Smelting Limited.

William Archibald

William Archibald, manager of Consolidated Mining and Smelting of Trail, B.C., is generally considered the father of business aviation in Canada. He earned his flying licence at the age of 53 and began applying his new-found skills in the operation of CM&S. He was also a long-time supporter of de Havilland and, according to the records, must have spent much time at Downview signing aircraft purchase documents. As early as May 8, 1929, he bought his first private Cirrus Moth and later that month ordered two Moths for company operations. He began a training school within the company for pilots and ground crew, which was rather a novelty at the time and proved successful. When the Puss Moth came on the scene, Archibald acquired one of the first and extended his business trips to include the whole of Canada.

Two more Puss Moths went to C.M.&S. in 1930 and 1934, followed by a Dragon on floats in 1935. In 1935 Archibald's use of aircraft for business was recognized when he was awarded the Trans-Canada (McKee) Trophy. In 1936 Consolidated bought a new Hornet Moth. The boss moved to two engines when he and his chief pilot, Page McPhee, arrived at Downsview on July 16 to take delivery of the Dragonfly, the first twin-engined executive aircraft in Canada. Three Hornet Moths followed in 1937 and the company turned its Dragon in on a Rapide in 1938. It also rounded out its DH stable that same year with a Fox Moth.

It was obvious from the start that Archibald was a good customer. His involvement with aviation and his reputation in the business world had earned him a place on the DHC board of directors on January 29, 1934. His only leave was a short period in the war years when the Canadian Government managed the plant, but he continued as a director until November 11, 1949.

The handover of its Rapide to the *Globe and Mail*. Newspaper officials and DHC employees gathered for the ceremony. (Globe and Mail)

The Flying Newsroom

A short-lived venture into early corporate aviation began in June 1937 with an impressive christening at de Havilland's Toronto plant on Sheppard Avenue. The man behind it all was a self-made financial genius who had learned his trade in the mining fields of northern Ontario. George McCullagh had arrived on the Toronto scene earlier in the year as publisher of the newly formed *Globe and Mail*. His partner in the venture was another wealthy mining man, William Wright, and it was clear the new paper would take a special interest in mining. Wright remained silently in the background, but the outgoing McCullagh planned to keep in close personal touch with the north by air.

On June 10 he purchased a D.H.89 Dragon Rapide, CF-BBG, and had it outfitted at Downsview for northern travel deluxe. It was named the *Flying Newsroom* and Toronto pilot Jim Crang was hired to fly mining reporters and analysts anywhere in Canada on wheels, skis and floats. Don Murray was given leave from DHC to accompany the plane for servicing and maintenance. The ceremony in Toronto included speeches from Phil Garratt, Col. Douglas Joy (district inspector of the DOT) and pilot Jim Crang in full uniform. McCullagh told of his ambitions for the airplane and invited his wife to formally christen the Rapide. As soon as all flight tests were completed, the *Flying Newsroom* went on floats at Fairchild in Longueuil and headed for the mines of northern Ontario.

CF-BBG returned to the Toronto waterfront Air Harbour on August 21 amid great publicity. Other trips were planned for the next day and refuelling began at 6 o'clock in the

evening. One tank was filled but as the hose was moved to the other side, a spark from the nozzle ignited gas fumes from the empty tank into a ball of flame. The wood and fabric plane did not last long and all that could be done was to float it away from the dock and let it burn. It was a severe setback to George McCullagh's enthusiasm and foresight, but he returned with a second private aircraft after the war, Grumman Mallard CF-EIZ.

RCAF overhaul work tapered off in 1936 but Phil Garratt was launching a drive to obtain civilian repairs. When he received a call from Roy Brown, head of General Airways, that their Fox Moth CF-API had gone through the ice and sunk in the Ottawa River, Garratt's reply was prompt: "Salvage all you can and get it to us on a truck. I'll guarantee to sell it for more than the repair costs." It was a sorry looking load of parts that arrived some time later but API was reborn in 1937 looking like new. Recalling the incident years later, Garratt said, "George Blanchard was our woodworking expert in those days and he practically lived in that Fox Moth fuselage."

Another call from General Airways involved their Bellanca CH-300, CF-AEC; it had been severely damaged. It looked like a writeoff but "What could de Havilland do?" Garratt's reply was the same: "Send it down. We'll repair it at cost; it will keep the plant busy." When the wreck arrived in a boxcar on February 26, 1935, it was in bad shape. The sternpost was gone and the sturdy Bellanca undercarriage, looking somewhat like a bridge, was punched high into the cabin. The wings and assorted controls were in reasonable shape and were soon spread around the shop for repair. Russ Borrett, the welding specialist, and a helper worked steadily until the fuselage again took shape. By summer, AEC was back together again and, according to the test pilot, flew better than ever.

Three DHC workers with the *Flying Newsroom:* Author Fred Hotson, Don Murray and Reg Corlett. (Hotson Col.)

(Below) When the ceremonies were over and tests completed, the *'Newsroom* flew to Fairchild for a change-over to Edo floats. It is shown on the Toronto Air Harbour ramp. A fire after its first northern flight put a sudden end to this operation. All that remained were floats, engines and skeletal remnants. (C.D. Long)

Wings for the Mounties

One of the early visitors to the new plant on Sheppard Avenue was the distinguished Major General Sir James Howden MacBrien. He later became head of the Royal Canadian Mounted Police and was the man who gave wings to the Mounties. Sir James was one of the most energetic aviation

Engineer C. Don Long joined de Havilland out of university. An avid photographer, he recorded much DHC history. During the Tiger Moth period, he took this photo of the engineering staff: Peter Gooch, Bill Jackson, Bruce Douglas and Bill Calder.

enthusiasts of the era, a lifetime soldier and an accomplished private pilot. His full and exciting career went back to the South African war, followed by a tour in the Royal Canadian Dragoons and Australian Light Horse. In World War I he was made a brigadier general of the 12th Infantry C.E.F. and was mentioned in dispatches six times. Promoted to major general, he became Chief of General Staff Overseas Military Forces of Canada, 1919-20; Chief of the General Staff Military H.Q. Ottawa, 1920-23; and Chief of Staff, Department of National Defence, 1923-28. He had at one time been general manager of Canadian Airways Limited and he became Commissioner of the RCMP in 1931.

His position as president of the Aviation League of Canada (a group of air-minded enthusiasts) and first president of the Canadian Flying Clubs Association brought his name to the attention of Sir Charles Wakefield in England. Sir Charles had earlier made a gift of a Moth to the Toronto Flying Club and he now sought to recognize MacBrien and the Aviation League in a similar way for the work he was doing. A new metal-fuselage D.H.60M Moth arrived in Canada for MacBrien's personal use as a gift from Sir Charles Wakefield and was registered CF-AAA to the Aviation League of Canada on June 15, 1929. The general made good use of the aircraft during the next five years for he loved to travel. The all-white Gipsy Moth was seen regularly at aviation functions from coast to coast. Phil Garratt used to tell the story of one such flight when the general was

asked to attend a flying meet to mark the opening of the new Moncton airport. In view of General MacBrien's position in the RCMP, the episode can only be labelled "The Case of the Unluckiest Smuggler."

On the day in question, military promptness and a good tailwind brought the RCMP Commissioner and his Moth to Moncton much earlier than expected. His arrival was to be part of the program so the committee asked him to leave for a while and arrange his return as part of the opening ceremony. This posed no problem for the general and soon he had landed in an out-of-the-way field with nothing to do but wait out the clock. MacBrien made good use of the time by conducting a detailed inspection of the ground in preparation for takeoff. As he strolled across the grass he came upon a few old boards covering an irregular depression. His curiosity got the better of him, and when he probed the situation further, he discovered a cache of illegal liquor.

It was the illicit liquor traffic in eastern Canada that helped put the Mounties in the flying business. The need for air mobility had been felt for many years and patrols in conjunction with the RCAF had been going on in British Columbia and New Brunswick since 1928. Better mobility was badly needed in northern Canada, where weeks of travel by land did little to speed law enforcement. In 1932 the incident of the "Mad Trapper of Rat River" drew worldwide publicity and emphasized the value of the airplane in police work, especially in remote areas. The 29-day manhunt in the Arctic for the man who had killed one Mountie and wounded another was one of the first cases in which an aircraft was called in to assist overland patrols.

During the same year the RCAF was asked to organize air patrols with single-engined Fairchild 71s on both coasts, using RCMP observers. Prohibition in the U.S. had brought a rash of rum-running in the eastern provinces. Drug traffic along the British Columbia coast was also a problem, even in those days. As the need for aircraft patrols increased, the hard-pressed RCAF found their involvement increasingly burdensome. Only 154 aircraft were on strength with the RCAF at the end of March 1936. This was reduced to 135 aircraft one year later with eight of these unserviceable. Ian Mackenzie, defence minister in the new Liberal government of 1936, was under pressure to decrease RCAF participation in the civil operations of mapping and patrol. The military won their point and, although it was a timely break for the RCAF, it meant that the RCMP had to shift for themselves.

Commissioner MacBrien was a firm believer in close headquarters contact with all outlying RCMP posts. In 1936 he completed a historic, four-week, 11,000-mile (17,700 km) inspection trip, using a float-equipped Fairchild 71 on loan from the RCAF and piloted by F/L R.C. Gordon. Later that year he was one of the first to evaluate the new de Havilland D.H.90 Dragonfly. Its size was ideal for patrols and the two engines seemed more appropriate for the long over-water flights. Four Dragonflies were promptly ordered for the RCMP.

The plan for the new Air Division went forward quickly with the signing of the order and DHC soon found itself involved in this interesting project. An RCMP detachment moved into North Toronto on April 1, 1937, taking quarters in the second story of the Post Office building on Montgomery Avenue. A flight refresher course was started at the Toronto Flying Club under chief flying instructor, R.W. "Ray" Goodwin weeks before the large boxes of aircraft parts began arriving at the Downsview siding. The eight RCMP pilots assigned to the new wing had a variety of previous flying experience – four were from the RCAF and four had flying club backgrounds.

Excitement grew at de Havilland as they began assembling the Dragonfly wings and building up the engine nacelles, and they soon came to know the men who would be flying the aircraft. In charge of the operation was Superintendent R.E. Mercer, Officer Commanding "O" Division in

Toronto. The pilots were Staff Sergeants T.R. Michelson and M.P. Fraser; and Sergeants R.H. Baker, G.F. Hart, W. Munro, L. Dubuc, P.M. Grant and W.E. Barnes (the last five doubled as mechanics).

The de Havilland demonstrator Dragonfly CF-BBD had been flying since October 1936 and was used for familiarization flights and instruction. Ray Goodwin, who later became Director of Civil Aviation, Department of Transport, was checked out on the aircraft by de Havilland's general manager. He began instructing on the Dragonfly at the Toronto Flying Club field at Dufferin Street and Wilson Avenue. April 19 provided the only awkward incident in the conversion program. Staff Sgt. Michelson was doing practice landings when his plane veered dangerously close to aircraft on the hangar line. Sitting in the Toronto Flying Club Puss Moth CF-CDM with the engine running was Dr. Easson Brown, prominent Toronto physician, and his daughter, waiting to go aloft for a pleasure flight. To the doctor's dismay, the Dragonfly headed straight for him. Michelson managed to brake his new charge, but not before it had straddled the nose of the Puss Moth and forced it into a distinct crouching position. The main damage resulted from all propellers turning at the moment of impact. The Puss Moth received considerable wing damage and never flew again. Its metal propeller cut through the plywood side of the Dragonfly, breaking Michelson's left leg. The accident caused considerable activity at the factory. John Slaughter was sent over to the flying club to put a new panel in the side of the Dragonfly and Phil Garratt flew it back to the plant for further repairs. It later emerged as CF-MCP, the third in the series. The first Dragonfly, CF-MPA, in its dark blue fuselage

Major General J.H. MacBrien, who headed the RCMP during the purchase of the Dragonflies, took an active part in the Aviation League of Canada, the Air Cadets and the flying club movement. (Via RCMP)

The RCMP's modern Dragonflies had electric starters, radio, a landing light and plush seating. CF-MPA later served with the RCAF as 7626. It was "reduced to spares" in 1943. (C.D. Long)

(Right) The only incident during RCMP training at the Toronto Flying Club happened when Staff Sgt. Michelson veered into a taxiing Puss Moth. (Via C.D. Long)

and yellow wings was delivered to the Mounties on May 5, 1937. CF-MPB followed on May 29, MPC on July 15 and MPD on June 26. For simplicity and identification, each was named for a flower coinciding with the last letter of the registration: *Anemone, Buttercup, Crocus, Dandelion*.

At the end of the training program, the planes went to Moncton to take up anti-smuggling patrols over the Gulf of St. Lawrence, the Bay of Fundy and the waters off Nova Scotia. This had a distinct and immediate effect on rum-running in the area. Sergeant W.E. Barnes, who later became a captain on Trans-Canada Air Lines, put it down to their use of radio, a considerable innovation at the time. The easy contact between the searching planes and marine cruisers soon put a damper on coastal smuggling.

With Sgt. Barnes as pilot, General MacBrien left Ottawa on June 19, 1937, for an inspection trip across Canada and back. The route took them to Kapuskasing, Winnipeg, Regina, Edmonton, Calgary, Lethbridge, Grand Forks, and Vancouver. Barnes noted in his log book: "Sir James is a

damn good man, but guess who was boss?"

Of the eight Dragonflies that came to Canada, six were taken over by the RCAF for twin-engine training at the start of the war. These were the DHC demonstrator, three from the RCMP and two new ones that had not been sold. AYF continued with Consolidated Mining and Smelting, while the fourth RCMP machine was sold to Leavens Brothers. Two Dragonflies were written off in RCAF service and four were eventually returned to civilian use. They all slowly retired from service. The last to go was CF-BFF, which sank through the ice on the Ottawa River on December 21, 1949, while with Gold Belt Air Service of Rouyn, Quebec.

Imperial Airways *Cambria*

August 1937 had been a busy month with the Tiger Moth production line starting to take shape on the hangar floor. In fact, it had been a good summer all around. The Mounties had departed for the east coast with their new

Dragonflies and the yellow Dragonfly CF-BFF had been adapted for floats at Fairchild. Now it was Canadian National Exhibition time when Toronto life quickened with programs at the waterfront, including aviation. This year the "Ex" was to feature a visit from Imperial Airways' giant Short flying boat *Cambria*, G-ADUV, making a special side trip from its experimental Atlantic trials. Nothing that size had ever flown into Toronto before and its arrival on Lake Ontario before thousands of Exhibition visitors was to be something of a spectacle. One of the employees recalled:

It was the talk of the shop that day, and I remember we were all disappointed that we had to work. The arrival was scheduled for five o'clock in the evening and we had adjusted our minds to the fact that we would have to hear about it on the radio that night. We saw Mr. Garratt leaving with a group about three o'clock and commented that there were some advantages, after all, in being the boss. I was working on Tiger Moth jigs at the time and got home as quickly as possible to hear the radio news.

It was evident that we had missed quite a show, for the Cambria *had experienced difficulty at the lakefront and had knocked off one of its wing floats. Sure enough, in the papers the next day were pictures of the flying boat being towed to the Toronto Harbour Commission dock and the story of what happened. Little did we know at the time that, being the only aircraft factory in Toronto, we would be called upon to do the repairs. It turned out to be quite an exercise!*

The story in the papers made it clear that the *Cambria* had landed at right angles to the wind and provided spectators with an exciting few minutes. It arrived at 5 p.m. as scheduled and, after circling the Exhibition grounds, began its approach over the Dufferin Street buildings and the Exhibition flagpole. The flag on the pole indicated a westerly wind but, because the approach was to the south, old-time boat pilot Roy Maxwell was heard to exclaim: "Good Heavens, he's in for it!" According to reports, the flying boat hit with a cloud of spray and, with its left wing in the water, swung slowly around facing the crowd. Captain Powell, the flying

The Imperial Airways *Cambria* in difficulty off the Toronto waterfront. It was towed to the docks, dangling one float, and later to Toronto Island for repairs. In the second photo *Cambria* is tucked into a lagoon at the Island, where a de Havilland work party removed the damaged sections and made repairs. New parts were shipped from England. (*Globe and Mail*, C.D. Long)

The only D.H.94 Moth Minor in Canada before the war is shown at Downsview. The Minor was a sleek, all-wood trainer designed during 1937 as a Gipsy Moth replacement. Production was cut short at 100 in 1939 when the pressures of war descended on the British company. Another Moth Minor, CF-ADO, came to Canada via Australia after the war. (F.W. Hotson)

boat skipper, claimed in an interview that he had hit an object in the water, but E.L. Cousins, manager of the Harbour Commission, countered that he had two boats sweeping the area for two days before the arrival.

Next day de Havilland was asked to repair the damaged *Cambria*, now tied near the coal piles – under guard – at the foot of Cherry Street. Frank Warren took Reg Corlett and Don Murray to begin a long stint at the Toronto waterfront. It was a case of removing all the damaged components, repairing torn sections of metal and ordering new parts. Imperial Airways sent a new float and parts via the *Queen Mary* to New York, whence they were brought to Toronto by truck. Working on such a large, all-metal airplane (now moved to a

secluded bay at Toronto Island) was a new departure for DH Canada, which had been dealing almost exclusively with wooden aircraft.

"You can just imagine us," recalled Don Murray, "bouncing around in a boat, trying to put metal patches on the underside of this big wing. Reg and I had just about got one piece of dural skin in position when it slipped and fell into the water. We poked around in the weeds with a stick but didn't have much luck. I spotted something shining and stripped off to my shorts and dived in, scraping around in the mud until I felt it. I brought up the piece but found it had been scratched, so we had to make another. This is the way it went, often into the night. I remember I was working late one night and couldn't stay awake. I went to Frank Warren and asked if I could have some time off to curl up and have a sleep." After 10 hectic days of work the *Cambria* was airworthy again and Captain Powell and his crew made their departure. Before leaving for Montreal they said thanks to the de Havilland staff with a flight over the hangars at Downsview.

Hornets for the RAF

A transaction involving D.H.87 Hornet Moths which might be classed as a "boomerang sale"

For WWII, Hornet Moth CF-BFK became No. 5600 in RAF Transport Command. In 1946 it returned to the civil registry as CF-DIP. (J. Reed via Jack McNulty)

took place in 1939. When the first Hornet arrived in Canada in 1936 it was sent to Fairchild for seaplane floats designed by their chief engineer, Francis Hyde-Beadle. The Hornet's side-by-side cabin and two doors made it handy for float operations. Its performance on water compared favourably to the Fox Moth of the same period.

Four years later, in 1939, a call came from the British Air Ministry inquiring about the availability of Hornet seaplanes. They were needed for a hurry-up program training seaplane pilots, and their folding wings facilitated stowage on board ship for special assignments. The inquiry could not have come at a more opportune time as four Hornets were at Downsview awaiting customers; three bore Canadian registrations and one was still in its crate. CF-AYI had belonged to Frank Trethewey in 1936 but was back with DHC a year later. The demonstrator CF-BFJ had sunk at its moorings in Toronto Harbour in 1937 but had been rebuilt ready for sale. CF-BFN had been tested on floats and was also up for sale. The three active aircraft went off the Canadian register in May 1939 and subsequently emerged as Ministry nos. P6788, P6785 and P6786 respectively. Hornet serial No. 8134 was not yet on the Canadian registry but was fitted with floats and shipped as P6787. They were all flown extensively at Felixstowe in England and were later restored to wheels. Two survived the war and ended on the British civil registry. Ex-Canadian BFJ became G-AHBL and ex BFN became G-AHBM.

There was secrecy surrounding the British Ministry Hornets, but the program was successful enough that when war broke out, British naval officials commandeered all existing Hornet Moths in Canada. One that got caught up in the order was CF-BKF, which sported an RAF roundel and the number 5600. It served in Canada with RAF Transport Command and was stationed at North Bay, Ontario. It was returned to the civil register after the war as CF-DIP.

Besides its regular landing strip, Fairchild had this natural ramp sloping down to the St. Lawrence River. The combination proved ideal for the Rapide changeovers. The only D.H.90 Dragonfly fitted with floats, CF-BFF, had its float engineering done at Fairchild. (C.D. Long)

A 1938 view showing DHC plant additions made in the hope of more Tiger Moth orders. The space proved useful once the war began and further expansion took place. (DH)

Company picnics during the late 1930s always included a ball game. Here is Phil Garratt in his typical role as umpire. Harry Kentner is at bat and Russ Borrett is catcher. (C.D. Long)

When war broke out in 1939 de Havilland Canada was one of the smallest aircraft companies in the country. Although employment fluctuated considerably during the years leading to the war, the numbers at Downsview always remained small compared with other manufacturers. If old photos of company picnics are any guide, DHC had 30 employees in 1935 and 52 in 1936. The Tiger Moth contract boosted the total to 195 by the end of 1939, still well below close competitor Fleet Aircraft Limited at 519. Montreal consistently led the Canadian aircraft scene in manpower and continued to do so during that critical year of 1939. Canadian Vickers Limited employed 450 and Fairchild Aircraft Limited totalled nearly 1,000. Canadian Car and Foundry of Fort William employed 700, while Noorduyn Aviation Limited of Cartierville, near Montreal, had a rather small group of 140. National Steel Car Corporation Limited opened its new factory at Malton, northwest of Toronto, in 1938 to build Westland Lysanders and from the beginning had more employees than its neighbour at Downsview. Throughout the build-up of military business,

CHAPTER THREE

THE WAR YEARS

de Havilland Canada continued to serve its civilian customers and was not involved in building other companies' airplanes.

Most Canadian manufacturers were building aircraft under licence and in 1938 a new organization emerged to supply Handley Page Hampden bombers for the Royal Air Force. This came about as the result of a British air mission investigating Canada's potential in their own air armament program. A central company was formed, known as Canadian Associated Aircraft Limited, to contract directly with the British government. Assembly factories were built in Montreal and Toronto, with six companies supplying components. DHC was too busy to join the Hampden plan and Phil Garratt preferred to stick with the DH family of aircraft. The six subcontractors – Fleet, Canadian Car, Fairchild, Ottawa Car, Canadian Vickers and National Steel Car – already had orders involving Hawker Hurricanes, Bristol Bolingbrokes, Supermarine Stranraer flying boats, Northop Deltas and Westland Lysanders. In Vancouver, Boeing Aircraft of Canada Limited was building the Blackburn Shark.

With all this activity, the RCAF order in 1937 for 26 Tiger Moths was a small piece of the business in a country verging on war, but everyone at Downsview believed an additional contract would follow. As a production program, construction of the Tiger Moths went well, but by the time the last Tiger was delivered on April 12, 1939, no new order had appeared. While de Havilland was delivering their first Tiger Moths to the Department of National Defence, Fleet added another 10 Fawn IIs to the RCAF inventory.

Shutting down the production line came as a shock for de Havilland after such a promising start in manufacturing. Some modest help came in the form of repair work, for in spite of the earlier letter from Ottawa that no more Gipsy Moths would be overhauled, 12 arrived at the plant for reconditioning. The contract specified that after overhaul the Moths were to be turned over to the flying clubs "under a new RCAF training scheme." Fortunately de Havilland England came through with an order for 200 Tiger fuselages to supplement their own production; otherwise lay-offs would have been considered.

Members of the British mission on an inspection tour of aircraft plants in Canada: Phillip C. Garratt, general manager, de Havilland Aircraft; Sir Robert Brooke-Popham of the British Air Mission; Robert S. Magor, president, National Steel Car; Air Marshal Sir Christopher Courtenay of the British Air Mission; and F.S. Amos of Arthur Balfour Limited. (Hotson Col.)

Engineering work went ahead, improving the Tiger Moth (now called the D.H.82C) with wheel brakes and a fully castering tail wheel instead of a skid. Elevator trim tabs were introduced, similar to those on the Hornet Moth, along with numerous refinements suggested by the RCAF. The last overhauled Gipsy Moth in the government order was turned over to the Regina Flying Club in August 1939 – then, suddenly, Canada was at war.

The Tiger Moth jigs were beefed up in anticipation of further orders, but the only delivery during that historic September was a Dragon Rapide to Quebec Airways. It was a unique experience, to have a war in progress with management considering temporary furloughs. Admittedly Ottawa had a hectic program on its hands as it put the country on a wartime footing, but it was a frustrating period for the DHC board of directors. The most likely prospect for work seemed to be the British Commonwealth Air Training Plan, which was announced December 10, 1939, and went into force seven days later.

Fleet and de Havilland Canada were primarily producers of training aircraft in the 1930s and were therefore dependent on government orders for survival. Each had its civil types to sell, but the impetus to start manufacturing on a large scale did not come to either company until the war was in its fourth month. Light trainer orders were balanced between the two companies but it could hardly be called industrial mobilization.

When the trainer contracts were finally placed, Fleet received a contract for 404 Finches in January 1940, while DHC received an equal order for Tiger Moths in February. After a 10-month lapse, the Tiger production line started

One of the first Canadianized RCAF Tiger Moths, showing new features such as the simplified three-piece engine cowling, the reinforced wing walkway, padded instrument panels and sliding "greenhouse" canopy. The model shown has the winter pad to insulate the exterior oil tank. (C.D. Long)

(Above) The Menasco Pirate 4 was fitted to the Tiger in case the flow of Gipsy Majors from England was curtailed. It was heavier than the Gipsy with less horsepower. As it had a generator attachment, 10 of the 136 built were used as wireless trainers. They were designated D.H.82C2 but called Menasco Moths by the RCAF. (C.D. Long)

(Left) The fabric shop ladies apply tape along the ribs of Tiger Moth wings during the busy days of 1940. (National Museum of Science and Technology)

D.H.82C fuselages are assembled while completed models are prepared for flight. (A.W. Gilford)

(Left) Tiger Moth engine installation took on a production atmosphere as Gipsies continued in good supply. Eddie Loveday guides an engine while Jerome McNamee works the crank. (DH2008)

again with the improved D.H.82C model, powered with the Gipsy 1-C engine of 140 hp, built in England and supplied by the British Ministry of Aircraft Production. Propellers were made in Canada by the Laidlaw Lumber Company, Toronto, and S. and S. Propellers Limited, Winnipeg.

By April 1940 Tiger Moths from Frank Warren's production line were rolling again into an enlarged flight department. One of Canada's veteran pilots, G. Ralph Spradbrow, joined the company as chief test pilot. He had been a career officer in the RCAF, a bush pilot with Dominion Skyways Limited, and more recently the private pilot for John David Eaton, head of the T. Eaton company's chain of department stores. Soon the plant was in full swing again, moving slowly into overtime work and eventually to round-the-clock operations. This sudden reversal of affairs raised the need for considerable expansion in land and housing.

Garratt's executive assistant for the past year had been W. John McDonough, whose task was to develop 96 acres (39 hectares) of newly acquired property into a full-scale airport with paved runways. A section bordered by Dufferin Street on the east and Wilson Avenue on the south was bulldozed into oblivion. Houses were demolished and trees felled in

THE DE HAVILLAND **DH** AIRCRAFT OF CANADA

(Above) A line of D.H.82C Tiger Moths prepared for delivery by the author in the spring of 1941 and photographed while awaiting RCAF crews. (F.W. Hotson)

(Left) Pilot Ralph Spradbrow flies Tiger Moth 5020 in this famous DHC publicity photo. This trainer served in the BCATP from June 1941 till April 1944, then was scrapped. (C.D. Long)

(Below) Early D.H.82A Tiger Moths at Camp Borden, Ontario, in the early days of WWII. No. 249, built in 1938, later was converted to a D.H.82C. (Jack McNulty)

the name of the war effort. The need for additional hangar space produced two new brick and steel assembly bays directly south of the original plant.

The Anson

The Commmonwealth representatives who met in Ottawa to set up the BCATP chose the Avro Anson as their basic twin-engine trainer. It had been used early in the war, but was obsolete as a fighting machine. Ansons were to be supplied from surplus British stock and later from components manufactured in England. The first used Ansons to reach Canada arrived on the de Havilland siding on Saturday, February 25, 1940, ready for assembly. An eager group of employees, working through the weekend, got them into the air by Sunday afternoon and delivered to the RCAF on Monday morning. A steady flow of British Ansons continued to stations across Canada, bringing a certain war urgency with their gun turrets and camouflage paint. Some even had bullet holes, testifying to their hasty withdrawal

from action over the English Channel. DH Canada assembled 264 British Mk.Is, but they hadn't seen the last of the Avro Anson.

Under the training plan, Anson components were supplied from the U.K., except for wings, which were made in Canada because of their wood content and size. Even the metal fittings for the wings came from England. With the spring 1940 crisis in Europe and the sudden evacuation of Dunkirk, the supply of British Ansons to Canada was suspended. This presented an immediate supply crisis for Commonwealth training; Ansons would have to be manufactured in Canada – and quickly.

A number of plans were considered at the highest level that would involve a large portion of the Canadian manufacturing industry. A crown corporation, Federal Aircraft Limited, was formed almost overnight, headed by Nova Scotia businessman Ralph P. Bell, to organize and manage this huge undertaking. Bell was president of Pickford and Black Ltd., a shipping company on the east coast with interests in fishing and lumber. He was drafted to his post as a "dollar-a-year" man in the executive committee of the Minister of Munitions and Supply, Hon. C.D. Howe. Bell became the first president of Federal, charged with administering the Anson program. The new organization was formed June 24, 1940, with headquarters in the Insurance Exchange Building on St. James Street, Montreal.

The first task was to find an American-made engine to replace the English Cheetah, but the major U.S. companies were already over-extended. Finally the Jacobs L6MB of less horsepower (330 hp for the L6MB against 335 hp for the Cheetah IX) was adopted for the Canadian model, to be called the Anson II. Canadian Vickers were given the assignment to engineer the Jacobs conversion and the task of doing the first installation fell to de Havilland Canada. While this was going on, Federal Aircraft put together a huge subcontracting program composed of five final assembly and manufacturing companies along with four supporting companies.

Final assembly and manufacture

Canadian Car and Foundry Company Limited, Amherst, N.S.

The de Havilland Aircraft of Canada Limited, Toronto, Ont.

MacDonald Brothers Aircraft Limited, Winnipeg, Man.

National Steel Car Corporation Limited, Malton, Ont.

Ottawa Car & Aircraft Limited, Ottawa, Ont.

Supporting companies

Canadian Car and Foundry Company Limited, Montreal, Que.

Boeing Aircraft of Canada Limited, Vancouver, B.C.

Cockshutt Plow Company Limited, Brantford, Ont.

Massey-Harris Company Limited, Weston, Ont.

Canada's aircraft manufacturing industry, which before the war was struggling to survive, now had to cope with unprecedented growth. There was much movement from company to company of men with experience, who found themselves in a world that lumped airplanes with land vehicles and farm equipment. One such transfer worked in de Havilland's favour because it brought the eminent Francis P. Hyde-Beadle to Downsview along with the Burlison brothers, George and Bill. Hyde-Beadle was one of the most respected aeronautical engineers in the country with a professional background that went back to the first days of flight in England. He began his career at the famous S.E. Saunders company, where he built racing motor boats. He was one of

the first six technical people to join the old Army Balloon Factory at Farnborough, the name of which was changed in 1911 to the Royal Aircraft Factory. Its first test pilot was none other than Geoffrey de Havilland, who was developing his first designs for the government. This was about the time de Havilland and Hearle's first aeroplane had been designated the F.E.1 and "DH" took "H-B" for his first flight in the machine. With a background of high-speed boat hulls it was only natural that Hyde-Beadle would move to flying boats, which became his design specialty. He designed an amphibian for Saunders in 1921 and Schneider Cup seaplane floats for Gloster. In 1928 he moved to Fairchild in the U.S. and later to the newly organized Fairchild plant in Longueuil. He held an associate fellowship in the Royal Aeronautical Society and was a member of the U.S. Institute of Aeronautical Sciences.

When National Steel Car set up at Malton to build Hampdens and Lysanders, Francis Hyde-Beadle left Fairchild to become chief engineer. He brought with him a number of Fairchild experts but it was a strange "non-aircraft-oriented" world he encountered. In the language of a later day, he became "disenchanted" with management at Malton and was welcomed with open arms by de Havilland. By a stroke of good fortune (for DHC) he persuaded his two top men to join him in his move to Downsview. The Burlison brothers were veterans of Canadian Vickers and Fairchild. George moved into production while Bill took a leading part in the growing inspection department under Bill Rouse.

A similar story involved Richard J. "Dick" Moffett, a highly qualified aeronautical engineer of English background, who became disenchanted with Federal Aircraft and was welcomed at de Havilland Canada. Moffett had come from Britain to Canadian Vickers in early 1928 as a stress engineer during the successful period when they designed and built six Vancouver flying boats. He became manager in 1930 and held that position throughout the Depression years when the staff went down to four. In 1935 he brought the company to life again with RCAF contracts for the large, all-metal Northrop Deltas and Supermarine Stranraers (they built 20 of each).

As war threatened, Vickers joined Canadian Associated Aircraft to build Hampdens and became involved in the Anson program at the declaration of war. Dick Moffett became general manager of Federal Aircraft on July 22, 1940. This story is best told by Douglas A. Newey, who was Moffett's assistant through the depression years and who left Vickers to accompany him to Federal:

Anson final assembly at Downsview. (DH)

It quickly became apparent that Federal Aircraft was by no means a "happy ship." Unfortunately it turned out that Moffett was not satisfied with arrangements at Federal and was very soon in a small war, particularly with Ray Lawson, who had been appointed by the government as President of Federal after Ralph Bell went to Ottawa as Director General of Aircraft Production.

 Mr. Lawson, while undoubtedly a very successful businessman, knew nothing about aircraft and quickly succeeded in antagonizing the entire aircraft industry, which reciprocated with the idea that the infant, Federal Aircraft, should be strangled and mercifully put out of the way before it got its eyes open. Moffett endeavoured to resign August 7th but was not allowed to do so. He resigned again on Sep-

(Left) R.J. "Dick" Moffett in a postwar photo while associated with Canada's Atomic Energy Board. He served two and a half years as production manager during the Tiger Moth and Anson period. (Via R.J. Moffett)

(Right) W.J. Jakimiuk, who led wartime engineering at DHC. He stayed on after the war to take part in the Chipmunk and Beaver programs. (DH1317)

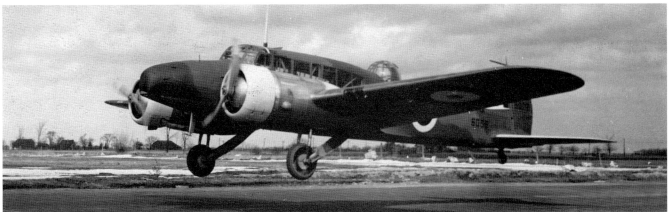

Anson 6093 was one of 75 Mk.Is converted to Mk.IIIs with Jacobs engines. It was photographed on a test flight at Downsview. (DH)

tember 18th and finally compromised by undertaking to build the prototype Anson at de Havilland, where he had already secured employment as Production Manager – as soon as he could become released from Federal Aircraft.

Fortunately, someone in Ottawa saw the light and succeeded in securing the services of Mr. A.W. Newman, at the time chief mechanical engineer of Canadian Pacific Railway, as director of engineering and production. From that day, Federal Aircraft proceeded to go into business and set about building the Anson without more than the normal mistakes that can be expected from such an ambitious project under war conditions. One of the first things Mr. Newman did was to accept the resignation of Dick Moffett, therefore releasing him to take over his duties with de Havilland and clearing the air for all concerned.

Moffett left Federal in November and settled in Toronto on Christmas Day, ready for his new job. He brought with him a well seasoned veteran, Ed Forrest, and suddenly DHC had a formidable factory management team – their own old-timers plus the cream of Vickers/Fairchild experience. On his arrival at Downsview, Moffett saw that the existing ma-

chine shop was completely inadequate. He had a new one set up and furnished with the latest equipment. He delegated clear-cut responsibilities on the Tiger and Anson lines, with Frank Warren in charge of the Tigers and George Burlison steering the Ansons through. In a search for talent within the existing plant, he put Bill Houston in charge of all woodwork, Reg Robinson in charge of machine shop and elevated George Blanchard to the new position of production control.

The first Jacobs engine conversion was carried out by de Havilland on an Anson Mk.I using Vickers drawings. It was completed quickly and test flown by Ralph Spradbrow on January 9, 1941. The DHC contract called for the production of fuselages, engine nacelles and wing root fairings, together with the assembly of Ansons from other subcontracted components. All test flying and preparation of the 375 units would be done at Downsview.

A massive hiring program was begun under Garratt's brother-in-law, Edgar H. Featherstonhaugh; almost everyone who applied received a try, from musicians to carpenters, piano tuners and school teachers. There had always been a number of ladies in the fabric shop, but as time went by more were hired. Since 1934 Toronto's Central Technical School had started many a student on a successful career at de Havilland. The war quickly boosted Central's output, with most of the graduates headed for Downsview and a set of DH overalls. In spite of the influx of new workers, the transition to aviation skills went quickly.

A solid base had been established during production of the first batch of Tiger Moths, along with strict discipline and high standards. Bill Calder as works manager ran a tight ship during that first program and had much to do with the high quality of workmanship that prevailed. Bill Rouse and

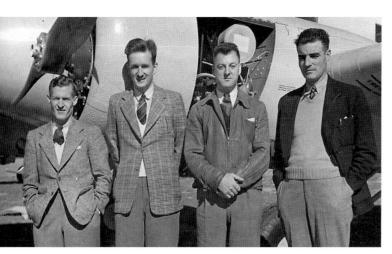

Four DHC test pilots during the Anson period: Ralph Spradbrow, Jim Follett, Frank Fisher and Mike deBlicquy. (DH)

Bill Burlison added new men to the inspection team and were joined by L.A. Taylor and John Macdonald as AID (Air Inspection Detachment) watchdogs. A training section under former Central Technical School instructor D.D. Flett was established for the upgrading of employee skills. New brick buildings smelling of concrete and fresh paint were ready by the fall of 1940 to accommodate this activity.

Because of the work done converting the first Anson to

Jacobs power, a batch of 75 Mk.I Ansons arrived (less engines) for similar treatment. They were promptly converted and went out as Anson Mk.IIIs. Along with the Anson bombers from Britain were 38 Fairey Battles needing assembly. The plant was now on a full wartime footing and coping successfully with the month-by-month expansion. The production of Anson fuselages got so far ahead at one time that they were hauled up into the ceiling for storage. The shop poet laureate even put the subject into verse:

> The ships come pouring off the line
> At such a dizzy pace,
> And then go soaring for a time
> Until they take their place
> Beside the incompletes,
> That hang from up above,
> Awaiting wings, and other things
> That all good airmen love.
> For without motors, wings and tails,
> They cannot turn and dive;
> Let's hope that they can hit the trail
> By Nineteen Forty-Five.

By the end of 1941 Ansons and Tigers were rolling in quantity from the production lines for delivery to the Department of Munitions and Supply. A quarterly report to end the year mentions a Tiger production rate of 60 per month and an additional order for 200 machines.

The Polish Connection

Another name entered the DH Canada scene in the summer of 1940, one that was to have considerable impact on the company for the next 10 years. Wsiewold J. Jakimiuk was the first of many who made their way to Downsview when Poland fell to the Nazi onslaught. He had been chief engi-

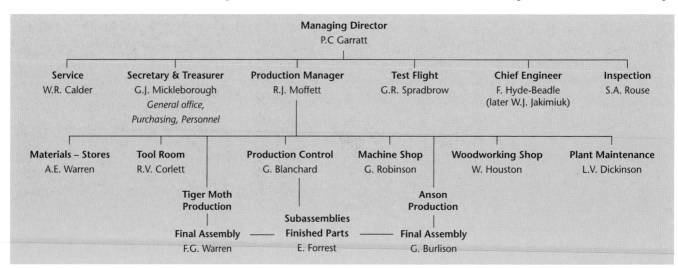

neer at the National Aircraft Factory in Warsaw and was the designer of Polish PZL fighters and a successful commercial transport. He was well known to the parent company in England and during prewar days of their all-metal D.H.95 Flamingo they had journeyed to Poland to consult with Jakimiuk. He was an engineer's engineer, European by culture and upbringing, proud and serious, and exuding confidence based on experience.

An agreement between the Canadian government and the Polish government-in-exile opened the way for the transfer to Canada of dozens of Polish aeronautical engineers who were either in active service with or at the disposition of the Polish Air Force. The arrangement looked ideal on the surface but because governments cannot function even in wartime without red tape, entanglements developed over payments for transportation and other trivial matters. At this point DH England cut through the red tape by guaranteeing the cost of transportation of the Polish war guests to Canada. The cost of some $200,000 was quite a sum at the time but was all later repaid by the engineers. W.Z. Stepniewski, writing years later, said, "I believe that de Havilland's guarantee was largely due to the confidence they held in Jakimiuk and his professional reputation."

Stepniewski and Waclaw Czerwinski were the first to join Jakimiuk out of an eventual total of 40. Both were senior engineers with aircraft designs to their credit and were to make substantial contributions to the Canadian effort.

"When we arrived," continued Stepniewski, "Jakimiuk was already well-established, both technically and socially. He had become a member of the prestigious Granite Club – an exceptional feat for a newcomer in the ultra-conservative, very English Toronto of those days. In addition to all his technical qualifications, Jaki spoke English well and could, in an almost opera-quality bass-baritone, sing a vast repertoire of songs from operatic arias to folk melodies. He had a charming, good-natured, French-English wife, Mary, whose memory can never be erased from the hearts and minds of all Polish engineers and their wives who were fortunate enough to have met her socially."

Waclaw Czerwinski had been one of the leading designers of gliders and high-performance sailplanes in Poland (as well as an advanced twin-engined trainer called the Wyzel). After working a few months at de Havilland he suggested forming a gliding club within the engineering department to design and fly their own glider. His idea was enthusiastically accepted by members of the design office and the management, including Phil Garratt who took a special interest in the project. Members of the club spent two nights a week on their own time for six months completing the drawings for what was later to become the Sparrow. The glider was built in the experimental shop under Bill Burlison and the first flight was completed by Czerwinski in the spring of 1942. It was a utility type glider of simple construction. Many who were in the club look back on the project as an educational challenge, a diversion from the pressure of the war effort and a complete success. It led to the later collaboration of Bev Shenstone and Professor Tom Loudon in producing the Wren and Robin gliders and Harbinger sailplanes, a distinct contribution to the development of the gliding movement in Canada.

Czerwinski brought another specialty to the North American aircraft industry, the expertise to form plywood sheets in a variety of complex curves. He had developed the science in his wooden trainer design and looked over the Canadian Anson, then under construction, to see what could be made simpler and less costly with formed plywood. He started with wing fairings and engine cowlings and it was not long before his efforts caught the eye of the National Research Council in Ottawa. They were conducting a drive to save metal of all kinds and to turn, wherever possible, to wood.

Gliding club members included, left to right, R.R. Cutter, Ian Lounsbury, Jim Morelli, Osmo Kolkka, Lloyd Meyer, C.D. Long, W.J. Jakimiuk, W. Czerwinski, Tracy Rozelle, J.W. Satterthwaite, Ben Etkin, K. Korsak, Andy Carrick, T. Taregynski and Lyle Leckie. (via C.D. Long)

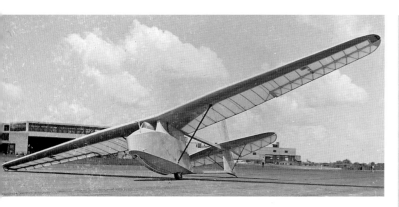

Under the guidance of the Polish experts, the Sparrow glider provided an ideal recreational wartime project. (Via C.D. Long)

Bud Hay explains the intricacies of glider flight to two of the ladies. (Via C.D. Long)

He soon found himself working on a project for the National Aeronautical Establishment to build a North American Harvard wing entirely of wood. The NRC concentrated on a wooden fuselage for the same aircraft. DH Canada had too much work at the time to get into the manufacture of small wooden parts, so a new company was formed in the fall of 1942 to concentrate on this specialty. Canadian Wooden Aircraft Limited was organized and financed by a Polish Lawyer, H. Styjkold, with Czerwinski as technical manager. They set up their first shop in the small Mason and Risch Piano factory and later moved to a larger plant on Sorauren Avenue. Many of the Polish experts joined the new company, whose products were almost entirely for the de Havilland war effort. First it was the Ansons, saving thousands of pounds of precious aluminum with their wooden components. When the Mosquito came along the shop was invaluable for the fabrication of nacelle side panels, pitot masts and even hydraulic tanks.

When the need for long-range tanks arose for the Mossie, Canadian Wooden Aircraft took on their most difficult but rewarding task. They devised a smoothly streamlined slipper

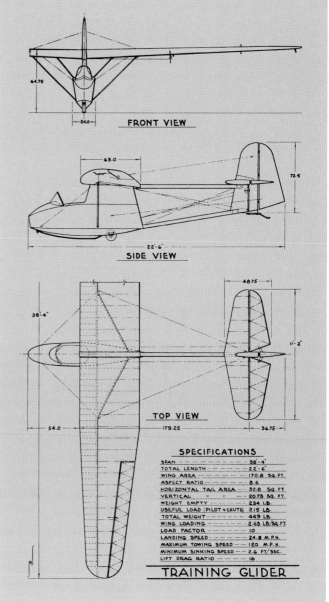

The Sparrow training glider was designed and flown by DHC employees in their off hours. Direction and design assistance came from the Polish gliding experts, particularly Waclaw Czerwinski. (Hotson Col.)

tank from veneer panels cut to size and shaped to the necessary compound curves in hot steam pressurized tanks (autoclaves). The process was unique in Canada and delegations from Britain and the United States came to observe it. A report from the Ministry of Aircraft Production and the United Kingdom Wood Mission paid glowing compliments to Czerwinski's process: "All our members were impressed by the methods you have adopted for producing the Mosquito drop tank, as we have not seen, previously, anything of a similar nature on such a scale. We admired the artistry by which you made difficult problems look simple, and thought that your war effort was an excellent one."

Central Aircraft

DHC had always worked closely in prewar days with Ottawa's National Research Council on experimental projects – the building of streamline skis for the Rapide was a typical case – but when the war came such projects only complicated factory planning and interfered with production. About this time Phil Garratt faced a major plant expansion. He discussed it with his assistant, W. John McDonough.

McDonough had been in and out of Canadian aviation for years – as a mail pilot, prospecting and bush flying in northern Canada. He had test flown the first Noorduyn Norseman and since early 1939 had been assisting Garratt in a number of jobs, most recently the new airport layout. When the company was confronted with these new requests for highly specialized projects, the answer became obvious: the work should be organized under a separate company banner away from the manufacturing problems yet in a close relationship with de Havilland. A subsidiary company, Central Aircraft Limited, was formed with headquarters in London, Ontario. McDonough would be manager, and the challenge of highly specialized engineering assignments attracted Francis Hyde-Beadle immediately. W.J. Jakimiuk had just arrived at the company and could certainly look after engineering at Downsview. A former Trans-Canada Air Lines Captain, Harry C. Umphrey, had recently applied for work in the test flight department and accepted the role of chief pilot in the new company. These three and a few hand-picked specialists made their way to London and were soon involved in experimental war projects both large and small. What started as an overflow operation soon had projects of its own. One was the design of a set of skis for a Lockheed Ventura intended for liaison with the underground in Norway. There would be many more special assignments when the Mosquito came to Canada.

The D.H.98 Mosquito flies for the first time at Hatfield with Geoffrey de Havilland Jr. at the controls. (DH4928)

Birth of the Mosquito

While expansion was the order of the day at Downsview, events were taking place in England that would affect the lives of thousands of Canadians. In great secrecy, de Havilland England was designing not only a revolutionary aircraft but a whole new concept of aerial warfare. They called it the Mosquito and its sting was to be felt by the enemy in ever-increasing fury for the balance of the war. Design work began as a private venture in 1939 in an old Hertfordshire mansion. There was more opposition than support from a sceptical Air Ministry.

The quickening pace at Downsview during the first year of the war was commendable on all counts, but nothing could compare with the feverish development of the Mosquito back in England. None of the workers on the Canadian Tiger Moth line on November 3, 1940, had even heard of the Mosquito, let alone that, heavily wrapped in tarpaulins, it was leaving Salisbury Hall that day on the back of a lorry. They had no idea of the excitement at Hatfield 22 days later as the new plywood bomber took to the air under the guiding hands of the founder's son. It was not until Geoffrey de Havilland Jr. began demonstrating the sleek new prototype that Ministry brass were convinced enough to start placing orders. Manoeuvrability on one engine was spectacular, as was its speed of 380-390 mph (610-628 km/h) at 30,000 ft. (9,100 m). It was originally planned as a light bomber, but later proved itself in high-level photography and intruder operations. Enthusiasm intensified at Hatfield as the Mosquito advanced through the testing stage, but there was still much convincing to be done. It was a closely guarded secret to most, but Canada's Minister of Munitions and Supply, C.D. Howe, was one of the first Canadians to see a demonstration of the new aircraft. The demonstration took place on December 29, 1940, only 15 days after the dynamic Howe had been rescued in mid-Atlantic from the torpedoed *Western Prince*.

About the time the Sheppard Avenue plant was beginning production of Jacobs-powered Anson trainers, a key

event took place in England that was to decide the future of the controversial wooden bomber. The date was April 20, 1941, when a top-level demonstration was convened at Hatfield for Air Ministry officials and Chiefs of Staff. Geoffrey de Havilland Jr. flew the Mosquito superbly that day and sent a new wave of hope through the hard-pressed British high command. One of the most enthusiastic guests in the audience was America's General Henry Arnold, who in those days of strained U.S. neutrality was an extremely concerned observer of events in Europe. This veteran airman sized up the Mosquito's potential immediately and received top-level co-operation from the British. He was given data on the machine for U.S. evaluation, but his interest met a wave of resistance from the military and manufacturers on his return home.

Five American companies were asked to evaluate possible manufacture in the U.S. – Fleetwings, Beech, Hughes, Fairchild and Curtiss-Wright. They were unanimously opposed to the aircraft. A blunt appraisal by the respected Beech organization summed up their collective views: "It appears as though this airplane has sacrificed serviceability, structural strength, ease of construction and flying characteristics in an attempt to use construction material which is not suitable for the manufacture of efficient airplanes." Even the growing operational successes of the RAF did little to change the American stand on the Mosquito. However, plans to build the Rolls-Royce Merlin in the U.S. went forward without a hitch, for it was needed in their own North American P-51 Mustang.

Fortunately, the debate on the merits of plywood airplanes did not continue. Even while the Americans deliberated, plans were finalized for mass production of the Mosquito in England, Canada and Australia. It was almost with a sigh of relief that the U.S. investigation died, and was replaced with a healthier "back the Canadians" approach – particularly with the supply of Packard Merlin engines.

Canada to Build the Mosquito

By late 1941 Canada's contribution was figuring heavily in the North American "Arsenal of Democracy." The British Commonwealth Air Training Plan was shipping trained flight crews to fight over Europe. Canadian Pacific Airlines helped put together a trans-Atlantic ferrying organization under C.H. "Punch" Dickins which was now fully operational as RAF Ferry Command. The decision to build the Mosquito in Canada brought an immediate response from the parent company. A mound of drawings and vital parts for 25 aircraft were shipped to Canada along with a com-

An early meeting on the Canadian Mosquito brought together Ralph P. Bell, Director General of Aircraft Production; Harry Povey; Doug Hunter; and Phil Garratt. (DH JH50)

pleted Mk.IV model as a production sample. The urgency of the situation was realized when Hatfield's general manager Lee Murray arrived from England on July 30 to examine every detail of the Canadian potential. Murray was well known to the seniors in the staff, for he had been their general manager from 1933 to 1936. He spent a busy month in Downsview and Ottawa, which culminated in the British Ministry of Aircraft Production order for 400 Canadian-built Mosquitoes, the bomber version powered by the Packard Merlin 31.

The announcement of a British order was followed 10 days later by the arrival of W.D. "Doug" Hunter and Harry Povey with bundles of drawings and microfilm. The two were quite impressed with their first trans-Atlantic flight, which allowed them to leave England on Thursday and begin work in Toronto on Saturday. Povey was a jovial dynamo who had been involved with the Mosquito from the beginning. He had joined the company in 1924 and was described as "an aircraft production engineer without peer." Hunter had started as a draftsman with the Graham White Aviation Company in England and had been chief technical engineer at de Havilland since 1925. He was always immaculately dressed, spoke quietly and punctuated every conversation with "quite!" Both were to figure heavily in the trials and tribulations at DH Canada during the next three challenging years. Their arrival coincided with a new threat to the program – shipping losses in the battle of the Atlantic. In the first shipment, a two per cent loss in vital drawings was experienced, but it was only a sample of what was to come. On September 13, a flyable Mk.IV, DK287, was shipped from Liverpool for Halifax, but arrived after a series of delays with such shipping damage that it required extensive repair. Vital castings suffered from salt corrosion and many irreplaceable assemblies ended up at the bottom of the Atlantic.

Povey's first move on arrival was to press for a separate

plant to build Mosquito fuselages. Bill Houston was selected to head the group and given a vacant building at 888 Dupont Street, formerly occupied by Baldwin-Beehive woollen mills. He took one look at the pile of microfilm and asked for an assistant to translate them into full-size profiles. Lofting was a new departure for DH Canada but a young draftsman, G.M. "Bill" Kelley, tackled the project on October 14 with considerable success, translating the curves from drawings to huge sheets of plywood on the floor. During the same month the Massey-Harris Company in Weston contracted to build the wings. An English fuselage jig arrived at Dupont Street on December 9, permitting the first fuselage shell and a Canadian jig to be completed two and a half months later.

It was during this period that R.B. "Bob" McIntyre began his long association with de Havilland through the newly formed Aircraft Division of Massey-Harris. McIntyre had grown up in Toronto and, after graduating from the University of Toronto in 1936, went to Cambridge University on a Massey Fellowship. In 1938 he lectured at the University of Toronto and two years later joined Massey-Harris.

James S. Duncan, head of the giant Massey farm machinery company, had responded to Canada's call to arms by steering his organization into war work. First it was the 1940 need for Anson wings which transformed their Weston Road plant within weeks into a woodworking establishment. The new aircraft division was headed by Morley Lazier. Bob McIntyre was chief engineer and Harry Proctor, who had been on loan from DHC to Fleet Aircraft and later National Steel Car, became chief inspector. Other de Havilland specialists moved over to broaden the aeronautical

experience: Bob Blanchard, George Lawrence and, later, Harry Beffort.

The Massey group built up a formidable production record of Anson wings and were the first invited to build Mosquito wings. Recalled Bob McIntyre:

Depending on how you look at it, we got off to a good start with Harry Povey. On his first visit to Weston Road he began telling us we should build our jigs of wood, like de Havilland England. We had already started building ours of metal and made the observation that there were probably more important problems that needed his attention back at Downsview.

We promised our first Mosquito wing by mid-May and delivered ahead of schedule. We always were ahead of schedule with Mossie wings, to the point where we had to store them until needed. The switching around from one variant to another caused us problems for it meant modifying the stored wings before delivery.

The Wooden Bomber

Volumes have been written about the birth of the DH Mosquito and its struggle for acceptance at senior levels, and even more about its unique construction. The use of wood for medium-to-large aircraft was not uncommon but de Havilland led the world in this type of construction – an art that was slowly giving way to metal. The Mosquito was to be the last fling by DH in entirely wooden monocoque design after the racing Comet, the Dragonfly and the Albatross. Decades later the wisdom of combining these special skills

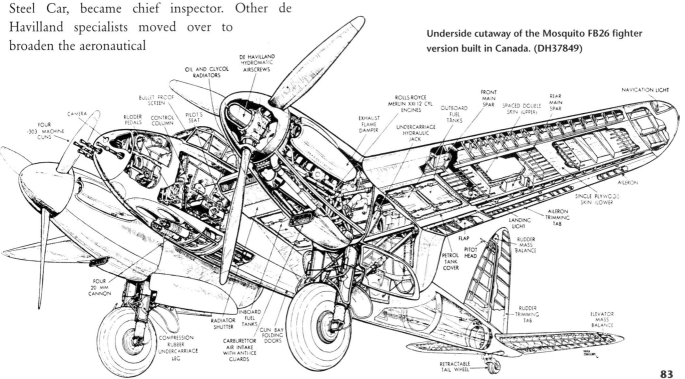

Underside cutaway of the Mosquito FB26 fighter version built in Canada. (DH37849)

with non-strategic materials and trades, under the pressure of war, has been applauded.

The Mosquito, as many were to find, was no ordinary aircraft. The Canadian model was to be predominantly the Mk.XXVI and the only information coming through to Downsview was that it was an all-wood, mid-wing monoplane, for a crew of two, powered by twin Packard Merlin engines built in the United States under the Rolls-Royce patent. The general optimism as they started the project was well-founded, for DH Canada had boosted its staff 140 per cent in one year. They were a cohesive, production-oriented group, but this Mossie was not the orthodox construction they had learned. Everything about it was new.

The construction of the Mosquito fuselage: First, plywood sheets were pressed over a concrete form, glued into position and dried with infra-red light. In the second photo, the two half-shells of the fuselage have had interior equipment added before being glued together along the top and bottom centrelines. Then, the finished fuselage with components was assembled. (NFB, NMST, NFB)

The fuselage had an oval, tapering cross section, built in two halves and joined along the top and bottom centre lines. A stiff monocoque (stressed skin) construction was obtained by using two layers of plywood sheeting glued together with a balsa wood filler. Wherever concentrated loads occurred, spruce or birch inserts were glued between the plywood skins. Occasional wooden bulkheads provided reinforcing and stiffening. The thickness of the fuselage shell was $^{7}/_{16}$ inch and was constant throughout. Birch 3-ply was used in the heavily stressed sections while the nose was 2-ply spruce.

The wing being built by Massey-Harris was a one-piece cantilever structure consisting of two box spars extending over the full span. The covering was of stressed plywood skin, reinforced by span-wise wooden stringers. Ten self-sealing fuel tanks were housed within the wing and were accessible through detachable panels on the underside. The flanges around these openings were of spruce with 3-ply birch while the stringers were of Douglas fir, with ash wherever additional strength was required. Wood screws were used throughout the structure and were driven while the glue between the joints was still wet. The finished wings were attached to the fuselage by four main bolts after being fitted with hydraulically operated ply-covered flaps and metal-covered ailerons.

Like the wing, the tail plane and fin obtained their strength through a box structure and stressed plywood skins. The elevators and rudder were of "Alclad" metal with fabric covering on the rudder and metal sheeting on the elevators. The two nacelles housing the 1,525-horsepower Packard Merlin 31, 33 or 225 engines were finely streamlined and completely enclosed the main wheels in flight. The tail wheel also retracted, making the Mosquito very streamlined in flight.

Much about the Mosquito was unique, from the two big spinners in front to the distinctive de Havilland fin in the back, and even the coolant radiators, which were housed within the forward section of the wing profile between each engine nacelle and the fuselage. Armament varied as the war progressed, but the Canadian Mk.XXVIs mounted four 20mm guns in the underside of the fuselage, four .303 machine guns and a camera gun in the nose. Space was provided for two 500-pound bombs. Two more could be carried under the wings. The crew operated behind a bullet-proof windscreen in a tubular cockpit covered in Plexiglas. Their working space was minimal, to provide overall streamlining – the only major complaint from the operational crews.

By March of 1942 the parking lots at Downsview were expanding to accommodate 2,400 employees, and a new cafeteria had replaced the early circus tent. There are stories told of that tent cafeteria, but none to compare with its suc-

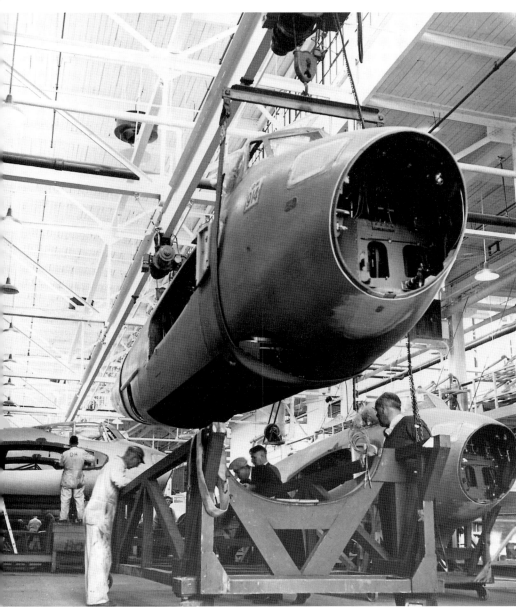

cessful transition to an airborne vehicle one summer night in 1940. The event took place during a violent storm which had three of the boys on duty fighting desperately with the tie-down ropes. One was carried aloft before he bailed out and let the elements take over. Next day the sun shone on a novel open-air luncheon.

On May 5, 1942, Phil Garratt left for meetings in England on one of the early RAF Ferry Command flights. It was a cold, dreary trip from Dorval in a dim, windowless Liberator but he was warmed by the thought that he carried with him a contract for an additional 1,100 Canadian Mossies, financed by United States Lend-Lease. With the total order now 1,500 and the test model nearing completion, Garratt's nine days in England were busy with planning. By then, high-level priority battles between the services were beginning to plague the parent company, where demand was running ahead of production. Garratt received a first-hand briefing close to the drama of war and a forewarning of similar problems ahead for the Canadian company. It was during this meeting that special mark numbers were set aside for the designation of Canadian variants, beginning with VII and ending with XXIX. A production schedule was set, calling for eight aircraft in 1942 and passing 50 per month in June 1943.

Back in Canada, Harry Povey was conducting a frantic search for new plant equipment, particulary in forming and pressing metal. Negotiations with subcontractors were in high gear, requiring constant compromises between British and North American machine standards. The drive to build the first test aircraft

The first production Mosquito from the Canadian line was flown initially by Ralph Spradbrow, then used by Geoffrey de Havilland Jr. for displays in Toronto and on the U.S. tour that followed. U.S. top brass liked the performance of the Mosquito, but clung to a dislike of wooden aircraft. (DH 7372)

proceeded as planned with a typical demonstration of wartime urgency. When the Boeing company was unable to meet the schedule for tailplanes, John Slaughter built a couple of sets at Downsview to keep the project on time. The first Massey-Harris wing arrived on May 9, 1942. In just 11 months the Canadian prototype, KB300, was ready for flight.

Canadian Mossie Airborne

The secrecy surrounding the Mosquito provided increasing problems as the day neared for the test flight. Such an occasion called for a celebration and the hard work of the past year deserved formal recognition. Phil Garratt sent a query to the ministry asking if they wished to publicize the coming first flight of the prototype, adding a cautious note that he "wouldn't be hurt or annoyed" if there was to be no ceremony to mark the occasion. The reply from Munitions and Supply was an enthusiastic approval, for they felt it would be "a milestone in aircraft production in this country" to have the flight recognized. The date was set for the afternoon of September 23, 1942, with invitations sent to high ranking officials and military leaders. The plan was for Geoffrey de Havilland Jr. to come over to do the flying; after all, he had conducted the early type testing and his spectacular flying displays had been a major factor in promoting the aircraft.

Little thought was given to British weather during the early planning for the event, but it proved a major factor when the day arrived. The September weather was ideal in Toronto for a celebration, but completely foul in England, where Geoffrey Jr. was preparing to leave on an RAF Transport Command flight. When news reached Downsview that he would be delayed, there was no turning back. "The show must go on." Attention shifted immediately to DH Canada's chief test pilot, Ralph Spradbrow, who so far had been busy

Peppy Burrell, engineer from DH England, and Ralph Spradbrow, chief test pilot for DH Canada. They first flew KB300 on September 23, 1942. (DH)

P.C. Garratt introduces Geoffrey de Havilland Jr. to DHC employees after he flew the first Canadian Mosquito. Also on stage is A/M L.S. Breadner of the RCAF. (DH JH372)

with Tiger and Anson testing. Fortunately, F.H. "Peppy" Burrell of Hatfield's test department was serving as liaison engineer at Downsview and had "Sprad" well briefed on the Mossie. When all was ready, the two took their places in the cockpit of KB300 and taxied to the end of the runway. When the Mosquito took to the air it was not the rolling climbing display that had become the trademark of the younger de Havilland, but it brought grins of satisfaction from all who saw the event as a red-letter day in the company's history. The fact that a Canadian was at the controls seemed all the more appropriate.

Public relations headaches increased with this momentous event, for although most publications adhered to the government request for no publicity, others tried to get around the ruling. In the words of one participant, "all hell broke loose" when a station newspaper at No. 5 SFTS, Brantford, reported the Mosquito's first flight in detail. Other magazines demanded the same privileges and reams of futile correspondence resulted. An official world press announcement on September 26 of a Mosquito raid on Oslo relieved the pressure and soon a notice went out admitting that the Allies *did* have a new high performance airplane and it *was* being produced in Canada.

When Geoffrey de Havilland Jr. arrived at Downsview six days after the first flight, he put on his own brand of demonstration, wringing out the Canadian model. The employees, who were given time off to witness the event, had never seen such a display. First it was a steep climb off the runway until he was lost from view, then a low-level pass over the hangars, followed by a series of well-executed rolls.

During Geoffrey de Havilland Jr.'s visit to Canada, he met Governor General the Earl of Athlone (left) and Canada's production czar, C.D. Howe. (DH 8238)

Many citizens of downtown Toronto saw the Mosquito for the first time that day and the people back at Downsview witnessed Geoffrey's specialty – climbing rolls with one engine feathered. After 15 minutes he came down to be welcomed by Air Marshal Breadner, Phil Garratt, John McCurdy (the first man to fly a heavier-than-air flying machine in Canada) and 4,000 employees.

One month after the first Canadian Mosquito flight, Geoffrey demonstrated KB300 to the doubting Americans at Wright Field, Ohio. He returned to Bolling Field, Washington, and Naval Air Station, San Diego, in December, where he remained until the end of the year. A novel plan was devised to move the Mosquito around the country as Geoffrey was unfamiliar with the North American airway system. The countryside was new to him, but he was used to flying formation. Captain Jim Follett of Trans-Canada Air Lines had just joined Test Flight. As he was thoroughly current on the airways, he flew the support team in a Lockheed Hudson. Geoffrey de Havilland, with Peppy Burrell as crew, simply flew in formation.

Convincing the Americans

It took more than young de Havilland's spectacular flying to sell the doubters south of the border, but more and more American officers became enthusiastic after flying the aircraft. In another combined Canadian/British effort to convince the Americans, an English-built Mosquito was put at their disposal for an all-out evaluation. This was the original Mk.IV that had come to Canada aboard ship as a model for Canadian production. It flew to Wright Field in March 1943 but was lost shortly thereafter due to an engine fire. The crew bailed out, but the accident only reinforced the arguments of the anti-Mosquito group. They complained about the cramped cockpit and the small escape hatch and clung to their dislike of plywood construction. In spite of the opposition, the U.S. Navy and the Marines wanted the type badly. The Mossie's range was beginning to impress the strategists, and its speed advantage over the P-38 had been demonstrated.

Perhaps the greatest support for the Mosquito came from a new source that brought weight from the top of the high command. Col. Elliot Roosevelt, son of the U.S. president, began flying a British Mk.IV with the 5th Reconnaissance Group early in the African campaign. He was impressed and his reports provided the operational back-up needed to convince the test and development boys back home. The advantages of a twin-engined fighter were also catching on among the hardened proponents of the single-engine school. Suddenly, as had happened in England, the Mosquito was in demand. Unfortunately at this critical time Canadian production was badly behind target and causing concern in Ottawa.

Pilot Ralph Spradbrow had done an excellent job of filling in on the first flight of the Mosquito, but the time had come for him to broaden his experience and learn the testing techniques of

Fighter ace Buzz Beurling poses with some of "the girls" on his visit to the Mosquito production line. (DH

Hatfield. He left for England in late 1942 but was almost immediately confined to hospital for a serious ulcer operation. To fill the gap at Downsview, DH England prepared to send out Pat Fillingham for test flight duties in Canada. The year ended on an encouraging note with a cheery Christmas letter to all from manager Phil Garratt. Addressing what he always termed the "DH Family" in a year-end letter of 1942, Garratt expressed great confidence in his team, as he outlined the challenges of the coming year. "In the past 11 months," he said, "we have produced 362 Ansons, 550 Tiger Moths, overhauled 119 aircraft and 178 engines, including modifications to 209 Jacobs engines; all of this on top of the development work on the Mosquito." He could have added that the first flight of the Mosquito had also been on time.

The cold January of 1943 began a bad year for both Garratt and DH Canada. The war was in its most critical phase; the demand for Mosquitoes grew daily. Even as the first Canadian machine flew, the British shadow factories had delivered 450 to hard-pressed RAF squadrons. On the Canadian side Harry Povey was struggling with the inevitable production compromises while trying to cope with the erratic flow of material from England. On two occasions batches of valuable drawings covering variant changes were lost at sea; vital hydraulic assemblies never reached their destination at Downsview. More parts were coming from England than most people in the plant realized, for some of the subcontractors were still not ready with their components. Even without the losses at sea, the experts could tell there would be a gap in production after the first 25 aircraft. These snags were compounded by yet another penalty of war – the battle among the commands for priorities. Original MAP contracts called for Canada to produce the bomber version, but this was later changed to include the fighter-bomber, FB Mk.XXI. Almost as an afterthought, Canada was asked to produce its own dual-control trainer while in the midst of

converting to the two-staged Packard Merlin. It was obvious that pressures were building at Downsview.

By now Ralph Bell had moved from Federal Aircraft to be Director General of Aircraft Production, reporting to the minister, C.D. Howe. In 1941 Bell had pushed for the production of the fighter Mosquito instead of the unarmed bomber. The about-face by the British Ministry of Aircraft Production in ordering the fighter-bomber brought out his natural reaction, "I told you so!" He saw it as a major production problem and expressed his views in a letter to Deputy Minister Charles Banks in England. "I am sorry that we ever touched the thing, for it never would have been done without my very enthusiastic support. So far as I am concerned, it is the last time I will have a thing to do with English aircraft in Canada." He sent a similar long memo to C.D. Howe, April 13, 1943, with assorted correspondence so that his boss would "have all the facts." By mid-April only 12 Mosquitoes had been produced with 14 more on the production line. Only seven had been officially accepted.

Senior Mosquito engineering personnel: Left to right, back row: C.D. Long; W. Burlison; W.K. Aykroyd; W. Jackson; R.B. McIntyre; J.H. Houston; front row: W. J. Jakimiuk; W.D. Hunter; F.H. Burrell. (DH8237)

There is no doubt that relations between the Department of Munitions and Supply and de Havilland Canada were becoming strained. Garratt went to England for meetings in February, followed in March by Povey and Hunter. The Director General of Aircraft Production was becoming increasingly impatient. Hatfield responded by sending out their general manager, Lee Murray, on a full-time basis in November 1942. His prestige and knowledge of the Canadian scene had a stabilizing influence, but the underlying problems continued. In April another variant problem arose – the conversion of machines for USAAF reconnaissance.

The Allied war effort was at the stage where all countries were working closely on matters of supply. The RAF and RCAF were juggling their own drastic needs to release reconnaissance Mosquitoes to the U.S. Weighty exchange points were to be gained in a share of the heavy bomber production that was growing south of the border. U.S. Army Air Forces personnel began to appear on the flight line at Downsview, where a new brand of Mossie emerged from the paint shop bearing the "star and bar" instead of the usual roundel. These American F-8s began to find their way into the U.S. photo reconnaissance pool, but only in small numbers – 40 were delivered from Downsview.

For having "hit the silk," Gerry Wooll and Tim Stone receive their Caterpillar Pins from J. Grant Glassco. This pin, recognizing the part played by the humble silkworm, was created by the Irwin Parachute Company of Fort Erie to honour those saved by parachutes. (DH)

(Right) Wooll's Mosquito burns in a farmer's field. (DH)

While these changes were taking place, the plant bulletin recorded activities around the company with everything from softball tournaments to weddings. The *de Havilland Mosquito* had been launched in 1941 by personnel manager "Feathers" Featherstonhaugh, assisted by Ivan Kirkhouse, Doug Higgins and Joe Holliday. In the summer of 1942 it recorded the visit of an RCAF bomber pilot, P/O Johnny Highman, DFC, of Saskatchewan, who did a morale-building tour of the plant. On February 22, 1943, Canada's number one ace, F/O George "Buzz" Beurling, DSO, DFC, DFM and Bar, was given an official welcome. He toured all the departments, posed for pictures with the ladies and was given a Mosquito flight by test pilot Fillingham.

All the drama that Hollywood attaches to test flying descended on the flight operations office during the late afternoon of April 26. A terse radio message from F/L Gerald R. Wooll at 4:30 p.m. informed operations that they were returning from a routine test at 20,000 ft. (6,100 m) over the east end of the city and that smoke was coming from behind the starboard nacelle. Moments later another message explained that while feathering the propeller a fire had broken out and that he and his observer/mechanic, T.J. "Tim" Stone, were taking to their parachutes at 17,000 ft. (5,200 m). Their position near the lakeshore caused some concern and, while chief pilot Spradbrow alerted the harbour police, pilot Jim Follett rushed to prepare a Grumman Widgeon in case the two should land in the lake. Stone released the emergency door and jumped first with no problem. Wooll trimmed the machine and eased himself through the same opening and soon he too was falling free under a canopy of silk. Both had fears of drifting into the lake but were able to speed their descent enough to remain over land.

Tim Stone landed without any trouble at Research Enterprises near the Don Ravine and was approached by a guard

A study in Mosquito cockpits: the British model (top) with the P6 compass and the turn and slip needles; and (bottom) as made in Canada with U.S.-style instruments. (DH980 & DH1241)

who thought it was a Victory Bond stunt. When he learned that the unheralded arrival was the real thing, he took Stone to the cafeteria for a cup of tea. Wooll, on the other hand, had the bad luck to land on a set of railway tracks near Dawes Road and found it difficult to get his footing. He was dragged a few feet before he could spill the 'chute, damaging his wrist and picking up a cinder in his chin.

The flaming Mosquito, scattering debris for miles, plunged into the farm of Arthur W. Mason. Two local farmers took Wooll to the de Havilland first aid office. While he was getting his cuts and bruises bandaged, a big arm appeared around his shoulder. It was Phil Garratt coming to ask how he felt after the harrowing escape. "I've been wanting to meet you, Mr. Garratt," said Wooll, "Sorry I had to pick this way to do it." Wooll spent the next day in Christie Street Military Hospital but was soon ready to test more Mosquitoes. The trouble was traced to a faulty exhaust manifold leaking flames to a propeller feathering line. When the prop was feathered the ruptured line acted like an oil burner and the flames took over.

Shortly after the Wooll incident, Pat Fillingham left Downsview to take up test flying duties with the Australian de Havilland company, which was now getting into production. Jim Follett was appointed chief pilot and Spradbrow became flight liaison officer to Doug Hunter.

At the signing of the first labour agreement on June 7, 1943: C.V. Coulson, president of Local 112, UAW; P.C. Garratt, managing director, DHC; J.C. Adams, secretary, Industrial Relations Institute; Frank Irvine, chairman of the office committee, Local 112; Richard Frankensteen, international v-p, UAW; and Morris Jackson, chairman of the bargaining committee, Local 112. (DH469)

C.D. Howe Takes Over

The underlying stresses and strains in management were unknown to most wartime DHC workers and were unappreciated by those more concerned with their own advancement. Throughout the first two years, Plant One had produced Tiger Moths under Bill Calder and later under Frank Warren. Plant Two operated as a completely separate unit, turning out Ansons under George Burlison, with Dick Moffett as overall production manager. Both lines had produced ahead of schedule, but now that all were required to unite in one project, a new set of responsibility problems arose: who would share the honours of command? Harry Povey's weight as the British production expert, plus the fact he had been sent out by the English company, put him in charge of "all production departments." Garratt asked Moffett and Burlison to work under Povey, but both stoutly disapproved of his production methods, particularly in the construction of jigs. George Blanchard adroitly summed up the differences some 40 years later in one sentence. "Dick and George were used to the North American way of doing things, Harry Povey the British." Management changes were tried in a frantic effort to cope with sagging production and keep up with the daily directives. It was no longer a case of a small plant grown bigger, for Canadian government investment in everything from buildings to equipment had now become a dominant factor. Little of the prewar plant remained. The same owner/government also held responsibility for the British order for Mosquitoes under the Department of Munitions and Supply. Aircraft production was solidly in the hands of the Director General, Ralph P. Bell, who was the undisputed boss.

Through the spring of 1943 government production officers at Downsview sent such pessimistic reports to Ottawa that Bell's executive assistant, Fred T. Smye, visited the plant to size up the situation for his superior. He was given cooperation by everyone from Phil Garratt down and freedom to contact anyone. "Things were a real mess," recalled Smye years later, "and as an illustration, I found three different officers who told me that they were responsible for production." Smye wrote a report of his findings, which were reviewed in a tension-packed meeting at Downsview presided over by Director General Ralph Bell. The de Havilland board rejected the report, expressing confidence in the plant management, but Bell took a very tough stand. He and the government were holding the board responsible, he said, and called for a prompt reply to the findings.

It was time for the board to do some investigating on their own and it was agreed that there was a production problem at Downsview. Garratt remained steadfast in his view that the existing management could provide the answer and that was that! The spotlight then fell on director J. Grant Glassco, who had been on the board since February 2, 1940. Glassco was a prominent Toronto lawyer and member of the firm Clarkson, Gordon, Dilworth and Nash. He was a government appointee and one of C.D. Howe's "dollar-a-year" men.

Two weeks after the critical meeting in Downsview, Glassco called Ralph Bell seeking an appointment. The request was immediately granted and Glassco went to Ottawa carrying the divided opinions of the DH Canada board. The two went to see C.D. Howe for a decision.

There is no doubt that Howe was the most powerful man in Canada at the time. His authority on matters of war supply

J. Grant Glassco and Vincent Massey during the latter's visit to de Havilland Canada. Massey was Canadian High Commissioner in London. Lee Murray, DH England representative, is in the background. (DH M1260)

was supreme. He reacted in his typical abrupt style to rearrange management at Downsview in a number of areas. The first step was to have an Order in Council (PC. 4668) passed appointing J. Grant Glassco controller of de Havilland Canada, to be head of an advisory committee and administer the company. An extraordinary meeting of the board of directors was called by Ralph Bell, who attended as the head of aircraft production, Department of Munitions and Supply. Others in attendance were R.A. Laidlaw, P.C. Garratt, L.C.L. Murray, J.G. Glassco, W.M. Archibald, J.D. Woods and G.J. Mickleborough. Laidlaw chaired the meeting and Mickleborough acted as secretary.

Ralph Bell stated the purpose of the meeting and read the wires and cables on the subject of Mosquito production. Copies of the Order in Council were tabled, explaining the action the Minister had taken. Bell was careful to stress that these drastic steps were taken solely by the Department of Munitions and Supply and were not made on the recommendation of anyone connected with the company. P.C. Garratt would remain de Havilland representative in Canada and members of the existing directorate, R.A. Laidlaw (chairman), Bethune L. Smith and J. Douglas Woods, would serve with Glassco on the committee. Bell asked that extreme care be used in announcing the management change to employees.

An announcement by the parent company backed Garratt's authority by naming him a director of de Havilland England and appointing him their official representative in Canada. This letter was read to the directors' meeting of July 29, 1943. Instructions from Ottawa forbade any liaison between de Havilland Canada and the former general manager, who set up a new office in the Bank of Commerce building on King Street in Toronto, staffed by his secretary of long standing, Ann O'Neil.

The New Broom

In another significant move from Ottawa, C.D. Howe brought in W. "Bill" Stewardson from the minister's home riding of Fort William to act as the new works manager. Stewardson was a tall, lean man, described as hard-hitting and production-wise. He had been six years with Canadian

Bill Stewardson, who took over as works manager in 1944, came from Canada Car in Fort William, where he had been involved in the manufacture of Hawker Hurricanes. (DH206)

Car and Foundry, four and a half of them as shop superintendent on the Hawker Hurricane being manufactured under licence at Fort William. He was received with mixed reactions at DHC for, although he was a friendly person, he swore a lot and, according to one report, "scared the hell out of everybody." He was brought in under pressure of war and tackled the project as he saw it. John Slaughter, who worked as his assistant for the rest of the war, recalled:

Stewardson was what we needed in the shop at the time. He had this rough approach, but he knew what he was talking about. He had been all over North America learning production techniques to build the Hurricane, whereas, we had never been outside Downsview. In spite of his profanity, he was not a drinking man. He was well read, didn't socialize and just lived, ate and slept aircraft production. He had a three-point philosophy on the subject: good tooling, good processing and good parts control. He wouldn't let anything stand in the way of these objectives. He spent the first two weeks in Downsview just walking around observing before he went into action. I remember his comment during one problem when he exploded, "There's still too many bosses around here – we've got to get it down to one." Former plant manager Dick Moffett and his assistants George Burlison and Ed Forrest, who had achieved such a fine record with the Anson production at the end of 1942, resigned to accept other positions in the aviation war effort.

In July a new man was appointed as assistant to controller Glassco. George A.D. Bear had been a WWI RAF ground crew and worked his way up in the automobile trade to become manager of Ontario Automobile Company. He was moved to de Havilland by Ralph Bell from Clyde Aircraft Limited of Collingwood, where he had been serving as president. The director described him as decisive, dynamic and straight-speaking. He had a knack of dealing with people in large groups or small and hit it off right away with Stewardson.

In December 1942, six months before the Canadian government stepped in, only four Mosquitoes had flown at de Havilland Canada. By December 1943, the output hit 20 per month for the first time and this put the total over 100. In keeping with Stewardson's plan to "get the bosses down to one," Harry Povey had been asked to return to England in October 1943, with the announcement that George Bear would become general production manager. The war was into its fourth year and few of the original DH Canada staff remained. Phil Garratt was sitting out the war in downtown Toronto. Bill Calder, Frank Warren and the "old guard" were now in secondary positions – or other wartime work. Don Murray, Fred Hotson and George Neal left to fly at the Air Observer Schools. Francis Hyde-Beadle, George Burlison, Dick Moffett, Ed Forrest and Harry Povey had all come and gone. Perhaps the only member of the Anson period still in any position of authority was Bill Burlison, who managed the experimental department. For some time the major de Havilland presence in this purely government environment

Downsview airport during the expansion in 1944. The original Dufferin Street runs north from the corner of Wilson Avenue (lower left) and a new east-west runway is in preparation. The Toronto Flying Club buildings can be seen off Wilson Avenue (lower right) where the TTC subway terminal now stands. (DH690)

was Lee Murray, assistant to the controller, who stood like the Rock of Gibraltar throughout the whole troubled period. Doug Hunter and W.J. Jakimiuk along with their engineering personnel were able to remain outside production's political battles.

The parts problem began to ease by the fall of 1943, as the North American suppliers came to grips with their assignments, but the last quarterly report for that year showed little improvement in production. "Although the controllership installed at de Havilland Aircraft has materially improved the management of the company," it read, "this improvement has not yet resulted in the production of Mosquitoes." These were troubled times for everyone in the plant as promotions and demotions took place without pattern or precedent. Employee morale was at a new low, complicated by a dispute over union participation. From 1941 to 1942 de Havilland was in the favourable position of operating their own internal union headed by Tom Caskie. In 1943 a series of elections put in UAW-CIO representation after a long, sometimes bitter struggle. C. Vince Coulson was made president of the new Local 112; Frank Irvine was named chairman of the office committee.

As requested by Ralph Bell, care was taken in breaking the news of the management change to the employees; it

was dispensed in small doses. The gentle approach was evident in the subsequent issues of the *de Havilland Mosquito*. The June 1943 issue welcomed Bill Stewardson as works manager and at the same time offered best wishes to R.J. Moffett, "who leaves to assume the post of Chief Engineer with Canadian Propellers, Limited, Montreal." Nothing was mentioned of George Burlison, who had resigned some time earlier. Page seven showed a photo of Phil Garratt on June 7 after signing a labour agreement, but no mention that he vacated his position three days later. The only word of top management change came in the July/August issue announcing that George Bear had joined and, again in March 1944, that Harry Povey had returned to England. Finally in the May/June issue of 1944 (10 months later) a message on the second last page announced "Change in Management." In June 1943 P.C. Garratt left and became a director of the English company. J. Grant Glassco became the executive in charge at DHC. In October 1943 Harry Povey returned to

England and G.A.C. Bear became general production manager. Since that time top management has been: Glassco, Bear, W.D. Hunter, L.C.L. Murray and T.G. Dalglish."

Deliveries Begin

Once Mosquitoes began flying regularly at Downsview it became clear that the east-west runway was too short for safe operations. The approach areas across Dufferin Street were cleared to permit maximum use of the runway and, as a temporary measure, stoplights were placed north and south of the approach path. The lights were activated to halt road traffic whenever an aircraft was on final approach but this arrangement was far from satisfactory. Meetings were held with the City of Toronto for permission to enlarge the airport boundary eastward.

A report in the *Toronto Star*, August 22, 1944, stated that an alternate road 2,000 ft. (610 m) to the east of Dufferin Street would be built at the responsibility of the Federal government. A stipulation was made at the meeting that Dufferin be returned to its original status north of Wilson unless a civic airport was continued on the property. Controller Bob Saunders – later Mayor of Toronto and Hydro Chairman – offered the opinion that the old Dufferin Street would never be reopened to highway traffic. On November 24, 1944, the last house on Dufferin Street between Wilson and Sheppard was moved to make room for the airport.

The first few deliveries of aircraft went to No. 36 Operational Training Unit, RCAF, in Greenwood, N.S., but the time had come to test the Canadian-made Mosquitoes in action. The long flight over 2,000 miles (3,200 km) of ocean required the design of long-range tanks. The task was taken

(Above) The delivery of the first five Mosquitoes called for a formal ceremony. As the result of a Victory Bond drive, each aircraft carried the name of a Canadian city. (DH 516)

(Right) Arnold Gorman and Fred Holterman stand beside a trans-Atlantic long-range fuel tank. This component was produced within 21 days of receiving the drawings. (British Aerospace 21273)

in hand by W.J. Jakimiuk and his engineers, who soon designed a 200-gallon (910 litre) tank to fit snugly into the Mosquito bomb bay. In a major effort of co-operation by the shop specialists, the first tank was ready for installation 21 days after the drawings were received. Five such tanks were prepared for the first series of trans-Atlantic deliveries.

One of the first five Canadian Mosquitoes delivered overseas, flies with one engine feathered. (DH)

As part of the public relations efforts of the day, delivery of the first overseas machines was coordinated with the drive for Victory Bonds. In July a number of government officials, including Ralph Bell, came down from Ottawa for a unique ceremony – the christening of the first five Mosquitoes for the Royal Air Force. The aircraft were named after the Canadian cities with the best sales records in the recent loan drive. The *Acton*, KB328; the *New Glasgow*, KB162; the *Moose Jaw*, KB329; the *Saskatoon*, KB160; and the *Vancouver*, KB161 (all Mk.XXs) were lined up in front of the assembled employees for a formal unveiling. In a fitting ceremony including people from all the cities involved, the aircraft were turned over to the Dorval-based RAF Transport Command.

The *Acton* was the first to reach Hatfield, piloted by P/O J.G. Uren with navigator F/O R.C. Bevington. It arrived August 12, 1943, closely followed by the *New Glasgow*, ferried by an American civilian crew. Both aircraft used the Newfoundland-Greenland-Iceland route under ideal summer conditions. By November others were safely in Britain, but further problems arose: the RAF would not accept the Canadian solid windshields. They were all sent to No. 13 Maintenance Unit RAF, Henlow, for installation of shatterproof glass. It was not until December 2, 1943, that the first of the Canadian group went into action. The *Vancouver* earned this distinction with a raid on Berlin which was completed successfully by Canadian pilot F/L G.W. Salter in spite of engine troubles and frozen controls. The *New Glasgow, Moose Jaw*, and *Vancouver* all served with 139 Squadron before being written off in operations.

To now Downsview visitors had been mostly war heroes in support of the bond drives. The fall of 1943 brought a new group whose interest in the Mosquito was to have considerable bearing a few years later. A delegation from the Nationalist Chinese Air Force was given a cordial welcome and a plant tour under the direction of Lee Murray.

The five trans-Atlantic deliveries ended 1943 on an encouraging note, with Canadian production inching upward. Now that preliminary details had been worked out with RAF Transport Command, the stage was set for a wholesale movement of Mosquitoes. Regular deliveries began in the summer of 1944, with weather being the major difficulty. Pat Fillingham returned to Downsview from Australia in April of the new year on his way home to England. His instructions were to assist with the ferry planning and deliver a Mosquito himself in the process. It was June before he finally departed Dorval and, as with so many of the northern deliveries, he took 11 days en route. Mosquitoes began mixing with the Mitchells and Dakotas along the northern staging route and, although there were snags along the way, they were all lumped together as a matter of routine. There were no major incidents, but if the planners thought they were in for clear sailing, they were mistaken. This relatively easy summer on the Atlantic was later described as "living in a fool's paradise." The next series of headaches for de Havilland Canada came from a completely unexpected source – long-range deliveries.

Trouble on the Atlantic

As the weather became colder over the northern route, reports of low operating oil temperatures were received, along with increasing instances of oil cooler failures. One complete engine failure occurred to KB452, October 18, 1944, and another to KB489 on the 24th. These incidents resulted in wild rumours among the ferry crews, who on more than one occasion shut down an engine unnecessarily when oil gauges gave false readings. The starboard engine failure on KB489 was of a major nature with a push rod through the crankcase. This presented a new concern for that engine was the only source of generator power. All radio was lost when the battery was exhausted during feathering but the aircraft was fortunate in reaching its destination at Narssarssuaq,

Four members of the DHC service team seconded to RAF Transport Command to monitor Mosquito deliveries: Bruce Glassford (Belém), Jerry Irvine (Nassau), Eddie Jack (Natal) and Bill Duck (Rabat Salé). (DH)

Greenland. The pilot, T.L. Clark, ended his report on the incident with, "As the result of my experiences, I suffered from nervous shock and was taken to hospital at BW-1."

A delegation from Dorval, including a Packard Merlin representative and the chief RAFTC maintenance foreman, was sent over the northern route to give special instructions to the maintenance people but the troubles persisted. Suddenly, on November 12, KB504 was lost between Gander and Greenland. An SOS was received but no details emerged. On November 30, KB535 disappeared between Goose Bay and Greenland without even an SOS. To add to the pilots' jitters, an Operational Training Unit Mosquito crashed near Summerside, P.E.I., in a snowstorm.

The problem of unexplained disappearances, coupled with the engine failures, was compounded by the unreliability of the oil temperature gauges. The possibility that a starboard engine shut-down would also exhaust the battery helped to bring about a major decision. Deliveries over the northern route would cease for the time being and be replaced by the longer, warmer South Atlantic route. Arrangements were made for de Havilland service engineers to be stationed along the key points of the route. Jerry Irvine went to Nassau in the Bahamas, Ed Jack to Natal in Brazil and Bill Duck to Rabat-Salé in Morocco. On the morning of December 15, 1944, 22 Mosquitoes were dispatched by RAFTC through the well-used southern bases.

The next day two of the machines, KB626 and KB620, disappeared without trace within 40 minutes flying time of Belém. These involved seasoned ferry crews under good weather conditions. A sudden explosion which prevented even the sending of an SOS was suspected. It set the experts thinking that the previous disappearances might not have been weather-related after all. The next day KB634 landed at

Zanderij Field on one engine; KB378 set down in the Caicos Islands under similar conditions. These incidents, combined with the previous losses, were unprecedented within Transport Command – particularly for crews still on the route. An order went out grounding all Mosquitoes in the system until further notice. Rumours were as widespread as they were unreliable and feelings ran high.

The problem took on a new urgency, calling for drastic action. A priority meeting was convened under Air Commodore G.J. Powell, Administration Officer RAFTC, on December 19, at Dorval Headquarters of 45 Group. Representatives from de Havilland Canada were Doug Hunter, Peppy Burrell and chief pilot Jim Follett. Thirty-two people joined in the tension-packed discussions in Dorval, which ranged from the serious disappearances to minor snags. Known facts were explored in a step-by-step process, with action delegated wherever applicable.

Even though cold weather conditions on the North Atlantic were first blamed, it became obvious that other possibilities should be investigated. The pilots were now paying more attention to their snag sheets and even the smallest problem was suspect. The oil coolers were given special attention, as were the reports of gasoline fumes in the fuselage. A series of monitored tests were flown to record the explosive potential of gasoline fumes in the cockpit. It was found that an explosive mixture could be brought about following a dive and steep climb and the blame was traced to a poorly positioned venting tube. The snag was quickly corrected but not all the ferry pilots were convinced this was the answer.

Oil temperature and pressure gauges in waiting aircraft were to be removed and bench tested for accuracy. Reports of toppling gyros and bottoming instrument panels were to be checked. Damaged engines, removed after failure, were to be sent back to Packard for a complete post-mortem. Stainless steel exhaust stacks that were burning out on long flights were to be replaced by the much more exotic Inconel. On top of it all, the weather-related incidents were explored in detail. Every flight henceforth must be conducted in visual flight conditions when possible.

Even with this multitude of directives, five hours of additional flight testing was ordered before every delivery. This effort to establish pilot confidence in the aircraft

Mosquitoes lost on trans-Atlantic delivery flights
KA100, 153, 197, 237, 259, 260, 316, 317, 968 and KB119, 196, 230, 296, 313, 340, 370, 457, 504, 506, 535, 536, 562, 575, 589,592, 593, 620 and 626.

One of the first Mosquitoes to leave Canada, the *New Glasgow*, loads for a bombing run over Europe. (DH642)

would be undertaken by Central Aircraft of London, Ontario. Transport Command pilots from Dorval were detailed to assist in this sudden workload, shuttling aircraft between Toronto, London and Montreal. Frank Baillie of RAF Transport Command had been working liaison with Test Flight at Downsview for some time and supervised every phase. The London organization expanded overnight to become the finishing depot for Mosquitoes. This arrangement continued into the final days of the war and proved to be a wise one.

The ferry problems brought another senior officer of the parent company to Canada for consultation – Major Hereward de Havilland, brother of the founder and one-time manager of the Australian branch. Hereward had provided engineering liaison between the company and the operating squadrons since the birth of the Mosquito; his quiet, thorough manner earned him the reputation of a true diplomat and trouble-shooter. He arrived in Toronto on February 26, 1944. Major Hereward concentrated on the operational problems and took more than the average interest in the move to mechanize the entire production line.

Production Increases

The Mosquito line was to be the ultimate in production engineering, making use of all the latest volume manufacturing techniques. It was planned around a system introduced at the Hurricane plant in Fort William in which sophisticated, self-contained carriages moved along a conveyor track. Each carriage acted as a "jig" to mate components and move them through the assembly bays. Each had platforms to give access to every possible work area on the aircraft, with racks for components and small parts storage. Transfer tracks moved semi-completed aircraft between the bays and returned the empty cradles to the start of the line. At the first station, the wing, complete with engines, was placed in position and the fuselage was lowered onto its mounting brackets. From there the assembly inched its way around 2,400 ft. (730 m) of track as the work shifts came and went. At the final station an overhead crane lifted the finished Mosquito for movement on its wheels to the paint shop. Production bosses Stewardson and Bear were behind this mechanization planning, but putting it into operation was the responsibility of L.V. "Dick" Dickinson, head of plant engineering. The carriages were called corvettes, which soon brought the system the unofficial title of "Dickinson's Navy." By March, Hereward de Havilland was to see all three bays full even

MOSQUITO'S-EYE VIEW OF MECHANIZED ASSEMBLY LINE

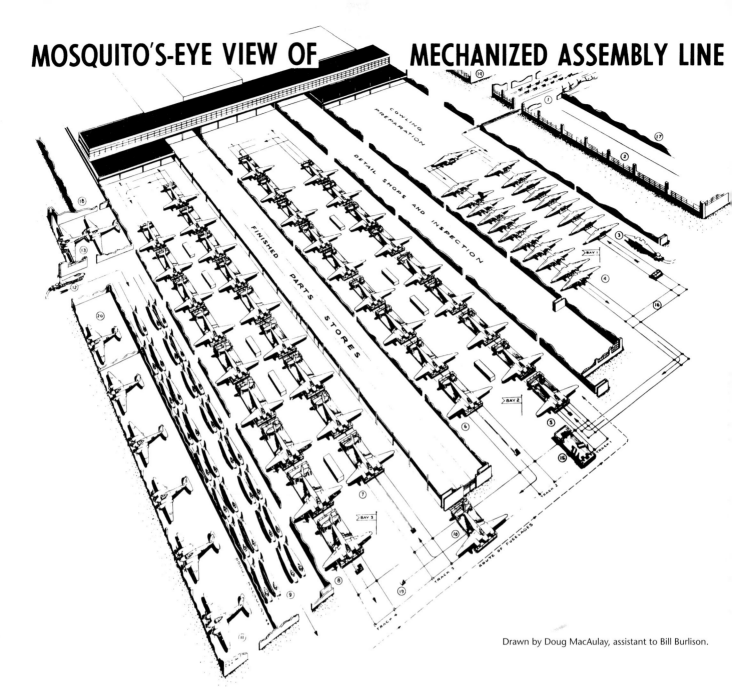

Drawn by Doug MacAulay, assistant to Bill Burlison.

A mechanized final assembly line at DHC was started for the Mosquito in June 1944. It occupied the two large assembly bays (2 and 3), each approximately 600 feet (180 m) long and 130 feet (40 m) wide. The line made a "U" circuit in Bay 2 and another in Bay 3 to give a length of 2,400 feet (750 m) from the start where wing and fuselage were mated. Transfer tracks outside the building moved semi-completed aircraft between Bays 2 and 3 and returned empty cradles to the start of the line.

The line accommodated 39 carriages. Assembly and installation, functional tests and inspections were organized into stations along the line. Carriages had multiple electric and compressed air outlets, compartments for larger components, and parts kits. Platforms gave access to all working areas.

1 Engine and propeller assembly shop.

2 Receiving room for engines and propellers.

3 Point at which wing is transferred from truck to wing buggy.

4 Wing, now complete with engines and radiator assemblies, is transferred to first position of main assembly line.

5 Wing meets fuselage on carriage at start of main assembly line.

6 Carriage, after chain-driven "U" circuit through Bay 2, moves via transfer track to first position of bay 3 assembly line.

7 Carriage entering assembly line in Bay 3 for its final "U" circuit.

8 Final position of assembly line at which the complete aircraft is hoisted from the carriage, ready for the paint shop and test flight.

9 Fuselage assembly lines and travel route to position No. 5 (see above).

10 Carriage (with plane) en route to Bay 3 on transfer track located outside building.

11 Trainer assembly bay.

12 Fuselage on truck entering fuselage assembly lines.

13 Experimental hangar.

14 Plant No.2 - Fitting, welding and small assemblies.

15 Empty carriage en route to position No. 5.

16 Return track for empty wing buggies.

17 Paint shop.

18 Experimental shop.

19 A winch for drawing carriage (with plane) up an incline from Bay 2 to Bay 3.

20 Experimental hangar No. 2.

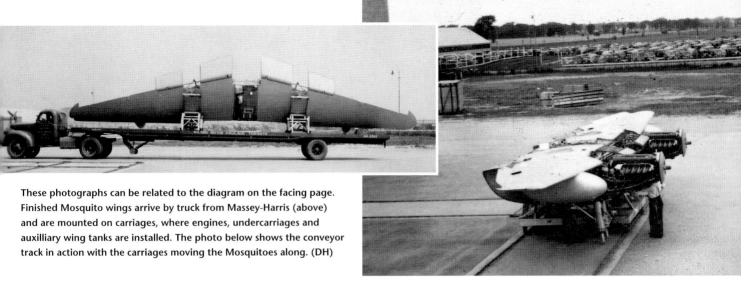

These photographs can be related to the diagram on the facing page. Finished Mosquito wings arrive by truck from Massey-Harris (above) and are mounted on carriages, where engines, undercarriages and auxilliary wing tanks are installed. The photo below shows the conveyor track in action with the carriages moving the Mosquitoes along. (DH)

More than 1,100 Mosquitoes came off the line at Downsview. (DH9648)

before the start of the sophisticated mechanization – with 80 aircraft produced that month. The movement became so good at one point that flight test backed up.

As far as Transport Command was concerned, Mosquito movements slowly returned to normal, even though pilots tried to steer clear of the type. Captain Don McVicar, who was an RAFTC training pilot, recalled: "Any of the crews I met in the hall would literally disappear before my eyes," he said. "I'd turn my head and they would be gone."

On September 17, 1944, a message from C.D. Howe announced the resignation of Grant Glassco, who was returning to private business. Howe praised him as an outstanding administrator who had served without remuneration for the duration of the war. "Mr. Glassco has given all his time and talents to the problems of the Mosquito production. He has encountered and surmounted many difficulties

Dick Dickinson, head of plant engineering, was responsible for the Mosquito conveyor system. (DH M259)

and problems and it is only with regret that I have accepted his resignation." In the same notice, George Bear became plant manager, to serve with the existing directors in what would now be known as the "Control Committee."

The celebration of the new year 1945 brought a more relaxed feeling to management and workers, for the flow of parts from 200 contracting plants had become routine. The production of fuselages, so well launched by Bill Houston at Dupont Street, at one time exceeded demand. They were stacked side by side in a corner of the hangar until needed and provided an excellent opportunity for one enterprising young lady. She sought the seclusion of a fuselage to set up a temporary branch of the world's oldest profession. From all reports business became quite brisk when word got out that it was "the second fuselage from the end." But this show of private enterprise was short-lived. It is not known whether one of the patrons talked too much or an alert guard noticed the increased traffic.

Bill Houston cut back on production of fuselages at Dupont Street to balance the flow, but maintained control of all wood fabrication techniques among subcontractors, particularly the gluing and testing. Downsview had become a huge assembly centre, putting together the labours of 15,000 Canadians from coast to coast. Production quotas were assured once Dickinson's Navy began operating and the problem areas then became testing and delivery. With the steady flow of Mosquitoes, Central Aircraft at London became a busy modification centre. With so many hours of testing and re-testing, the number of pilots under Harry Umphrey eventually grew to 14. Delivery incidents were considerably reduced as a result but they were not completely eliminated. DHC had taken a major part in the clean-up program but was also on the receiving end of a lot of criticism and innuendo. The pressures of war overshadowed the fact that the Mosquito was not designed for the vagaries of Atlantic weather and that the art of ocean flying was still relatively new. The significance of the whole Mosquito ferry saga can be seen in the fact that by VE Day RAFTC had delivered 646 of them to England.

By early 1945 many Canadian Mosquitoes were credited with 50 or more sorties over Europe. They played a major role in the night offensives that characterized the latter months of the war. They took part in 31 consecutive night raids on Berlin while serving with 139, 162, 163 and 608 Squadrons. Other operational squadrons with which they served were 109, 128, 142, 578, 627 and 692. Some went to the Admiralty for special duties, while others were dispatched to the Middle East. Closer to home Mosquitoes served with No. 133 RCAF at Patricia Bay, British Columbia, No. 7 OTU at Debert, Nova Scotia, and No. 8 OTU at Greenwood, Nova Scotia. No. 133 Squadron was a home defence unit patrolling the B.C. coast for Japanese fire balloons.

'Shop' Lifting

Every wartime factory needed security practices, particularly with anything involving aircraft. Most employees realized this, but others looked upon it as a challenge to "beat the system" and try a little petty larceny. The sport became even more attractive with the government involved and everything movable seemed "fair game." A book could probably be written about the illegal "expropriations" that go on, during and after all wars, wherever human nature and authority mix, and de Havilland Canada in WWII was no exception.

A company vise seemed to be the ultimate challenge; but few who tried for this prize outdid the ingenuity of the "turkey raffle caper." As the story goes, an enterprising worker made his way through the security gates at quitting time with a parcel from which dangled two turkey legs. He made a great play of his luck that day in winning the department raffle and might have won his acting debut if the package hadn't come apart just at that moment and deposited a hefty vise at the guard's feet. On another occasion a railway serviceman came into the guard house carrying a vise he had found beside the railway tracks. The culprit was never identified, but when management heard of the find they felt that anyone who could throw a vise that heavy 15 feet from the boundary fence should win some kind of prize – even if he didn't get to keep the vise.

Then there was the employee who worked in the mould-

Canadian Subcontractors for the Mosquito

Aircraft Hydraulic Company – *jacks*
Aluminum Company – *aluminum alloy castings*
Boeing Aircraft Company (Canada) – *tailplanes*
S. F. Bowser Company – *parts and assemblies*
Canadian Power Boat – *fuselages and flaps*
Canadian Pratt & Whitney – *propellers*
Canadian Westinghouse – *metal elevators*
Cockshutt Plow Company – *undercarriages, rudders and elevators*
Delaney & Pettit – *casein glue and adhesives*
Dominion Chair Company – *control fittings*
Dominion Oilcloth & Linoleum Company – *sheet metal parts*
Dominion Screw – *bolts and bushings*
Duplate Glass Company – *canopy tops and windshields*
General Motors Canada – *fuselages*
Gutta Percha – *parts and assemblies*
Hoover Company – *propeller pitch mechanisms*
Humber Engineering – *tail fins*
Kelsey Company – *wheels*
Lysaught Dominion – *propeller spinners*

Massey-Harris – *wings*
McCord Company – *radiators*
Robert Mitchell – *aluminum alloy castings*
Moffats – *fuel tanks*
O'Donnell Mackie – *torque tubes*
Otako Company – *tailwheel assemblies*
George W. Reed & Company – *hydraulics and fuel tanks*
Research Enterprises – *parts and assemblies*
Sparton of Canada – *instruments and indicators*
Stone Franklin – *bomb winches*
Toronto Metal Spinning – *small parts*
Universal Cooler – *tanks*
York Button – *small parts*

Tooling by: Myers Engineering, Otis Fensom, Aurora Engineering, Duplate Tool, Canada Cycle and Motor, Precision Tool
From Packard Motor Company in the U.S.A.: Packard Merlin engines

A U.S. Army Air Forces F-8 Mosquito emerges from the hangar. A molded plywood slipper tank is under the wing. (DH1501)

One of the first of many dignitaries to visit DHC was the popular HRH, Duke of Kent. Phil Garratt is in conversation with the Duke. Behind is Ralph Bell, Director General of Aircraft Production. (DH JH 50)

(Below) Movie actress Joan Fontaine unveils the Mosquito named in her honour during a 1944 plant visit. (DH239)

ing shop making the forming dies. They used a metal called "kirksite" that had a low melting point and was quite valuable. An alert guard noticed that this chap carried his lunch box differently each night. Sometimes it would swing light and easy, while at other times it looked heavy with no swing at all. On one of the "heavy" nights he was asked to "open up" and, sure enough, inside was a neat block of kirksite, just made to fit. A search of his home revealed quite a number of these carefully made bricks awaiting a buyer.

Celebrities and Ceremonies

From the beginning of the war effort, de Havilland Canada welcomed many celebrities who mingled with the workers on the production line. The Duke of Kent dropped by during the early stages of the Tiger Moth program, as did a number of flying aces. They all did their part to publicize the sale of Victory Bonds, but none could match the glamour of the visitor who was driven up to the front door on May 14, 1944. All eyes strained to catch a glimpse of the beautiful movie star Joan Fontaine, who had come to christen a Mosquito in her honour. She was given a royal welcome, not only for donating her time to the bond drive, but because she was a member of the famous de Havilland family and cousin of the founder. Managing director Grant Glassco led a huge crowd as their guest unveiled Mosquito KB273, named *Joan*, followed by a tour of the factory that rivalled any Hollywood production.

By fall 1944 the staff was approaching the 7,000 mark, and many of the early problems were only a memory. The Victory Loan drives were still active and pressure mounted for a full-scale family day at the factory. One of the prime

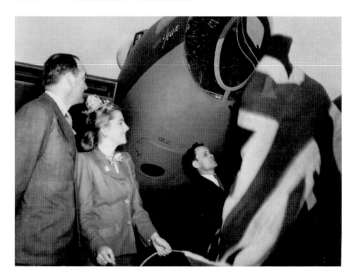

movers was the active WWI veterans group under longtime employee Charlie Powell. Charlie led the company ex-servicemen in forming their own branch of the Canadian Legion, whose project during the past year had been the preparation of a de Havilland memorial to record the names of employees who lost their lives in the war. The six-foot stone cairn topped with a bronze Mosquito over a world globe was erected in a garden area outside Plant 1. An aluminum faceplate bore the names of the DHC honour roll.

The unveiling took place on Family Day, October 8, 1944. Thousands of cars jammed the narrow roads leading to the plant. It was the first such large event and the organizers soon found themselves parking cars in open fields and sideroads. The tour of the factory and the dedication of the memorial cairn went off in fine style. Padre Sidney Lambert of Christie Street Military Hospital officiated at the solemn wreath-laying ceremony. Charlie Powell read the honours list, followed by Taps and a moment of silence. The flag-draped memorial was uncovered by Mr. and Mrs. G.H. Baker, whose two sons had once worked for de Havilland and had lost their lives with the RCAF. (The memorial later was moved to the office entrance of the plant).

A ramp had been constructed, allowing guests to mount a few steps and view a Mosquito cockpit. The long line-up proved the aircraft's popularity and acted as a prelude to the flying display to follow. Three Mosquitoes performed to perfection, but a sudden rain forced many to take cover, including the announcer, Woody Walden, who continued his commentary under a flatbed truck. Scheduled addresses by general manager Bear and the president of Union Local 112 were cancelled, but a display of the de Havilland glider by B. Baronowski was completed as planned. A rain-soaked RCAF band brought the day to a close with the national anthem. Two other occasions were found during that month to show the de Havilland flag, starting with a subcontractors' preview day on October 6 and a salute to the air cadets on the 15th. The latter activities were conducted under sunny skies and totalled 4,500 officers, NCOs and air cadets. Guests that day included Air Marshal W.A. "Billy" Bishop, senior officers of the RCNVR and Toronto Mayor Fred Conboy. The events started with a march-past with Air Vice Marshal A.T.N.

The de Havilland Canada war memorial cairn, with its famous bronze Mosquito ornament. (DH851)

"Tom" Cowley taking the salute at the reviewing stand. A conducted tour of the plant was followed by a drumhead service and the highlight of the afternoon, a flying display featuring three Mosquitoes and the DHC glider. As the glider landed from its display, the cadets were bussed to their form-up area, where a round of doughnuts and milk ended their action-packed day.

Another opportunity to get acquainted with the subcontractors was arranged for Sunday, January 21, 1945, when 1,200 members of the Massey-Harris company of Weston came over to see what was being done with all the Mosquito wings they had been building. This time it was overcoat weather, but they were treated to another flying display and tour of the plant. On April 19, 1945, movie actor Pat O'Brien visited Downsview to help launch the 7th Victory Loan Campaign. Once again there was a plant tour with a hangar ceremony and flying display. O'Brien removed a large Union Jack from the nose of RCAF Mosquito KB171, serial No. 750.

The Final Year

By the end of 1944 the Allies were finding stubborn resistance in Europe, even though victory was only a matter of time. A long, nasty battle was forecast in the Pacific after the expected European surrender. As it happened, 1945 proved to be the final year for DH Canada's war effort, but instead of a glorious ending, the year was marked by a number of fatalities that hit close to home. Two days before Christmas, Jack Rogers and his observer, Arthur Copp, found themselves with a jammed aileron on a routine flight. This started a dramatic exchange with the control tower on what procedure to follow. The crew got permission to jump but the final decision was left to the captain, who felt he could get his craft down safely. The wheels-up approach seemed to be proceeding well but the Mosquito suddenly nosed over in a nearby field and crashed, killing both occupants. The investigation revealed the dreaded spectre that always haunts the aircraft manufac-

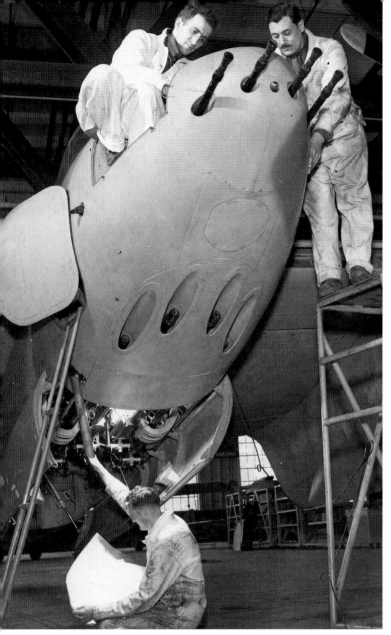

The two variants of the Mosquito manufactured in Canada were bombers and fighters. Here the machine guns and cannons of a fighter are shown, along with the side crew door. On the bomber the crew entered from below (see photo on page 86). (DH196)

engineer Jakimiuk to one of the more difficult staging points, Bluie-West-One (BW 1) Greenland (now Narssarssuaq). Every problem tended to revive the ferry rumour mill, particularly the Mosquito's lack of de-icing equipment.

In the summer of 1944, during the delivery clean-up program, a young Torontonian had joined the company as assistant to Lee Murray. The 30-year-old Woodrow "Woody" Walden had been circulation manager for *Canadian Aviation*, and when he joined Murray in a liaison capacity had just completed two years as an Anson pilot flying navigation students. He received a check-out on the Mosquito and became involved with the ferry problems at Dorval. The company backed his request to do a delivery himself, which was agreed to by Transport Command. He was allotted aircraft KB593 and briefed with radio/navigator Tom Scotland for a flight via Gander and the Azores.

The weather on arrival at Gander presented one of those nasty frontal situations over the Atlantic. This had a number of Mossie crews nervously holding over, waiting for a break. At the first sign of clearing, the air force crews were ordered to go and had no alternative, but most civil crews balked, considering the weather still unsuitable. Walden, carrying the DH banner, found himself in an extremely touchy position, particularly as it was his first Atlantic crossing.

The atmosphere in the Met office that March 6, 1945, grew as chilly as the outside air when Walden decided to go despite considerable opposition. He teamed with Jim Henderson, who was on his sixth Mosquito delivery, and they planned to go over together in radio contact. Henderson recalled:

There were about 23 crews in Gander at the time, and we had been holding 10 days for weather. Woody asked if he could go with me so we taxied out together. He went back with an engine temperature problem and got off 10 minutes later than I. We never did make radio contact. It was clear weather when we left but after an hour or so we were in haze at 15,000. A weather alert came from Gander when we were two hours and 40 minutes out and I climbed to 23,000 without finding a top. I noticed the shiny glint of ice on the wing so I figured it was about time I headed back to Gander. I was just starting a slow turn when the old girl stalled from under me and it took a dive to 10,000 feet before I could regain control. Six crews went out that day; some got through and some went back. All were accounted for but Walden, and I imagine he got into the same conditions we did. I was asked to be on the court of inquiry.

This tragedy less than a month before VE day further damaged the Mosquito's Atlantic reputation and did nothing to solve the ferry problems.

turer – faulty workmanship, compounded by an inspection slip-up. A circular wooden plug covering an inspection opening was lacking a simple retaining screw. The plug vibrated out of position, jamming the aileron. Quality control had waged an on-going battle from the beginning, but this glaring incident brought a new drive with explicit photographs posted throughout the plant telling everyone exactly why the aircraft had crashed.

In spite of the gloom and remorse that started the year, production was on schedule, even if ferry flights were still giving trouble. The company was making a determined effort to resolve every snag that cropped up in this touchy area. One step was a round-trip visit by chief aeronautical

In a spectacular near-fatal incident, April 17, an air bottle exploded in KA970 as it approached Scotland, tearing a seven-foot hole in the side of the fuselage. An exciting wheels-up landing ended the episode successfully, but the aircraft never flew again. It did not console anyone that the fault was traced to a pressure regulator which froze at altitude

Mosquito No. 1,000 off the production line got a lot of attention, including from 11 of the women who contributed to the war effort. (DH47217)

and let go as the crew descended into the warmer air of Prestwick.

From the early spring of 1944, a celebrated British Mosquito toured Canada in support of the huge Victory Loan drive. "F for Freddie" had been featured in a movie, had survived 213 operational missions over Germany and was accompanied by its crew: F/L Maurice Briggs, DSO, DFC, DFM, and F/O John Baker, DFC and Bar. Ed Jack of de Havilland, who had been seconded to Transport Command, acted as their service engineer. The aircraft's schedule brought it to Downsview on May 6, where Bill Burlison's experimental test crew touched up its ruffled paint and primped it for a western tour. "F for Freddie" arrived in Calgary with a superb demonstration, May 9, and was scheduled to repeat it the next day as wind-up to their tour. Eddie Jack was to ride right seat on the 10th but felt a strange nausea after climbing into the cockpit. The regular crewman, Johnnie Baker, promptly replaced him for takeoff, on what the service pilots used to call a "legalized beat-up." The spectators were thrilled again, but tragedy struck, when "Freddie" ticked a wing on the control tower and went hurtling to the ground. Jack had watched the performance from the control tower and was just going downstairs when the crash occurred. It was two close calls in one day for the colourful Eddie Jack.

In April 1945 tragedy struck the flight department again with the loss of two pilots. Both had only recently

joined flight test and were delivering a Mosquito from Toronto to Washington. F/L T. Murray Mitchell, DFC, came to DHC as an experimental test pilot after an operational tour on Mossies. W.G. "Gord" Hiltz had been a civilian pilot at No. 1 Air Observers' School at nearby Malton. Their aircraft was cleared from Malton late in the afternoon and crashed 20 minutes later in high terrain between Attica and Varysburg, in New York State. Weather was blamed.

There was great rejoicing with VE Day May 8, 1945, but the effort to finish the war in the Pacific continued. How this would come about was of little concern to the factory workers, but it was conceded by most that their years of war employment were coming to an end. Some gave the matter little thought as long as the war with Japan continued, for they had adapted to the comfortable routine of daily challenges and regular pay cheques.

With improved efficiency on the production line, at the start of 1945 a total of 1,700 had been laid off, but when the main lay-offs came they were swift and devastating. On

The celebrated "F for Freddie" (RAF serial LR503) visits Downsview. It had flown 213 operations with 105 Squadron. It is shown with Bill Burlison's crew, who checked it over for the ill-fated trip to Calgary. (DH)

August 28 the balance of the Mosquito contract was cancelled; only 18 on the line would be completed. A notice went out the same night that 3,000 workers would be laid off immediately on a seniority basis. The suddenness caught everyone by surprise, particularly the union heads, who sent a delegation to Ottawa and petitions outlining their suggestions to the Minister of Munitions and Supply, C.D. Howe. They demanded that Ottawa begin immediate conversion to civil work and that the employees receive one month's severance pay for each year of service. The workers at de Havilland were not alone, for similar notices were going out in all the plants building aircraft: 4,000 at Noorduyn, 2,000 at Victory Aircraft, 1,200 at Massey-Harris, 825 at Central Aircraft. There was talk of mass protest meetings and the employees of Clyde Aircraft in Collingwood even threatened to remain in the plant until Howe stated his plans for their company. The rows of unfinished Mosquito bombers made for dramatic articles in the daily papers, with photos of Downsview housewives discussing their future – and their mortgages. It was an emotional time, punctuated by the surrender of the Japanese in September. C.D. Howe issued a typical government statement that "all existing war plants will be converted to civilian production at the earliest possible date." Most soon realized it would be a long time before there would be many jobs at DHC and busied themselves looking for other work.

The transition was not without a little drama here and there, for many were reluctant to leave. One workman in the fitting shop insisted that he was still needed and should go on a little longer. He used every ruse possible to stay on the job, until a search of his orderly work area revealed the reason. Most of the parts he was making had nothing to do with aircraft. Under his bench was a neat production line of fixtures for table lamps. When confronted with the evidence, his excuse was that he could not quit yet for he still had orders for 200 sets.

Sample issues of the DHC plant magazine, aptly named *Mosquito*. This monthly publication kept employees up-to-date about local issues and the success of their aircraft in combat.

By August the company made an agreement with the government to do commercial work and there was the obvious overlap of new planning and finishing the Mosquito line. The biggest job would be putting the Mossies into storage. By September the long ordeal of war was over; the workmen packed their tool boxes one last time for employment in other fields. Test pilots Jim Follett and Gerry Wooll combined to test the last Mosquito, KA534, on October 13, and by the end of the month the once-full parking lots were deserted. The noise of Packard Merlins in the circuit seldom broke the silence that descended over Downsview.

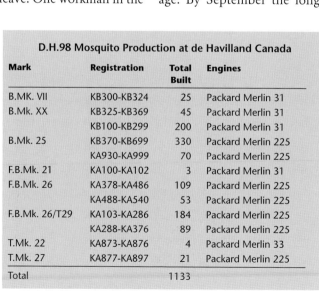

Mark	Registration	Total Built	Engines
	D.H.98 Mosquito Production at de Havilland Canada		
B.MK. VII	KB300-KB324	25	Packard Merlin 31
B.Mk. XX	KB325-KB369	45	Packard Merlin 31
	KB100-KB299	200	Packard Merlin 31
B.Mk. 25	KB370-KB699	330	Packard Merlin 225
	KA930-KA999	70	Packard Merlin 225
F.B.Mk. 21	KA100-KA102	3	Packard Merlin 31
F.B.Mk. 26	KA378-KA486	109	Packard Merlin 225
	KA488-KA540	53	Packard Merlin 225
F.B.Mk. 26/T29	KA103-KA286	184	Packard Merlin 225
	KA288-KA376	89	Packard Merlin 225
T.Mk. 22	KA873-KA876	4	Packard Merlin 33
T.Mk. 27	KA877-KA897	21	Packard Merlin 225
Total		1133	

CHAPTER FOUR

A NEW START

The last days of hostilities on both fronts were busy ones for de Havilland. Woody Walden had gone missing over the Atlantic two months before VJ day and the disastrous news of the crash of "F for Freddie," two days after victory in Europe, had stunned everyone back at the plant, while the flight of Mosquito 1,000 in July had been greeted with excitement. Though preparations for peacetime projects had gone on informally, it was not until three months after VE Day that formal government permission was received to do commercial work again. Mosquito production was phased out rapidly as attention went more and more to postwar projects. The peace that so many had prayed for had come.

Throughout the days of turmoil that surrounded the Mosquito in Canada, engineering and experimental work went on almost unnoticed at Downsview. To the casual observer, de Havilland's 98th design seemed simply a British aircraft under manufacture in Canada with decisions made in England, but the complex Mossie, with its thousands of components and its ever-changing variants, did not conform to any such concept: a skilled engineering capacity, backed by an equally competent experimental department, was needed from the very beginning. While all eyes were on production at Downsview and the glamour of operational reports of this outstanding aircraft, DH Canada built an engineering capability that was to prove a key factor in the competitive years ahead.

Every new Mosquito problem, be it the type of glue or the fitting of a U.S. bomb sight, was turned over to engineering. Rocket projectile fittings, revised bonding and trans-Atlantic fuel tanks, all had to be designed, tested and applied to the production. Every new mark of Packard Merlin engine added hundreds of engineering man-hours, what with rocker box breathers, tropical air intakes and carburetor de-icing. The use of North American hardware on a British design provided a constant challenge which involved everything from ball races to nuts and bolts. The fact that the subcontractors did not have aeronautical engineering experience only added to the responsibility of the experts at Downsview.

The men who headed these departments were seasoned professionals in their respective fields and ideally suited to their tasks. The bulk of engineering fell on the shoulders of "Jaki" Jakimiuk, whose background of experience in Poland had already been well proven. His presence had attracted many of his expatriate countrymen who were respected for their design skills and drive. To head this group on the experimental side was Bill Burlison. His years in Montreal when that city led the country in aircraft manufacture provided an ideal background for the position. Hovering over it all, like a maestro in an orchestra, was Doug Hunter, an engineering administrator steeped in the parent de Havilland tradition.

These were creative people whose daily conversations revolved around new methods and new projects, and as early as 1943 part-time study began in a corner of the plant on a boxy-looking, high-wing passenger plane with an in-line Gipsy engine. A couple of plywood cockpit mock-ups were even built to form a basis for their discussions. A low-wing trainer was

Some of the postwar planners in front of the Sheppard Avenue office: A.F. MacDonald, R. Bannock, G.J. Mickleborough, W.D. Hunter, G.C. Ross (of DH South Africa), P.C. Garratt and H.R. Smyth. (DH 47631)

1. The original curved roof hangar brought from Mt. Dennis – after its second move, across Sheppard Avenue.
2. The first factory building with the tall chimney, built on Sheppard Avenue in 1929.
3. Two economy metal hangars built in 1938 – one used as a paint shop, the other for storage.
4. The first de Havilland addition, to accommodate Tiger Moth production.
5. The main plant built by Federal Aircraft for Anson and Mosquito production.
6. Cafeterias.
7. Painting and spraying bay.
8. The first flight test hangar, later removed to accommodate a new runway.

A view immediately after the war showing how war construction grew around the original DHC building. That section is still recognizable with its black roof and chimney. The wooden hangar with the curved roof (also black) has been moved for the second time to the cluster in the foreground. (DH 688)

also in their talks and a model of their collective ideas graced the desk of their boss Jakimiuk. This was the situation as everyone adjusted to a postwar world. It was also the time for DHC to begin putting this design capability to work.

The Overhaul Business

By April 30, 1946, the de Havilland portion of the plant was officially returned to the company from government control and Garratt was securely back in his corner office. The rest of the building complex was to be administered by DHC under a series of lease-purchase arrangements with Ottawa. The problem now was to put the hangars to use.

Ever mindful of the struggling thirties, Phil Garratt went shopping for overhaul work and it was not long in coming. The Netherlands bought six Catalina flying boats from Garratt's friend C.R. "Peter" Troup of Aircraft Industries of St. Jean, Quebec. The extensive refurbishing could only be done at a large plant with access to a large body of water, so de Havilland got the work. A complete overhaul depot was set up at Toronto Island Airport for these big "boats" and soon quotes were being asked by many customers. Such "bread-and-butter" contracts added a new dimension to de Havilland's recovery program, broadening plant skills and building stability.

A deluxe Canso conversion for a South American company done as part of DHC's postwar overhaul program. (Hotson Col.)

Overhaul contracts brought DHC badly needed cash, and kept a core of the wartime labour force current with their skills. Here a Catalina is being overhauled at Toronto Island Airport. (DH M10)

(Left) From 1946-56, 68 Cansos were overhauled at Downsview. DHC Canso experts here are (left to right) Jack Ball, Fred Jackson, John Aitken, C. Beatty, Alex Hughes, Hank Warner, Bill Hall, Bill Bozanin and Norm Davis. (DH 9730)

Routine and uninspiring as overhaul may have been, the revenue from these contracts was responsible for DH Canada's healthy recovery after the war. Fairchild of Canada, by comparison, attempted to bolster its return to civil aviation with pre-fabricated housing and went out of business in 1948.

The overhaul of Catalinas at Toronto Island in 1946 led to a steady flow of similar Canso work, which was the backbone of the overhaul program for the next 10 years. The Canso line started with six conversions for the Danish Air Force. Canadian Pacific Airlines needed four for northern Quebec and war hero Johnnie Fauquier needed two for mining exploration. Rexco had one outfitted for South America and another was done in a deluxe configuration for Rich-

Cansos for the Danish Navy completely refurbished and awaiting delivery at Downsview. (DH 1947)

mond Exploration. Eleven were converted for the RCAF.

Business Expands

The British D.H.104 Dove came on the market in the latter part of 1945 and was a good replacement for the Rapide. Because of the Rapide's early acceptance in Canada, hope was high for Dove sales. The first aircraft from the Hatfield production line came to Canada in 1946 and was shown around the country by sales manager A.F. "Sandy" MacDonald as CF-BNU. It was used for some time to fly executives for Imperial Oil, but they

The first commercial helicopters entered the Canadian market right after WWII. DHC initially held the Canadian agency for the Bell 47, company rep Bill Jackson being in charge. Here he flies Santa Claus in a PR stunt. Some war-surplus Anson Vs are beyond. DHC soon left the helicopter market to concentrate on its own products. (DH)

never put it into regular service. Serial No. 15 also came to Canada for testing on floats, but proved less than satisfactory due to limited power. Eventually 14 Doves came to Canada, but its greatest success in North America was in the U.S., where it was marketed by the Riley Aeronautics Corporation.

Twenty-six North American Harvards went through the shops in 1948-49, along with two rare birds, a Fairchild 71C bushplane and a Vickers Valetta transport. From 1951- 54, 50 Avro Lancasters were overhauled while 16 others were modified. The Grumman G21A Goose was much in demand for executive conversion and four were completed. Eight Douglas DC-3s were overhauled as were 10 Canadair North Stars. A North American B-25 Mitchell went through the shops along with 13 Noorduyn Norseman Mk.IVs.

The move by the RCAF in 1948 to obtain 86 D.H.100 Vampires put the company into jet maintenance. The whine of jet engines was new to Toronto but, with all the assembly and overhaul taking place at Downsview, jet flying in the area became routine. Russ Bannock flew the first RCAF Vampire in February 1948 and DHC test pilots became pioneers in pure jet propulsion. From 1949-56, 71 Vampires went through their overhaul cycles at Downsview and 60 received 400-hour inspections. By the time overhaul work dried up in 1956, a total of 340 aircraft of 15 types had been processed.

DHC's first postwar connection with its parent was promoting the Dove executive plane and feeder liner. Several were sold in Canada, including CF-GBE, seen in the colours of petroleum giant Sunoco. (Government of Ontario)

Fred Buller Joins

If pragmatism is the "philosophy which tests the validity of all concepts by their practical results," then Fred Buller was pragmatic. He was educated in western Canada and his roots in aviation began with W. Leigh Brintnell at Edmonton-based Mackenzie Air Service. He had great admiration for Brintnell but by 1943 the time had come for a change. Buller left for Ottawa, where he offered his services to the war effort. Thus began a series of moves that brought him into the de Havilland sphere of operations.

He went first to Central Aircraft, where Francis Hyde-Beadle was resident aeronautical engineer. As part of the war

Aircraft Type	1946	1947	1948	1949	1950	1951	1952	1953	1954	1955	1956	1957	1958	1959	Total
Chipmunk							3	3	4		3	7	3		23
Beaver – Civil										1	4	6	1	2	14
Beaver – L20a										44	75	42			161
Beaver – L20												6			6
Otter – Civil											1	5	3	1	10
Otter – RCAF											14	21	1		36
Dove							3	4	2	2	5	1	1		18
Heron								1		1		2		1	5
Canso	1	17	9	21	10	8	2								68
Dakota			1	6	1										8
Harvard			20	6											26
Lancaster						9	28	10	3						50
Lancaster – Mods							11	5							16
Norseman								13							13
North Star									5	3	2				10
Vampire				2	13	11	8	4	18	12	3				71
Vampire – 400hr					27	28	5								60
Anson			1	1											2
Catalina	6														6
Comet									2						2
Fairchild 71C				1											1
Goose		1	1	1	1										4
Mitchell						1	1								2
Rapide		1													1
Valetta				1											1
Total for year	7	19	31	34	30	57	73	51	39	63	107	84	15	4	614

program, Central was involved in producing Mosquito fuselages and test-flying Mossies before delivery. At the age of 53 Hyde-Beadle was suffering from a recurrent heart condition and his doctors advised him to cut down his activities. This was easier said than done for an engineer of his stature, and Ottawa agreed that he should have assistance. Buller was sent to London, which involved him immediately with de Havilland engineering staff, the ferry problems and bringing Mosquitoes up to delivery status.

On December 14, 1943, Francis Hyde-Beadle died in London, ending an outstanding career in aeronautical engineering. Fred Buller took over responsibility and, in doing so, impressed his counterparts at Downsview. During the fi-

Fred Buller came to de Havilland after years with Mackenzie Air Service and Central Aircraft. His talents were welcomed on the design team from the Chipmunk to the Dash 7. He was the 1971 McCurdy Award winner and was made a member of Canada's Aviation Hall of Fame. (Via Betty Buller)

nal weeks of the war Bill Jackson offered Buller a position at de Havilland. He moved to Toronto and hit it off immediately with de Havilland's Jakimiuk because of their similar views on metal aircraft construction. The two began experimenting with metal laminates and before long Buller began taking part in discussions about a trainer and a cabin utility plane.

Doug Hunter understood the mandate that his boss Phil Garratt had given him and was pleased with the staff that was developing under his command. Besides Jakimiuk and Buller, he had Bill Jackson, with DH Canada since Tiger Moth days, Bob McIntyre, who had moved from Massey-Harris midway through the war, Bob Klein, another University of Toronto graduate serving as chief stress engineer, and Jim Houston, whose entire career had involved engines and propellers. Jim travelled with his father a great deal in the years between the wars and was in England about the time the de Havilland Technical School was organized. He became one of the first graduates of this prestigious institution and began specializing in the new art of controllable pitch propellers. When the war came he took a major role in modifying early British fighter aircraft with the latest propeller techniques to keep ahead of similar German technology. He came to Canada during the Mosquito program as propulsion expert and remained in this capacity – through seven Canadian designs – until his retirement in 1976.

The Fox Moth Reborn

The shutdown of the Mosquito line had a traumatic effect on the lives of thousands as they scrambled back to peace-time living. All the wartime empire-building and jockeying for position ended in a new quandary – how to stay in aviation at all. The coming of peace put the de Havilland originals in the spotlight again for Phil Garratt was back in command with the full support of de Havilland England. He

The postwar Fox Moth production line at Downsview, where wood-working skills were again in demand. (Hotson Col.)

seldom discussed the C.D. Howe-Ralph Bell edict that had sent him into isolation for 26 months. The subject came up one day in England during a discussion with W.F. Shaylor, who used to fly Moths with Garratt at Mount Dennis. Shaylor was now a fellow director of DH England and they were discussing a situation with similar political overtones. "What do you do in a case like this?" Shaylor asked, and Garratt came back with one of his short answers that held a lot of meaning: "Just sit tight and saw wood."

Garratt wanted to steer the company back into producing small civil aircraft and saw the Fox Moth as an ideal interim type until new designs could be developed. It was a proven workhorse for which a market still existed, and the fact that it shared many components with the Tiger Moth meant that it could be put into production quickly using recycled Tiger parts. The Fox Moth was described as the first aircraft to support itself financially in the air and had the reputation as an economical performer in the years before the war. It used Tiger Moth mainplanes, tail unit, undercarriage and engine mounting. The only different component was a deep ply-wood fuselage with a four-place cabin between the wings. It had adapted well to floats and skis during the 1930s and

proved itself in the Canadian bush. The prewar models had the Gipsy III engine but the new D.H. 83C to be built at Downsview would have the 145 hp Gipsy Major IC.

One of Garratt's first moves was to re-appoint Bill Calder as works manager, where he had been before the Mosquito shuffle. Bill had always viewed the wartime staff as tempo-rary help and had ideas about how he would get things back to normal. First he would remove all the stools from the benches in the fitting shop, wage scales would go back to their prewar standard and new employment numbers would be issued to postwar help of his choice. While top-level planning went on in the upstairs office, a new world was opening on the shop floor on Sheppard Avenue.

It was a dramatic period for those who received Bill Calder's nod of approval. Typical of those returning was Alex Downey, who had been in charge of Tiger Moth en-gine installation in the early 1940s. He returned to DHC after a stint with the Canadian Army to take part in the final days of the Mosquito. He recalled the early postwar days:

Bill asked me if I wanted to join the new company, and his offer was 90 cents an hour — the amount I had been making on the Tigers. After a long haggle, we settled for $1.10 and I was given the new number five. Bill took me to the old dope shop, where he wanted to set up engine overhaul. He opened a cupboard full of Gipsy engine parts

This Fox Moth was sold in May 1946 to Mssrs. Sponarski and Roderick of Rainy River, Ontario. Within a few weeks it was wrecked taking off at Nestor Falls. (DH)

and my first job was to reclaim a thousand spark plugs that he had squirrelled away during the war years. Jack Hall joined me and we were soon rebuilding Gipsy Major engines to the latest specifications.

It was about this time that I got involved in the Fox Moth, for John Neal had been invited back and was rebuilding Arthur Fecteau's Fox, CF-ATX, that had sunk. Jack Hall and I were told to study all the Tiger Moth parts that were compatible with the Fox and get ready for a very important trip. It all seemed so secretly "hush-hush" as we waited with our bags one cold, grey morning for a pick-up at the corner of St. Clair and Dufferin Streets. At the appointed hour, along came Bill Calder with his wife in the front seat and we dutifully took our places in the back. We had no idea where we were going but seemed to be heading in the direction of Montreal.

Bill drove like he had never heard of a comfort stop and it didn't help our predicament to have Mrs. Calder on board. He didn't believe in restaurants either and it was fortunate that we had brought some sandwiches along. The trip was memorable for more reasons than our bladder discomfort for in Montreal we collided with a cyclist and draped the rider across the hood of the car. I was afraid the police would be involved but all Bill could say was, "Look at the mark he put in my fender." Our eventual destination turned out to be Cap-de-la-Madeleine and, as we drove down one of their narrow streets, someone threw a brick on the top of Bill's car. We arrived ex-

Alex Downey's early connection with de Havilland involved the Fox Moth program. He is shown demonstrating a wingtip replacement for the later Chipmunk. (Hotson Col.)

hausted at the hangar of the former No. 11 EFTS with about 200 Tiger Moths lined up.

Our job, Bill told us, was to remove all components that would be used for a Fox Moth and prepare them for shipment to Toronto. After a one night stop-over, the Calders returned to Toronto but, somehow, nothing was mentioned about what we would use for money while we did the job. Jack and I worked like beavers to remove wings, tail sections and fittings according to instructions, and a couple of woodworkers came down from Toronto to pack the stuff into boxcars. All we left in the hangar was a row of Tiger fuselages stripped down to the engines and we made our way back to Toronto on the CNR with a lovely choice of washrooms.

When the boxcars finally arrived in Downsview, Calder came storming into our shop asking, "Where are the engines?" We had never been asked to remove the engines and no message had been sent. A phone call to Cap-de-la-Madeleine confirmed that the demolition boys had taken a sledgehammer to everything that was left, including the engines, so there was no use going back there. The problem was overcome when Ab Warren went to a depot in Fort William and soon we had plenty of Gipsy Majors for a full-scale overhaul program.

It did not take long to set a Fox Moth production line into operation. There was plenty of war-surplus plywood, and woodworking skills, after the Mosquito years, were of a very high order. Design improvements to the Fox Moth included a larger cabin door, a three-part engine cowling, a bubble cockpit canopy and a reinforced cabin floor. With so many of the Cap-de-la-Madeleine components on site, the first Fox was flying very soon. The test flight department had dwindled to one man but George Turner, who used to fly Mosquitoes and spent part of his time in the engine shop, was available to take the first D.H.83C CF-BFI-X into the air on December 5, 1945.

Fox Moth Customers

The first customer for the new Fox Moth was A. Fecteau Transport Aérien Ltée. of Senneterre, Quebec. Arthur Fecteau was an old friend of de Havilland, having begun operations with his brother in 1936 using one of the early wooden Cirrus Moths. From 1943 he operated British-built Fox Moth CF-ATX from his base on the Bell River, near Senneterre, flying the local Indians and fur traders throughout northern Quebec. By 1945 ATX was back at DHC for a

Arthur Fecteau operated a Moth and a Fox Moth before the war, then bought the first postwar Fox Moth. Sold on DH products, he soon added the Beaver (1948) and Otter (1952). CF-BFI had several owners after leaving Fecteau. It was wrecked on takeoff at Parent, Quebec, on July 21, 1958. (Bombardier)

friend, but his total assets fell considerably short. The attitude of this clean-cut young man made quite an impression in the meetings that followed and he was soon sitting down with George Mickleborough working out the details of a contract. "I remember I made payments to the Industrial Acceptance Corporation to the tune of $515.64 a month," said Ward years later. "I'll never forget that number as I had to work so hard to get it together every time."

complete rebuild just as Fox Moth production was beginning. Fecteau liked the Fox so much that he bought the first production model, CF-BFI, in January 1946 and operated it until September 1950. By then he had his first Beaver and went on with Beavers and Otters to become one of the most successful bush operators in Quebec.

The saga of the Fox Moth cannot be told without the story of serial No. 29 and its proud owner, Maxwell W. Ward. Max Ward grew up in Edmonton with aviation as his dream and a desire to emulate the feats of Dickins, May and Berry. He won his wings in the RCAF in 1941 and, although he wanted an overseas posting, he spent the war on training assignments across Canada. After his discharge he investigated aviation possibilities around Yellowknife. He visited de Havilland in August 1946, arriving in Sandy MacDonald's office with his mind set on a Fox Moth. He had his war bond savings, some $1,500 and a loan from a

The story of his early hardships and eventual success is the history of the one-time world charter airline Wardair. When other bushplanes were built at Downsview in later years, Ward was back for Beavers, Otters and Twin Otters. This association was demonstrated again in 1977 when Wardair became one of the first customers to place its confidence in the Dash 7. He operated two in the Arctic before withdrawing from bush flying to concentrate on his holiday charter business.

The Fox Moth provided everything Phil Garratt had hoped for. It gave DHC a chance to renew its acquaintance with old commercial customers and make new friends in the business. DHC's first exports were Fox Moths. Sixteen went to four countries, and by the time the program closed in 1948, 53 had been built. A set of components was combined by Leavens Bros. of Toronto in 1952 with equipment from the original CF-API to produce CF-EVK. Fox Moths became museum artifacts although a few were still flying. Max Ward had a replica of his original Fox built in the 1980s and donated it to the National Aviation Museum in Ottawa.

The start of DH Canada as an exporter came in 1947. India and Pakistan bought 11 of 35 Fox Moths built that year. (DH)

Max Ward's original airplane was the D.H.83C Fox Moth CF-DJC. Max operated it until 1949. (DH)

Dick Hiscocks Joins

Shortly after the test flight of the all-Canadian Fox Moth, Phil Garratt had a visit from a young man who had worked at the plant as a summer student. Richard D. Hiscocks was a Torontonian who had built model airplanes of such quality during his schooldays that he won numerous prizes in local competitions. One of these awards in 1928 was a flight in a Gipsy Moth at the Mount Dennis flying field with test pilot Leigh Capreol. Dick obtained summer employment at Downsview during 1936 to augment his engineering studies at the University of Toronto. He worked on assembly of the *Globe and Mail* Rapide, helped with the RCMP Dragonflies and generally made himself useful. Upon graduation he broadened his studies in England and, with the help of Phil Garratt and Lee Murray, found himself in the manufacturing mainstream at DH Hatfield. The shop experience was rewarding but his efforts to study technical reports and advanced aerodynamics fell short of his expectations. An offer from the National Aeronautical Establishment of the National Research Council in Ottawa drew him back to Canada, where he soon established himself with leading scientists.

With the war the number of experimental undertakings doubled at NRC and Hiscocks' talents were directed to wood replacement projects in case of a metal shortage. He took a major design role in the wooden Harvard and a new wooden Anson Mark V, with a plywood bonded fuselage. This typically Canadian Anson was eventually built in great numbers by MacDonald Bros. and Canadian Car & Foundry.

The highlight of Dick Hiscocks' career with the NRC came when he was named a member of Canada's scientific delegation to Britain at the end of hostilities. It met with similar groups from Allied countries reviewing aeronautical advancements and interrogating German scientists in an unprecedented exchange of information. It was in this exhilarating environment that new concepts of wing design and flap arrangements excited Hiscocks. He projected them into his dream of the ideal bush airplane and became even more enthusiastic. It was this interest that brought him for the third time in his career to see Phil Garratt. The meeting expanded into discussions with Hunter, Jakimiuk and Buller, who were now well into the design of what was to become the DHC-1 Chipmunk. They listened intently to Hiscocks' reasoning and were impressed; he was asked to join the team.

A New Primary Trainer

On one of his first postwar trips, Francis St. Barbe was at Downsview and could not take his eyes off the trainer model on Jakimiuk's desk. He saw it as an ideal Canadian project, based on his seasoned view of the world market. He took a positive approach, as reported by Martin Sharp in his book *D.H., An Outline of de Havilland History,* with the comment, "If you make a good trainer I'll sell it." Everyone paid attention to St. Barbe's words for they were based on the

R.D. "Dick" Hiscocks' connection with de Havilland went back to the summer of 1936 when he was a University of Toronto student. His expertise in aerodynamics was reflected in the company's line of STOL utility aircraft. He was the first McCurdy Award winner in 1954 and became a member of Canada's Aviation Hall of Fame in 1998. (Via Bettie Hiscocks)

company's long-range strategy; the Tiger Moth was now 14 years old and no longer a strong competitor in the light trainer market. Design enthusiasm ran high and all attention was directed to the trainer. By October 1, 1945, Bill Burlison and Reg Corlett began laying out the contours on large sheets of brown paper. On October 31 a go-ahead order was issued for two experimental machines.

At this stage, the design office had dropped from a wartime 700 to 30 people. The adjustment had been slow and orderly. The key men in the department made the transition from war to peace without even changing their desks. The ball game had changed in favour of design and it was the engineers' turn at bat. Their team had been carefully rounded out with new specialists, and experiments were started, particularly in metal techniques.

The year 1946 found the Fox Moth production line and the experimental shop alive with action. Jakimiuk's team of draftsmen was turning out drawings for the trainer at a great rate while Bill Burlison's men were making parts and devising jigs as they went. Bob McIntyre was project manager, coordinating all departments and planning eventual production. Design responsibilities were spread throughout the engineering department, with Bill Jackson doing the front fuselage, Fred Buller the rear fuselage and undercarriage, Jack Greeniaus the

wing, Len Trotter the controls and John Mazur the stressing. Jim Houston managed power plant responsibilities, Jack Ball the electronics, and Jack Satterthwaite the sketching and layouts. The team was outnumbered by the staff on overhaul work, but developed a sense of purpose with the realization that a new era had come to DH Canada. The growing drafting responsibilities produced a core of personnel for the years ahead – people like Norm Bell, George Luesby, Bill Kelley, Dick Nelson, Simon Gung, Jack Anderson, Bill Somerville, Art Wynne and Doug Ward. Jakimiuk and Buller were pleased that they were winning the battle for all-metal construction. Production of detailed parts began on December 21, 1945, only a few months after the go-ahead, and the aircraft was ready for test in May of the following year.

The DHC-1 reflected the widespread change to metal, stressed-skin aircraft construction. The fuselage was all-metal, as were the fin and tail plane. The wing had a single spar with a stressed-skin leading edge and fabric sections. The control surfaces and flaps were of metal construction, fabric covered. The two cockpits, in tandem arrangement, were well-suited to the military style of instruction and were enclosed with a built-up Perspex canopy.

As the little trainer took shape everyone began calling it the Jakimiuk in deference to the chief designer and his leadership in the project. The subject of a name came up officially during lunch one day in the executive dining room. Garratt had been watching the chipmunks at his cottage the day before and felt that would be a good name. Everyone liked the idea as it sounded so much like Jakimiuk.

During the first week in May 1946 an ocean liner

The first DHC-1 Chipmunk takes shape in Bill Burlison's experimental department during 1946. The ready availability of war-surplus Gipsy Majors from Tiger Moths spurred on the Chipmunk project. (DH)

Pat Fillingham at the controls of Chipmunk No.1 during the first flight on May 22, 1946. This aircraft soon went to DH in England, becoming G-AKVE. (Right) The Chipmunk's tandem cockpits. (DH, Hotson Col.)

ploughed westward through the Atlantic bringing a new member to the expanding DH Canada family. On board was Fred Plumb, a factory man from Stag Lane days when the company's star was rising. He had taken a major role in building the first Mosquito. Although he had no specific assignment in Canada, he was hoping for a senior position in the growing Canadian staff.

Also reporting for duty was W/C Russell Bannock, DSO, DFC and Bar. He had been chosen by Francis St. Barbe to become test pilot and operations manager at Downsview. Bannock had been in the RCAF from the start of the war. Although most of his service career had been in training and administration, he destroyed 11 enemy aircraft and 19 buzz-bombs in only 11 months of action over Europe. He commanded 418 "City of Edmonton" Squadron and led Canadian pilots in the number of buzz-bombs destroyed.

The Chipmunk Flies

As the time drew near for testing the Chipmunk, arrangements were made to have Geoffrey de Havilland Jr. over from England to do the first flight. The first flight of a de Havilland aircraft, wholly designed in Canada, was a historic milestone and aroused considerable interest in England. Geoffrey Jr. was unable to spare time away from Hatfield, so delegated Pat Fillingham for the job. Two others – Bob Loader and Martin Sharp – were on board the TCA Lancaster with Fillingham as it headed for Canada on May 17, 1946. Loader had been the first general manager of the company in Canada and was now head of the advertising

company, Samson Clark & Co., which handled de Havilland promotion. Martin Sharp had held many positions in the British company and since May 1937 had been publishing the in-house publication, the *DH Gazette*. Fillingham went to work acquainting himself with the Chipmunk. On May 22, 1946, he took it aloft for the first time on a 60-minute flight.

In test programs, the excitement usually takes place in the

Russ Bannock demonstrated the Chipmunk to private and military customers. (DH9865)

At F.E.N. St. Barbe's request, the first Chipmunk was packed and shipped to England for evaluation. (Below) Staff at Hatfield look over the new Canadian trainer. It was received with such interest that U.K. production was started and 1,014 were built. (Hotson Col.)

air, giving the pilot a chance to exercise his trade. With the Chipmunk, everything was routine, but some excitement was generated in one of the after-flight discussions. The usual procedure at the end of the day was for the engineering heads to gather in Jakimiuk's office to discuss the progress of the test program. One spring evening the group was listening to test pilot Fillingham, who sat smoking his pipe and tapping his ashes nonchalantly out the open window. The problems of the day were minimal, but as everyone prepared to leave a curl of smoke was noticed rising from below. The awnings on the lower window were burning. The engineering hierarchy tackled the emergency without delay. Fred Plumb was early on the scene with a fire extinguisher, closely followed by Jakimiuk. Unfortunately Jaki turned his extinguisher upside down while tucking it under his arm as he hurried to the burning awning. By the time he reached Plumb, the nozzle was spraying foam in every direction. Most of it landed on Fred's dark suit, which provided a disinct colour contrast. The fire was quickly brought under control, and although Plumb was a bit annoyed at first, he soon saw the funny side and joined the general laughter.

A minor modification to the rudder control was the only change made during the initial Chipmunk flight testing. The second test machine flew on June 30, 1946. The program with the first two hand-built models went surprisingly well until

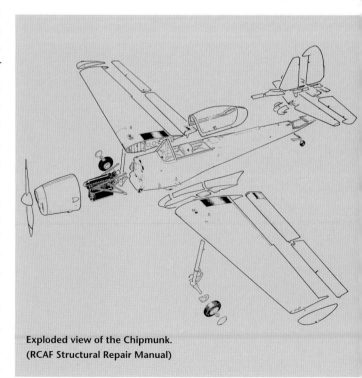

Exploded view of the Chipmunk.
(RCAF Structural Repair Manual)

(Above) Chimunks and Beavers being assembled at Downsview. (Howard Levy)

(Left) DHC experimented with various Chipmunk modifications. Here the prototype has a smaller rudder. Skis also were tried. (Jack McNulty)

In 1951 a 190-hp Lycoming was tried in a Chipmunk. The larger frontal area cancelled any advantage of extra power and no further work was done. (Jack McNulty)

Director Alan S. Butler was a key booster of DH Canada and the Chipmunk in the postwar years. (Hotson Col.)

January 19, 1947. Test pilot Charles Stockford had been working with Alex Downey for most of that week, completing data on a series of spin trials. They were slowly adjusting the loading for each stage and the time had come for the farthest aft

condition. Because of the position of the weights, Downey did not accompany Stockford on the flight.

Stockford did his series of manoeuvres in the sky north of Downsview. All went well until it came time for the final spin recovery. The Chipmunk entered the spin quickly enough but it was obvious from the ground that it was taking much too long to recover. Witnesses thought it was going to plough straight into the Dufferin Street farm of Thomas Bowes but it partially levelled off at 25 feet with no chance for a normal landing. The propeller dug into the frozen ground and one undercarriage leg went through the wing. CF-DJF-X bounced once and travelled 100 yards across the snow-covered field. The wing and fuselage were severely buckled and the engine dislodged. The 34-year-old, ex-RCAF pilot was taken to Toronto Western Hospital with a fractured skull and other injuries. He recovered but his injuries precluded any further test flying for the company. The loss of test aircraft No. 2 was a blow to the program, even though the criteria on spins were firmly established.

Fred Plumb's arrival in the midst of the Chipmunk program brought a shuffling of responsibilities on the manufacturing side. His background in the shops at Stag Lane and Hatfield made him a natural choice to take over Chipmunk production. The move relegated Bill Calder to the service department, for Bill Matthews was running the Canso overhaul. Frank Warren was then moved to plant superintendent under Plumb. The responsibility charts were beginning to move again – almost like 1941.

News of the successful Chipmunk certification soon reached St. Barbe in England, whose reaction was "Let's have one over here." The test machine was the logical demonstrator for Britain and CF-DIO-X was crated and shipped. On arrival it was quickly assembled by the staff at Hatfield, who were anxious to pass judgement on the new Canadian product. Pat Fillingham was soon flying it over the fields of Middlesex and demonstrating it around the country as G-AKEY. The RAF began a series of tests with a view to making it their primary trainer. It was a fitting climax to Fillingham's association with the Chipmunk that he won the prestigous King's Cup race around England in 1953 in G-AKDN.

The Chipmunk became the primary trainer of the RCAF and a number were issued to Canadian flying clubs by the Department of National Defence for refresher training. The DND/RCAF order totalled 113, with 79 going to the RCAF and 34 to the flying clubs. There were only five private sales in Canada but major exports included 41 to India, 22 to Egypt and 18 to the Royal Thai Air Force.

The RAF adopted the Chipmunk as its trainer for the volunteer reserve and 1,014 were built in Hatfield and Chester, according to Fisher, Brown and Rothermel in *Chipmunk: The First Fifty Years* (Air-Britain). The Duke of Edinburgh and Prince Charles trained on RAF machines. Sixty additional Chipmunks were built at the Portuguese Government OGMA factory under licence. The DHC-1 thus became the first Canadian design built under licence abroad. Chipmunks remain popular sport planes around the world.

The Great Chinese Mosquito Caper

Although official records show 1,133 Mosquitoes completed at Downsview, 100 had not been accepted by the RCAF when the war ended. In late 1945 these and 110 other war-surplus Mossies were put in storage at a number of airports. It was not long before the War Assets Corporation had a customer for them. The *Globe and Mail* of May 20, 1947 carried a note that 100 Mosquitoes, valued in excess of $30 million dollars and stored at de Havilland, were to be sold to the highest bidder or scrapped. In 1944 a delegation from China had visited Downsview to evaluate the Mossie. They were back again in the summer of 1947 ready to negotiate a purchase. Little detail remains of the transaction. An official report of July 12, 1948, mentions the agreement by War Assets to sell the Mosquitoes to China for $5 million "where is – as is." A total of 300 would be made available although it was noted that some were not serviceable and were reduced to spares. Four hundred spare engines would be made available plus some operating equipment. M.L. "Mac" McIntyre, in researching the subject for the Canadian Aviation Historical Society, puts the number at 205 Mosquitoes reaching China, but there are many gaps in the record. DH Canada became involved immediately, particularly the new works manager, Fred Plumb. His experience with the British Mosquito in the experimental stages and the challenge of a foreign assignment drew him away from Downsview. Under a contract with the Chinese government, he was to manage the transfer of aircraft to China and oversee their reassembly. DH Canada assistance was going to be necessary in both training and supervision. By mid-October, in what must be a historic record of sorts, a Mosquito "disassembly" line was established in Bay 1 to ready the aircraft for packing and crating. An item in *Canadian Aviation* speculated that the aircraft were being purchased for $10,000 to $15,000 each and that the whole deal ran to about $12 million. The Canadian government took great pains to avoid publicity, emphasizing that it was simply a commercial sale. No mention was made of Chiang Kai-shek and his battle with the Communist forces. The transaction between the Canadian and Chinese governments came under close scrutiny by the American advisory group in Washington.

While the wings and fuselages were put in protective cocoons in the hangars at Downsview, the neighbours must have become curious when they saw Mosquitoes flying regularly again. The original plan was to have all the flight training done in Toronto by ex-RCAF Mosquito pilots. This began in the cold month of February 1948. Fifteen Chinese Air Force pilots, making the transition from nose-wheeled B-25 Mitchells, found the tail-wheeled Mosquitoes and the Downsview snowbanks intimidating.

A Canadian-built Mosquito on duty in China. (George Stewart)

The high-performance Mossie, with its tendency for a tail swing on takeoff and landing, gave the Chinese a hard time. When seven aircraft had been written off, mostly in the snowbanks, the plan was changed to have all training done in China. Word quickly got back to their homeland that a Mossie was a "wicked" airplane and the pilots promptly named it "Lin Tai Yu," after a legendary empress who was beautiful but wicked. The Toronto-trained pilots must have been travelling under a shadow; they later accounted for nine more prangs back in China.

As the components were prepared for rail shipment to Halifax and their long ocean voyage to Shanghai via the Atlantic and the Suez Canal, a group of technical specialists was chosen to go to China. Eddie Jack was foreman. He was given veteran Mosquito experts in each of the trades. Jim Crowe was an RAF squadron leader with lots of Rolls-Royce engine experience, while Les Abiss, also from the U.K., was a former inspector from DH England. Bill Morgan would look after radio and electronics, while Bill Hall covered hydraulics. George Smith, a long-time member of the Mosquito test flight department, would manage the flight line and be joined in May by another veteran of the service department, Bruce Glassford. Ground crew comprised Don Lewis (crew chief), John Howlett (engines), Geoff Williams (hydraulics), Ernie Croydon (electrical), Bill Mann (airframe) and Ed Slater (armament). Their function was primarily to instruct the Chinese but it did not always work out that way.

Flight training started in Hankow on April 12, 1948. In the first two months there were 13 accidents, including a number of fatalities. Canadian pilots had their share of thrills but managed to survive the unique training conditions and the change in environment. The Chinese set up a training unit of their own in Tazang but in eight days wrote off five aircraft. As the accidents were still mostly in ground handling, Eddie Jack built them a taxi trainer. It had heavy steel braces from each undercarriage leg to the fuselage, but even that was wrecked when it ran off the runway. A report reached de Havilland through Ottawa that the project was going badly on all fronts: the shipping losses had been high, the aircraft were badly packed and so on. The author of the report also noted that during a demonstration and flypast for the military brass, one Chinese Air Force general was noted sitting in the back seat of his car practising on a mouth organ. Numerous other problems reached Garratt's desk, prompting him to send Alex Watson over to act as supervisor and chief inspector.

There was more training than combat because the Mossies were not suited to that kind of war. Chiang Kai-shek's forces were equipping with sophisticated surplus WWII equipment which was no match for the guerrilla tactics of the Communist forces (a lesson that was later to repeat itself in Vietnam). The Canadians knew little of activities at the front except that the situation was getting worse. The Communists were advancing, the currency was failing and the non-Chinese were beginning to leave the country. On December 10, Peking fell and by the 17th word came for the de Havilland contingent to "get out." Some exciting scurrying took place during the next few days. Most of the DH team took the Refugee Special, a two-day train ride to Hong Kong, and eventually reached home.

Alex Watson and George Smith were asked to stay a little longer than the rest, with no idea what would come next. On one occasion they were rushed to the airport in a jeep crewed by stern-looking soldiers. On arrival, they found a DC-4 with three engines running and one that refused to start. The Canadians were marched to the balky engine with the simple instruction to "fix it." They managed to get the engine running and later learned that the plane was carrying the last of China's gold and valuables to Formosa. Finally DHC arranged for Watson and Smith to board a special DC-6 flight from China, but Watson got another request at the last minute to stay behind. It was hard to argue with all the soldiers around, the sound of gunfire in the distance and the aircraft loading for departure. With some help from the crew Watson managed to make a last-minute dash to the taxiing aircraft and escaped in the confusion.

When de Havilland came to Canada in the 1920s, it was with the humble D.H.60 Moth. The market was ready for just such an aircraft. Canada's original Moths fared well, especially with flying clubs, the OPAS and the RCAF. Veteran DHC test pilot George Neal restored this 1931 D.H.60G, flying it first on June 16, 1962. He later sold it to Moth expert Watt Martin. CF-AAA is shown during a visit to the National Aeronautical Collection at Rockcliffe on June 10, 1967. (Larry Milberry)

The D.H.60 evolved into the D.H.82C Tiger Moth, adopted at the beginning of WWII as an important RCAF trainer for the British Commonwealth Air Training Plan. Tiger Moth contracts helped establish DHC as a leading Canadian manufacturer, pointed the way to advanced projects like the Mosquito, and did much to prepare DHC for the postwar era. Surplus Tiger Moths later worked in the bush, tided over flying clubs till they could find new equipment and, with the passage of time, became valuable classic airplanes. Here ex-RCAF Tiger Moth CF-COU departs Ignace, Ontario, in September 1994, while en route to Winnipeg from an airshow in Thunder Bay. (Richard Hulina)

A Downsview-built Fox Moth, CF-DJB worked in the bush into the early 1960s. Wardair then displayed it at air shows. After a crash at Toronto it again was restored, this time with a new fuselage, and the wings of CF-BNO. After some more demonstration flying it was donated to the National Aviation Museum, George Neal ferrying it there from Toronto on May 15, 1989. Here it is flown by Watt Martin. (Jack McNulty)

The Chipmunk brought DHC into the modern era. From 1946 1,291 were built in Canada, the U.K. and Portugal. Here George Neal taxis DHC's demonstrator CF-FHY at Oshawa, Ontario, on June 18, 1961. His passenger was DHC engineer Dick Batch. (Larry Milberry)

(Above) The Chipmunk served the RCAF/CF from 1948 to 1971. A hundred were used, most of which survived to reach the civil market through the Crown Assets Disposal Corporation. In the 1970s Chipmunks in fly-away condition were sold by CADC for $2,000-$3,000. Twenty years later one in good condition was worth about U.S.$75,000. These Chipmunks were at the basic training school at CFB Borden in March 1969. (Andy Graham)

(Right) Postwar and wartime trainers. Chipmunk C-FBXK flown by Hank Dielwart and Tiger Moth C-FPOW flown by Peter Stewart were photographed near Sudbury on August 28, 1988. (Larry Milberry)

Chipmunks visit Downsview on June 26, 1997, to welcome two others being flown around the world commemorating the end in RAF service of this great trainer. C-FCXP is in the 1950s colours of flying club Chipmunks used in refresher flying by RCAF reserve pilots. (Kenneth I. Swartz)

(Left) R.V. "Reg" Corlett took many famous DHC publicity photos. This one of RCAF Chipmunks in a graceful loop is typical. The Professional Photographers of America chose four of his DHC photos for a special award during a conference in New York in 1956. (DH)

(Below) Art Scholl's highly modified Chipmunk. Besides its powerful Lycoming GO-435 engine, it sported a retractable undercarriage. Here Art was at Toronto Island Airport on September 2, 1971, to perform at the Canadian International Air Show. Following Art's death, N13Y was donated in 1987 to the National Air and Space Museum at the Smithsonian Institution. (Larry Milberry)

(Right) Airshow performer Frank Ryder's Super Chipmunk N13DW (U.K.-built, ex-VH-KFA) was familiar to millions of spectators around North America. N13DW had a 295-hp Lycoming GO-480. Frank is seen along the Scarborough Bluffs in east Toronto on August 30, 1991. (Larry Milberry)

(Below) Several Canadian Chipmunks were modified to the Continental IO-360 engine, the first being CF-CYT-X. Jean-Paul Huneault did seven such conversions. Here CYT was at Orillia, Ontario, on July 17, 1971. (Larry Milberry)

(Below) DHC did a variety of postwar work. While turning out Fox Moths and Chipmunks, it had many overhaul and conversion projects. There also were sales and service for the D.H.104 Dove and support for the RCAF's first jet fighter, the D.H.100 Vampire. The Dove and its offshoot, the four-engine Heron, were sold all over North America. This Dove, owned by Timmins Aviation of Montreal, was at Malton in October 1963. (Al Martin)

(Below) The RCAF took 86 Vampires from 1948-56. These were assembled and test flown at Downsview. Thereafter DHC supplied Vampire parts and overhauled their Goblin engines. Ex-RCAF Vampire N41J, owned by Bill Lamberton of Seattle, was seen at CFB Comox with two DHC-5 Buffalos on April 18, 1991. (Larry Milberry)

CHAPTER FIVE

THE UBIQUITOUS BEAVER

Of airplanes destined for aeronautical immortality alongside the Douglas DC-3, the DHC-2 Beaver must be one. Even after a number have been retired to museums around the world, the demand for this half-ton flying truck remains as strong as ever. Any aircraft that boosts its original selling price of $27,000 to $275,000 (and climbing) after 51 years must hold something more than the secret of eternal youth. Certainly it was the right airplane at the right time, but analysts through the years credit a fine design team, a bit of luck, and a first-class quarterback calling the signals. The fact that it was all done without government help makes the accomplishment all the more outstanding in light of later industry trends.

There is no doubt that a new Canadian bushplane came into the early postwar discussions of Garratt and St. Barbe, but to launch the project immediately would have been premature. It would take some time to test the design team, get a production staff together and still generate enough income to meet the weekly payroll. These objectives were tackled on the three-pronged front of overhaul, production and design.

The Fox Moth revival gave the plant a production line almost immediately and it was not long until the growing overhaul business took care of the wages. The bushplane idea was shelved for the time being with Garratt's approval. The engineers and draftsmen, under Jakimiuk, made short work of the Chipmunk design with only seven months, 22 days from the first lofting to test flight. The study of a side-by-side fuselage for the Chipmunk was under way, but a sudden order came halting any more engineering work on the trainer. It was time to revive the bushplane study – without delay!

To appreciate the background of the Beaver story, it is necessary to go back to prewar days at Downsview and the modification of

British aircraft to Canadian needs. Whereas U.S. planes were predominantly of steel tube construction with wooden wings, the British concentrated on all-wood construction. This was never practical in the harsh Canadian weather. Most DH England designs were biplanes, which made them difficult for bush loading or manoeuvring on floats. The conversions carried out by the small Sheppard Avenue shop were successful in spite of these handicaps, but the style of the ideal bushplane was firmly established with the Fokkers, Fairchilds, Bellancas and the Norsemen. DH Canada had experience rebuilding all of these types before 1939, so the postwar staff were well-acquainted with bushplane fundamentals.

One aspect of the Beaver equation that cannot be ignored was the move of general manager Phil Garratt away from the Mosquito program in 1943. The seclusion of his downtown office allowed him more time to think about the company's future. He had been through the days of Canadianizing Rapides and had taken on almost impossible rebuild jobs in the late thirties to keep his men busy. He was the right man to dream of a new bush design, even though he freely admitted he was no engineer.

Competition

While DH Canada engineers were busy with their Chipmunk, Fairchild of Montreal were designing an aircraft specifically for the Canadian north. This was the F-11 Husky, which flew for the first time on June 14, 1946. The Fairchild name had been formidable in the bush before the war and it now looked as though they had stolen a lead on de Havilland. The Husky had a novel, all-metal fuselage with rear-loading and a Pratt & Whitney R985 engine. To cap it all, Fairchild had interest from Frank MacDougall, flying deputy minister of the Ontario Department of Lands and Forests.

Frank A. MacDougall, the 1963 McKee Trophy winner, was a key supporter of aircraft in forestry. As Ontario Deputy Minister of Lands and Forests, he took a major role in the development of the Beaver, backing that interest with orders. (Hotson Col.)

A Fairchild Husky in Toronto Harbour about 1950. The Husky competed and lost against the Beaver for an important OPAS contract. (Hotson Col.)

Providing that the aircraft met his department's requirements, he would order 25. MacDougall was heading a drive to replace the department's aging Stinson SR-9s. He liked the size and performance of the Stinson, but the pounding it took in forestry work caused cracking in the wing support tubing. One Stinson had shed its wings in flight because of this problem and there had been other close calls. They managed to live with the situation during the war when suitable replacement aircraft were not available. Now they were in the market for new equipment. Fortunately Lands and Forests had been a longtime customer of de Havilland, dating to the purchase of Moths in 1927. Frank MacDougall made the same verbal offer to Garratt for 25 machines, but by the time design started on the new project at Downsview, Fairchild had 50 flying hours on the prototype Husky.

Little paper work was exchanged during these negotiations between DHC and the Ontario government because MacDougall was a direct man who believed in the straightforward personal approach. Recalling the period years later, he explained that he took Hunter and Jakimiuk for a flight in an OPAS Stinson at Algonquin Park. "I wanted to show them what to shoot for in their new airplane," he said. "I showed them the plastic covers we used to inspect the wing support fittings on the Stinson and told them, 'Just design it so the wings don't come off!'" To those seasoned engineers, MacDougall's words must have represented a novel way of expressing a design definition. MacDougall elaborated on his theory that bushplanes should be built stronger than the average and have at least a 20:1 strength factor. "Doug Hunter paid attention to me," he recalled, "which was quite impressive, particularly as I knew nothing about designing airplanes. I met him on the ferry at the Toronto Island one day and he told me he had strengthened a support in the tail because of my suggestion. I always thought he was a pretty good engineer after that."

An early drawing of the Beaver concept showing pleasing lines similar to the Chipmunk and with an in-line engine. (DH)

Robert B. McIntyre (engineering) and T. Wes Hurley (sales) discuss plans for the DHC-2 Beaver in March 1945. (DH B5)

127

The first official act to set the Beaver in motion was a DH document signed September 17, 1946, authorizing preliminary engineering studies. These began on the 20th, leading to a wooden mock-up on November 20. The decision was made on December 4 to build one prototype and the appropriate internal sales order was issued that day. The project was well launched by spring, but selecting an engine became more of an issue. The Gipsy Queen 50, delivering 295/330 hp, was still undergoing tests in England. It had not been proven in service and the horsepower hardly fitted the "half-ton truck" the designers had in mind. If it was ready in time, would the supply of production engines be adequate? What about spare parts and product support? The questions mounted.

Doug Hunter had been made director of engineering by Phil Garratt, who was often described as a boss "who was not one to meddle." He liked to give complete authority to his appointees and he was not going to change now. Hunter's engineering roots were decidedly British, and he had strong diplomatic contacts with the parent company. It is understandable that he favoured not only the English engine, but metric hardware as had been used with the Chipmunk. Chief engineer Jakimiuk headed the design team of Dick Hiscocks, aerodynamics; Fred Buller, design; and Jim Houston, propulsion; with Bob McIntyre acting as liaison between the office and the shops. They were designing to a number of new concepts and doing a good job with the in-line engine profile of the Gipsy and a proportionate fuselage. They were going for complete metal construction, which was rather a new departure for a bush airplane.

Fred Buller had a clear mandate on the type of construction, while Dick Hiscocks was to replace the RAF airfoil section originally chosen with one of his own. This was the curve he had calculated as the result of his

studies in England and closely resembled the NACA 4416. His other concepts, including a 15-degree droop to the ailerons when the flaps were fully down, were also to be incorporated. Buller's approach to airframe construction was to use steel from the engine to the firewall, heavy aluminum truss frames with panels and doors throughout the front seat area, lighter trusses toward the rear and all monocoque construction aft. The method proved itself in the Beaver and was later extended to the Otter in even more complex form.

Punch Dickins Joins

The healthy sale of Fox Moths through 1946 had placed A.F. "Sandy" Macdonald in the role of sales manager. As the design details of the Beaver began to take shape, he sent a few letters to prominent bush pilots outlining the project and soliciting their comments. One of those receiving his letter was C.H. "Punch" Dickins, whose experience in flying the bush went back to his days with Western Canada Airways in 1928. He had conducted many pioneering flights in the north, won a McKee Trophy for his efforts and was a logical choice for such a survey. Like many in the postwar period, Dickins was pondering his future about the time he received the letter. It rekindled his interest in the concept of an all-Canadian bushplane. Punch felt strongly on a number of points, particularly the choice of engine. He could not see any future in a Gipsy for the bush and prepared a carefully considered list of other recommendations.

Early in 1947 he delivered his answer to Phil Garratt in person, for he was not only well known at Downsview but always a welcome guest. Garratt took him to lunch, as was his custom, and the two had a long chat about many things. On January 10 it was announced that the dean of Canada's bush pilots had joined de Havilland Canada and was to become a director of the firm.

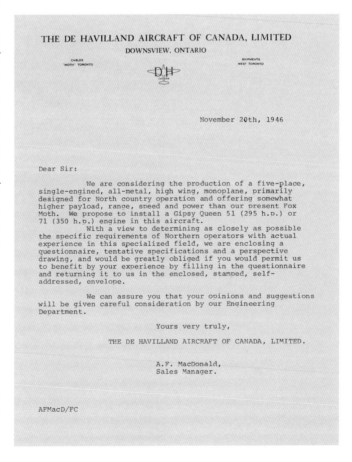

This letter accompanied the questionnaire sent to bush pilots by A.F "Sandy" MacDonald soliciting their views on the Beaver concept. (DH)

A Major Decision

The choice of engine was becoming a controversial topic. The matter came up at a luncheon meeting one day in Montreal between Phil Garratt and his friend James Young, president of Canadian Pratt & Whitney. Young announced a breakthrough in his own company, for it had recently managed the certification of surplus R1340 Wasps. Most of these had been made under licence, outside P&W control. There

The prototype Beaver fuselage is tested under landing loads during July 1947. (DH B35)

was some doubt that Pratt & Whitney headquarters at Hartford would approve them for civil use, but Canadian P&WC vice-president John Drummond convinced his parent company and the Canadian government to approve the engines, providing all parts were overhauled and certified as airworthy. The Longueuil plant was beginning to process R985 Wasp Juniors from surplus Anson Vs across the country. At two engines per Anson, there was a good supply.

James Young argued with Garratt against using the Gipsy in any new de Havilland bushplane. He cited the difference in power between the two engines and forecast supply problems with the manufacturer so far away. To back his argument he offered a ready supply of Wasp Juniors and pointed out that the competing Husky used this engine. These arguments gave Garratt much food for thought as he flew back to Toronto in his yellow Hornet Moth.

About this time rumours were circulating that all was not well with the Gipsy Queen program. It was reasonable that Garratt should send Hunter and Jakimiuk overseas to check the situation and make a decision. Hunter knew there was opposition to his choice of engine so he issued strict instructions to his subordinates that nothing was to be done on the subject until his return. The climax to the growing drama came one morning while the ship carrying the two senior engineers was in mid-Atlantic and Garratt sat alone in his office pondering a new wire from Hatfield. The prototype engine had broken down on the test stand; the problem was solving itself.

In the midst of his deliberations, Garratt looked out of the window and noticed Fred Buller going across Sheppard Avenue for an early lunch. He put the telegram in the desk and went down the stairs in the direction of the cafeteria. There were few in the lunch room and Buller was sitting at a table, all alone, staring into a bowl of hot corn chowder. He was one of the engineers unhappy with the prospect of the Gipsy Queen, particularly where it related to his responsibilities. Garratt joined Buller and the conversation soon came around to the new plane and its engine.

No mention was made of the message from England, but Garratt questioned the possibility of using the Wasp Junior. He reasoned that seaplanes in the past never did have enough power and that he could get plenty of these engines from Pratt & Whitney by making a phone call to James Young. Buller was slow to reply. He was inwardly elated that the boss was taking this approach but was exceedingly cautious in view of the directive he had received from Hunter. When he was sure "PC" was serious, Buller admitted that it would be practical to switch to the P&W engine and it could be accomplished even with two-thirds of the aircraft already designed. He was told to check out the details and report. In a meeting that followed Buller required only minutes to gain unanimous approval from the other engineers and the results were duly reported to Garratt that afternoon. The answer was an immediate go-ahead. The crisis was over.

New problems were to be expected under the circumstances but design changes went forward without delay – a new engine mount, a higher undercarriage to provide propeller clearance, strengthening the wing, repositioning the oil tank. The work was well advanced by the time the senior engineers returned from England and no further comment arose at any level regarding the choice of an engine.

The design program had other hurdles to overcome. A small, all-metal plane was a bit of a novelty and much about it would be new to an old-time bush engineer. The use of flap for take-off and the combination of droop ailerons raised more than one eyebrow in the trade. Knowledgeable

The first flight of the Beaver was on August 16, 1947. From the time Russ Bannock strapped on his parachute harness, through the engine run to lift-off, eager support crews appreciated the importance of this event. (DH 9772-2)

people heard of the proposal and sent word to the DH general manager that they were "heading for trouble!" Garratt and Hunter were dubious, but an agreement was reached to leave the system intact for the test program. A simple linkage between the flaps and the ailerons performed so effectively on the test that nothing more was said on the subject.

The choice of a name was much easier and was once again decided at the executive dining room table. When the subject came up everyone agreed with Garratt that the DH Canada line should be named after Canadian animals and that calling the trainer the Chipmunk had been appropriate. It did not take long to relate the hard-working beaver to the bushplane they had in mind; even before coffee was served everyone agreed.

The Beaver Flies
On a hazy afternoon, August 16, 1947, the prototype Beaver, CF-FHB-X (combining the initials of F.H. Buller), was test flown by operations manager and chief test pilot Russ Bannock. After all the pressure of last-minute changes in design, the test flight was almost anti-climactic. The fuselage that had been designed for 300 hp now had 450 hp in the nose; everyone expected good performance. There were two flights on the day that de Havilland STOL was born, one a 20-minute hop when Bannock landed to check an oil supply problem and the other of one hour.

With Bannock's early flights completed, the urgency was to get the aircraft on floats as soon as possible. Six weeks af-

ter the first succesful hop, Russ turned float certification over to George Neal, whose association with DH Canada went back to 1936. He had his private pilot's licence in those days and, because of his previous automobile experience, was given engine overhaul and test stand duties. Like many who were flying actively before the outbreak of war, he went into full-time flying with the Air Observer School movement. He trained at No.1 AOS Malton and was posted to Chatham, where he became a senior member of the staff, in charge of all test flying. With 4,000 hours in his flying log and his reputation for getting things done, George was welcomed back to Downsview in 1945. Once again he specialized in engine overhaul, but this did not last long. His flying experience was called upon more and more, what with Dove flights, Chipmunk tests, Fox Moth deliveries, a Rapide for South America and now the Beaver.

On a major design project, problems sometimes come from the most unexpected sources. Fred Buller recalled one such case that provided embarrassment for a very good customer – the Ontario Department of Lands and Forests. Shortly after the department's decision to purchase the Beaver, orders went out to start building hangars at all the district headquarters in northern Ontario. Somehow their construction people picked up the wrong dimension of the Beaver wingspan. It was only after the work was well under way that the doors were found to be four feet too small. Buller and Hiscocks got a frantic call inquiring if the wingspan of the new aircraft could be decreased, which was unthinkable for more reasons that one. In the interests of diplomacy they referred the question to Phil Garratt, who set their minds at rest with a simple reply: "Leave it with me." The problem disappeared promptly and the Beaver wing dimension remained intact.

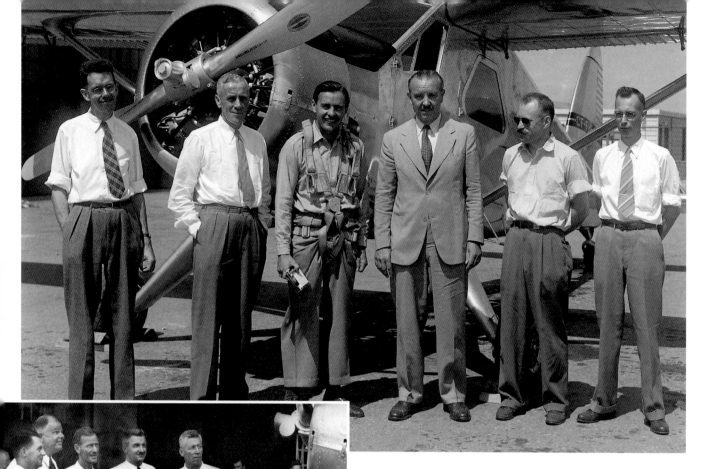

(Above) Some of the key personnel in the Beaver story. Left to right: Dick Hiscocks, Doug Hunter, Russ Bannock, Jaki Jakimiuk, Jim Houston and Fred Buller. (DH23885)

(Left) Punch Dickins, Phil Garratt, Sandy MacDonald, Pat Reid and Frank MacDougall with the prototype Beaver. (DH39411)

There was a certain amount of urgency in the Beaver test program as the Fairchild Husky had already been demonstrated to Ontario's Frank MacDougall. The deputy minister was withholding his judgment at the time and was soon invited for a Beaver evaluation flight at the Toronto waterfront. George Neal allowed the veteran forester to fly the plane in every configuration and gave him a convincing demonstration of the use of flap for take-off. MacDougall came away impressed with the Beaver's performance and promptly placed an order for four. The Ontario forestry people never did buy a Husky. Only 12 Huskies were built and soon the proud name of Fairchild vanished from the Canadian scene.

In June 1947 limited production of 15 Beavers was approved, followed by the issuing of shop drawings on August 5. The first aircraft from this batch, registered CF-OBS, was test flown February 5, 1948, and delivered to Lands and Forests on April 26. The production model of the Beaver varied considerably from the prototype. When FHB first flew it had short exhaust stacks on each side. The final configuration had a collector ring directing the exhaust to the heater underneath. For some time surplus Anson V heaters were used with much success. The original fin and rudder, looking much like the Chipmunk's, soon had an added dorsal fairing tapering gracefully to a position midway down the back of the fuselage. A very distinctive feature of FHB when it first flew was soon modified: the original windshield sloped back behind the leading edge of the wing which curved to meet it. A raised windshield soon replaced the original and allowed a smoother airflow around the cabin and tail section.

Production Beavers had a functional, rugged look with a square-sided fuselage and sturdy undercarriage legs. The strut-braced wing was of constant chord with large-span, slotted flaps. It had two doors up front and two large removable doors in the cargo/passenger area. There was accommodation for six and the pilot: three on a hammock seat across the back, two on single seats and one beside the pilot. There was room for light baggage behind the hammock seat and a

George Neal flies CF-FHB over the Toronto waterfront. An experiment was under way investigating airflow around the wing root and windshield. This resulted in a new windshield line (right) that blended with the cabin roof. (DH)

suitable door for loading long objects. All but the pilot's seat could be removed for carrying freight. With the bush operator in mind, the fuel was stored in easy-to-reach tanks under the floor. All controls were simple, with flaps that were operated by a hydraulic hand pump under the pilot's seat.

Beaver and Chipmunk Sales

A new aircraft type provides exciting times in any company and the birth of the Beaver was no exception. Certification came March 10 and the four Ontario Department of Lands and Forests aircraft were delivered quickly. Further orders followed which brought their total to 16 before the year was out. Laurentian Air Service in Ottawa was the first commercial aviation company to put the Beaver to work, while the Quebec North Shore Paper Company was the first private corporation to order one. The Manitoba and Saskatchewan governments, along with the federal Department of Transport, soon followed Ontario's lead with orders in 1948.

On June 1, Punch Dickins put his prestige in western Canada to work with an extensive tour with FHB. He was delivering the machine to Russ Baker of Central B.C. Airlines and touched down at all the important bases along the way to show off the new aircraft. He combined with Stan McMillan to do another demonstration flight on skis during the following winter via Sioux Lookout, Kenora, Lac du Bonnet, The Pas and all stops to Edmonton. Established

veteran bush pilots such as Matt Berry, Stan McMillan and Arthur Fecteau began operating the Beaver. Colourful contractor Harry McLean bought aircraft 42 for his personal use, flown by his pilot, Dick Preston. During the Leduc, Alberta, oil rush of 1949 Russ Bannock was sent west to try his luck in that area and ended up selling 12 aircraft.

While the Beaver was getting the lion's share of attention, Chipmunk sales were building slowly. True to St. Barbe's prediction, most of the early ones went to faraway places, but many countries that might have bought the little trainer could not handle the hard currency requirements. India proved to be the best customer until 1949 and interest grew throughout the Commonwealth. Britain's Royal Air Force liked the sprightly little trainer and it was at this time that the decision was taken to build the Chipmunk under licence at Chester, England. Bill Kelley and R. McLeod from the Downsview engineering office went to England to work with the Chipmunk team at Hatfield and Chester. Their first night in England was almost their last. Dick Hiscocks was already in Hatfield working on the project but, because his

CF-FHB went straight from being the Beaver demonstrator to airline service in British Columbia. It spent its life in the west, retiring after 33 years to National Aviation Museum in the summer of 1980. (DH)

hotel was full, the lads from Canada were sent to a small hotel on the outskirts. Arrangements were made for the next day's work at the design office. When they did not show up at the appointed hour, Hiscocks became worried. By telephone he learned that the new arrivals were recovering in hospital from near asphyxiation. The gas heater in their room had malfunctioned and they were lucky to be alive.

The Wayward Dolly

Whenever de Havilland old timers talk of "dollies" they are referring to the unique system they devised to deliver Beavers to the waterfront on floats. In prewar days it was always a high insurance risk towing fragile aircraft fuselages through Toronto traffic to the air harbour. Another couple of trips

with wings, floats and an assembly crew made the process costly and time-consuming.

With these recollections and a little experience with Fox Moths, it was decided that there had to be a better way. A dolly was built to accommodate a float-equipped Beaver. It was aimed down the runway for takeoff and was designed to run in a straight line until the aircraft lifted clear. Russ Bannock made the first takeoff into a stiff breeze but the

The first takeoff using the single-tail-wheel dolly went well. (DH)

On the second delivery, with no wind, the dolly took to the grass while the Beaver lifted clear. (DH)

DIRECT HIT !!!

On the day Phil Garratt brought out some friends to watch, the dolly swung at the intersection and demolished the boss's Studebaker.

A later four-wheeled dolly provided more stability and had a brake which came on once the weight of the aircraft was removed. (DH)

next attempt on a calm day nearly ended in disaster. George Neal was delivering the second OPAS machine. He had hardly begun rolling when the dolly began to veer in a direction of its own. By the time it was off the runway, George had enough control for a very short takeoff. Modifications were made to the vehicle, but a headwind was deemed necessary as part of the procedure.

Thirty-four successful takeoffs were made in the days that followed, always being careful that a headwind was blowing, until one day Phil Garratt brought out some friends to witness the event. He parked his car back from the intersection and the group walked to a vantage point from where they could watch. This time there wasn't much wind and the dolly misbehaved again. It stayed on the runway this time and George had to improvise another short takeoff. There was no danger to the onlookers but they stood transfixed as they watched the dolly circle around and score a direct hit on the boss's Studebaker.

George commented in later years that he caught a glimpse of something wrong and flew over the field to assess the damage. He called Mr. Garratt from the Island Airport to ask about the car and was told it was a complete writeoff. The incident was the talk of the shop for a while and the engineers made sure everyone knew it was not one of their designs. The result was a fully-approved order to the engineering department and a four-wheeled dolly was built with brakes to bring it to a stop after the liftoff. There were no more mishaps and the same procedure was used in later years to deliver Twin Otters to the waterfront.

Beaver Superiority

After a year of Beaver operations, Russ Bannock headed to Edmonton with a demonstration aircraft. He was renewing his acquaintance with western life when he read in *Aviation Week* that the 10th Search and Rescue Squadron USAF was expanding in Alaska. The "10th" was commanded by Colonel Bernt Balchen, famous Norwegian Arctic pilot, and they were currently using Cessna 195s on floats and skis. They were looking for something capable of carrying 1,000 lb. (450 kg). Bannock got busy with a letter to Balchen offering a demonstration of the Beaver. August 1 found him in Anchorage working from Elmendorf Air Force Base. It was a pleasant month with the "10th." Balchen had a skilled group working in a demanding, rugged requirement. The officers were impressed with the Beaver's performance and were continually thinking up new challenges – including fishing trips. The ultimate turned out to be a greyling river some 100 miles (160 km) east of Fairbanks. Up to then it had only been ap-

One of the north's legendary pilots, Colonel Bernt Balchen (centre), is introduced to the Beaver in Alaska. He is shown with Russ Bannock and entrepreneur Charles Babb. Bannock's visit stirred U.S. military interest in the Beaver. (Bannock Col.)

proached by a tortuous overland trail. "Could the Beaver go in?" Russ agreed to a flight with six people, including Brigadier General Gaffety and Balchen himself. The winding greyling river presented a formidable challenge, for although there would be no trick in setting down, the test would come in getting out again. While the officers were fishing, Russ marked out the deep-water channels with a series of sticks as he planned his takeoff. The fishing was terrific that day, which only added to the gross weight for takeoff. When the time came to leave, Russ was able to rudder through the channel onto the step for a convincing takeoff and return to Fairbanks.

On the strength of the month's demonstrations, Balchen ordered 10 Beavers, along with a glowing recommendation of the aircraft for other military tasks. In due course, a request went through to Washington for the purchase of 22 aircraft which promptly ran into fierce opposition. American manufacturers were up in arms, citing everything from single-source restrictions to the Buy America Act. The argument drew increasing Congressional fire along with considerable nationwide publicity. Any decision for orders, it was decreed, must come as the result of a competition.

Later, in 1950, the argument was compounded by a new factor – the U.S. Army's interest in the Beaver. Bannock read, once again in *Aviation Week*, that Colonel Louis Compton, Commander of the Artillery Board, was considering larger aircraft for liaison and utility duties. Soon Russ was at Fort Bragg, N.C., amazing everyone with the go-anywhere, carry-everything agility of the Beaver. The Army immediately wanted this rugged performer to replace their Piper Cubs, but ran into the same arguments about buying outside the country. New fuel was added to the long, bitter argument and served to bring the matter to a head. The USAF and the U.S. Army arranged fly-off competitions; the winning aircraft in this new single-engine class would be designated the L-20. Bannock and his crewman, Norm Davis, were looking forward to any kind of fly-off, for by now they were well-versed in U.S. service requirements. They felt that they had a considerable lead over any opposition.

A New Approach to Sales

In December 1950, a total of 13 aircraft signed in for the long-awaited competitions, the first to be held at Wright Field, Dayton, Ohio, for the USAF, the other at Fort Bragg,

N.C., for the U.S. Army. Cessna fitted a bigger engine in their "195" and Beech put two in their Bonanza. Aero Commander had their new twin-engine prototype. Probably the most serious competition would come from the prototype Helio Courier, which was specially designed for short take-offs. Numerous old-timers, including Bellanca and Noorduyn, showed up, along with a new contender called the Atlas. The de Havilland team of Bannock and Davis spent three months on the scene, supported on occasion by Dick Hiscocks, Fred Buller and Alex Watson. The discussions seemed endless but the action picked up during the flying displays. Every conceivable test manoeuvre was devised, including landings and takeoffs over a 50-ft. (15 m) barrier. The DHC-2 Beaver breezed through them all and was spectacular in the latter category.

With the first round at Wright Field firmly "in the bag," the aircraft moved to Fort Bragg for the second challenge. The Army had their own series of tests but, once again, the most points were given for short takeoffs and landings. This time the Beech twin prototype, trying to match the Beaver's landing distance, might have come close if it had not pushed the landing gear through the wings in the resulting crash.

Some of the contestants in the competitions held at Dayton, Ohio, and Fort Bragg, N.C. Clockwise from the bottom left are the Ryan Navion, Atlas, Aero Commander, Bellanca Skyrocket, Beaver, and the Cessna 195. (Best Col.)

The attending crowd quickly dragged the aircraft from the test area and, although it was clearly out of the running, the question arose as to what to do with the remains. Of all the companies in the competition, Bellanca and de Havilland were the only ones with attending service personnel. George Taylor of Bellanca and Norm Davis of de Havilland looked the situation over. Fortunately, Davis had a wheel and tire of the right size, which he loaned to the cause. They then visited the local junk yard and acquired a few pieces of rusty angle iron; a trip to the hardware store for bolts and hacksaw blades was next, then they went to work on their competitor's aircraft. They first locked the gear in the down position, then reinforced the damaged areas with angle iron. After installing the spare wheel, the aircraft was ready for a ferry flight to the factory. "We received a nice thank you letter from Beech when they returned our wheel and tire," Davis recalled.

The U.S. Army trials were another victory for de Havilland's stubby-nosed workhorse, which opened the way to an eventual flood of orders. First of all, six production models were taken "off the shelf" for wide evaluation, including with Balchen's search and rescue squadron. Next it was 100 planes for the USAF tactical force, then a series of orders for the U.S. Army. The military version was called the L-20; it had only a few changes from the civil model, such as a larger pilot seat and roof windows. To manage this new contract Russ Bannock became director, military sales.

While a lot of attention was going to the sale of the DHC-1 and DHC-2, life on the production floor had not been neglected. Chipmunk manufacture had been first organized by Fred Plumb, and when he left for the Chinese Mosquito contract, Bill Burlison took over. The supply of manpower from the overhaul shops allowed an orderly buildup of the Beaver line, which averaged 30 aircraft a year for the first three years.

1. COLD AIR DUCT
2. OUTSIDE AIR TEMP. GAUGE
3. FLIGHT INSTRUMENT PANEL
4. RUDDER TRIM WHEEL
5. DEFROSTER
6. FLAP INDICATOR
7. ELEVATOR TRIM INDICATOR
8. COWL SHUTTER CONTROL
9. ELEVATOR TRIM WHEEL
10. ALTERNATE COMPASS POSITION
11. COMPASS POSITION
12. RADIO COMPASS
13. PROPELLER LEVER
14. COLD AIR DUCT
15. THROTTLE LEVER
16. DEFROSTER
17. MIXTURE LEVER
18. FRICTION DAMPERS

19. RADIO PANEL
20. ELECTRICAL SWITCH PANEL
21. CONTROL COLUMN THROW-OVER LOCK
22. ENGINE INSTRUMENT PANEL
23. OIL TANK FILLER
24. CO-PILOT'S RUDDER PEDALS
25. FUEL AND OIL EMERGENCY SHUT-OFF LEVER
26. OIL CONTENTS LABEL
27. STARTER BRUSH RELEASE LEVER
28. ASH TRAY
29. ATTACHMENT POINT FOR CO-PILOT'S SEAT
30. CABIN HEAT GRILL
31. WOBBLE PUMP
32. FLAP HYDRAULIC HAND PUMP
33. CARBURETTOR AIR LEVER
34. CABIN HEAT CONTROL

35. FLAP SELECTOR
36. FLAP HYDRAULIC RESERVOIR AND FILLER
37. ATTACHMENT POINT FOR PILOT'S SEAT
38. PARKING BRAKE
39. RUDDER PEDALS
40. HAND FIRE EXTINGUISHER
41. PRIMER
42. BRAKE TOE PEDALS
43. HOT AIR FOOT DUCT
44. FIRE EXTINGUISHER PANEL
45. ALTERNATE COMPASS POSITION
46. STARTER PANEL
47. FUEL SELECTOR
48. OIL DILUTION SWITCH
49. STARTER CLUTCH
50. FLIGHT CONTROL SWITCH
51. MASTER SWITCH

The cockpit of the civil Beaver. (DH)

year for the first three years. The welcomed sales to the U.S. military services suddenly drew everyone's attention to the manufacturing side of the company; some even doubted that the delivery schedules could be met.

Burlison took the challenge in his stride and began farming out small components to subcontractors. The assembly line was enlarged and shop management was reorganized. George Blanchard's role in production control increased

The cockpit of the military L-20 Beaver. Note the location of the flap selector and hydraulic pump under the left seat position. The L-20 differed in a number of ways from the civil Beaver. It had four windows in the cabin roof, a Y-type dual control yoke instead of the "throw-over" control in the civil model, and foot brakes in left and right positions (optional on civil models). Seats were of standard fibre to facilitate the use of parachutes. Due to a different carburetor, the L-20 primary quadrant controls were: (left ro right) power, pitch and mixture. In the commercial model the controls were: pitch, power and mixture. Army-type radio equipment was used. (DH)

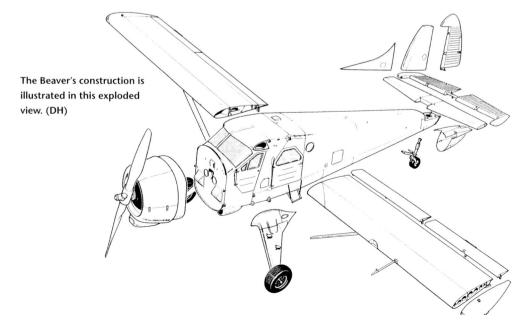

The Beaver's construction is illustrated in this exploded view. (DH)

daily. Phil Garratt had heard of Bill Stewardson's reputation from the war days and broached the subject of his return to DHC. "Phil suggested that I needed an assistant," recalled Burlison, "and mentioned Stewardson's name. I looked on it as an order, so contacted Bill, who had been working with the Ontario Department of Highways, and brought him back." John Slaughter, who had been Stewardson's assistant during the last years of the Mosquito, was invited to return and the new group soon developed into a formidable team. The delivery schedule of the U.S. Beavers left little time for any expansion program, however; the first unit was delivered on schedule and deliveries continued throughout the L-20 contract until the last one on May 6, 1960.

The six YL-20 evaluation Beavers, serial numbers 98, 99, 109, 110, 114, 115, were delivered without fanfare to the USAF in the spring of 1951. Once regular deliveries started to the USAF, a formal hand-over was organized. The date was November 13, 1951, and the resulting press headline must have been encouraging to everyone in the plant – "De Havilland Crashes the U.S. Aircraft Market." The story went on in a similar vein:

For the first time in its peacetime history, the United States of America accepted delivery on

L-20 Beavers for the U.S. Army go down the production line. (DH)

When General Eisenhower became president, he too travelled in Korea by L-20. Beavers in uniform carried exterior loads under the wings, laid telephone wire from tree to tree from under-wing canisters and transported ammunition to the troops. The more they coped with difficult jobs, the more they were used.

As the number of L-20s grew in Korea, the U.S. Army asked for a DHC field representative. Bannock offered the position to Bruce Best, who was then chief engineer of the Toronto Flying Club. As Best was also a licensed pilot, he checked out on the Beaver and was soon on his way to Ascom City in Korea, a big U.S. Army repair and maintenance depot.

It was a tough testing ground for any aircraft and much was learned to benefit future Beavers coming off the production line. A total of 17 modifications was recommended by Bruce Best during his year with the U.S. Army. By 1953 damaged L-20s piled up to the point where they were being shipped in bulk lots back to the U.S. on a plan called IRAN (Inspect and Repair as Necessary). It was easy for de Havilland to bid on IRAN work. Phil Garratt spurned a cost-plus arrangement and insisted on a low, fixed-cost contract, based on volume and improving performance. The contract was no sooner signed than L-20s began arriving from the U.S. and abroad. A few were flown in, but most arrived by truck or boxcar. Those used as ammunition carriers in the front line had taken quite a beating. A veritable

November 13th of a foreign-made military aircraft. Not since the war has the United States gone outside their own boundaries for procurement of military aircraft. The purchase of Beavers from de Havilland is a significant departure from the traditional policy and a new milestone in Canadian-American relations.

The ceremony was at Downsview Airport, Toronto, where in the presence of a large gathering of high ranking Air Force officials and industrial leaders, Canada's Defence Production Minister, the Right Honourable C.D. Howe, turned over the first de Havilland L-20A to the United States government. The aircraft was accepted by Major General Mark E. Bradley, Director of Procurement and Production, U.S. Air Materiel Command. The first two aircraft lined up that day for the ceremony were serial numbers 150 and 151 bearing the USAF registrations 51-16463 and 51-16464.

The Beaver Goes to War

By June 1952 a hundred L-20s were with the U.S. Army and it was not long until half were participating in the Korean War. The L-20 was promptly dubbed the "flying jeep" and its environment was the battlefront. It carried out thousands of medical evacuations, hauled supplies of all kinds, and ferried generals and an endless stream of congressmen up and down the front.

Bruce Best during his Korean tour. (Best Col.)

DHC pilot Dave Fairbanks test flies a typical U.S. Army L-20. Note the windows in the roof. (DH 8936)

DHC tech rep Bruce Best arranged this photo of a Korean-based L-20 at Haneda Airport (Tokyo) with a BOAC Comet that was passing through.

production line developed in Bay 4 totalling 16 aircraft a month with a tight turn-around schedule that pleased the U.S. Army. Five hundred and sixty-three eventually went through. The results were so satisfactory that a similar program was arranged in later years in which U.S. Army Caribous destined for Vietnam came to Downsview for special military installations.

A New Beaver

In 1952, discussions started on the advisability of a British version of the Beaver for European and "soft currency" countries. The British Army had expressed interest and there was talk of putting the aircraft into production in England. The English-built Alvis Leonides engine was available with 100 horsepower more than the Wasp Junior; it had accumu-

lated a good record of reliability installed in the British Provost and Prince. The physical dimensions were compatible with the Beaver and all performance estimates showed a Leonides-powered Beaver to be an attractive proposition as well as an engineering challenge.

These estimates suggested a shorter takeoff distance could be achieved, which prompted a further study to shorten the landing run. While awaiting a sample Leonides engine and three-blade, nine-foot-diameter propeller from England a larger fin and rudder unit was flight-tested on a Beaver with

The Beaver with the Alvis Leonides engine performed well, but not enough to warrant the added expense. The aircraft is shown with its British paint scheme and registration. (DH)

(Right) The Leonides Beaver in England, demonstrating a spectacular takeoff. (DH 7227)

the regular Pratt & Whitney engine. The new engine installations provided the usual problems of adapting British standard threads to American, but all these problems were overcome and George Neal took it up for its first flight on March 10, 1953.

The weight penalty worked out to 96 lb. (44 kg) in exchange for the added 100 horsepower, with the gross weight remaining at 5,100 lb. (2,315 kg). To shorten the landing run two simple steps were taken. The incidence was increased two degrees and Goodyear disc brakes were installed. Tests proved an increased top speed and rate of climb, and during the cooling tests the enlarged vertical tail surfaces were found more than adequate to offset destabilization. As the battle was now between increased performance and weight, a second smaller rudder was built and the previous dorsal strake removed.

A Canadian certificate of airworthiness was obtained and the aircraft was shipped to England for evaluation. The high-performance Beaver aroused enthusiastic comments in England but the cold economic facts did not justify the expense of any change in the aircraft. The Hatfield demonstrator, G-ANAR, had an interesting life in England and returned to

Canada many years later as the personal plane of Charles Robson of Oshawa, Ontario, now registered CF-CNR. The British Army, who were involved in the evaluation of the Leonides Beaver, bought 46 standard L-20s between 1960 and 1967.

Engine Overhaul

A major part of the postwar program was overhaul work. This got off to a good start and continued for the next 10 years, averaging 33 aircraft per year. A wide variety of types went through the shops, including everything from flying boats to jets. Overhaul had the double-barrelled advantage of providing a versatile shop capability along with a stable income. It did even more, for it led to the overhaul of engines and an early move into the turbine age. DHC had overhauled Gipsy and Cirrus engines in prewar days and the engine shop was one of the first rehabilitated in 1945 to look after the Fox Moth program. As the volume of work grew, so did the size of the engines, but it was the arrival of the D.H.100 Vampire with its Goblin engine that brought new techniques to Downsview. Phil Garratt saw the need for

(Left) The British Army used Beavers in utility work. This one was doing aircraft carrier deck trials. (DH 14379)

(Top) Fecteau Transport Aérien of Senneterre, Quebec, was one of the first operators sold on the Beaver. Here is its base at Chibougamau in the late 1950s. Arthur Fecteau (shown above at right) is standing with his secretary-treasurer, Sylvio Ménard. (Bombardier)

(Right) While the L-20 was busy in Korea, other innovations were under way. This Beaver had experimental water-bombing tanks, a concept that later proved successful. (DH)

(Left) Beavers adapted well to aerial application work, spraying locusts in East Africa, spreading fertilizer in New Zealand, etc. This Beaver was spraying in India. (DH 8369)

Goblin overhaul facilities. He called in Bob McIntyre, who was in charge of Canso overhaul, and asked him to set up an engine division. McIntyre went to England to train and returned with some DH Engine Company personnel to start up a shop. Reg Corlett was delegated to establish a jet engine school and also went to England for training. By the time

Goblins started arriving, the department was organized and the staff made the transition to the new techniques. Later, when the RCAF purchased two D.H.106 Comet airliners, the shops were in an excellent position to overhaul the larger Ghost engines.

The division's big move forward came when the Mk.5 and

6 Canadair F-86 Sabres were built with Orenda engines, replacing the General Electric J47s. General Electric did not want to overhaul the Orendas and the Canadian government asked de Havilland to carry out the work. Bob McIntyre later recalled that busy period: "At the height of the program, 30 to 40 engines would be in process on the overhaul line during a single week. The

George Neal test flies one of the RCAF's new Vampires in 1948. (DND)

key to the company's success was the establishment of a fixed-price contract which allowed the government to control its costs and allowed de Havilland to make a profit on the volume of work processed. The two test cells ran 24 hours a day and consumed a tank car of kerosene each day." With the Starfighter replacing the Sabre in the early 1960s, de Havilland's engine activity waned. When the company disposed of the last Gipsy engine work and spares to Standard Aero in the mid-60s, de Havilland Canada engine activities passed into history.

Royal Visitors

Early in October 1951 Princess Elizabeth and Prince Philip arrived for their first trip across Canada. They landed at Quebec City on the 9th and took part in festivities in four major centres involving rides in an open convertible through cheering crowds. The October weather was always threatening rain and a sudden shower on one occasion forced them to finish the trip in a closed car. The royal visitors were reportedly upset that the waiting crowd could not see them properly and took the matter up with their transportation office. The Princess suggested a Perspex canopy and Prince Philip even sketched a few ideas for the Army colonel.

The officer's next move was to approach the automotive industry – General Motors, Ford and Chrysler – for quotes on a canopy. The replies were not encouraging for the price ranged from $50,000 to $100,000 and the time required would be four to six weeks. When the news was relayed to Prince Philip he thought for a while and said, "Why don't we go to de Havilland? They are used to this sort of thing." It was not long before manager Phil Garratt got a personal phone call from Prince Philip, who explained the project and the preliminary sketches. Garratt ran it through his mind a couple of times, noting that it was Friday the 11th,

and said, "How long do we have?" "Monday," was the prompt reply and, after a few pleasantries, the general manager suggested that the car be sent up whenever it could be spared.

Phil Garratt called in Doug Hunter, who promptly formed a team to tackle the project. By the time the car arrived at the plant after work on Friday, Fred Buller from engineering and Bill Burlison from the shops had their key personnel ready to start work. In recalling the incident years later, Russ Bannock, said, "I knew the project was going on around the clock and went out on Sunday to see how the job was coming along. I was utterly astounded, for they had the canopy built and were fitting Chipmunk cockpit lights around the frame so it could be lit up at night." By Monday the car went out of the plant complete with canopy, ready for the rest of the royal tour. "It was an amazing accomplishment," said Bannock, "and to think that de Havilland got nothing for it except a personal 'thank you' from Prince Philip and a nice letter."

The Plexiglas canopy designed and built during a weekend for the 1951 cross-Canada tour of Princess Elizabeth and Prince Philip. (DH 10251)

(Above) The first Vampires to operate in Canada make an imposing line-up at Downsview. (DH)

(Right) George Neal with Battle of Britain ace Douglas Bader beside a Vampire. Bader represented Shell Oil aviation products. (DH)

(Below) Vampires, Harvards and Cansos going through the overhaul bay at Downsview. (DH)

The Turbo Beaver

Years later, in the 1960s, after the Beaver had long been established as a workhourse, United Aircraft of Canada (later Pratt & Whitney Canada) introduced the PT6 turbine engine. This technology was developing rapidly. Turbine engines, with their greater efficiency and higher power/weight ratio, were taking over from pistons. DHC was working closely with UAC, and some Canadian bush operators were expressing interest.

The engineers at de Havilland became involved early in the life of the PT6. DHC received the contract to convert a standard RCAF Beech 18 as a PT6 test bed. Bill Billings was in charge of the engineering, which included a special nose mount. Preliminary test flying was done at Downsview by Bob Fowler. Then the aircraft was turned over to John MacNeil, P&WC's chief test pilot, who did the engine calibration flying.

This introduction to the light turbine era started many a huddle among the engineers at de Havilland, particularly those associated with the experimental STOL Otter. They wanted to round out the test program with a pair of PT6s, knowing that the benefits would be worthwhile. DHC's involvement in the PT6 provided an inside track to new engine data. The PT6 seemed tailor-made for DHC designs; it was not surprising that the company began getting customer enquiries. Pacific Western Airlines, for example, considered converting their piston Beavers to turboprop power. The first meeting on the subject was in December 1962 and correspondence continued through March of 1963. A DHC kit was considered so that operators could modify their own aircraft, but by March 14, when a complete proposal for a turbine Beaver was issued, the project had grown in complexity. Changes, besides the engine and nacelle, would include a new fin and rudder, and a 28-inch (71 cm) fuselage extension forward of the wing. This allowed two more passengers and under-floor storage for an extra 29 Imp. gal. (132 l) of fuel. Payload would be 157 lb. (71 kg) more than a standard Beaver at ranges up to 500 miles (800 km). Economical cruise speed would rise, but gross weight would remain at 5,100 lb. (2,315 kg). The PT6A-6 produced 550 shp, against the R985 Wasp Junior's 450 hp, giving excellent takeoff performance. This was attractive to the Ontario Department of Lands and Forests, which could add dozens of smaller lakes

The PT6 engine mount for the Beechcraft testbed was engineered by de Havilland. (DH 13123)

The test crew on the first PT6 flight: J.A. MacNeil of Pratt & Whitney (left) and R. H. Fowler of de Havilland. (DH 13072)

for routine operations. Ontario considered converting their existing Beavers.

While PWA bowed out of proceedings, an April meeting of DHC's management committee approved three months of design to determine the necessary modifications and a 16-

The first flight of the DHC-2T Turbo Beaver on a cold December 31, 1963. (DH 17017)

plane program was approved. Prototype CF-PSM-X (to record the initials of project engineer Peter S. Martin) flew on the last day of 1963 with Bob Fowler and "Jock" Aitken.

Ontario became the main Turbo Beaver operator, taking the first of 17 on June 4, 1965. But the extensive improvements involved in conversion, along with the costly turbine, made the Turbo Beaver very expensive. It still had to compete with its piston cousins and these were now becoming available at good prices from surplus U.S. Army stocks. Turbo Beaver sales slowed enough in 1967 that Hawker Siddeley (the owner of DHC) closed the production line.

The final configuration of the Turbo Beaver tail can be seen in this view of demonstrator CF-ROM and prototype CF-PSM-X. Sixty Turbo Beavers were completed by DHC, mostly for Canadian customers. (DH)

DHC's main Beaver sales were of L-20s to the U.S. Army. They were needed for search and rescue in Alaska, then, in large numbers, for the Korean War. The majority (more than 900) wore standard camouflage, as seen in these photos. First, an L-20 on a photo flight near Downsview. Then, 56-405 (Beaver No. 1149) delivered in September 1957 is seen in a European setting. Finally, bearing government disposal serial UD077, 56-4425 is shown in 1975 at Davis-Monthan Air Force Base awaiting a buyer. Hundreds of surplus L-20s were sold to civil operators during the 1970s, and many came to Canada. (DH, Swartz Col., Ben Knowles)

The Beaver is at home on wheels, skis, wheel/skis, floats or amphibious floats, but we naturally envision it on floats. C-FDIN was photographed at Sioux Lookout by bush pilot Richard Hulina in May 1997. Beaver No. 68, it first appeared on the Canadian Civil Aircraft Register in 1951.

(Below) A classic Rick Radell set-up photo of Beaver CF-QQE over Georgian Bay near Manitoulin Island in September 1996. Gary Schroeder, owner of Birch Island Lodge, was at the controls.

(Left) Piloted by Marg Watson, C-FIUU heads north on June 9, 1992, from Sudbury to Solace Lake. There Marg's passengers spent some relaxing hours reeling in lake trout, then enjoying a delicious shore lunch. This Beaver's previous owners included Labrador Mining and Exploration. (Larry Milberry)

(Right) Ski Beaver C-FODB of Austin Airways on the Albany River at Ogoki Post, Ontario. This was in March 1975, before a new airstrip was put in, allowing Twin Otters and Beech 99s to reach this tiny Indian reserve. In 1998 ODB was with Parry Sound Airways, serving Ontario's Georgian Bay region. (Larry Milberry)

(Below) Trippier Air of Ear Falls, Ontario, had drooped leading edges, STOL wingtip extensions and wing fences retrofitted to Beaver C-FLUA. As sold in 1998 by AOG Air Support of Kelowna, this performance-enhancing Baron kit cost U.S.$23,000 installed. Here LUA (bought new in 1959 by Arthur Fecteau) was at Red Lake Seaplane Service in July 1995. (Larry Milberry)

With the Canadian North supplied with modern airstrips, and with helicopters available all year to serve isolated camps, Beavers and Otters now fly mainly in the summer tourist trade. Here is Red Lake Airways' Beaver AQJ in hibernation over the winter of 1991-92. AQJ had begun in 1957 as L-20 No. 56-4411. (Larry Milberry)

(Left) In the 1960s-70s the B.C. coast had many independent operators flying Beavers and Otters. Here Bill Pogue flies Gulf Air Beaver C-FFHT near Campbell River. In the 1980s, most such carriers were absorbed by Jim Pattison of Vancouver. He welded them into a province-wide operation, Air BC, which eventually became a regional carrier with Twin Otter, Dash 7 and Dash 8 turboprops. It gradually spun off its local services, giving rise to a new era of independents. As to FHT, it was Beaver No. 55. In earlier years it had flown with coast operators like BC Airlines and Trans Mountain Air Services. In 1998 it was with Tweedsmuir Air Services of Nimpo Lake, B.C. (Kenneth I. Swartz)

Coast pilot Sandy Parker snugs L-20 Beaver C-FWAC into the dock at Kitkatla following a 41nm flight from Prince Rupert on August 2, 1993. (Larry Milberry)

(Above) Otter, Beavers and Cessnas wait for the morning fog to lift in this Prince Rupert scene from August 1993. Soon they dispersed to destinations on the coast, and out to the Queen Charlotte Islands with passengers, freight and mail. (Larry Milberry)

(Right) Harbour Air's C-FOSP is launched at Vancouver International Airport on April 13, 1992. Beaver No. 1501, it went new in 1962 to Canadian Collieries Timber Air Services of Vancouver. Later it served West Coast Air Services. Note the tow vehicle. Clapped-out Oldsmobile Toronados, Cadillac Eldorados and other front-wheel-drive cars and light trucks often evade the wrecker by being cut down for wheeling float planes around. (Larry Milberry)

Beaver N9762Z near Seldovia on Alaska's Kenai Peninsula in June 1975. Bill de Creeft started Kachemak Air Service in Homer in 1967. He bought N9762Z from Kenmore in Washington in 1970, logging 14,000 hours with it over the next 25 years. Then it became C-FYEX of Atlin-based Apex Air Charters. (Jack Hayes)

C-FOBU, the fourth Beaver, at a mineral exploration camp on Crescent Lake in northern B.C. in June 1980. OBU had started with the OPAS, then went to Omenica Air Service of Burns Lake, B.C. (Kenneth I. Swartz)

(Above) Beaver C-FIGF flew in 1956 with Fleetwood Logging of Vancouver, then went in 1960 for a long stay at BC-Yukon Air Service of Watson Lake. Here it was with Vancouver Island Air at Campbell River in July 1988. A decade later VIA still operated Beavers – in the second view IGF is seen again at Campbell River, but in its 1997 colours. (John Kimberley, Lenn Bayliss)

(Right) Amiskwi Air's C-FJOM in for maintenance at Vancouver in May 1990. Previously with mining developer Karl J. Springer, PWA, Northern Mountain Airlines and Northern Thunderbird Air, this was the 1024th Beaver. In 1998 it was with Sterling Pacific Air of Vernon, B.C. (John Kimberley)

(Left) Some of the hundreds of ex-military Beavers on the civil market await restoration at Kenmore Air Harbor in Washington in 1989. The nearest is sprayed with "1606", which probably is the constructor's number. If so it's the Beaver delivered on August 12, 1965, to the Zambian Air Force. (Gary Vincent)

(Right) C-GAEE, Beaver No. 724, was made up to resemble an old-time bushplane for its role in the movie *Never Cry Wolf*, shot in B.C. in the early 198os. In the 1970s it was with Laurentian Air Services, an important Beaver and Otter bush operator. AEE was one of dozens of surplus L-20s renovated by BM Aviation of Lachute, Quebec. (Below) AEE in more regular service with Taku Air. Beyond is historic Atlin, where gold was mined for decades. (Gary Vincent)

(Left) Some Beavers were modified for aerial survey. C-FTUR-X of Ottawa-based McPhar Geophysical shows an array of electronic monitoring gear in this 1974 photo. In the 1990s TUR was with the Quebec operator Air Mont-Laurier. When the Beaver appeared in 1947, it sold for $21,000. A half century later the market had changed. In 1998, for example, Tsayta Aviation's Beaver C-GIJK, with 17,650 airframe hours, was noted for sale on the internet for $275,000. (Gary Vincent)

CF-HGZ was one of many corporate Beavers. Often these served natural resource companies. Shell Oil used HGZ in the 1950s-60s in Alberta and the NWT. Later it worked for BC Airlines, Air West Airlines, Trans Provincial Airlines and Harbour Air. (Al Martin)

Beavers were sought by operators around the world. Typical were HK-1104-G (right) delivered in 1953 to the Colombian government (note the optional long-range belly tank). Then (below), a desert Beaver in Arabian colours. Even in the 1990s Beavers were being exported far afield. In 1996, for example, Turbo Beaver C-FLPF was sold in Sweden as SE-LEV. (Swartz Col., Benner Col.)

DHC planes found a warm welcome in Australia and New Zealand. From 1990-98 the Australian register noted 30 Chipmunk, 20 Beaver, 3 Otter, 15 Twin Otter, 2 Dash 7 and 25 Dash 8 aircraft. For 1998 the New Zealand register listed seven Chipmunk, six Beaver, three Twin Otter and four Dash 8 aircraft. In New Zealand the Beaver was valuable for spreading fertilizer over sheep grazing lands. Here are typical Australian Beavers: VH-IDD with spray booms, and Aquaflight's VH-IMR used in the Queensland tourist trade. (Benner Col., Vincent Col.)

Powered by the PT6 turbine, the DHC-2T Turbo Beaver flew in 1965. It became a workhorse with the OPAS, but only 60 initially were sold. What held back sales? The price was steep, the concept of turbines for bushplanes was new, and piston Beavers were plentiful at good prices. Shown is prototype CF-PSM, which served DHC as a demonstrator for years. Here pilot George Neal and passenger Jim Genes were deplaning at Downsview on June 10, 1973. Following a landing accident, PSM was donated by Bombardier to the Canadian Bushplane Heritage Centre in Sault Ste. Marie. (Larry Milberry)

CF-OEA of the OPAS (Turbo Beaver No. 3) at Toronto Island Airport in September 1965 with Beaver CF-ODG and Otter CF-ODW with a centre-line water bombing tank . These famous OPAS machines eventually moved on, OEA to the Manitoba Government Air Service, ODG to Cargair of Quebec, and ODW most recently to Points North Air of La Ronge, Saskatchewan. (Larry Milberry)

Turbo Beavers like C-FETN, used for years by Toronto's Eaton family, were ideal for trips to the cottage and sport fishing. Here Russ Bannock was flying ETN at Sudbury in September 1997. Note the extra cabin windows compared to PSM. Early Turbo Beavers had the 550-shp PT6A-20, but in the 1980s, by when operators were sold on the idea of turbines, the 680-shp PT6A-27 came into vogue. In the 1990s, many Beavers were being converted to the PT6, mainly at Viking Air in B.C. and Kenmore Air Harbor in Washington. (Larry Milberry)

Eccentric-looking Alaskan Beaver N754, originally delivered in 1958 to the Cuban Air Force, was a turbine with a difference. Instead of a PT6, it used an Allison C250-B17F. Ken Swartz photographed it at Anchorage, one of the world's bush flying capitals, in May 1987.

(Left) Converted on the production line in 1953 to a 550-hp Alvis Leonides, Beaver No. 80 spent its early years in the U.K. Eventually it returned to Canada as CF-CNR (for owner Charles Norman Robson). Here it is at its base in Oshawa in June 1976. In the 1980s CNR went to the missionary organization Wings of Hope, which assigned it to Bolivia. Once its engine ran out of hours, CNR was abandoned (even though it had only about 2,000 airframe hours). Richard Wagner brought it to Wisconsin, then sold it to Bob Retterach, who restored it as N115LA. Gone was the famous Leonides, in its place a 600-hp PZL. N115LA, based in 1998 at Lino Lakes, Minnesota, also had a set of Wipaire 6100 floats. (Larry Milberry)

(Right) The only one of its kind, Australian Beaver VH-AAX was neatly modified with a Garrett TPE331-61 turbine. AAX had been shipped from Downsview to de Havilland of Australia in March 1960. In 1998 it was with Sydney Aerial Tours of Bankstown, New South Wales. (Vincent Col.)

Operators who chose the PZL over the R985 or PT6 found their "new" Beavers to be superb performers. Note the four-blade prop in this 1996 view of Démolition Outaouais' PZL Beaver C-GBUL in the Ottawa River. (Andy Graham)

The Beaver richly deserves its place of honour in aviation history. In Canada CF-FHB, the first Beaver, is in the National Aviation Museum (above). U.S. Army L-20 No. 51-6263 flies on at the U.S. Army Aviation Museum (left) at Fort Rucker, Alabama. Delivered in early 1951, this was the third U.S. YL-20. An Otter and a Caribou complete the museum's tribute to de Havilland Canada. (Andy Graham, Larry Milberry)

CHAPTER SIX

THE OTTER YEARS

With the sale of 1,692 Beavers to 62 countries around the world and the large military numbers involved, the question has often been asked, "Why did the RCAF never buy any?" According to all accounts, the answer is simply that they found it too small for their requirements. They still had a lot of Norsemen, the size of bushplane they preferred. The argument that the Beaver was too small may never be settled, but the resulting deliberations led to the next DHC model – the Otter.

It was only reasonable after the initial success of the Beaver that thoughts should turn to something bigger, possibly the size of the Norseman and Bellanca. Other potential customers backed the RCAF view, particularly the Ontario Department of Lands and Forests, who liked the Beaver but wanted something bigger. The RCAF was serious enough to take part in the research funding.

By 1950 the basic concept for a new type was evolved, mainly under the original Beaver design group, but his time Jaki Jakimiuk was not involved. A call had come from Hatfield during the engineering lull that followed the Beaver for design assistance with the Heron, Comet and Vampire. Jakimiuk headed a Downsview team to England: Charlie Bishop, Jack Greeniaus, Bill Heaslip, George Luesby, Al Marten and John Mazur. They worked on the Vampire

night fighter. Jakimiuk resigned while in England to join the French company Sud Aviation. The other Canadians returned by September 1950 to work on the DHC-3.

Late in 1950, specifications were laid down for the DHC-3, then called the King Beaver. It was to have Beaver takeoff performance with twice the payload and $2^1/2$ times the cabin volume. This was formidable considering that there was only 33.3 per cent more power to do these wonderful things. This time, however, they would have access to new technology, along with the proven Pratt & Whitney R1340. On November 29 a factory instruction was issued for a design start and construction of a single prototype. It was an encouraging time for the 40 engineering staff – their Chipmunk had sold 122 copies and was being manufactured under licence in Britain, and Beaver sales were going well with deliveries nearing 100.

Another Major Decision

Market surveys on a bigger aircraft were in agreement with the Wasp engine and fuel tanks under the floor as in the Beaver. The once-disputed linking of the aileron and flap was approved without question. Punch Dickins felt an engine/propeller combination compatible with the Norseman would be a good sales point when talking to operators, but Dick Hiscocks insisted on the geared version of the "H" Wasp for maximum engine efficiency. Garratt approved the decision but was immediately confronted with a supply

The prototype Otter prepares for its first flight on December 12, 1951. Test flying resulted in the vertical tail being enlarged. (DH)

Pilot George Neal after testing the first DHC-3 Otter at Downsview in December 1951. (DH)

Two exhaust ejectors on each side, below the pilot door, are a distinct feature of the Otter. In the cockpit is Prince Bernhard of the Netherlands, on a visit to Downsview. (DH 8111)

problem. Only a few of these engines had been manufactured during the war especially for the Australian Wirraway. A world search was conducted with the aid of Canadian Pratt & Whitney and a used aircraft entrepreneur, Charlie Babb. The search covered four continents and took on all the aspects of a detective mystery. Fifty engines were found in Sweden, sufficient for a start. Phil Garratt said, "Why don't we go ahead. I think I can talk my friend Jim Young into making the components. I know he would like to get into the manufacture of engines." The "old boy" system went into operation again and another crisis was over.

While the prototype Otter took shape, a factory order for 15 machines was issued, encouraged undoubtedly by the recently announced Beaver sales to the U.S. military. Pre-production orders were taken from the Ontario Department of Lands and Forests along with some from a new-found market – the booming oil industry in Alberta. A push was on to get the new plane, now called the Otter, into the air in less than a year from the start of the design. George Neal, now chief test pilot, accomplished this objective on a cold December day in 1951. A busy year of test and development flying followed. The guidelines imposed by limited power had forced a maximum effort in all areas of engineering. Fred Buller's airframe design had the lowest structural gross weight of any aircraft in this class up to that time. The large

British aviation cartoonist Christopher Wren picked the occasion of the DHC-3 Otter flight to show some members of the team that shaped the aircraft. (*The Aeroplane*, April 17, 1953)

The interconnected slotted flap and droop aileron of the Otter are shown in this sequence: (1) both in the normal flight position; (2) half flap with a partial droop to the ailerons; (3) the flaps fully down and maximum aileron droop. (Industrial Pictures via R.G. Halford)

fuselage was smoothly streamlined and could almost be described as a wide-bodied bushplane. A double slotted flap was introduced as an improvement over the Beaver system; and then there was the geared engine. The complicated gearing added to the overall weight but allowed the "H" Wasp to swing a larger propeller at lower rpm. It resulted in a slower air speed at altitude but gave the desired extremely short takeoff run. The novel ejector cooling cowls were employed to squeeze maximum efficiency from the engine along with some augmented thrust. The gross weight of the first Otter was 7,200 lb. (3,266 kg). This grew with later models to above 8,000 lb. (3,629 kg).

The added torque of the large propeller on the geared engine could destabilize the aircraft in extreme yawing manoeuvres. To overcome this tendency, an increased fin area was added which remained standard on all production Otters.

Certification came on November 5, 1952, with the delivery of the first production aircraft to Hudson Bay Mining & Smelting the following day. Imperial Oil was the next customer to receive an Otter, only days ahead of the Ontario Department of Lands and Forests. The RCAF received its first machine on February 14, 1953, the first of an eventual 63. Maxwell Ward ordered Otter No. 5 but had to await his charter licence before he could put the airplane to work.

The Honourable Brooke Claxton, Minister of National Defence, announced on May 21, 1952, that Philip C. Garratt had been awarded the Trans-Canada (McKee) Trophy. The trophy was first presented in 1927 to the "person rendering the most meritorious service during the year in the advancement of aviation in Canada." It had been donated by the late Captain James Dalzell McKee to commemorate his first seaplane flight across Canada. A presentation was made by Chief of the Air Staff Air Marshal W.A. Curtis at a meeting in the Seigniory Club, Montebello, Quebec, in November 1952.

The Comet in Canada

One spring day in 1952 Punch Dickins was in Ottawa, making the rounds. He dropped in on his bush flying friend "Lewie" Leigh. Group Captain Z. Lewis Leigh was Director of Air Operations RCAF and, like Dickins, a winner of the McKee Trophy. Punch had come to talk about de Havilland's D.H.106 Comet jetliner and the two were soon discussing the possible role of jet transport in the RCAF.

Phil Garratt is presented with the McKee Trophy by Air Marshal W.A. Curtis at a CASI banquet on November 11, 1952. (CPR)

The first RCAF Comet at Ottawa's Uplands Airport, May 29, 1953, the day it arrived in Canada. (CF PL57344)

The meetings prompted a further study and that summer Dickins and Leigh visited Hatfield for a closer investigation. RCAF interest was confirmed with the purchase of two Comet 1As, making it the first air force in the world to operate jet transports. The first air force crew was F/L C. Brown, F/L M.D. Broadfoot, S/L J.D. Dixon (Captain), F/L K.A. Wark and W/O C.W. Baine. They were trained in England by BOAC.

RCAF Air Transport Command was the envy of its USAF counterpart and the Comets were welcomed regularly in New York and Washington. They ran into opposition at first from airport authorities because of the jet noise factor but soon the opposition dwindled as their visits became routine. They crisscrossed Canada working closely with the DOT on the subject of jets and piston transports in the air traffic system. When all Comets were temporarily grounded in 1954 following several accidents, the hours on the RCAF machines were below the critical point. Many modifications were carried out at Downsview, however, while the problem was being investigated. Both aircraft were converted to the IXB model in 1957 and served until their retirement in 1965. During the Comet years in Canada, Harry Hunter of the DHC service department was technical representative and RCAF liaison officer.

A New Building

With Beaver sales booming, the Otter coming along and overhaul work taking a good portion of the hangars, lack of space became a problem. The solution came when the Crown offered DHC $5.5 million and a 96-acre (39 hectare) parcel of land on the southwest corner of the airport on a 99-year lease, in exchange for the de Havilland buildings at the north end. The government needed these buildings for a new RCAF station. Phil Garratt accepted and plans went ahead for a new factory and offices. Bill Burlison had responsibility for the new building and, after a quick look around similar factories in the United States, could see that his budget would be tight. He evolved a novel system of using squared plastic to compare existing space with that needed in the new plant. With the help of Reg Corlett he went back and forth to the managers, having them plan their own areas. There was a bit of cutting and trimming when the proposal went to management, but after considerable re-arrangement of the squares, the project was turned over to architects Sheppard and Powell.

The next few months were busy ones for Burlison, who reflected later that they were the most rewarding in his career:

We had our problems, of course, but made many moves that proved successful over the years. We were able to install overhead mobile cranes, which we never had before, use automatic doors, and even put a door on both ends of Bay 4. I received a lot of opposition to this idea but it proved very flexible as we moved to bigger aircraft. One thing

161

The factory at the south end of Downsview airport nears completion. Beavers, two Lancasters, a Vampire and a Chipmunk are parked around the flight test hangar. Construction and the move during 1953 were planned so that all operations continued without interruption. (DH A272)

that worked well was the small supply train that moved parts through the aisles to the various work areas. It was particularly useful in transferring Ab Warren's stores department to the south plant in only one move. We transferred one department at a time, usually over-night, and every bench, cupboard and tool box would be sitting in its new spot ready for the shift next morning. It got a bit rough in the cold weather but everyone co-operated and we only slipped production of one aircraft during the whole transition. We knew the building was too small when it was built and that additions would soon be needed, but we got maximum value for our dollar, with $6 per foot for the ground floor and $12 per foot for the upper stories.

By the end of January 1954 most of the structure for the new building was up and the move from the north plant was in the planning stage. The flight test hangar opened first, then the cafeteria, followed by the shops and offices. Francis St. Barbe had taken great interest in the proceedings and was over from England at the end of February to have a look around. The cafeteria was operational and it seemed a good idea to have the first party in the new building in honour of their visitor.

The $8 million plant covering 10 1/2 acres (4.25 hectares) was connected to Wilson Avenue during the summer of

The original Downsview plant and wartime additions after it became an RCAF base. To the right are the original DH buildings, many times extended. The wartime complex where the Mosquitoes were produced can be related to the diagram on page 98. Note the RCAF C-119 transports and the lone Tracker. (DH 11016)

W.C. "Bill" Burlison was key to engineering and management through the war years, the Chipmunk/Beaver transition period, to production of the Caribou and Buffalo. He was a major player in planning the new quarters at the south end of the field and the Grumman Tracker program that was announced a month later. He is a deserving member of the de Havilland Canada Hall of Fame. (DH 1393)

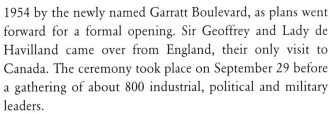

1954 by the newly named Garratt Boulevard, as plans went forward for a formal opening. Sir Geoffrey and Lady de Havilland came over from England, their only visit to Canada. The ceremony took place on September 29 before a gathering of about 800 industrial, political and military leaders.

After a detailed tour of the new plant and a flying display, the guests gathered in the flight test hangar for the official ceremonies. It was a proud day for Phil Garratt, who introduced the guests on the speakers' platform that afternoon. Representing The de Havilland Aircraft Co. was Sir Geoffrey de Havilland, president of DH Canada, and Francis T. Hearle, the recently retired chairman at Hatfield. Another well-known member of the de Havilland enterprise was Major F.B. Halford, chairman and technical director of the de Havilland Engine Co. Limited. Representing the Canadian government were the Hon. C.D. Howe, Minister of Defence Production, and the Hon. George Marler, Minister of Transport. On the military side were Lieutenant General G.G. Simmonds, Chief of the General Staff, Canadian Army; Air Marshal C.R. Slemon, Chief of the Air Staff, RCAF; Major General F.R. Dent Jr. of the USAF Air Materiel Command; and Vice Admiral E.R. Mainguy, Chief of the Naval Staff, RCN.

An impressive gathering on the front steps of the administration building at the formal opening of the south plant. Left to right: Phil Garratt, managing director DHC; George J. Mickleborough, secretary treasurer; Francis T. Hearle, recently retired as chairman of DH England; Lady de Havilland; Sir Geoffrey de Havilland; W. Doug Hunter, director of engineering; Punch Dickins, director of sales; and Russ Bannock, director of military sales. (DH 839)

(Below) Three dynamic personalities: C.D. Howe, in a characteristic pose, stands between Sir Geoffrey de Havilland and P.C. Garratt in front of the company Heron at the opening of the new plant. (DH 829)

In his address Phil Garratt paid tribute to C.D. Howe for the untiring interest and assistance he had always given the aircraft industry. Howe, in performing the official opening ceremonies, recalled his association with de Havilland from the time of the first building being erected at Mount Dennis. He spoke also of the "great initiative and resourcefulness of the company management," adding that he was speaking from personal experience. He stressed the part that the company had played and continued to play in the "Canadian Century." Sir Geoffrey de Havilland, in a rare public appearance, paid tribute to the progress of the Canadian company and concluded, "One gains a sense of the great future that lies before Canada, and of the stability of the country in its handling of great national resources and responsibilities."

DOUG HUNTER
Dir. of Engineering

'SANDY' MACDONALD
Sales Manager

BILL CALDER
Service Manager

GEORGE MICKLEBOROUGH
Sec. Treasurer

The de HAVILLAND AIRCRAFT of CANADA Ltd.
TORONTO

PHIL C. GARRATT
Man. Director

'PUNCH' DICKINS
Sales Dir.

RUSS BANNOCK
Dir. Operations & Military Sales

KWIK KAFÉ

10c.

GROUNDED

Christopher Wren was in Canada in 1953 doing cartoons on each of the aircraft manufacturing companies for a special issue of *The Aeroplane*. When Wren arrived at Downsview, Phil Garratt had just issued a notice that employees were spending too much time around the new coffee machine, with the threat that if this continued, the machine would be grounded. That was all Wren needed as a theme, as he included the management of the time in his cartoon – and the coffee machine. (*The Aeroplane*, April 17, 1953)

The Grumman Tracker

The variety of overhaul work that played such a role in DH Canada's postwar recovery required a versatile management. As contracts manager, George Neely was constantly dealing with new customers, both civil and military. The need for modifications on customer conversions moved Len Trotter from the Chipmunk design team in 1945 and for the next five years he specialized in contract engineering.

Early in 1954 the Royal Canadian Navy indicated that they were prepared to order a quantity of new Grumman S2F Tracker anti-submarine aircraft to replace their aging Avengers. There was talk of a quantity order along with the fact that they might be built in Canada. Neely and Trotter discussed the possibility of de Havilland involvement but were sceptical in view of Phil Garratt's reluctance to become involved in building other companies' airplanes. Meetings between the Canadian Department of Defence Production and the Air Industries and Transport Association about a national manufacturing plan went ahead during the summer of 1954. Neely represented de Havilland's interests in the negotiations, and when the news broke it was sudden and complete. Instead of being an "also ran," DH Canada was to be the prime contractor for the new RCN aircraft.

Len Trotter went immediately to Bethpage, Long Island, as DHC representative in contract negotiations. Shortly af-

ter the new Downsview plant opened, the Tracker plan was publicized. It was to involve several participants. The wings would be built by Canadian Car and Foundry of Fort William, the rear fuselage section by Canadair in Montreal, the tail by Enamel & Heating Products of Amherst, N.S. and the engine nacelles by MacDonald Brothers Aircraft of Winnipeg. The undercarriage shock struts were to be made under licence by Jarry Hydraulics of Montreal, the nose undercarriage and tail bumper by Dowty Equipment of Ajax, and the bomb-bay doors, hatches and covers by Fleet Manufacturing of Fort Erie. As prime contractor, de Havilland Canada would build the forward fuselage and the pilot's compartment, assemble the aircraft, look after the installation of the electronic gear and test the aircraft for RCN acceptance. The $100 million contract was the biggest since WWII. Even the engines were to be manufactured in Canada. At one stage converting the aircraft from Wright to Pratt & Whitney engines was considered in order to provide work at CP&W. The Department of Defence Production instead negotiated with the Curtiss-Wright Corporation for 400 Wright R1820 Cyclones to be built under licence by CP&W. The RCN bought one U.S.-built S2F-1 as the test model. The all-weather, twin-engined Tracker was to have the most sophisticated electronic gear in the hunter/killer role and be capable of carrying a variety of weapons.

The Grumman CS2F-2 Tracker assembly line at Downsview. (DH 5472)

Everyone at de Havilland, especially Phil Garratt, was pleased at the prospect of a new production line. His comment was quoted in the February 1955 issue of *Canadian Aviation*: "It is not only good business, but as the largest and most complicated aircraft DHC has yet undertaken, it is a most interesting project. Our whole organization feels quite keenly about the CS2F-1 and looks forward to the first model off the line."

Representing the company on the business side in all contacts with Grumman, the RCN and government was George Neely. Bill Burlison managed production and Len Trotter was project engineering coordinator. Promotions and new employment followed hand-in-hand as everyone tackled the new challenge. The first strike in the company's history put a dent in the schedule, but in May 1956 the first Tracker was tested. George Neal and Tony Verrico took RCN number 1502 into the air on the 31st and it was delivered to the Navy in a ceremony on October 12.

The aircraft resembled the U.S.-built Grumman model in

Representing thousands of Canadians who helped produce the Tracker are some of the men who supervised its assembly. Left to right: Bill Bozanin, Bill Stewardson, Art Bradley and Charlie Cobb. (DH 5170)

structure and flying qualities. The electronic gear, including the tail boom and special radar, was Canadian. Production went well in the new plant and deliveries continued at a regular rate. From serial No. 43 on, a number of RCN modifications were incorporated. Later 17 of these aircraft were passed to the Royal Netherlands Navy.

Although records show 100 Tracker aircraft delivered from the de Havilland production line, only 99 were fully manufactured in Canada. The extra aircraft was the Grumman-built machine used in the development program and rebuilt later as RCN number 1501.

Years later, when Bill Burlison was asked to summarize the project, he admitted that it was a large program for such a small number of aircraft with the U.S. manufacturer so close to the border. "It was a good project for Canadian aircraft manufacturers," he added, "and a good deal for de Havilland. We worked well with Grumman and were exposed to a company with a higher technology. We learned more about big jigs and production methods during this period than ever before. We were able to upgrade things on the Beaver and Otter lines a dozen different ways because of our association with Grumman."

The Tracker served the RCN and CF well and even when some were declared surplus, they found a new role as forest fire bombers. The Ontario government, in conjunction with Field Aviation Co. Limited, worked to incorporate a chemical retardant tank and release system. The test model returned to de Havilland in 1976 to be flight certified in its new category.

DHC-built Trackers served in the anti-submarine role aboard the aircraft carrier HMCS *Bonaventure* from 1957 to 1969. Then they operated ashore at Summerside, P.E.I., and Shearwater, N.S., doing fisheries and sovereignty patrols. Canada retired the Tracker in 1990. (DH 4435)

Another Success Story

Throughout 1953 and 1954, 50 Otters were delivered to a variety of customers, both civil and military. Max Ward set a precedent by bringing a bushplane the size of the Otter to Yellowknife. His competitors were equipped with prewar types of varying shapes and sizes and were quick to pass judgement on the expensive new Otter. They were outspoken that it would never pay its way, but Ward had other ideas and set out to prove that the added efficiency of design and the reliability of new equipment was right for the north. Thirty years later he recalled:

I proved my point, and it wasn't long until my opposition saw the light and went for Otters too. The Otter changed the whole transportation picture in the Arctic and flying took a big step forward. This was the first time we could carry full sheets of plywood and it changed the living styles considerably. Prospectors spent less time making camp and more time prospecting. You could almost tell the camps that were built before and after the Otter came by the size of the plywood used.

I had a total of six Otters at one time and found de Havilland a great company to deal with. We had our problems but we always sorted things out. It was a great family company and it was always fun to come to Toronto and have lunch with Phil Garratt at the big round table in the dining room. It became a sort of company symbol.

In Norway, Widerøe Flyveselskap A/S was the first foreign customer to catch Max Ward's enthusiasm for the Otter and bought the first of many in June 1954. A link greater than the Arctic Circle joins Norway and Canada, for much has been similar in the development of aviation. By 1934 both countries had entered the bush flying era. That year, the brothers Viggo and Arild Widerøe founded Norway's first flying concern. They began using Waco, Stinson and Bellanca airplanes in a seasonal pattern much like in Canada. After the war, when it became necessary to start all over again, Viggo maintained his preference for the robust single-engine bushplane. His introduction to the Otter was by chance. He was at Oslo airport as George Neal arrived with the Otter on a demonstration tour. Thus began a long, successful relationship with the Otter and de Havilland Canada. It was not long until Widerøe's neighbours, the Royal Norwegian Air Force, were also buying Otters for search and rescue duties out of Bodø. Other customers in 1954 included Imperial Oil, the RCMP and Laurentian Air Services. By 1955 the RCAF had 34 Otters.

A typical piece of DHC advertising. The art was by R.W. Bradford, who later was curator of Canada's National Aviation Museum. (DH)

Arctic Rescue..

Mid winter 1961. A U.S. Air Force crew has crash landed a C47 on sea-ice in the Hudson Straits off Resolution Island. Their mayday call is picked up 200 miles away by Pilot Kenneth Dempster of Wheeler Airlines.

The light is failing as he lands at the scene. There is insufficient space for a normal take-off. With 14 people and equipment aboard his DHC-3 Otter, Dempster starts his take-off down wind—hits an ice hummock—swings his overloaded plane into wind, and succeeds in achieving an amazing take-off under extremely difficult circumstances.

Back at Resolution airstrip, Dempster sets the crippled aircraft down—with its landing gear damaged—without further mishap.

For distinguished conduct, heroism and exceptional judgement, Pilot Kenneth D. Dempster was awarded the United States Air Force Exceptional Service Award.

Pilot Kenneth D. Dempster, Wheeler Airlines, wearing U.S.A.F. Exceptional Service Medal following presentation by U.S. Ambassador Livingston T. Merchant.

the **STOL** *Otter... designed and built by*
de Havilland Aircraft of Canada
downsview   ontario
Western Sales and Service: Municipal Airport, Edmonton, Alta. • Pacific Coast Sales and Service: Vancouver, B.C.

Otter vs Helicopter

By any standard, the Otter had made a commendable start but the U.S. Army had not shown its usual interest. Russ Bannock kept the sub-

Max Ward introduced the DHC-3 Otter to the far north and proved that it was right for the times. Here is a view of old and new types of winter transportation. Later, the dogs gave way to snowmobiles. CF-IFP was Otter No. 73. In 1998 it was flying in Manitoba with a 1,000 hp Polish PZL engine. (DH 52287)

ject alive, checking regularly with the director of Army aviation in Washington. The Army liked the Otter, but recollections of the controversy surrounding the Beaver order were still fresh in everyone's mind. Any purchase would involve a competition and there were no competitions coming up for medium-sized aircraft in the fixed wing category. As the two men talked it occurred to the director that Exercise Skydrop II at Fort Bragg between two helicopter types was scheduled for late summer of 1954. "If de Havilland would make an Otter available for operation Skydrop II," he said, "it could be slipped into the contest and provide an interesting comparison from everyone's point of view." An Otter was made available with a team composed of pilot Doug Givens, Russ Bannock and maintenance engineer Bob Irving. It was a gruelling month's work, taking part in every conceivable form of military support. The Otter proved immediately that it could operate in confined spaces hitherto restricted to helicopters. Observers could see that it was carrying bigger loads from nearly all the same areas and doing so with relative ease. The helicopters were plagued with mechanical delays, but the Otter went through the month with nothing more than daily maintenance.

The Army was bubbling with enthusiasm at the Otter's performance under such competitive circumstances but they were not the only ones watching. By coincidence the Army Corps of Engineers were in search of a special aircraft for a project of their own – an extensive mapping assignment north of the Brooks Range in Alaska. Both Army interests combined to spark a quick purchase of six Otters. These were

RCMP officers accept the log books for Otter CF-MPP from Buck Buchanan, September 28, 1954, while Geoff Priestley looks on. (DH 9269)

to be off-the-shelf civil machines for a series of evaluations, particularly in the Alaska survey. The first was turned over on January 25, 1955, followed quickly by the others.

The U.S. Navy did not wait long to put in their order, for they too had been impressed at Skydrop II. They needed the Otter for the Antarctic, where the U.S. was taking part in a multi-national exploration program. The U.S. flag was being carried by the Navy, which started with four Otters. This increased to 11. By the time the first Antarctic Otters were delivered in early 1956, they had proven themselves on both sides of the Arctic Circle.

The First Strike

The issue of a shop union did not come up at de Havilland until 1941, during Anson production. The first inroads were made when the employees were handed union leaflets at the corner of Sheppard and Dufferin as they left for home in the evening. There was still much of the family spirit throughout the plant and it was unanimously decided that an employee relations committee be formed under Edgar "Feathers" Featherstonhaugh to meet regularly on shop problems. It functioned successfully for some time but changed during Mosquito days to an employee-run UAW-CIO local.

As the staff grew following the war, the same union continued to represent the workers, and by all accounts the relationship went well. However, pressures built by 1955 to the point where negotiations between company and union became difficult. The meetings that year stalled on one major issue: the union insisted on seeing the company books. Phil Garratt stayed clear of involvement, but his years of struggle to provide employment left him a little biased on the management side of the argument. Finally, negotiations reached the point where George Bird, head of the UAW in the U.S., came up to meet local union officials and company representatives. Garratt agreed to attend one meeting. The preliminaries were dispensed with by about mid-morning and all made their way to the table as befitted a meeting of such importance. The proceedings were opened by Bird with a formality that indicated years of practice.

At the first indication of a

Canadian Pacific Airlines found its two Otters useful on the West Coast. Both were active in the north in the late 1990s with other owners. (Below) A trio of early U.S. Army U-1A Otters before delivery. (DH 1761, '1609)

The Otter instrument panel. (DH 2633)

moved to an office in the Eglinton-Bathurst area. For many years de Havilland had retained legal title to the dormant Central Aircraft Limited which had been used during the war as part of the Mosquito program. The engineering staff simply reported for work each day at the new address as members of Central Aircraft. The strike left a lot of non-union people immobile but a bad forest fire season in northern Ontario made work for the pilot staff. Those who could, assisted the Ontario Department of Lands and Forest in aerial firefighting. Dave Fairbanks recorded 73 hours of such work, flying a Beaver and Norseman in what he later described as some of the toughest flying in his career.

Trans-Antarctic Otters

The Otter arrived on the aviation scene while there was still a lot of old-fashioned glamour connected with flying, particularly in exploration. The histories of exploration aircraft make interesting reading and none more typical than the story of serial No. 126. In July of 1956 an RAF crew arrived to ferry this special orange-coloured Otter to England. The aircraft had been purchased by the British Commonwealth Trans-Antarctic Expedition as part of the upcoming International Geophysical year. Forty nations were to combine their efforts during 1957-8 for a scientific exploration of the south polar continent.

The expedition was the brainchild of Sir Vivian Fuchs, who dreamed it up in 1954 while waiting out a blizzard in Graham Land, Antarctica. Its purpose was to mount a combined Commonwealth effort to complete the first surface crossing of the Antarctic from Shackleton Base on the Weddell Sea to McMurdo Sound on the Ross Sea. It was to be supported by Great Britain, New Zealand, Australia and South Africa and financed by a mixture of government and private donations. The New Zealand portion would be headed by the famous conqueror of Mount Everest, Sir Edmund Hillary, using a Royal New Zealand Air Force Beaver.

The RAF supplied a crew of four, plus two supporting Auster single-engined planes and miscellaneous radio equipment. The Otter was to be the only one operated by the RAF, which used it for the next two years with outstanding success. It was fitted at Downsview with a 177-gallon (805 l) internal tank, giving it twice the normal endurance, and prepared for the Atlantic flight. S/L John Lewis was com-

discussion, Phil Garratt was up on his feet. "Just a minute," he said, "before we waste a lot of time, let's get a couple of things straight. We know nothing about strikes, you do. We don't want a strike, you do. We don't know how a strike will hurt us, so that is up to you. If the question to be decided here is whether you can see the company's books, the answer is no! I don't know what you are going to do, but I think I'll go have a drink." And he walked out.

Everyone was dumbfounded; glances went from one to another. Doug Hunter became red in the face; silence was complete for the better part of a minute. The meeting continued and a strike decision was called. It was the end of June and the first strike in the company's history. When told of the decision, Garratt's comment was, "They'll be back by September – it gets pretty cold then." It was Armistice Day, November 11, before the strikers returned – a day that Garratt felt was significant – and it was getting cold.

It turned out to be an awkward strike. The union tried to keep everyone from entering the plant except supervisory personnel. To avoid trouble, the engineering department

This scene at de Havilland in 1954 shows a mix of activity. Beavers, Otters and Chipmunks are being finished, while down the line an RCAF North Star and Vampire are being overhauled. The nearest Otter on the right, No. 42, became CF-MPP. It served more than 30 years with the RCMP. In the late 1990s it was N234KA with Kenmore Air Harbor in Washington state. (DH 145)

mander with F/L Gordon Heaslip, FSgt. P. Weston and Sgt. E. Williams. Navigator S/L Robert Seymour was along to work out the details of their Atlantic crossing.

Their route from Downsview was Goose Bay, Labrador; BW-1 at Narsarssuaq, Greenland; Keflavik, Iceland; Prestwick, Scotland; ending at Hatfield. Here the Otter was winterized to expedition specifications with a heavy-duty battery, a radio altimeter, a SARAH (Search and Rescue Aircraft Homing) beacon and receiver, a radio compass and a Bendix Polar Path Gyro. Otter 126 now took on the identification XL 710, was crated and was put aboard the ship *Magga Dan*, which set sail from London on November 15, 1956.

The International Geophysical Year began on July 1, 1957, and ended in December 1958. The exercise was a harsh proving ground for some 22 other Beavers and Otters. The U.S. Navy was handling much of the United States' commitment and had been taking part in Operation Deep Freeze since February 1, 1955, making preparations. They started with four Otters and added nine the following year. Australia, New Zealand, Chile and Japan all had Beavers. By early January 1957, the British Commonwealth Otter arrived at Shackleton Base on the Weddell Sea with Sir Vivian Fuchs and his party. The same RAF crew under S/L John Lewis continued with the aircraft, this time without the services of navigator Seymour.

On the other side of the continent Sir Edmund Hillary was setting up his headquarters at Scott Base on McMurdo Sound. The plan was to establish a sub-base between Weddell and the South Pole and move from there to the polar crossing. Sir Edmund, in the meantime, would arrange for depots from the Pole to Scott Base and assist during the balance of the mission. Otter XL 710 surveyed the preliminary route during 19 flights, each averaging 6 1/2 hours. It set up a depot 300 miles (480 km) closer to the Pole, later called South Ice Base, and stocked it for the next summer's drive.

During the winter of 1957 the Otter was stored and covered in a pit. With the approach of summer in September it was made ready for support of the Fuchs' land mission. When the party moved out, Shackleton Base was closed and operations centred for the next few weeks on South Ice Base. Once again when the land party left for their push to the South Pole, S/L Lewis and his crew supported them until it was time to join Sir Edmund Hillary on the other side of the continent. This flight required a little waiting for weather, but they got away on January 6, 1958. Their effort was historic as it was the first attempt at a non-stop crossing of Antarctica in a single-engined aircraft.

They passed the overland party after two hours and reached the South Pole station 2 hours, 40 minutes later.

(Right) A New Zealand Beaver carries sleds underwing during Antarctic operations. (All via DH)

One of the Australian Antarctic Beavers is poled to shore.

(Right) Members of the expedition pose with a Beaver and an Otter.

The British Commonwealth Trans-Antarctic Expedition Otter alongside a Beaver. XL710 eventually worked its way back to Canada as CF-PNV.

Otter 55-3272 (serial No. 118) with experimental aerial surveillance radar pods. It served the U.S. Army from 1956-74, then became CF-BEP with AirDale of Sault Ste. Marie, Ontario. (DH 6292)

(Right) Early in the quiet Otter experiments an external exhaust system was used. Later, a silencer inside the cabin was combined with the five-bladed propeller in a U.S. Navy research program. (DH 5207)

Exactly 11 hours, 1 minute after takeoff, XL710 touched down at Scott Base, a flight of 1,430 statute miles (2,300 km). The Otter continued to work with the New Zealand Beaver throughout the rest of the party's overland mission until the expedition was triumphantly welcomed at Scott Base headquarters.

The end of the expedition did not complete the history of Otter 126; it simply changed allegiance, joined the U.S. Navy and took on the number 147574. In its original orange colour it served from July 1958 to April 1960, flying 148 hours for VX-6 Squadron in the Antarctic. When New Zealand needed an aircraft to replace a Beaver, a USAF C-124 Globemaster flew the Otter to Wellington for overhaul at de Havilland Aircraft Company of New Zealand. By then it only had 408 hours. It flew in RNZAF colours for the first time in November 1961, ready to return to Antarctic duty. Before the new identification, NZ 6081, could be installed, politics and a change of policy by the New Zealand Department of Defence brought another stage in its career. The closing of their Antarctic flight detachment rendered the Otter surplus and it was put up for sale by tender under New Zealand registration ZK-CFH.

Georgian Bay Airways of Parry Sound, Ontario, tendered a bid, bought it sight unseen and had it shipped to Montreal. The registration changed to CF-PNV in March 1964 in time to do a summers's work along the Hudson and James Bay coasts, working from Moosonee. Most of its life in Ontario was spent on amphibious floats or wheel-skis, fulfilling a number of contracts from the resort areas of Muskoka to Frobisher Bay.

In December 1969 PNV moved west to La Ronge Aviation in Saskatchewan, where it worked for the next six years. There it suffered its only major damage. On May 14, 1976,

while taking off from the strip at Lynn Lake, it stalled due to improper loading and fell back onto the runway. There were only minor injuries to the nine people on board but the aircraft was withdrawn from service and its registration cancelled. Old 126 had now served 20 years and looked as if it was destined for retirement as a crippled derelict in the back of a hangar. A new career loomed when title of the aircraft was transferred to Cox Air Resources of Edmonton.

Spy Otter

In May 1957 an interesting experiment was conducted at Downsview for the U.S. Army under a contract to test a "spy plane" Otter. The object was to obtain complete silence and involved a large, five-bladed, fixed-pitch propeller. It didn't have the performance of the standard propeller (in fact it was very restricted) but with the exhaust muted in a series of noise dampeners the aircraft was exceedingly quiet. George Neal and Bob Fowler flew the test series and described the uncanny silence inside and out. There was no sound but the internal clatter of the engine, a sound that is usually well hidden in the regular configuration. The propeller never went past the experimental phase. (Years later six-bladed

The visiting Comet 3 at Downsview during a brief stopover in December 1955. It was back later for repairs. (Left) First officer Peter Bugge and Captain John Cunningham. (DH 2390, DH 3855)

props were used on the Dash 8 Series 400.) In a companion exercise about the same time, a special 360-degree radar installation was tested in a U.S. Army Otter involving two radomes, one on each wing.

Team Work

Those who knew Phil Garratt always marvelled at his tact and diplomacy when dealing with the people in the plant, particularly when there was something difficult or out of the ordinary to be done. He would usually prefix his request with "When you have time…" or "Wouldn't it be nice…" but when the company's reputation was at stake, a sort of mutual understanding took over. One old-timer in the shop summed it up in a few words: "We got to know Phil Garratt because he would come down on the floor and talk to us."

One such occasion was the visit of the Comet 3 to Downsview in 1955. The pressurization problems of the earlier Comet 1s had been rectified after an exhaustive program and the parent de Havilland was sending the new model on a flight around the world to re-establish the airliner's prestige. The Canadian portion of the trip involved Vancouver, Toronto and Montreal before the final dash home to England. The flight in Comet G-ANLO had gone amazingly well with John Cunningham, de Havilland's chief test pilot,

and Peter Bugge as second pilot. R.W. Chandler was radio/navigator. A number of the world's top airline captains rode on various legs, along with DH sales personnel and seven aviation specialists in everything from aerodynamics to engines. The landing at Downsview on December 18 was a courtesy stop, giving recognition to the Canadian branch of the family. A good crowd was on hand to meet the sleek jet as it arrived from Vancouver and the crew, who only two days before had been basking in the sunshine of Hawaii, were treated to a cold Ontario Sunday. Full opportunity was given the Toronto and Montreal airline executives to inspect the Comet during the next two days before its flight to London on the 22nd.

Shortly after takeoff from Dorval that night, the Comet 3 experienced its only mechanical problem of the tour. The jet pipe of No. 3 engine became detached and the subsequent blast blew the large engine cowling doors open. After dumping fuel, Cunningham landed at Montreal. Here the decision was made to remove the damaged doors and make a three-engine ferry to Downsview for repairs. After his retirement in 1980 John Cunningham recalled:

Looking back to that December, I well remember the remarkable effort made by the Downsview staff, over Christmas, in repairing the damage done to our Comet. The weather was bad on the 23rd, but I eventually arrived on three engines at Malton Airport because Downsview was below operational limits. I was driven to the de Havilland plant and met by Phil Garratt and Russ Bannock, shortly after dark. Phil was pouring me a welcoming drink but, before I was able to accept, I looked out of the window and realized that the visibility had improved somewhat and I could see lights on the other side of Downsview. We checked with the Met. office at Malton who said there would be a temporary lifting of the cloud and an improvement in visibility. We dashed back to Malton, got NLO fired up on three engines and took off. I remember flying down the expressway until we saw the lights of the airport. And so it was that our Comet arrived back at Downsview on the night of the 23rd, ready for repairs. I was finally able to accept Phil Garratt's offer of a drink.

By a lot of hard work over Christmas, the DH Canada team cleaned up the engine bay, bolted the jet pipe back to the engine, repaired and refitted the engine bay doors so that on the 27th we left for Dorval. We took off on the night of the 27th and, after a six hour, 20 minute flight, arrived at London airport. We flew to Hatfield later that morning and gave a press demonstration flight there the next day – a fine tribute to the splendid work put in by the DH Canada team. I have many happy memories of my visits to Downsview since 1946, but Christmas 1955, when Peter Bugge and I enjoyed the day with Phil and Jessie Garratt and family, will always remain in memory.

A forest fire rages as an Otter of the Ontario Department of Lands and Forests is readied for another mission. Otter CF-ODL served with the Ontario government from May 1953, frequently as a water bomber. In the 1990s it was flying with Knobby's at Sioux Lookout, Ontario. (DH 7770)

Bill Bozanin was on the repair crew that Christmas and remembered it as a hectic but exhilarating experience: "We had a team organized as soon as we heard about the problem and went to work the moment the Comet was pushed into the hangar. From six to eight of us worked around the clock with little time off to sleep. Bill Stewardson kept us supplied with coffee and snacks, but I recall that we were all able to make it home for our Christmas dinner. There was a lot of damage to the rear of the nacelle but we got it all cleaned up on the 26th and then they were off for Montreal." As a pleasant postscript to the affair, the world flight won John Cunningham the U.S. Harmon International Trophy for 1955.

Tragedy and Hard Work

With the unfortunate strike behind them in 1956, everyone settled down for a productive year. The first Tracker was close to its test flight and the Beaver and Otter lines were moving favourably again; military deliveries were getting back into full swing. During mid-February this new surge of optimism was shattered by the crash of a U.S. Army Otter and the loss of four lives – all within sight of Downsview. It was the first fatal accident since the war at the DH Canada field involving an aircraft manufactured at the plant. When the control tower phoned in the first news that an Otter had broken up in the air, a sombre group gathered in the general manager's office. It was February 14, and three of the dead were U.S. Army pilots from Fort Riley, Kansas, who had arrived only the day before to start flight training. Bill Ferderber was the DH Canada pilot killed. The aircraft they were flying was No. 92 with U.S. Army markings 53252.

Ferderber spent the morning with Major A.G. Aticisson and Captains J.P. Dowling and C.E. Durand preparing for their familiarization flight. They had been in the air about an hour in the Downsview area at approximately 3,000 ft. (900 m) when security guards saw a wing separate from the Otter and the remains spin down into a field. The fact that it came apart in the air was serious, in view of the fine record and the 75,000 hours of flying time Otters had accumulated.

Forty members of the company engineering staff were soon joined by experts from the RCAF, DOT, National Research Council, USAF, U.S. Army and U.S. National Advisory Committee for Aeronautics. Fred Jones of the Royal Aircraft Establishment, Farnborough, England, was also there to help put everything in sequence, go over every square inch of wreckage and determine what failed first.

Some idea of the task they faced can be determined by the records of the photographic department alone. During the investigation some 2,200 photographs were produced, 2,100 ft. (640 m) of film and 5,000 ft. (1,500 m) of oscillogram recording film. Photos were made of all the structural static tests and over 1,500 ft. (460 m) of film were taken in the air to record flight manoeuvres during the aerodynamic trials. Aviation artist Bob Bradford was brought in to piece together, in graphic form, the logical sequence of events and present a step-by-step interpretation of the aircraft's fatal plunge.

The suspected cause was an inadvertent release of flaps. A series of tests was conducted by pilots George Neal and Bob Fowler in a reinforced Otter in an attempt to duplicate the situation. Neal and Fowler, securely strapped into their specially instrumented Otter, arranged bunts on signal, which George could manage with relative ease. After a series of these he reasoned that, although recovery was within the capability of the pilot anticipating the manoeuvre, the abnormality of the original case, coupled with the surprise element, would render recovery out of the question. A contributing factor would undoubtedly have been the forward centre of gravity condition since it was a training flight. It is not difficult to picture three keen students, one in the copilot's seat and two by the cockpit door, looking over his shoulder.

The investigation was going on almost around the clock when a second Otter accident was reported. The location was Goose Bay, but the circumstances were all too similar – a training flight, a sudden bunt and a breakup. Fred Buller and Dick Hiscocks went to the scene. They gathered fresh evidence, adding to what already was known.

With everyone giving the investigation the highest priority, the details slowly emerged. The primary cause was metal contamination holding a valve in the wing flap jack open. When the pilot selected the flaps up, there was no restriction in the hydraulic circuit and the flaps retracted immediately. With the extreme downwash suddenly removed from the tail, the nose pitched down with disastrous results. Combined with the element of surprise and the forward centre of gravity, this caused overstressing and an immediate breakup of the wing.

In the Toronto accident, the wing had passed under the fuselage and made sufficient contact with the fin area to completely remove the tail section. After long months of investigation, the details of the accident finally settled into place. DHC set to work to eliminate any such future occurrence. An interlocking mechanism coupled an elevator tab to the flaps, automatically compensating for any abrupt changes of trim without pilot input. The same device was used later in the Twin Otter.

The Move to Missiles

Shortly after the Tracker program was announced, a new division at Downsview led de Havilland Canada into the sophisticated field of missiles. It all started because of the close ties with de Havilland Propellers Limited, leaders in British missile technology. The new Guided Missile Division at DH Canada was able to provide the Canadian government with technical units drawing on British missile experience and technical know-how. The classified nature of the work meant little publicity. Not much was known, even in Downsview, of what went on behind the doors marked "Secret." The new division played a major part in the Tracker program with the installation of the intricate avionic equipment.

The sphere of this new operation included control engineering, electromechanics, optics and infrared studies, as applied to guidance, auxiliary power, fusing, missile ancillaries and fire control. The division took part in the Velvet Glove and Sparrow II missile programs. It also took part in U.S. Navy missile developments, always classified "highly secret." Two specialist areas for the Canadians were missile auxiliary power units and infrared calculations. Specialty work was started on inverters and alternators. It was the only integrated infrared research and application capability in Canada. The department worked in conjunction with de Havilland Propellers on the Firestreak air-to-air missile, used on the Sea Vixen.

In 1960 the name was changed to Special Products Division, embracing all the former activities and expanded to include the operations of the former Engine and Propeller Division at the north plant.

The STEM

Throughout the late 1950s, de Havilland was earning a reputation in the art of forming sophisticated metals into difficult shapes. Bob Prout was always taking on these new challenges, but a call he received at a quarter to five one evening from Dr. Phil Lapp of the Special Products Division had him stumped – temporarily. The next morning Lapp explained that de Havilland had acquired the rights to produce an idea that had been patented by George Klein of the National Research Council. He wanted a long metal strip that would coil in and out like a carpenter's rule and form a rigid pole. "Once I knew what he wanted," recalled Bob, "I figured we could do it and headed back to the shop. It took quite a while, but finally we made it work and it became STEM (Storable Tubular Extendable Member)."

The success of STEM was immediate. The de Havilland self-erecting antennas went on to become an important element in every subsequent U.S./Canada space satellite program. In its final form, STEM consisted of a stowage drum, an unfurling element, a drive pinion and a guide roller. It was designed for either motorized extension and retraction or self-extension in which the tightly wound metal tape used its inherent energy to propel itself and form a 360-degree tube as it extended. STEM devices also served as land antennas, vehicular masts or even hand-held exploration communicators. They varied from 15 inches (38 cm) to 850 feet (260 m).

A companion project added to the Division's prestige when they built the hull for Canada's first satellite, Alouette I, also equipped with STEM antennas. A 75-foot STEM unit was produced for the Canadian Javelin rocket tests.

To ensure a Canadian presence during the installation of the Boeing Bomarc missiles in Canada, a consortium company called DCF Systems Limited was formed. DHC's Special Products Division was the lead member, with CAE (Montreal) and Ferranti Packard (Toronto) as the other participating companies; their initials formed the name for the new company. The 30 to 40 Canadians from the consortium assisted Boeing in installing the Bomarcs in their shelters at North Bay, Ontario, and La Macaza, Quebec, in 1961 and 1962. The bases were turned over to the RCAF upon their completion.

In 1962 the facilities of the Special Products Division were expanded by the acquisition of Canadian Applied Re-

The idea for an extendable antenna came with the building of the Alouette. The STEM (Storable Tubular Extendable Member) was a coiled spring that shot out on command like a carpenter's rule to a distance of 75 feet. (DH 41215 via W. Turner)

(Below) The once-secret 300-lb. (136-kg) Alouette or S-27 Topsider Sounder in its final stages ready to launch. The structure was an oblate sphere covered with silicon cells to convert the sun's rays into electricity. The preliminary work under the direction of Ottawa's Defence and Telecommunications Establishment (DRTE) began in DHC's north plant and later moved to new quarters at Malton. (DH 26342 via W. Turner)

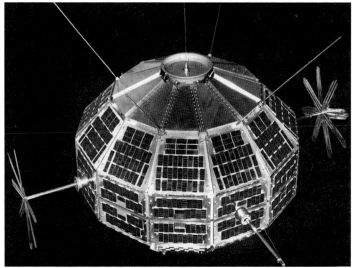

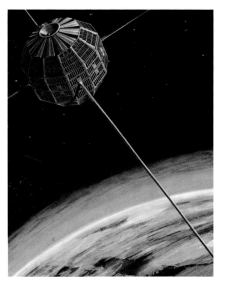

(Left) A view by artist D.A. Kletke of Alouette in orbit, with STEM antennas extended. The satellite was built to explore the ionosphere.

search, a company formed in 1947 as part of the Avro complex. The combined organization, under the new name SPAR (Special Products and Applied Research) was headed by vice-president Doug Annan. They took over 260,000 sq. ft. (24,000 sq. m) at Malton and employed up to 600 people.

In a few years Larry D. Clarke moved from contract administrator to manager of SPAR. By then the division had built up considerable as-

Otter 3682 runs up atop its test stand. This experiment gathered STOL data while the Otter remained on terra firma. (DH 7472)

sets and equipment, but throughout the troubled years of the Douglas contract (dealt with later) had always operated in the background. Clarke came up with an offer to purchase the division for $1,350,000, which was approved by Hawker Siddeley. From 1969 SPAR became a separate entity with Larry Clarke as its head. A number of de Havilland specialists accompanied him. They moved to the forefront of the space industry. In a tough environment SPAR continued to mix sound business with scientific ability. One of their finest accomplishments is the remote manipulator system or Canadarm, used successfully on the space shuttle.

Slower STOL

While the Otter's reputation grew, others were watching its progress on the scientific side – those who wished to probe more deeply into STOL technology. The National Research Council and the Defence Research Board in Ottawa had always worked closely with de Havilland on the aerodynamic aspects of STOL. With the advent of the Otter they sought to explore further.

Discussions on the subject between the Canadian Defence Research Board and DHC as early as 1956 resulted in a joint research program. It revolved around existing Otter technology and went deeper into the areas of slow flight and steep approach. A report at the time spelled out their reasoning: "The purpose of the DRB/DHC program is to assess the aerodynamic performance, stability and control problems of STOL aircraft with the object of finding new refinements in the art." RCAF Otter 3682 was modified for a program that was to have three stages. The beam-type landing gear, looking like small floats, was capable of absorbing steeper descent touch-down speeds. The tail was high out of the propeller slipstream and used butterfly-type elevators. In the initial stages, measurements were made of the aerodynamic characteristics of the Otter in its standard configuration. Next, a series of novel aerodynamic features was planned to study slipstream deflection and boundary layer control.

Looking like a huge bat, Otter 3682 flies along the taxiway behind DHC's flight test hangar. Trackers beyond await delivery to the RCN. (DH 11217)

The STOL Otter with the modified tail, special undercarriage and fuselage-mounted J85 turbojet. Note the intake for the J85 atop the fuselage. (DH 15070)

absorption. The major change was the installation of a General Electric J85-GE-7 turbo jet in the rear fuselage with the jet exhaust directed out each side through fully-modulated diverters. A control in the cockpit enabled the pilot to direct the jet thrust forward or back. This configuration examined in-flight reverse effects in combination with slipstream deflection. Test pilot Bob Fowler did the flying during 1961 and 1962 with encouraging results. A speed as low as 48 mph was obtained.

In the slow-flight experiments a large bat-wing flap was installed. Then the aircraft was mounted on a stand and towed behind a truck at 35 mph to study the flight characteristics close to the ground. These experiments determined the type of gear and the size of the larger tail section still to be designed. When the aircraft was ready for flight trials, George Neal conducted a series of short flights close to the ground, then at altitude, gathering data. This series terminated in 1960.

The second stage used modified Otter wing flaps and had the undercarriage strengthened to twice the standard energy

About 200 hours had been logged when Pratt & Whitney announced the PT6. Fowler's involvement in test flying this engine opened new avenues of thought at de Havilland. The engines were not available commercially, but two test models were rented and installed in the experimental machine. With the slipstream from two propellers plus the effect of the vectored-thrust J85, a wide range of data could be recorded. The program terminated in 1965; by then, talks had started on the design of a twin-engined Otter. The twin-engine configuration was the most noticeable feature to emerge from the experimental program. The greatest advantage was the data and experience gained during 300 hours of flying in the slow flight regime and its relation to STOL landings. Bob Fowler's contributions were in the interpretation of human reactions to steep descent and the co-ordination needed for landing in this configuration. The experimental Otter added considerably to the company's depth of STOL technology that was later reflected in the product line.

Otter 3682 with twin PT6 engines, an internal J85 turbo jet, and its unique undercarriage. This was the first fixed-wing twin application of the PT6. (DH 19154)

The Export Business

As assemblers of British-made products from 1928 until the war in 1939, DHC's sales objectives lay naturally within Canadian borders. Even postwar sales were planned around the Canadian market until circumstances forced a broader outlook. The first indication that the rest of the world was interested came with the sale of 13 Fox Moths in 1947-48 to India, Southern Rhodesia and New Zealand. When the Chipmunk went into production, 90 of the first batch went for export. The design was even exported to the U.K. so it could be built there for the "soft currency" countries.

A large department packed and crated Beavers for shipment around the world. The first 100 went mainly to the hungry Canadian market from 1948 to 1951, with only 18 to the United States and abroad. Of the second 100 delivered, 65 were exports. The same general pattern developed with the Otter, where exports jumped from 34 in the first 100 to 88 in the second. Sales continued strongly into the 1950s.

Two new offices sprang up because of the U.S. military commitment to the L-20 Beaver. W/C Derry Wray managed the increasing business at Ottawa, while Col. Joe E. McDonald was U.S. liaison in Washington. When Derry Wray died in 1951, Garratt approached Donald L. "Buck" Buchanan, who was secretary-manager of the Royal Canadian Flying Clubs Association, and invited him to become the Ottawa representative. Buchanan obtained his early education in Guelph and was in editing and publishing before the outbreak of war. He joined the RCAF in 1940, serving as a flight instructor first at Mount Hope, then at Oshawa, Dunnville and Trenton until 1943. A posting overseas to 419 Squadron put him into Lancasters; later he moved to 420 Squadron on Halifaxes in July 1944. He became a squadron leader, served as flight commander of 420 and won a DFC before his discharge in July 1945. He took up publishing briefly again but returned to aviation in 1946 to manage the RCFCA.

Buchanan's chores with DHC in Ottawa were many: from DOT liaison and chasing contracts through the government maze to entertaining guests. The main sales responsibilities rested at headquarters with Russ Bannock as director of military sales and Punch Dickins as director of civil sales. A.F. "Sandy" MacDonald was sales manager but most of the orders from outside the country came through DH agents around the world shared with the parent company.

In April 1955 Sandy MacDonald took over public relations and Buck Buchanan moved back to Downsview as sales manager. This was the unprecedented growth period with over 800 Beavers and 75 Otters in operation. When a

Russ Bannock

Buck Buchanan

George Hurren

Geoff Priestley

Tony Verrico

John Shaw

The de Havilland Canada sales team at its formation in 1960. When Punch Dickins retired, vice-presidents were Russ Bannock and later Buck Buchanan. (DH)

major sale to Malaysia began to drag, Buchanan asked for the services of G.V. "Geoff" Priestley, who up to that point had been doing contract administration at a desk outside Punch Dickins' office.

The volume of paper work, which grew as shipments increased, and the wide geographical coverage held a message for Buchanan that he could not ignore. "The Canadian and U.S. orders were easily managed from Toronto," said Buchanan, "but when the amount of paperwork on some of the foreign sales began to equal the weight of the airplane, we had to get a little more efficiency into our dealings with new customers." Under the arrangements existing at the time, the solicitation of new business in the foreign field was handled by DH area representatives, whose services and costs were shared with the parent company. The same applied to agents who held exclusive sales rights in their respective countries. Buchanan recalled:

The DH area representatives were experienced, able and energetic, but they had interests other than DH Canada to serve. We also enjoyed close ties with our agents but they, too, had other principals to serve. We were relatively new boys in the game and often wondered if we were getting the dedication to the DH Canada cause that we wanted. The development of international business clearly indicated that we get out and beat the bushes on our own with representation directly from the Downsview headquarters.

In 1960 a Beaver order for the Ghana Air force was a typical case and proved to be a turning point in our sales approach. It started shortly after the world tour with an early morning telephone call I received from an old fishing friend, Air Commodore Fred Carpenter of the RCAF. Fred was at the United Nations in New York on business and indicated that there was the possibility of a sale to Ghana. I rushed to New York and that afternoon I was introduced to the general commanding the armed forces of Ghana. He was visiting his country's mission at the UN and before the day ended, I had negotiated the sale of 14 Beaver aircraft. The general and his staff were in the process of establishing the Ghana Air Force and discussions indicated the likelihood of requirements in the near future for Otter, Caribou and Chipmunk aircraft as the new service progressed.

When the contract documents were ready I sent Geoff Priestley to Accra for the signing. He was fully briefed on the situation and, in addition to the signing, visited the Ghana Air Force main base at Takoradi. We became involved with the development of their air force, which netted us two million in Otter sales and a Caribou order of five and three quarter million dollars. The Ghanaians also bought Chipmunks from England to become the first organization, civil or military, to operate all our Canadian types.

Buchanan now received approval to broaden his international coverage and enlarge his sales staff. Geoff Priestley took charge of Africa and the Middle East, while Tony Verrico moved from the test flight department to begin a search for customers in the Far East. John F.B. Shaw joined the company after a career on helicopters with the British military. Buck selected him for South America, which involved learning Spanish. Shaw tackled the assignment in two stages. First he took a university language course in Toronto; then he lived for 12 weeks in the homes of the agents in Caracas and Bogotá, where only Spanish was spoken. He combined his new-found knowledge with his flying background and was soon selling DHC products to 14 countries in South America.

The North American market remained strong but was becoming a special field. Buchanan brought George Hurren from Ottawa, where he had been managing company affairs since 1955. Like Buchanan he had considerable wartime experience and associated himself with the Royal Canadian Flying Club movement. He was manager when he was asked to take over the Ottawa office of DH Canada, filling the role Buchanan had vacated. Hurren's sales responsibilities at Downsview began with Canada and slowly enlarged to encompass North America and the Caribbean.

The marketing team that began in the early 1960s remained relatively intact for the next 20 years. The salesmen became as well known in their territories as they were at Downsview: Tony Verrico and Peter Adams in the Far East, Geoff Priestley in Africa, and John Shaw in South America. George Hurren looked after Canada and the U.S., and all reported through Buchanan to the vice-president sales, Punch Dickins. The group built up a remarkable record, with exports growing from 40 per cent in 1960 to 85 per cent 10 years later. In the period after 1970 when Buchanan became vice-president of sales, yearly sales averaged $60-80 million with a peak in 1976 of $130 million.

Beaver 1000

On November 10, 1956, the company joined in a happy ceremony to present Beaver number 1000 to "the Boss" in recognition of his years of leadership. The registration was to carry his initials, CF-PCG. During the preliminaries leading to this gala occasion, Phil Garratt was asked what colour he wanted on his personal aircraft. The reply was a typical Garratt quote: "You can paint it any colour you like as long as it is yellow!" One year later the parent de Havilland company paid him a similar honour with a full directorship in the British company.

All of these accolades brought out a new round of Garratt stories. He was typical of the old school that managed with a father image, a firm hand and an adroit smile. Responsibil-

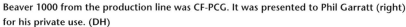

Beaver 1000 from the production line was CF-PCG. It was presented to Phil Garratt (right) for his private use. (DH)

ity charts were not for him, and when asked for his methods, he said simply, "I run the company and my managers can come and see me at any time." Bill Burlison was a typical manger of the period who was in charge of production. "There was no one between Mr. Garratt and myself," recalled Bill, "and he made it clear I could go to him any time I liked. This was quite true, but you can be sure I checked everything out at my own level before I would dare call on him for a decision. Only Phil Garratt could make such a system work!"

It was not a period of marathon meetings. Most important decisions were made over the big round table in the directors' dining room. Often when an awkward situation arose, Garratt would invite the participants to dinner at the Granite Club and by morning the problem would usually be settled. He tried to keep everything simple and was a great believer in the personal approach. He discouraged any memo of more than a page, and once when someone offered to lend him a book, his quick reply was, "But I have a book."

The early de Havilland world organization made a policy of recognizing long-service employees at 10-year intervals. Here the new Canadian members of the 20-year club gather in 1957 to receive their scroll, pin, £20 and a subscription to the *Gazette.* From left: Harry Kentner, Bill Duck, Bill Houston, Bob Wright, Gordon Fatherby, Phil Garratt, Simon Gung, Harry Johns, Howard MacDonald, Herb Bennett and Sam Creelnan. (DH 7556)

In early 1998 there were 134 Canadian-registered Otters, more than in the 1950s-60s. In this summer 1995 scene, Randy Winters flies C-FAPR of Ignace Airways over Bell Lake northeast of Ignace, Ontario. The 31st Otter, APR had begun in 1954 with the Royal Norwegian Air Force. It served until 1967, then went to Widerøe Flyveselskap A/S. In 1971 it returned to Canada, first with Laurentian Air Service of Ottawa. (Richard Hulina)

Otters frequently serve tourist operators, carrying cottagers, fishermen and hunters to favourite spots. C-GLQX rolled out early in 1960 as a U.S. Army U-1A. It later served the U.S. Civil Air Patrol in Alaska, then came to Canada in 1977 for Gander Aviation. Next it was with Lindbergh's Air Service in Cochrane, Ontario, then Air Wemindji, a First Nations operator in northern Quebec. (Andy Graham)

(Above) Beavers and an Otter at the Air Saguenay base on Lac Sebastien, north of St-Honoré, Quebec, in June 1989. (Richard Beaudet)

(Right) C-GLCW in for a check at Sault Ste. Marie in July 1991. The 172nd Otter, it served the U.S. Army 1956-74. Eventually it came to Leuenberger Air Service of Nakina, Ontario, and in 1997 was converted to a PT6A-34. In 1998 it was flying alongside turbo Otter C-GLCS and piston Otter C-FSOX. On extended 7170 floats and with other mods, LCW had a gross weight of 8,367 lb. (3,800 kg), compared to the standard 7,967 lb. (3,600 kg). It had flown more than 16,000 hours by mid-1998. Leuenberger liked to fly each of its Otters about 425 hours yearly. (Larry Milberry)

Gulf Air's C-FLCP, flown by veteran West Coast pilot Jack Schofield, cruises near Campbell River in September 1980. Originally delivered to the Ghana Air Force in 1961, LCP returned to Canada in 1974 to serve various operators. In 1998 it was with Mid Coast Air Services of Gibsons, B.C. Ken Swartz took this photo from Beaver C-FJBP.

184

Northern Wilderness Outfitters Otter C-GMDG gets an engine change at Fort Frances, Ontario, in June 1993. A 1958-model U.S. Army U-1A, it later served in Alaska with Frontier Flying Service, but returned to Canada in 1980. (Andy Graham)

(Right) A famous Otter role was water bombing, systems for which were developed at Sault Ste. Marie in the 1950s-60s by the Ontario Department of Lands and Forests, and by Field Aviation of Toronto. Each summer Otters extinguished many small fires, and fought larger ones in conjunction with crews on the ground and larger types like the Tracker and Twin Otter. Here Ontario government Otter C-FODP demonstrates water bombing at Toronto's 1975 CNE airshow. (Larry Milberry)

(Below) C-FWJB-X served the RCAF 1956-65, then went to Gander Aviation. Later it was with Gateway Aviation and Labrador Airways. After an accident and rebuild, it went to Airtech of Peterborough, Ontario, to become the first Otter with a Polish PZL engine. Test pilot Paul Hartman and Airtech president Bogdan Wolski made the historic first flight with a 600 hp PZL on February 12, 1980. Although the engine was lighter than an R1430, performance benefits were marginal, prompting Airtech to jump to the 1,000 hp PZL. WJB is seen at Hamilton on June 21, 1980, with the 600 hp PZL. (Dave Thompson)

Although noisier and harder on gas, Airtech's 1,000-hp PZL Otter has improved takeoff performance, higher cruise speed and requires less maintenance than an R1340. C-FODJ, the 14th Otter, began with the Ontario government in May 1953. After more than three decades, it joined Green Airways, a famous Northern Ontario operator. There it became a PZL Otter. It's shown in July 1993 at a tourist camp on Birch Lake near Red Lake. (Left) ODJ's pilot David Robertson en route to Birch Lake. By 1998 Airtech had done 15 1,000-hp conversions and was planning its first Otter with the new Orenda piston engine. (Larry Milberry)

(Below) The Otter adapted easily to amphibious floats. Although expensive, these opened new markets. A resort operator could meet guests at an airport like Thunder Bay or Prince Rupert, fly them out for fishing, then return them to the airport to catch their flights home. Coast pilot Uwe Ihssen photographed amphibious Otter C-FQRI at Port Hardy in August 1980.

This Australian Otter was at Stradbroke Island, Queensland, in 1998 still in the colours it carried for years with the Ontario Provincial Police. With the OPP it flew from Timmins, patrolling the vast, often-frigid Ontario northland. In 1997 another Canadian Otter made its way "down under" – C-FBEO of La Ronge Aviation. It became VH-OTR with Aquaflight Airways at Cairns in northern Queensland. (Lenn Bayliss)

Otter CF-IKT went to Canadian Aircraft Renters at Toronto Island Airport in January 1956. That year DHC delivered 115 Otters and 159 Beavers, so times were booming. Here IKT was with Austin Airways at Mount Hope, Ontario, in May 1967. It later was with Labair of Gander, and Newfoundland Labrador Air Transport of Corner Brook. For a while it used a 600-hp PZL, but poor performance saw it re-converted to the R1340. In 1985 IKT moved to Goose Bay Air Service, then went back to Labair. (Larry Milberry)

(Above) Otter C-FODL wore various colour schemes over the years since it was delivered in 1953 to the Ontario Department of Lands and Forests. Here it was at Sioux Lookout in 1997 on wheel-skis. (Richard Hulina)

(Left) CF-ODT started with the Ontario government, but later moved to White River Air Services. Here it was at Nakina, loading for a March 3, 1975, charter to Ogoki Post on the Albany River. Twenty years later it was going strong with Expeditair, a northern Quebec carrier. (Larry Milberry)

187

Many Otters served in aerial survey, mostly doing electromagnetic searches for mineral deposits. CF-IUZ-X carried its electronic equipment in underwing pods and in the fuselage, where an operator monitored readings. This work was done at low altitude, so the flying often was hard on both plane and crew. IUZ was photographed at Oshawa in July 1972. It later served with Air Roberval in northern Quebec. (Larry Milberry)

Most U.S. Army U-1A Otters flew in a standard khaki like these on detachment at Bosco Mantico, Italy, in 1957. This scene also includes a Cessna L-19 (nearest), an L-20 Beaver and some Sikorsky H-34 helicopters. (Dick Gleasure)

58-1696, one of the last two U.S. military Otters, served on utility duties at Goose Bay from 1963-75, where it was seen in March 1975. Declared surplus a few days later, it joined Newfoundland Labrador Air Transport in 1981 as C-GLJH. In the late 1990s it was in Manitoba with First Nations bush operator Sowind Air. (Larry Milberry)

Canadian Air Reserve Otters served for decades on wheels, skis and floats. These examples were with 401 Squadron at St. Hubert from the 1960s through the 1980s. (via Anthony Valenti)

RCAF Otter 3743 over the Sinai desert in 1957 while with No. 115 Air Transport Unit. It later was CF-WJB with various bush operators, then was the prototype PZL Otter. (CF)

(Right) Amphibious Otter 3691 was at Winnipeg in 1966 in standard RCAF search and rescue colours. In 1998 this Otter was N100BW with Rainbow King Lodge of Iliamna, Alaska. (Andy Graham)

(Left) No. 9405 refuels at Winnipeg in an Andy Graham scene from 1966. After 16 years in the military, 9405 be-came C-GSMG of Sioux Narrows Airways.

(Left) Otters 9413 and 3685 escort ex-RCAF Lysander R9003 over Toronto Island Airport during the 1968 CNE airshow. The Lysander, a progenitor of STOL design, had been restored by Barry Lapointe as a project honouring Canada's 100th aniversary in 1967. It later joined the National Aviation Museum. Otter 9413 ended its days in a July 1975 mishap at Duke of York Bay, NWT. After its career in search and rescue and with reserve squadrons, in 1971 3685 went for a tour to Gander Aviation as CF-QOQ. It also ended badly, crashing at Whitehorse while with Air North in 1981. But it was restored and in 1998 was with Air Saguenay. (Larry Milberry)

189

(Left top) A Downsview-based Air Reserve Otter doing float training in Toronto Harbour on November 10, 1973. In 1998 it was N26DE with All West Freight in Flat, Alaska. (Larry Milberry)

(Left) The turbo Otter began in 1972 with a short-lived conversion to a Garrett engine. Cox Air Resources of Edmonton followed with a PT6 version. Cox toiled for years without success. By the 1990s, however, PT6A-27 and -34 Otters had won support. With 750 shp , a turbo Otter offers improved performance, reduced maintenance, great cold weather starting, and a quiet cabin compared to the ear-shattering piston Otter. The supplementary type certificate for all the 1990s turbine Otter conversions was held by Vazar of Bellingham, Washington. In this view, Harbour Air turbo Otter C-GUTW takes off from the Fraser River at Vancouver International Airport in April 1992. Carrying a dozen sportsmen from the U.S., it was headed north to an exclusive salmon fishing resort. UTW was ex-RCAF 9423, built in 1960. Its career included stints with 4 Operational Training Unit and 102 Communications Unit (Trenton, Ontario); 116 Air Transport Unit on UN duty (New Guinea); 400 Squadron (Toronto), 424 Squadron (Hamilton) and 438 Squadron (St. Hubert). (Larry Milberry)

(Below) Turbo Otter C-FCMY of Central Mountain Airlines over Smithers, B.C., in 1991, with Hudson Bay Mountain beyond. With another operator, CMY was lost in bad weather on the B.C. coast in August 1996. (Grant Webb)

Turbo Otter C-FXUY, a Twin Otter and a Turbo Beaver, all of Air Tindi, are seen at Yellowknife on June 26, 1993. (Larry Milberry)

(Above) A DH-built Grumman Tracker of 880 Squadron flies over Prince Edward County, Ontario, practising for the CNE airshow on August 31, 1972. (Below) In the early 1970s Ontario's Department of Lands and Forests acquired several ex-RCN Trackers for conversion to water bombers. Field Aviation of Toronto designed the water drop system, while de Havilland did other engineering work. Tracker CF-OPX on fire-fighting standby at Kenora, Ontario, in July 1974. Ontario later sold its Trackers to Saskatchewan, where most still served in the 1990s. (Larry Milberry)

CHAPTER SEVEN

THE CARIBOU

If ever de Havilland Canada wanted to reflect upon when it came of age, the answer is somewhere in the Caribou program. In the wake of earlier successes, the decision to enter the big league with a large twin-engine design was accepted without a qualm by all concerned. Certainly the drama began with a formidable cast of players, but much was to be learned before the box office tallied the receipts or the final curtain fell. No project came closer to bankrupting DHC, yet the Caribou is credited with setting the company on the trail to world status in the industry.

Planning for the fourth DHC design did not happen overnight. With the Otter safely launched, the engineers began thinking of a twin-engined machine that would con-

tinue the workhorse heritage and incorporate their growing lead in STOL technology. Aircraft size did not bother the designers, but the choice of power plant did. As early as 1954 a study was conducted involving an airplane of 13,000 lb. (5,850 kg) gross weight with two P&W R1340s. It showed very little gain over the Otter and was dropped while still on paper. A second study set gross weight at 22,000 lb. (9,900 kg) with two 1,200 hp engines and transport carrier certification. This study was discontinued as commercially unattractive, but the search went on for a proper engine/airframe combination. Five power plants were considered; even a four-engine configuration was visualized. If the engine was a dilemma, so also was the choice of customer. The average Canadian bush operator would never be able to afford such a large aircraft and the big-money customer at Downsview was now the U.S. Army. The Tracker program was going well by this time and a feeling of optimism prevailed at all levels of the organization.

While deliberations for a new design continued, Russ Bannock, director of military sales, made regular trips to Washington. He was pleased to hear the glowing reports of Beavers and Otters in Army service and often heard, "This is what we want next." The ultimate in the Army's eyes, according to these discussions, was a three-ton tactical transport with rear loading. Fortunately this was in line with DHC thinking. With this limited input, the design team settled on two P&W R2000-7M2s of 1,450 hp each. This would allow a maximum weight of 28,500 lb. (12,825 kg). Turbine engines were ruled out, but an adjustable rear loading ramp with inward-folding doors was considered a must.

A general specification was drawn up in early 1957, complete with drawings, and presented to the right people on Bannock's next visit to the Pentagon. First impressions brought signs of interest along with an informal suggestion that Russ "stick around" for a few days. His vigilance paid off three days later when he was invited to meet with the Director of Army Aviation and the Secretary of the Army. Things moved quickly at this meeting, for Russ was confronted almost immediately with the question "How much for five and when could we get them?" This time it was Bannock's turn to

A 1954 painting by Robert Bradford illustrating DHC's concept for a twin-engine STOL transport with fixed gear and rear clamshell doors.

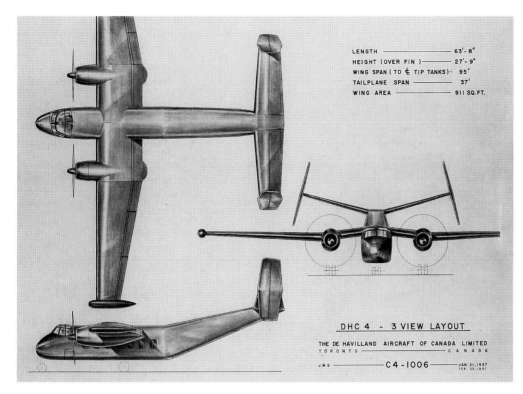

LENGTH ——————————— 63'- 8"
HEIGHT (OVER FIN) —————— 27'- 9"
WING SPAN (TO ₵ TIP TANKS)- 95'
TAILPLANE SPAN ——————— 37'
WING AREA ——————————— 911 SQ.FT.

DHC 4 - 3 VIEW LAYOUT
THE DE HAVILLAND AIRCRAFT OF CANADA LIMITED
T O R O N T O ——————— C A N A D A
J.W.S. ————— C4-1006 —— JAN. 21, 1957
FEB. 25, 1957

A January 1957 layout of the Caribou showing a preliminary twin tail arrangement. (DH 678)

place in Garratt's office during the next hour and Hunter returned the call to Washington with, "Phil says its OK." Within three months a Pentagon order arrived for the first five Caribous.

Design in a Hurry

Wind tunnel models were used to establish airfoil properties of the Caribou. Because of the suddenly crowded timetable, a unique method of testing was developed. The model, with all its connected gadgetry, was mounted on the front of a truck and driven up and down the runway. This worked so well that soon a similar system was flown on

say "stick around" as he headed for a telephone booth in the corridor and called Doug Hunter in Downsview. The urgency of the situation was impressed on the director of engineering along with the suggestion that the price be set at $500,000 each, with delivery in 24 months. Serious discussions took

the back of an Otter, giving a quick source of aerodynamic data. Two tail configurations were considered: a twin fin with an upswept stabilizer, and a more conventional single vertical tail. The latter was chosen along with a retracting undercarriage. Large, double-slotted flaps covered the whole

A scale model of the Caribou atop an elaborate framework on the prototype Otter. This provided quick aerodynamic information. (Right) A wooden mockup was constructed to confirm dimensions and was photographed with the lead team: George Neal in the cockpit, Dick Hiscocks, W.D. Hunter and Fred Buller. (DH)

(Above) Caribou No. 1 during the early stages of construction. (DH 2280)

(Left) The same Caribou, by now registered CF-KTK-X, on its first flight, July 30, 1958. (DH 8665)

(Below) The crew on the first Caribou flight: George Neal, Hans Brinkman and Dave Fairbanks. (DH 8678)

The Honourable George R. Pearkes, Minister of Defence (left), P.C. Garratt and Air Marshal H.L. Campbell were on hand for the Caribou media day. (DH 8862)

All the DHC types lined up for media day: Chipmunk, Beaver, Otter and Caribou. (Howard Levy)

span, with the outboards serving as ailerons, similar to the Otter. A good deal of attention was given to cargo loading and cabin size. The original layout drawings were dated January 21, 1957, and, in an effort involving nearly everyone in the plant, the prototype was readied for flight in the summer of 1958. On July 30 at 2:30 p.m. the test crew of George Neal, Dave Fairbanks and H. Brinkman took Caribou No. 1 on a two-hour first flight.

Exhilaration swept though the organization at this milestone. No one could begrudge the feelings of pride on September 17 when the press were invited to witness the Caribou in action. Even the British Comet was over to round

out the display and add to the excitement. The Chipmunk, Beaver and Otter performed in turn with emphasis on short landings and slow manoeuvring. Rain forced the guests into the hangars during the main event, but the Caribou performed anyway to rave reviews in the papers the next day.

A small run of 20 machines was begun, including the five evaluation aircraft for the U.S. Army, which now called the aircraft the YAC-1. There still were cries of concern from the U.S. aircraft industry and considerable opposition to the Army buying another Canadian-made aircraft, even though there were no competitors in the category. When the first of the Army machines arrived at test flight, it joined in the certification flying. This had reached the stage where the Department of Transport chief evaluation pilot was taking part.

The licensing standard for the Caribou was the U.S. civil certification rule governing twin-engined transports, then called CAR 4b. It was the world-accepted norm and was accepted by Canada's DOT, which began working regularly with DHC on the step-by-step procedure. Chief pilot George Neal and his crew were busy, for this was the first time DHC was breaking new ground in the certification of an original design in the 24,000-lb. (10,800 kg) gross weight, twin-engine class.

Testing progressed satisfactorily through 1959, even though equipment and techniques to do the job were not as

(Below) The second Caribou demonstrates its abilities to the military at Camp Borden, Ontario. (DH 9112)

Caribou CF-LAN with its original nose section and (below) with the 42-inch (107 cm) addition forward of the propeller danger line. This allowed an additional window. (DH 6094, 9457)

(Below) A view of Downsview looking northward during the Caribou period. The plant is in the foreground, with DHC's taxiway leading toward the runways. Runway 33-15 runs between the RCAF and RCN complexes at the top, while the shorter Runway 27-09 crosses the middle of the field. (DH 13721)

196

A typical installation of the R2000 engine on the Caribou. (DH 8332)

A Day to Remember

Tuesday, February 24, started like any other for Neal and Gadzos, who were pleased with the progress they were making. The dive presented no anxiety since Neal already had completed the same manoeuvre with the prototype. At 10,000 ft. (3,000 m) in their dive – at 265 mph (426 km/h) – a high frequency buzzing developed in the elevator control which Neal diagnosed as spring tab flutter. This excited the elevator, and even though speed immediately was reduced, excessive vibration continued.

At 180 mph (290 km/h) an audible structural failure occurred on the port elevator with a resulting change in the control column oscillations. Slowing the aircraft and even shutting off the engines made no difference to the fluttering elevator; the decision was made to abandon the aircraft. By then they had lost considerable altitude. Gadzos had some trouble with the escape hatch in the cockpit floor. When it did open, he went through with the push and hung upside down momentarily by his legs. George Neal prepared to follow, but paused for one more check – he shut off all switches and fuel, tucked his pencils and clipboard under the co-pilot cushion and jumped at 3,000 ft. (900 m). As the silk snapped open and quiet prevailed, he watched LKI continue on its final path with a flapping noise like a broken window blind.

sophisticated as in later years. The flutter tests, in which the aircraft is flown to its maximum designed dive limit, were completed to '4b standards and the program moved to stalls. Neal found the "power off" stalls borderline but controllable with aileron. They were written up as such in the general reports. The "power on" stall was limited to rudder control but considered within the bounds of certification at the time. A year-end meeting was held to summarize progress; Neal prepared a list of 24 items needed before finalization, including a stick-shaker stall warning.

It was during the early testing that a decision was made to add 42 in. (107 cm) to the cabin forward of the wing to obtain the proper centre of gravity range. This was introduced in serial No. 3, which joined the program as CF-LKI-X (U.S. Army No. 57-3079). The program was nearing the end and Neal was working with DOT test pilot Walter Gadzos in clearing up outstanding items. One was a repeat of the dive to 280 mph (450 km/h) to test for flutter due to the lengthened fuselage and the fact that additions had been made to tailplane trimming.

Caribou CF-LKI-X on the line in U.S. Army markings. Then, its remains near Uxbridge after the maximum dive sequence and the spring tab problem. The absence of fire allowed a quick diagnosis by the accident investigators. (DH)

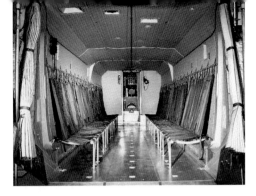

A typical military Caribou interior with folding troop seats. Then, a Caribou making a supply drop. Another loads jeeps and troops, while preproduction Caribou 73081 loads a Canadair CL-91 all-terrain vehicle. (DH, Canadair)

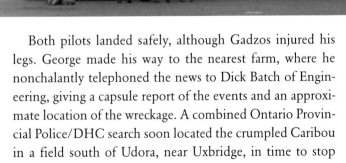

Both pilots landed safely, although Gadzos injured his legs. George made his way to the nearest farm, where he nonchalantly telephoned the news to Dick Batch of Engineering, giving a capsule report of the events and an approximate location of the wreckage. A combined Ontario Provincial Police/DHC search soon located the crumpled Caribou in a field south of Udora, near Uxbridge, in time to stop early arrivals from walking off with souvenirs. Thanks to George's presence of mind in shutting things down, there was no fire, even though the wreckage reeked of gasoline. Now the reporters who had been so kind on press day, had something a little more lively to work on. They cited the 4,000 jobs involved at Downsview and called Washington to see if the crash would kill the Caribou order. "Losing an air-

craft is nothing to get pan-
icky about," was the reply.
"We've lost a lot in the early
stages." One press call to
general manager Garratt asking if the company would
still continue to make the
Caribou brought a quick reply: "Why not?"

The evidence collected
under knowledgeable eyes
soon began to tell the story.
The details fell into place after the surrounding area had
been searched and all parts
returned to Downsview. On
March 29 the port elevator
horn and horn shield were
found north of Musselman's
Lake, 13 miles (21 km) from
the crash site. Another valu-

This Caribou was one of a pair for Kuwait. It shows typical improvements: the extended nose and modified wing, including stall bars, wing fences and drooped leading edge. This aircraft later returned to Canada as C-GVYZ. (DH 16189)

able find during May, in the same general area, produced
the spring tab strut from the port elevator and the tab balance weight. Added to the pilot's report, it was all the evidence the engineers needed to determine the cause and to
correct the fault.

It was a typical case of aerodynamic sleuthing and, like
most accidents, it began for the simplest reasons. Evidently
the longer control cable required by the lengthened fuselage
reduced the dampening of the spring tab in the elevator circuit, allowing both to flutter at a much lower speed than
those in aircraft No.1. It was enough to start the buzzing
George Neal felt and the high-speed control oscillations at
265 mph (426 km/h). The mass balances and strut found
near Musselman's Lake indicated that they were torn off
early in the sequence, aggravating the flutter and leading to
a failure of the tube that linked left and right elevators. From
then, the left side was free to flutter like a window blind,
even though George had some control with the starboard elevator. The extreme pull forces required to raise LKI's nose
at the height of the activity also uncovered a control column
fault. The control wheel pulled out of the column, forcing
George to switch to the co-pilot wheel. He found the aileron
controls jammed at this stage and the decision was made to
abandon the aircraft.

The incident proved a costly portion of the company's
learning curve with large aircraft, but the problems were
quickly diagnosed and put right. A larger washer corrected

the control column problem and a series of stiffening modifications eliminated flutter. Testing continued on the next
Caribou and Clay Staples of the U.S. FAA and an assistant
went up for a ride. The time was near when U.S. approval
would be sought. Staples' introduction was favourable, but
he did not agree with the criteria written up for stalls. He
insisted that they be completed using FAA procedures in the
approaches to stalls and actual stalling. The Caribou would
not meet these requirements, so a new program had to be
carried out. With only five aircraft on the order books, this
presented a crisis. Test pilot Bob Fowler and project engineer
Bob McIntyre took charge of the program; George Neal got
a much-needed holiday to recuperate from his harrowing experience over Uxbridge.

By mid-summer of 1959, U.S. approval for stalls was received, but the job had not been easy. Ted Johnson teamed
with Fowler in flying over 1,000 stalls in every conceivable
configuration. Bob McIntyre carried on the diplomatic role
with weekly trips to Washington, reporting regularly to the
FAA on the growing file of test data. The Caribou that
emerged was certainly the most stall-tested aircraft in the '4b
category. It now had wing fences, stall bars, a drooped leading edge and two stick-shaker stall warning devices.

When Canada's General Guy Simonds, Chief of Staff,
learned of U.S. Army interest in the Caribou (designed specifically for army support) he ordered studies within his own
command and pledged $2.5 million to de Havilland in sup-

port funding. The RCAF learned of the Army's sudden interest in large aircraft and promptly put a stop to the scheme. Fortunately for de Havilland and the program, financing went through just the same. The money was well spent, for during the Belgian Congo relief mission the RCAF came through with a quick order for four Caribous, designated CC-108-1A. This stop-gap assistance helped but no new orders came from the U.S., even though U.S. Army enthusiasm was a strong as ever.

An Exercise in Banking

In a few weeks the burden shifted to the director of finance, whose introduction to the Caribou problem had been unusual. Frank Stanley was returning to Toronto along Highway 401 after a few days away from the city. He had heard of the Caribou crash but did not know many details. Somewhere west of Oshawa he found himself driving behind a truck carrying unmistakable portions of a Caribou. He

A very important visit from the heads of Barclay's Bank, March 17, 1954. Left to right: F. Udell, manager of Barclay's in Canada; Russ Bannock, DHC; H.A. Stevenson, president, Barclay's Canada; Lord Portal of Hungerford, Barclay's England; Phil Garratt and George Mickleborough of DHC. (DH)

could hardly contain his curiosity until he reached his home telephone, little knowing he would soon become an active participant in the Caribou drama. The DH Canada financial position became so tight that the Royal Bank of Canada, with whom they had dealt for years, said, "No more money!" Frank Stanley, the man between the company and the banks, became very busy.

The banking industry has always depended on an understanding of risk capital, and here was a situation to test any bank. DHC's search for new support went as far as the Barclays group in England, where one of the directors was Lord Portal, Viscount Hungerford, ex-Chief of Air Staff, RAF. He had visited Downsview on May 17, 1954, where he had flown in the Otter and was briefed on company activities. The decision was placed with this ex-airman, whose judgments in the banking world, reputedly, were on a par with his wartime decisions in high command. He ruled favourably for DHC. This, according to hard-pressed Frank Stanley, saved the day. It was a major corporate move and changed DHC's banking pattern forever. The same group of banks, Barclay's-Canadian Imperial Bank of Commerce, continued to look after the company's banking under the capable direction of Frank Udell, who was with Portal on that 1954 visit to Downsview.

Royal Assignment 1959

Eight years after the incident of the plastic top for the royal car, DH Canada got another request involving the royal couple, this time, Her Majesty the Queen and the Duke of Edinburgh. Another tour of Canada was in the offing and the organizers turned to DHC for its demonstrator D.H.114 Heron, CF-IJR. Most of the flying for the tour was to be done with Trans-Canada Air Lines, but some airports were too small for their Viscount airliner. Since four-engined Herons formed a major part of the RAF Royal Flight, the call came from Ottawa, "Would it be possible for DH Canada to take part in some of the travel arrangements?" The timing was awkward, in the aftermath of the Caribou crash, but the reply went back that DHC would be pleased to help.

Test pilot Bob Fowler took the job and went through briefings with the RAF Royal Flight on matters of protocol. It was discreetly pointed out that Prince Philip, who was an experienced Heron pilot, would probably wish to fly IJR, but he should not be allowed to do so with the Queen on board. Fowler placed a call to the Caribou test program at the last moment and the assignment fell to Dave Fairbanks. He was joined by F/L Heath of the RCAF as co-pilot. With DHC service representative Terry Rawlins, they took the Heron to Whitehorse, Yukon, to be ready for a flight on July 19.

This was only months before the birth of Prince Andrew and, as the Queen was feeling indisposed that morning, Prince Philip proceeded alone on the day's itinerary. From then there was no doubt who would fly the plane and the question never came up. His Royal Highness simply took his place in the left seat and began starting the engines.

Fairbanks went along in the right seat for what turned out to be a very relaxed ride, completely devoid of any protocol. Prince Philip proved a good pilot, even though his radio transmissions favoured naval language rather than airways terminology. They flew first to Dawson, then Mayo, before returning that evening to Whitehorse. But the assignment was not over. After returning to Downsview, Fairbanks, Rawlins and Heath positioned themselves in Charlottetown, P.E.I., on July 29. On the morning of the 31st they flew the Queen and the Duke of Edinburgh to New Glasgow and, later in the day, to Sydney, N.S. This time Prince Philip joined the Queen and her lady-in-waiting in the cabin, along with LCmdr McPherson of the Royal Navy and Terry Rawlins. "It was a trip to remember," said Rawlins years later. "Everything went smoothly including hoisting the little flag over the cockpit as we taxied in. My introduction to the Duke didn't go so well, for I wasn't with him on the Whitehorse flight. He didn't know who I was. After I had attended to my duties at Charlottetown and climbed

The Heron demonstrator used by Queen Elizabeth and the Duke of Edinburgh in 1959. (DH 11795)

aboard, Prince Philip looked down the long cabin and said, 'Who the hell is he?' Fortunately the equerry explained that I was the engineer and I was allowed to stay." At the end of the day's flying the crew said goodbye to the royal couple and returned to Downsview for a late night landing.

Another Demonstration

Dave Fairbanks was a native of Ithaca, New York, and the son of a Cornell University professor. Early in the war he skipped school to hitchhike with a couple of friends to the Canadian border. They intended to enlist in the RCAF, but were turned back at Buffalo with only pennies in their pockets. Fairbanks' second attempt to become a pilot was a little more formal – he had his widowed mother's approval and in February 1941 enlisted at Hamilton, Ontario. He soon became a skilled pilot with 826 hours of instructing to his credit; but his dream was the action of an overseas posting. This came in 1943, when he joined an RAF Spitfire squadron in England. Soon he transferred to a Tempest squadron, where his targets were enemy aircraft, locomotives, road transport, ships and buzz-bombs. He was shot down while accounting for his 15th victory and spent two months in a German

Company demonstator, CF-OYE, which made the 1964 around-the-world sales tour. (Larry Milberry)

prisoner of war camp. Fairbanks was repatriated as a squadron leader with a DFC and two bars and joined de Havilland in 1955.

Although Caribou stall problems had been solved by mid-summer of 1959, promised orders from the U.S. did not come. Undelivered aircraft on the line provoked another crisis, which forced a showdown in the manner of the Beaver and Otter sales. The need for a competition was still being stressed by the opposition at the Pentagon but, because the Caribou had been designed specifically for the Army, there was no competing type. Finally, in desperation, Secretary of Defense Charles Wilson said, "Bring the plane down and demonstrate it."

If ever a trade became a polished art at de Havilland it was demonstrating STOL airplanes. The pilots in test flight used to call them "dog and pony shows" and every opportunity was taken to fly circuits for visiting guests on a short grass strip close to the hangars. The same kind of show could easily be moved to Washington. Dave Fairbanks, manager of flight operations, planned the demo with a flare that was to become his trademark. Permission was obtained from the FAA to use a parade square in Washington with a level, 900-ft. (270 m) grass section. Fairbanks arrived in a Caribou in front of the military observers, took on 32 troops, took off, circled and landed. He loaded again with cargo and vehicles and went through the same routine. Next day the procedure was demonstrated in every detail for General Howze, Secretary of Defense Wilson and a number of congressmen. The convincing display put an abrupt end to the debate – the Army could buy the airplane they so badly wanted and began ordering them in batches of 50. The U.S. Army certificate and designation AC-1 coincided with the official delivery of the first three machines in September 1959. Eventually 165 AC-1s were built.

The Caribou World Tour

During the dark days following the Caribou crash and the subsequent drain on company finances, many serious discussions took place about sales strategy. Seven months of flying had given everyone complete confidence that the Caribou was everything the engineers had predicted. With the number the U.S. Army might order in question, world sales certainly would be needed to make the project viable. It was time for the sales department to take centre stage. The spotlight fell on Russ Bannock, then director of military sales, and Buck Buchanan, who managed all international sales. Both were steeped in the sales expertise of the de

Havilland empire. They had the established worldwide agency organization of the parent company backing their effort, along with considerable experience in the export of Beavers and Otters. These had been delivered by ship, but now the company had a product that could fly oceans and navigate the world airways. Like any new concept, STOL had to be seen to be believed; the Caribou must be ably demonstrated worldwide, if it was to be sold. Bannock and Buchanan came to this decision early and soon had Phil Garratt's approval for a major tour. Planning was developed by correspondence, using the services of the de Havilland area representatives, along with the agents concerned. Whenever available, the assistance of Canadian government representatives, ambassadors, commercial counsellors and trade commissioners was requested. Planning was carried out by flight operations manager Dave Fairbanks and his staff, who arranged special navigational charts, clearances, manifest forms and crew visas, down to the careful selection of a spares package to be carried. It was to be the longest tour the company had ever attempted, covering 30 countries in the course of four months. It was timed to coincide with the first Caribou deliveries to the U.S. Army.

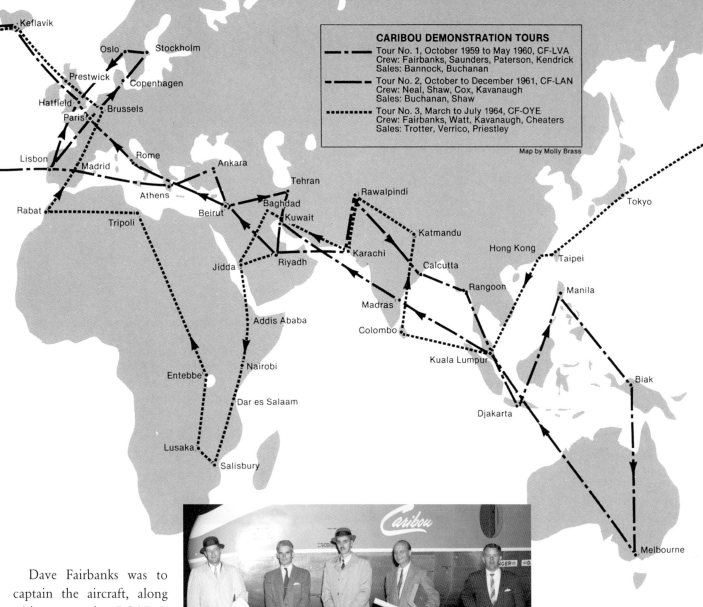

An early morning departure for the crew of the world tour Caribou. Left to right: Dave Fairbanks, captain; Mick Saunders, first officer; Dave Kendrick, engineer; Hans Brinkman, who joined the tour through Germany only; and Norm Paterson, engineer. (DH)

Dave Fairbanks was to captain the aircraft, along with a seasoned ex-RCAF pilot, A.W. "Mick" Saunders, as first officer. Two of the company's top maintenance engineers, Norman Paterson and Dave Kendrick, would accompany the flight, along with a sales department head to handle briefings. Russ Bannock would manage the first phase through part of Europe; Buck Buchanan would take command starting with Lisbon. Their mount for this ambitious program was Caribou No. 9, CF-LVA, with only 15 hours of test and demonstration flying in its log. The tour began on October 22, 1959. The weather was poor; then on arrival in the Azores, LVA required an engine change, with a new "power egg" flown in from Canada. They got away to Lisbon on November 2 and arrived in England on the 4th. Their British stop was Hatfield, where demonstrations were arranged in Germany, the Netherlands, Belgium and France, mostly to U.S. Army units there.

Log book entries began to match any flying carpet story. Throughout Portugal, Algeria, Libya, Greece, Turkey, Lebanon, Iran, Kuwait, Bahrain, Qatar and Oman they went, seeking out difficult landing strips to astound everyone with the Caribou's versatility. They preferred fields designed for Beavers and Otters, for usually nothing bigger had ever used them. Any DC-3 strip they called a "piece of cake." They sought instead high mountain clearings with difficult approaches. Each country provided a new challenge, in its fly-

The Caribou cockpit and instrumentation. (DH 10887)

ing facilities or geography. To Pakistan, India, Kashmir, Burma they went … to Thailand, Malaysia, Singapore and North Borneo. Their regular reports to Downsview made interesting reading and provided a special article for the parent company's *Gazette*.

Dave Fairbanks described the trip as "right out of an adventure book," with paradrops, food drops, loading and unloading vehicles, transporting passengers and awkward cargo. Life took on all the aspects of a travelling caravan – arrive, unload, meet the officials and arrange the details of a demonstration. The next morning, up at dawn to fly all manner of cargo to the smallest airstrips their hosts could find. They would climb with heavy loads on one engine, while observers sucked oxygen from primitive bottles and noted performance figures for their own enlightenment. When the show was over, they would pack up everything again and move to the next stop.

Sarawak in North Borneo, the Philippines, Dutch New Guinea, Australian New Guinea, Australia, Timor, Bali and South Borneo and back to Madras, India … they had now been away four months and were performing near-miracles, still on schedule, no delays and no sickness – until March 2. On that day Fairbanks visited the local hospital for what he thought were stomach cramps. He ended with an emergency appendix operation. A quick conference was called and an

immediate decision made: "Press on with the tour." Buck Buchanan took on a dual role. He had maintained his pilot's proficiency since his Lancaster days of WWII and by now had plenty of experience with the Caribou. Mick Saunders took over as captain and Buchanan moved into the right seat – it was business as usual. From Madras they travelled to Bombay and Karachi, followed by demonstrations in Kuwait and the deserts of Saudi Arabia. Then it was Syria, Lebanon, Greece and Italy.

Dave Fairbanks joined them again March 14 in Rome and they went on through Paris to England. This completed their schedule, but they made another swing through Germany, Switzerland, Denmark, Finland, Norway and Iceland before finishing with a flight back to Downsview via Frobisher Bay. In all, they had been away 221 days, travelled 50,000 miles (80,000 km) to 40 countries, and visited 154 airports. In 479 demonstration flights they had made 664 landings, carried 6,683 passengers, and feathered one propeller 500 times. The crew received an enthusiastic welcome home, for things had taken a decided upswing in the Caribou saga. The first quantity order of 50 U.S. Army machines had been received and word had just arrived that a set of turbine engines was to be installed in a Caribou. Three of the major purchasers of the Caribou – India, Australia and Malaysia – were visited on that first demonstration tour. It had been a very convincing display and one that prompted a similar world flight four years later.

The Resolution Island Airlift

Much of the DH Canada story has taken place far from the airport boundaries of Downsview. The whole world has been the testing ground. The nature of the product provides many a tale of adventure in faraway places. Most of the time it was the customer who built the reputation that surrounded DHC airplanes – the bush pilots in the Arctic and military crews on their support missions. DHC pilots often joined in the action, particularly on demonstration and proving flights. A typical operation originating from Downsview and involving DHC people was the Resolution Airlift of 1961.

Resolution Island lies off the southern tip of Baffin Island at the junction of Hudson and Davis Straits. It was one of the Distant Early Warning sites where Federal Electric Corporation was responsible to the U.S. on matters of supply. It had a 1,300-ft. (400 m) gravel landing strip, long enough for an Otter, but Nordair, the commercial operator on the contract, was suddenly faced with a 25,000 lb. (11,250 kg) airlift of bulky equipment from the main base at Frobisher Bay. It was a difficult job calling for STOL. Nordair contacted de Havilland engineering about using a Caribou.

To this time only six Caribous had been delivered to the U.S. Army and four to the RCAF; none had been used commercially. All had departed for sunny climes with only hot weather to worry about. When demonstrator CF-LAN was

leased to Nordair for the Resolution project, it was to be the first such operation in the Arctic. Bob Fowler would captain the flight, with Bill Weitzel of Nordair as first officer. The rest of the DHC crew was Norm Paterson, Bob McKenna and Len Trotter. Photographer Reg Corlett was along to record the event. The flight arrived at Frobisher on January 29, 1961. Frobisher was a DOT field with navigational aids, a 9,000-ft. (2.7 km) runway and a heated hangar. The other destination, even in the most flattering terms, could only be described as a wind-swept, snow-covered, ice-locked outpost, with an airstrip on the perilous hump of a high, narrow promontory. One end of the runway pointed to a sloping valley, while the other presented an 800-ft. (240 m) drop to the sea. For half the length, the airstrip was only 100 ft. (30 m) wide, walled by rock, well above the Caribou's wing tips. One windsock on a cabin gave the wind direction – it usually blew straight across the runway at an average 25 to 35 knots. Whiteouts were prevalent and the mixture

The Resolution Island approach, looking east. Circled is the area of the airstrip. (DH 13324)

The Caribou was vital to U.S. activities during the Vietnam War. Here locals do airport maintenance work as Caribous wait beyond. Then, troops board for operations, and a Caribou lands at a remote village. Although many Caribous were lost in Vietnam, most made it home. No. 62-4169, seen in the second photo, later served with the Hawaii National Guard. (DH)

of warm and cold ocean currents often blanketed the strip with fog. Maximum VFR conditions each day in January ranged from 7:30 a.m. to 3:30 p.m.

To complete the mission it took 15 days with six round trips averaging 2 hours 30 minutes flying time. It took 40 minutes to load at Frobisher, but only 12 minutes to unload at the strip using the large rear door. All unloading was conducted on the runway with the engines idling. At Resolution the average temperature was -31°C. At one time it went as low as -38°C (with no calculation for wind chill). The runway was of compacted snow and the turning space varied from precarious to non-existent. Caribou LAN did not have reversing propellers. Despite the handicap of strong crosswinds and turbulence, at no time did the Caribou use more than 700 ft. (213 m) of runway. The operation proved a test of men and equipment and a lot of data was acquired on the limits of the oil dilution system, and how equipment reacted to the cold-soaked Arctic environment.

A Caribou Tale

As the U.S. Army received more Caribous, their interest grew in the professional aspects of STOL. When the first Caribou with reversing propellers was tested by the U.S. Army in July 1960, the pilots sought every opportunity to use this feature. Representatives from DHC and the Army were conducting hot-weather evaluation at Yuma, Arizona, and the service crews often took off on their own for a little practice. It was during one such session that the rescue service got a call from a local farmer that an aircraft had crashed in the desert and disappeared in a cloud of dust. The helicopter rescue squad was alerted and began a search with fears that it might be the Caribou. It was a relief to all when the Caribou came in to land in the midst of the confusion. The helicopter flew to the so-called crash site and found only tire tracks in the sand. The cloud of dust that so alarmed the farmer had been thrown up by the mighty wash from the reversing props as the crew braked.

STOL In Combat

While Korea brought the Beaver into combat, it was

Vietnam that tested the Otter's ability under fire. The first eight U.S. Army U-1A Otters were assigned in 1963 to a small American combat contingent known as Farm Gate. More than 100 Otters eventually served in Vietnam in such roles as electronic eavesdropping. Throughout the war some 25 Otters were lost in action. Twenty others were transferred to Cambodia under U.S. foreign aid.

As U.S. military involvement in Southeast Asia began to grow in the early 1960s, the Caribou had its baptism of fire in Vietnam. The first arrived in the spring of 1962; in less than four years six squadrons were in use with the 834th Air Division. In January 1967 these were transferred to the 483rd Tactical Airlift Wing based at Cam Ranh Bay. For the duration of the war Caribous provided valuable airlift throughout South Vietnam in many combat operations, including the notorious siege of Khe Sanh. During the war 20 Caribous were destroyed in combat or operational mishaps. At war's end many were captured intact by the North Vietnamese, as three of the six American Caribou squadrons had been handed over to the South Vietnamese Air Force. Caribous served into the early 1990s in the USAF, equipping several reserve squadrons, and special units such as the Army's Golden Knights parachute team.

Another World Tour

By March 28, 1964, it was time for another Caribou world demonstration. This time the aircraft was CF-OYE with the crew of Dave Fairbanks, captain; Jack Watt, first officer; Bill Kavanaugh and Ron Cheaters, flight engineers. The sales team was Len Trotter, technical sales manager; Tony Verrico,

Canadian Forces Caribou 5322 in United Nations colours. The RCAF/CAF used its Caribou on general transport duties, search and rescue, and UN assignments in places like the Middle East and India-Pakistan. (CF)

Caribou 5320, with a special camera pod, used in filming Canadian scenes for the 1970 Osaka World's Fair. (Benner Col.)

regional sales manager Far East; Geoff Priestley, regional sales manager Africa. This time they went round the world east to west, starting their demonstrations at Tokyo and ending in Brussels. They visited 28 countries and flew 38,000 statute miles (61,000 km) with 200 demonstrations for a total of 320 flying hours.

RCAF Caribou Operations

Caribous gave good service to the Canadian military, particularly on United Nations duties. They were a vital aspect of UN air support in the Middle East. They supported UN observation teams into the late 1960s, running schedules to El Arish, Gaza, Beirut, Jerusalem, Cairo and Cyprus. RCAF Caribous also supported missions in Yemen and West Pakistan. On these duties life was far from routine. These were operational zones and real hot spots. On May 18, 1967, Caribou 5321 was intercepted by an Israeli fighter while flying from Raffa to Gaza and was in danger of being shot down. Captain Bob Simpson dived and evaded the fighter, which had fired warning shots. On another occasion an RCAF Caribou was destroyed on the ground during action between India and Pakistan.

A major Canadian Armed Forces operation took place in Peru after a disastrous earthquake in June 1970. When word of the trouble filtered out on June 7, Ottawa dispatched 424 Squadron Caribou 5327 from Trenton to Lima. It was the first international relief plane to arrive and began hauling medical supplies to a crude strip bulldozed from an orchard at the 8,700-ft. (2,610 m) level near the devastated town of Anta. Soon five CAF Caribous, with 70 personnel, were on the scene, each flying two return trips daily with supplies to the interior, then flying out the victims. In the first six days, 806 sick or injured were evacuated in 41 missions, and 90

tons of supplies were moved. The CAF relief operation under LCol. W.E. Butchart continued until June 26. It had functioned almost perfectly but for one minor landing incident. The efforts of 424 Squadron were roundly praised by relief organizations and a number of Peruvian and Canadian decorations were conferred upon many 424 participants. Ironically, when the Caribous returned to Trenton in late June, they were greeted by the first CAF Buffalo replacement, which had arrived June 23.

Persistent Caribous

In 1970 the CAF Caribous were sold to Tanzania, where they served for years. Many such overseas Caribous later worked their way back to North America to fly in such widespread regions as Central America and the Arctic. Canadian bush operators found that the STOL qualities built into the Caribou for the military, their rugged gear and loading capability, were ideal for northern freighting. Jean-Marie Arseneault, who had 5,500 hours flying Caribous for La Sarre/Propair in northwestern Quebec, described a typical operation: "The Caribou is ideal for outsize cargo. On one job we took a helicopter from Val d'Or in Quebec to Rae Point in the Arctic islands, a 2,500-mile (4,000 km) flight. The chopper was at work 26 hours after we left Val d'Or and the customer probably had the most economic air transport deal he could have found anywhere." Bob Ambrose of Kelowna Flightcraft also operated Caribous in remote parts of Canada. His first aircraft, C-GVYZ (ex-Kuwait Air Force), started work in March 1980. Much of its work was to the Cadillac Mine, 210 miles (340 km) north of Fort Nelson in the Yukon. Arseneault and Ambrose concurred on the Caribou. Not only was it a good all-round transport, but it would be around for a long time, especially with the advent of the PT6-powered version.

Army Aviation Develops

A study of U.S. military history during the 1950s shows a major trend to be the rise of Army support aviation. This began with the Beaver, for up to then the air arm had been restricted to small reconnaissance aircraft. Despite opposition by U.S. industry, the Army won the right to purchase all three de Havilland STOL types. The opposition they experienced only strengthened the Army's resolve, for they were using the aircraft effectively – in some cases spectacularly – and were proving their point. The Army developed a close bond with de Havilland, which was, in fact, designing specifically for the Army in a way no U.S. manufacturer had done.

Caribous destined for Tanzania, Malaysia and Australia. JWTZ later returned to the U.S. as N3262W with NewCal Aviation. Malaysia planned to keep its aging Caribous. In 1996-97 Airod overhauled eight of them. The Australian Caribou later was in Ecuador, Oman, Quebec and Panama. (Benner Col.)

Unfortunately the growth of Army aviation antagonized the USAF. During years of working with DHC, the Army developed its own brand of aviation, became very good at it, and was buying bigger aircraft. A confrontation was brewing because the Air Force felt its specialty was being infringed. The Army was confident that it had the situation in hand. Meanwhile, de Havilland remained friendly with both sides, avoiding inter-service politics. This was the situation in February 1961 when the announcement of a combined development program moved DHC into the turbine age and gave new life to the Caribou. Since 1957 General Electric had been developing a high technology engine under a contract with the U.S. Navy Bureau of Weapons. The T64 turboprop/turboshaft engine was designed for low fuel consumption, high reliability and ease of maintenance. It had a two-stage, high-efficiency generator turbine and delivered 2,344 shp plus 565 pounds of thrust.

General Electric were looking for a fixed-wing evaluation aircraft and had their eye on the Caribou. Soon a single-source contract was drawn up with DHC as a joint effort between the U.S. and Canadian governments. News of the program was welcomed by DHC engineers, who

The T64 Caribou in flight. It was later reconverted to R2000s. In 1998 it was operating in Mozambique with Interocean Airways, 40 years after its first flight. (DH 13928)

were in a slack period and down to a staff of 250. They had been considering turbine power for the Caribou and here was an opportunity to put their ideas to work under the watchful eye of their best customer, the U.S. military. Participants would be the U.S. Navy, under whose auspices the T64 was developed, General Electric's small aircraft engine department at Lynn, Massachusetts, and DH Canada, which was responsible for designing and carrying out the conversion, and conducting test flying. The RCAF would supply Caribou No. 1 as a test-bed airframe. This was the company's first experience with turbine power and the T64-GE4 fitted their requirements.

After considerable modification, RCAF Caribou 5303 emerged with its new turbine look in September 1961. Chief engineering test pilot Bob Fowler took it into the air on September 22 and continued with 220 hours of interesting flying. With the added thrust from the more powerful engines, great care had to be taken: it was possible to exceed design speed limitations with only one engine operating and to attain design dive speed with both engines in level flight. It took only three minutes to climb to 14,000 ft. (4,300 m). Needless to say all parties were pleased with the results. After the evaluation contract, Caribou 5303 was reconverted to its original configuration. It was active in Africa as a commercial transport in 1998.

The Changing Times

For over 30 years DH Canada lived under the proud banner of the British company, steeped in the prestige of Sir Geoffrey de Havilland (knighted in 1944) and his associates. The family image that Phil Garratt encouraged at Downsview was simply a reflection of a longstanding company philosophy that went back to Moth days. The pattern of DH management throughout the world, evolved from a set of old-fashioned values, was remarkable. It was not the later style of space-age aviation, but was ideally suited to the period. These happy circumstances could not last forever, but while they remained, few appreciated the uncluttered nature of the system at Downsview.

Martin Sharp, in his book, *DH: An Outline of de Havilland History*, summed up in one sentence the parent company's relations with its offshoots: "The central policy for each of the overseas companies had always been to serve aviation in the land of its adoption." The view continued through the war years. Frank Stanley, DHC's finance man in the 1950s, described this parent-branch relationship after the war: "The parent company never expected any returns from us, and resisted the efforts of British banks to acquire Canadian profits. DH England made loans to us from time to time and were repaid, but held the policy of ploughing profits (whenever there were any) back into the next design project. Their aim was self-sufficiency, not a source of head office revenue."

"The annual meetings with England were simplicity itself," recalled Russ Bannock, "and more like an annual family re-

Alan S. Butler (right), a director of the parent company, was a frequent visitor to Downsview. The others are Phil Garratt and, behind him, Russ Bannock, W. Jakimiuk and Doug Hunter. (Hotson Col.)

The British de Havilland board of directors after the retirement of Alan S. Butler. Left to right, rear: F.E.N. St. Barbe, W.E. Nixon. Front: C.C. Walker, Sir Geoffrey de Havilland and F.T. Hearle. (Via British Aerospace)

union. Whoever was over from the Canadian board would report on the year's work. Sir Geoffrey and his directors would ask questions, offer advice and that would be it. We would touch base with their sales group and ask a few questions of our own. It was always a very productive session."

While attention in postwar Canada was focused on the manufacture of large passenger aircraft and jet fighters – particularly Avro's delta-wing Arrow – Phil Garratt was moving de Havilland Canada along an unspectacular path almost of his own choosing. He used to enjoy a walk through his plant and complained once that the place was getting too big; he

did not know everyone any more. Once he recognized one of the sweepers and asked about the man's health. "My health's fine, Mr. Garratt," he said, "but they tell me I must retire next month due to my age. Is there anything that can be done, sir?" Garratt dropped in to see Frank Stanley on his way back to the office and argued the sweeper's case. His reasoning was simply that the man would be able to sweep the stairs just as well next year as this and it did seem a little unfair when the man wanted to keep on working. Stanley sympathized but suggested that the only option to comply with union rules would be to make the sweeper assistant to the general manager. No records exist of any such title.

Life in the engineering department during the 1950s was uncluttered, as is shown in veteran George Luesby's notes of the period. Luesby headed the drafting department from the war days and kept a diary of engineering highlights. Summarizing the times, he wrote:

The design team had become quite cohesive and all had a complete understanding of each other's capabilities, which contributed to a productive output. The computer had not yet been introduced; the manufacturing and skilled trades had the flexibility to permit rapid changes with a minimum of paper work. Moreover, the management heads were gentlemen of the old school in every respect. That applied to the parent company and here in Canada, where exercise of the humanities was combined with their foresight and good judgment. It permeated through the whole organization and the success of our products was a reflection of the people involved.

This was the family atmosphere that prevailed at Downsview to 1958, with the entire aviation industry in Canada on an upward swing. The advent of the Caribou was almost overshadowed by the high-profile Avro Arrow a few miles away at Malton, but de Havilland felt comfortable in its STOL niche. It felt confident in the move to larger aircraft, for it was basking in the success of its previous projects. The Chipmunk was now with seven air forces and numerous civil schools. The Beaver was making a name for itself in the Antarctic, where three newly discovered features – a glacier, a lake and an island – had all been named in its honour. The world press was telling of the Otter that flew non-stop across Antarctica, over the South Pole. Grumman Trackers were being delivered regularly to the Royal Canadian Navy. These successes seemed to reach a crescendo on the day the Caribou was demonstrated to the press – things had never gone so well. These were heady days in the Toronto area. The end was to come abruptly on February 20, 1959 – Avro Canada's Black Friday.

Black Friday

The employees at Downsview followed with interest news of the spectacular Avro Arrow and sometimes saw it fly. Even those who thought they knew the problems developing at Malton were shocked at the news of the sudden cancellation of the Arrow on what became known as Black Friday, February 20, 1959. But those at DHC had their own work to do. If any felt uneasy having such a calamity so close to home, history would prove they had every justification.

The gloom and doom that followed Black Friday has been told and retold with varying degrees of emotion. The traumatic effect on the industry as a whole was to continue past the first stage of shock. Few escaped some part of the Arrow backlash. To the remaining Avro officials and the skeleton staff at Malton, the job of cleaning up was depressing in the extreme. Here was a large plant with the potential for high technology, coupled with a production reputation that went back to WWII. How could it be brought back to life?

The sonic boom of halting the Arrow was felt on both sides of the Atlantic, particularly in the boardroom of the A.V. Roe empire in England. They had enough problems at home to deal with and simply told Malton to find something to do – anything. It was not the most inspiring assignment in industrial Toronto, moving into the competitive trades of pots, pans and home hardware. The construction of aluminum boats was started with little enthusiasm and less success. The once-proud Avro had been dealt a mortal blow. The whole industry mourned (although nearly everyone affected recovered before long and went on to other projects).

Dramatic events in the aviation industry seldom go singly, as was soon seen at de Havilland Canada. The shock of the 14,000 layoffs at Malton was still a topic of conversation when the first U.S. Army Caribou ploughed pilotless into the woods near Uxbridge. The backing of the de Havilland empire was needed in the months that followed to fend off financial disaster and put the project back on track. In the next two years, while both Toronto companies were adjusting, the Avro and de Havilland parents back in Britain were facing another kind of problem.

The British government chose this critical time to overhaul its aviation industry with a program of amalgamation. The longstanding names of A.V. Roe and de Havilland soon disappeared, swallowed up by 1966 in one giant company – Hawker Siddeley Aviation. Both remained for some time as the Whitworth Division and the de Havilland Division, but merged into Hawker Siddeley upon the recommendations of the British Defence White Paper. Sir Roy Dobson of A.V. Roe headed the new organization.

Although Canada had no part in the re-arrangement of the British industry, the repercussions were felt for years to come. Hawker Siddeley soon became a diversified group in Canada of which aviation was only a part; de Havilland Canada kept its name as a member of the group, but was now only a spoke in a much bigger wheel. Malton's Avroites in their haughty moments had often called DHC the "box factory" in reference to postwar Fox Moth production. Since the days of the wooden Fox, however, Downsview had forged a new identity with its successful workhorse airplanes. After the Arrow cancellation many Avro specialists were welcomed into the expanding DHC work force. The Tracker contract was a financial success and Caribou sales

A visit from the top brass at Hawker Siddeley, which now owned de Havilland. Left to right: C.H. Punch Dickins, DHC; Crawford Gordon of Avro; Russ Bannock, DHC; P.C. Garratt, DHC; Sir Roy Dobson, head of A.V. Roe; and Sir Arnold Hall, Hawker Siddeley. (DH 3139)

were now in high gear. The situation at the bank, under the watchful eyes of George Mickleborough and Frank Stanley, was slowly improving again.

Engineers to Britain

During 1959, contracts for U.S. military Beavers and Otters ended and Caribou costs grew to where cutbacks were made in engineering – the staff fell from a high of 400 in mid-1958 to a low of 225 in December 1959. In England the D.H.121 Trident jetliner was in the early design stages and the parent company requested engineering help from Downsview. A group from DHC, under M.C.W. "Mike" Davy, left in November and included K.J. Bullock, G.B. Jackson, G.A. Hilliam, Tony Liddell, A.J.W. Melson, Bill Snyder and Allan

Skeggs. Overseas, they took on an assortment of tasks, but most worked on the Trident empennage. They remained a year, returning in time to take part in the test installation of the T64 turbine engine in the Caribou. Another request from England about this time involved tool processing and co-ordination for the manufacture of the D.H.125 business jet. DHC's manufacturing engineering section sent Bill Simpson, Gordon Hogan, Derek Thoms, Roy Hickman and Tom Salsbury on loan to assist in that project.

A Caribou demonstration tour took place from October to December 1961. It included every South American country except Bolivia and Paraguay. George Neal was captain with John Shaw as first officer. Ben Cox and Bill Kavanaugh were the engineers and Buck Buchanan was in charge of sales. Though the tour went well, no Caribou sales resulted, since everyone was waiting for turbines. The tour, however, paved the way for later products. In the case of the Twin Otter, 100 sales resulted in a 23-year period. Three were presidential aircraft, and Peru, with 17, had the world's largest Twin Otter floatplane fleet. Argentina took some 20 Twin Otters.

The Thin Edge of the Wedge

If ever there was an opening line, "There I was minding my own business," it applied to the next round of events faced by Garratt and company at Downsview. It was mid-1962 and Sir Roy Dobson was in Canada for a critical board meeting. Things had been going poorly at Malton and the problem of what to do with the Avro plant was high on the agenda. Sir Roy's style was not the easy-going manner of Sir Geoffrey, nor did Hawker Siddeley necessarily agree to leave the Canadians on their own. A tough new policy had come to Downsview and a wily, free-wheeling leader was now in command. The subject of the Malton plant was not mentioned at the morning meeting – it was in the dining room later that things began to happen. After pre-lunch refreshments had been measured out, Sir Roy, gazing across the 96 acres of de Havilland property, opened the inevitable conversation. "Garratt," he said abruptly, "I want you to buy Avro."

Phil looked at the ice in his drink as he thought for a moment and replied, with his usual grin, "How much?" All ears perked at the sight of a couple of masters at work and Dobson replied with two words in his broad accent, "B-o-o-k value!" There was a brief silence, then, as if on cue, Frank Stanley said in a meek voice, "And what is 'book value,' sir?"

Once again, after a slight pause, Sir Roy launched a lead-

ing question: "How much do you have in the bank?" This proved a critical point in the conversation because the director of finance had to admit to a healthy balance of $12.5 million. "That's 'b-o-o-k value'!" said Dobson, and the deal was closed.

Once the sale was consummated and Dobson was back in England, management had to decide what to do with their new investment. Avro's boat building enterprise was not going well and by now sparrows were the only things with wings in the empty bays at Malton. Now de Havilland, the once humble "box factory," found itself in the driver's seat with more power than it had ever expected or wanted. Garratt received criticism in some areas for becoming involved in events that followed. It was becoming clear that he was no longer "the boss," and that the backlash of Black Friday had reached Downsview.

A July 1962 editorial in the respected *Aircraft* magazine put the change of owners at Malton in perspective:

Full Circle: The news early this month that The de Havilland Aircraft of Canada Ltd. was taking over the Malton facilities of Avro Aircraft brought to an end – just 16 years and 7 months after it started – the meteoric career of the Malton-based company.

The principal reason for Avro Aircraft's untimely demise was, of course, the cancellation three years ago of the Avro Arrow. This traumatic experience was one from which the company never recovered in even a small way. Undeniably the problems faced by the management were staggering, but even making allowance for this, the company's performance in the last three years has been disappointing. Post-mortem reveals that the feeling is very widespread that the Avro name is till anathema in Ottawa, and to a very large extent this was behind Avro Aircraft's failure to re-establish itself in the smallest way. The change of name of the parent company from A.V. Roe Canada Ltd., to Hawker Siddeley Canada Ltd., tends to suggest that not only the outsiders felt this was the case.

Nothing but Good: The takeover of the Avro facilities bodes nothing but good for the giant Malton complex, which has about half as much plant space again as de Havilland Canada operates at Downsview. This means that de Havilland Canada will now have expanded plant space in the order of 2.5 million square feet, about 30 percent less than Canadair, but nevertheless still impressive by any standards. More important, perhaps, than the Avro plant itself, is the variety of very modern manufacturing and production tooling which it contains. Giant stamping presses, skin mills, etc., many bought especially to handle the advanced fabricating techniques required for the Arrow, are now at de Havilland Canada's disposal.

The Bobcat

One of the first steps for de Havilland was to take stock of their new acquisition – its equipment, manufacturing potential and contracts. There were still CF-100s in the plant at Malton for servicing and the installation of ECM (Electronic Counter Measures) equipment. Alex Watson was project manager and, with Ron Gibson as project engineer, worked with Air Materiel Command in Ottawa to complete the contracts. There also were tip-tanks for the CF-104 to be made and a small contract with Republic Aircraft in the U.S.

Another project was far removed from aviation and eventually required the maximum in de Havilland ingenuity in the form of the machine shop expertise of Bob Prout. Bob was a veteran of the war years, going back to Ansons and Tiger Moths. He had worked closely with Reg Robinson in setting up the machine shop for Mosquitoes and had become a specialist in metal fabrication. He was asked to go to Malton to review a Hawker Siddeley project that had been in progress for 10 years, first at Canadian Car in Montreal and now at Malton. It was called the Bobcat and after all this time had become a controversial project. It was an all-purpose half-ton military armoured personnel carrier. It was an amphibious tracked vehicle, light enough for transport by air, yet strong enough to withstand the rigours of combat. When Prout sized up the project, he could see it was a long way from completion. The armour plate from England had not arrived, U.S. contracts were still unfulfilled and the gearboxes were untried. His report sparked a re-evaluation of the work and, as so often happens the such cases, he was "borrowed" from Downsview to take charge of the project.

The Bobcat became a major challenge for the next year with its all-welded construction, its amphibious skirts and complicated gearing. Finally, the 20 vehicles were completed and delivered to the prime contractor, Hawker Siddeley. From there they were turned over to the military for operational testing, but the Bobcat ended as one of those great ideas that never made it to the production line. By this time, Bob Prout was busy with a new contract at Malton building Douglas DC-9 wings.

People who knew Phil Garratt's method of operation and his dominant presence at Downsview could see a new problem growing in the complexity of Hawker Siddeley ownership. The successes from Chipmunk to Caribou had been accomplished with DHC almost supreme unto itself. It would be difficult to find any subsidiary that enjoyed such complete command of its destiny with the head man so completely "the Boss." But new names were entering the Canadian scene and new management structures would end the simplicity of the past.

When efforts to refloat Avro Canada proved unsatisfactory in 1961, Sir Roy Dobson managed to lure Theodore Jonathan "Ted" Emmert from the vice-presidency of Massey-Ferguson to become president and chief executive officer of Hawker Siddeley Canada. The move put Emmert and Garratt on an equal footing, both reporting to Dobson. The following year, when Emmert became president and chief executive of Hawker Siddeley Canada, it was a different matter. The two men, whose paths had hitherto never crossed, now were thrust together at the highest level. Observers knew them as different personalities from different backgrounds and speculated over how they would get along. Garratt was invited to the Hawker Siddeley Canada board and Emmert joined the board of DHC on August 16, 1962.

Ted Emmert was born in Illinois in 1915 and was educated at South Dakota and Washington universities. He

The controversial Bobcat during its unsuccessful field trials. It was one of the leftover projects that followed the Arrow cancellation. It never went into production. (Via R. Prout)

The de Havilland Aircraft of Canada Limited board of directors, July 1963. Left to right: N.E. Rowe, vice-president, engineering; R. Bannock, vice-president, military sales; C.H. Dickins, vice-president, sales; G.J. Mickleborough, vice-president/secretary treasurer; P.C. Garratt, chairman and managing director; T.J. Emmert, chairman, Hawker Siddeley Canada Ltd.; W.W. Parry, vice-president, legal counsel; O.M. Solandt, vice-president, research and development; F.A. Stanley, vice-president, finance. (DH 16163)

joined Boeing in 1935 as a production worker and in eight years became assistant to the executive vice-president. In 1947 he joined Canadair as director of organization, which took him to the office of vice-president and director within a year. In 1950, while still an American citizen, he was with Ford of Canada as executive vice-president. This lasted for nine years until Emmert became vice-president of Massey Ferguson – and thence to A.V. Roe Canada. His latest assignment involved more than aviation, for his portfolio covered such diversified companies as Avro Aircraft, Orenda Engines, Canadian Applied Research, Canadian Car Co., Orenda Industrial, Canadian Steel Improvement, Canadian Steel Foundries, Canadian Thermo Control Co., Dominion Steel and Coal Corp., and Canadian Steel Wheel.

The Douglas Wing Contract

Phil Garratt and de Havilland Canada had the ability to manage Hawker Siddeley's airframe commitments in Canada, while Orenda handled things on the engine side. Together they had the unenviable responsibility of restoring a normal state of affairs to the Toronto aviation scene. Larry Clarke began searching for a company interested in the Malton plant. By coincidence, Douglas Aircraft of California needed a DC-9 subcontractor with a suitable plant and a willingness to share the financial load. The Avro–de Havilland facilities at Malton seemed tailor-made. Partial manufacture at Malton would provide an excellent bargaining point in selling the DC-9 to Trans-Canada Air Lines, who were calling for Canadian content in any fleet replacement. The opposition, General Dynamics, with their

Canadair plant at Montreal, were certainly not in the running, so the DHC/Malton arrangement looked ideal. Douglas soon invited the DHC management team to Los Angeles to discuss an arrangement.

This was the first meeting between Donald Douglas Sr. and Phil Garratt, who reportedly got along well. A development-sharing contract was drawn up for construction of wings and rear fuselage components in Malton. It was the first of seven such DC-9 subcontracts. Each participant was to use its own capital to fund the engineering, tooling and qualification testing of its own components. Douglas would purchase the completed portions under a fixed-price contract covering a specific number of units. Payment would be completed on delivery of the aircraft to the airline. Each subcontractor was to share in the cost of aircraft certification testing, proportionate to its participation, this cost to be returned later as part of deferred payments. It all sounded straightforward and little was said at the time that Douglas (and therefore DHC) were competing for much the same market as the Hawker Siddeley Trident.

It was in March 1963 that the cost-sharing arrangement between Douglas and DHC was announced with all the fanfare that a post-Arrow industry could muster. A feeling of relief swept through Toronto at the thought of reactivating the troubled Malton plant, particularly with a partner of such international prestige as Douglas. Phil Garratt, however, was less enthusiastic – he never did like building parts for other people's airplanes. He admitted that his prejudice was personal. He also realized that opposition was mounting in the U.S. against foreign military purchases and, in the words of one director, "that Beaver, Otter and Caribou sales, would not last forever." On top of it all were the growing problems with his new bosses in England.

Garratt made his only trip to Malton, reasoned that there was more than enough to keep him busy at Downsview, and handed the management of the contract to Punch Dickins. Punch looked on the assignment with misgivings. It was not his kind of work, although he had a free hand and the pick of company personnel. Don Long became project engineer, while Bill Houston looked after planning and methods. Bill Burlison and Alex Downey left the Caribou line to manage production and inspection respectively. Bob Prout was already at Malton finishing the Bobcats and began checking out the machine shop potential. George Robinson became Hawker Siddeley's financial watchdog, while Larry Clarke, Doug Annan, Bill Jackson, Harry Beffort and Duke Riggs took other responsibilties in the newly-formed Malton Division. A recruiting campaign was begun for engineering and production personnel, particularly within the ranks of DHC itself. Promotions were the order of the day at Downsview as longtime specialists left for Malton. Plant enthusiasm was at an all-time high for new challenges were appearing simultaneously on four fronts.

Trouble at Malton

The contract with Douglas had started well, with good relations and plenty of know-how available. It soon became obvious, however, that the contract had been prepared too hastily. There were many hard-to-live-with clauses in view of the unknowns in the project, which cost millions before they were resolved. Douglas and de Havilland were 15 per cent short on their man-hour figures and the tooling estimate of $9 million was used up in the first year. The prime contractor, Douglas, did not have an easy time. The deep stall problem with T-tail jets was complicating the DC-9 program and causing delays. Just as production had settled down at three wing-sets per month, there was a sudden demand for five, then nine.

These roller coaster activities put a strain on management, even though life at Downsview was going surprisingly well. Hawker Siddeley Canada exercised its authority with two major moves to overcome the Malton problem. It brought in William B. Boggs on July 29, 1965, to be president of DH Canada. (Phil Garratt was to remain a member of the board). Their second move was to engage U.S. production expert Lew Whittier to take charge of Douglas wing production. Boggs rearranged his management team in an effort to boost production at Malton, allocating new responsibilities and sending over more people from Downsview. Douglas was happy with the workmanship on the wings – compliments were received from resident airline representatives – but deliveries fell behind. Comparisons were always being made between American and Canadian methods of manufacture and it was generally conceded that U.S. companies got more per man-hour from a worker than did their Canadian counterparts. Whittier took the U.S. approach and went through the plant drastically rearranging manpower. These moves did not sit well with the union, so more problems arose.

By September 1965 the situation at Malton had deteriorated to where even the once-happy relationships among top personnel were suffering. On the financial side, the problem fell under that part of the contract termed the "risk factor" and no money had yet been received from Douglas. When $50 million was needed at the bank to carry on, the situation became critical. Phil Garratt admitted that "we are in the wrong swimming pool," a typically brief and to-the-point comment. "We have got to get out." A proposition was made that Douglas buy out the operation or increase the agreed price. They chose the former, but DHC retained title to the property. The sad story was announced in the press that de Havilland Canada had relinquished its partnership with Douglas Aircraft in producing components for the Douglas DC-9 jetliner:

In 1962 the Avro complex came under de Havilland ownership. Here a set of DHC-built Douglas DC-9 wings awaits rail shipment to California. (DH)

DHC has been engaged in production of the wings, rear fuselages and empennages of the DC-9 at its Malton plant since July last year and has delivered a number of sets. But recent doubling of the aircraft's production schedule, plus increasing complexity resulting from the demand of various models in the series, have combined to require an investment twice that originally projected for the DHC portion of the program.

Accordingly, the two companies have agreed that Douglas should take over full responsibility for expanding DC-9 production, and the portion of the Malton plant devoted to the program will be leased and operated by Douglas Aircraft Co. of Canada Ltd. Initially the lease will be for five years, with option to renew for three terms of five years each. Douglas will reimburse de Havilland for its investment in the program; under the original arrangement, DHC would not have been paid for the components until the sale of completed aircraft to the airlines. DHC will be able to return to the concentration of its full resources on its expanding STOL utility transports and other projects.

they got into difficulty some years later and were forced to join with the McDonnell company, the Canadian operation was one of the points that did not sit well with the famous "Mr. Mac" of St. Louis.

A Cirrus Moth Story

In the early 1960s a project came along that involved a little nostalgia. The subject was a lowly Cirrus Moth, G-CAUA, being launched into a new career with Canada's National Aviation Museum. G-CAUA had been No. 15 on the company's original 1928 delivery list. It had been sold to International Airways Ltd. of Hamilton. In 1936 it became the property of Carl F. Burke of Charlottetown and spent the war in storage.

By the 1960s Carl Burke was managing director of Maritime Central Airways. Kenneth M. Molson, curator of the newly-formed National Aviation Museum, arranged that Carl donate his Moth and asked de Havilland to recondition it. A group of company staff with plenty of Moth experience worked on the project in their off hours,

D.H.60X Moth G-CAUA, presented to the National Aviation Museum by Carl Burke in May 1963, was put into mint condition by these DH employees: Kathleen Neal, Bella MacDonald, Tom Glasson, Ben Goul, Howard MacDonald, John Hall, John Slaughter, George Blanchard, Tom Hollinsworth and Jack Driscoll. (DH 15749)

Some de Havilland Canada work continued at Malton after Douglas took over, for there was still lots of vacant space. A large section of the office was maintained for new project engineering, including the hydrofoil and augmentor wing. The huge spares inventory, from Chipmunk to Buffalo, which had only recently been established under one roof in Malton, stayed there for a number of years. The hangars backing onto Derry Road were handy for storing Caribous and Twin Otters, but required a time-consuming shuttle service back and forth between the two airports, particularly with the growing traffic at Toronto International Airport.

During the months that followed the collapse of the Douglas contract, people continued to ask, "What happened?" Many maintained that DHC could have solved the production difficulties and maintained control of the property and the wing contract. Douglas was not anxious to locate in Canada, but had no alternative at the time. When

and by early 1963 they had old AUA back in pristine condition. Everyone agreed that the turnover to the museum should be a formal affair. Phil Garratt was proud of the effort and invitations were sent to the aviation fraternity for May 10.

The program began with Garratt introducing the company team who had done the reconditioning: George Blanchard, Jack Driscoll, Tom Glasson, Ben Goul, John Hall, Tom Hollinsworth, Howard MacDonald, Bella MacDonald, Kathleen Neal and John Slaughter. Ken Molson spoke to the audience as did Carl Burke, who ended by presenting AUA's log book to Mr. J.H. Parkin, head of the National Research Council. Parkin added his thanks on behalf of the museum and everyone adjourned to the cafeteria for refreshments. AUA suffered the indignity of being shipped by land to the National Aviation Museum, where it is viewed by thousands of visitors yearly.

(Above) The second prototype Caribou wearing its attractive early-1960s colour scheme. CF-LAN was used for engineering trials, type certification and as a sales demonstrator. Here it was taking part in the historic Resolution Island airlift in 1961. (DH)

(Right) As it was for the Beaver and Otter, the U.S. military was the main buyer of Caribous, designating them AC-1s (later CV-2s, then C-7s). Of 307 Caribous, 164 went to the U.S. Army. Here an early example, fresh from the paint shop, awaits delivery. (DH)

(Right) A U.S. Army Sikorsky CH-54 heavy lift helicopter of the 1st Cavalry Division slings a damaged Caribou from An Khe, Vietnam, in December 1965. Many Caribous were lost to enemy action and accident during the war. (U.S. Army)

Caribou 57-3082 was the fourth YAC-1 Caribou ("Y" for service test). It served for years at Fort Bragg, North Carolina, as a jump plane for the Golden Knights parachute team until replaced by an F.27 Friendship in 1985. After its retirement, 57-3082 was transported by C-5B Galaxy to Dyess AFB, Texas, where in May 1992 it joined the base historic air park. (DH)

(Below) RCAF 5322, the 11th Caribou, on United Nations duty in 1967. The RCAF/CF had nine Caribous from 1960-71. Upon delivery of 15 Buffalos, the Caribous were donated to Tanzania. Many later served civil operators all over the world. (Dave Lamb)

(Right) In 1963-64 Australia ordered 25 Caribous to replace its Dakotas. George Neal checked out the initial RAAF pilots at Downsview in February 1964. On March 17 the first three Caribous left for 38 Squadron in Richmond, New South Wales, arriving on April 22. Here A4-140 poses for a DHC photographer before delivery. It survived 2½ years of war in Vietnam and remained in service in 1998. By this time the RAAF planned to keep its Caribous for several more years. (DH)

DE HAVILLAND IN CANADA

Lenn Bayliss of Brisbane took these RAAF (35 Squadron) Caribou photos. A4-285 was practicing STOL landings. A4-234 was doing a nose wheelie – a notorious RAAF airshow gimmick – down the runway at Amberley.

(Below) One of DHC's grand publicity photos of the 1960s was this one of a Caribou, Otter and Beaver for Ghana. G401 was the 31st Caribou off the line. It later was purchased by U.S. interests and was re-sold to the Indian Air Force, becoming M2169. Only the GAF, RAAF and U.S. Army operated all three of these famous DHC types. (DH)

The Caribou was not widely used in Canada, where there always was a supply of affordable old propliners like the DC-3, DC-4, and C-46 to do the work. However, a few Caribous found work, always in some rugged hinterland. Here C-GVYZ, originally with the Kuwaiti Air Force, was delivering fuel for helicopters in northwest B.C. in July 1980. (Brent Newbery)

Years later C-GVYZ still was at work. Here it was with Air Tindi on DEW Line clean-up at Port Radium, NWT, on August 15, 1995. The job was to remove scrap from an old telecommunications site. In the second view Capt Tom Hanson is flying VYZ back to Yellowknife. In 1997 VYZ was sold in Florida as N112CH, where it freighted in the Caribbean. (Larry Milberry)

The Turbo Caribou uses PT6A-67Rs. Marketed by Pen Turbo Aviation, it offers the Caribou a new lease on life. Here Pen Turbo's N600NC flies near home base, Cape May County Airport, NJ, in November 1996. By March 1998 N600NC had logged more than 200 hours. Gobi Gobalian of Pen Turbo commented, "Our trust in the Caribou is fully justified. After all it is a de Havilland Canada product." (Howard Levy)

The T64 might have been a U.S. Navy development engine, but the Army were closely monitoring its test in the Caribou. They had ambitions to operate an advanced version capable of carrying vehicles and they now had a turboprop engine with the right performance. In keeping with Army policy of constant improvement, they presented their requirements in the form of a design competition. They specified a STOL transport able to carry the tactical loads of the Boeing Vertol CH-47 helicopter, including a Pershing Missile, 105 mm howitzer or a ³/₄ ton truck. Turbine engines, rear loading and a five-ton payload were specified. The company put its accumulated data into a proposal called the Caribou II and entered it in the competition during May 1962. The other finalists of 25 competing companies were Fairchild, Grumman and North American Rockwell. The evaluation took nearly a year, ending with a contract for DHC in March 1963 for four DHC-5 prototypes. The new airplane was to be developed for $22.5 million on a one-third share basis among the Canadian government, U.S. Army and DHC.

The U.S. Army were pleased with the arrangement but the USAF grew more restless. Design went ahead speedily, for the project, now called the Buffalo, was a natural extension of DHC's STOL line. It received the U.S. designation CV-7A and took only one year to bring to the testing stage. The Buffalo flew on April 9, 1964, with Bob Fowler, Mick Saunders and Bob Dingle as crew. Testing with the cooperation of the U.S. Army and Canadian government was toward FAA CAR 4b certification. All went well – by the time approval was obtained in April 1965, four prototypes were flying. It was then that Ottawa ordered 15 Buffalos for the RCAF, enabling the company to begin production.

Four evaluation models were delivered to the United States for comprehensive tests totalling 500 hours of flying. The military proving cycle was so trouble-free that a 90-day trial was ordered for two aircraft in a combat environment. The first Buffalo departed Fort Rucker, Alabama, on November 12, 1965, arriving in Nha Trang, South Vietnam, on the 17th. It was demonstrated on the 18th and went to work the next day, carrying 17,400 lb. (7,900 kg) of cargo and 112 pas-

CHAPTER EIGHT

BUFFALO DAYS

sengers in five hours of flying. The second Buffalo arrived on the 22nd and went into service two days later. Both aircraft teamed perfectly with the Caribous of the 92nd Aviation Company supporting operations in the Vietnam interior. The jungle airstrips varied from 1,000 to 3,000 ft. (300 to 900 m) and the support action involved cargo, troops, supply drops and LOLEX (Low Level Extraction, in which the cargo is pulled from the rear doors by parachute) deliveries, often on short notice. The test aircraft were an inspiration, for they carried greater loads and did everything with more flair than the Caribou. On low-level missions, under enemy attack, the Buffalo's steep descent and pull-up kept it out of the range of enemy fire.

The aircraft were deliberately put into front-line action. Loads of 10,000 lb. (4,500 kg) were routine. Air drops included ³/₄-ton army trucks and on one mission a Buffalo dropped 64 Vietnamese paratroops. When a special fuelling operation was called for, 45-gallon drums were hauled into a strip 25 drums per aircraft. A good day's work, according to one crew, was 60,000 lb. (27,000 kg) of cargo and 170 passengers in 4:50 hours of flying. Maintenance was reasonable for a new aircraft so far from home – only 10-15 per cent of the available spares were used. Operational commanders were pleased with such performance.

When the aircraft returned to Fort Rucker in mid-February, they had flown 605 hours with 416 sorties, carried 1,045 tons (950 tonnes) of supplies and 2,831 passengers. Both returned in serviceable condition with only minor damage recorded. The commander of the 5th Special Forces Group requested the Buffalo on a regular basis to support his units. This was never put into action for it came at a difficult time. The Air Force had not been idle throughout this period, for their stepped-up studies showed that they could meet logistical requirements with the Lockheed C-130 Hercules. This decision coincided with the arrival in Washington of a new Secretary of Defense, Robert McNamara. His background had been with the Ford empire and with a consulting company that had done work for the USAF. While de Havilland looked worriedly across the border at this turn of events, a compromise was reached between the two services. The Army would

With Caribous still on the line, Buffalo No. 1 takes shape at Downsview in early 1964. (DH)

acquire all helicopters for their tactical support and the Air Force would take over all fixed-wing operations, including Caribous that were still in the system (to be called the C-7A). The Buffalo got lost in the shuffle from then on; all liaison work with it ceased. It was a major setback for DHC to lose such a valued customer and such a large project with politics the only reason. The shock severely retarded further engineering development on the Buffalo. But production was under way and a search began for other customers. Deliveries of DHC-5A Buffalos to the RCAF began in 1967. These incorporated improvements developed from the Vietnam interlude. By 1968 sales materialized in Brazil, with two orders of 12 each, and Peru, which bought 16. Production was temporarily terminated in August 1972 with the delivery of aircraft No. 59.

As sales tapered off through 1972, more thought was given to improvements. If the U.S. Army's plans had been allowed to run full course, constant improvement would have been routine. It was also clear that the original specifications, written around STOL tactical requirement for rough terrain, were penalizing the aircraft in the normal transport category. Design criteria allowed much greater payloads from paved runways, resulting in two sets of performance figures. One would be an Assault STOL version at

(Above) Buffalo rollout day at Downsview. There were four pre-production U.S. Army aircraft. Although the U.S. ordered no more, these four had long careers in experimental and scientific flying. (DH)

(Right) Engineering and production heads at the Buffalo rollout on February 14, 1964. Left to right: W.T. Heaslip, N.E. Rowe, R.D. Hiscocks, W.C. Burlison, F.H. Buller, W. Bozanin and T.G. Higgins. (DH 17362)

(Below) Guests watch in amazement as a Buffalo makes a maximum-effort STOL landing on the grass at de Havilland. The taxi strip is lined with aircraft, mostly visitors. From the top are an Otter, Beaver, USAF C-131, Cessna 337, Heron, Beech Seminole, Caribou, Beech L-23F, Aero Commander L-26 and an RCAF Cosmopolitan. (DH 18152)

41,000 lb. (18,600 kg) gross weight for unprepared fields, the other at 49,200 lb. (22,300 kg) for paved runways. Once the decision was made, more than 60 improvements were incorporated, including anti-skid brakes, Beta control propellers and a new auxiliary power unit. The major change was the GE CT64-820-4, increased from 2,970 shp at sea level and 86°F (30°C) to 3,133 shp. This Buffalo was the DHC-5D and a new production batch was ordered to incorporate all planned improvements. Production resumed in 1976.

The amazing Buffalo, with its history of technical progress and political setbacks, continued in production until 1982. Like the Caribou it toured widely, recording sales in 17 countries outside North America. The year 1982 ended with the sale of 10 Buffalos to Egypt and brought the total over 18 years to 121.

A World Record

Buffalo No. 60 was used for prototype testing of the new "D" model and showed improved performance in all areas of flight. Pilot Tom Appleton was doing high-altitude handling at 30,000 ft. (9,100 m) and noted that his time in climbing to the test area had been exceedingly short. Reflecting on the higher flat rating of the new engine and the D-model's higher power-to-weight ratio, he realized the climb must have been close to a world record. A search of the figures revealed that the Group 2 climb record for turbo-

props in the unlimited weight class was held by the Lockheed P-3C Orion at 10 minutes, 26 seconds to 9,000 meters (29,500 ft.). He felt the Buffalo could beat this easily and requested permission to apply for a record attempt in conjunction with other high altitude Buffalo test work. He applied to the Fédération Aéronautique Internationale, the official world body on such trials, through the Canadian representative, the Royal Canadian Flying Clubs Association. By early February the necessary recording and calibration equipment was in place and on February 16, 1976, W.P. "Bill" Paris of the RCFCA was in attendance at de Havilland to act as official FAI steward.

The crew for the attempt in Buffalo C-GBUF-X was captain Tom E. Appleton, co-pilot W.E. "Bill" Pullen and engineer Barry Hubbard. Appleton lifted off at Downsview for a direct climb to 30,000 ft. (9,150 m). The tapes started to record from brake release and printed the times through every altitude. The flight took only 17 minutes from takeoff to

(Right) A 105 mm field piece and light truck go aboard a Buffalo during trials. (DH 23358)

(Below) A Buffalo does a demo STOL landing on a rough strip. (DH 32836)

The crew of the record-breaking Buffalo after completing the climb-to-height record on February 16, 1976. Barry Hubbard, Tom Appleton and Bill Pullen. (DH 43343)

touchdown and covered just 13 miles. Even without instrumentation and tapes they knew they had bettered the Orion's time. It turned out to be a margin of two minutes and 22.5 seconds The time to 3,000 meters (9,800 ft.) had been 2 minutes, 12.75 seconds; to 6,000 meters (19,700 ft.), 4 minutes, 27.5 seconds; and to 9,000 meters (29,500 ft.), 8 minutes, 3.5 seconds. These constituted three records in each of the two categories – one for the turboprop "unlimited" class and one for the new class (no previous record) for turboprops in the 12,000-16,000 kilogram class. During those 17 minutes of flying, Appleton and his crew had broken six "time to height" records and established the Buffalo as a top world performer.

The Bell-Bottom Buffalo

An interesting design project involving the Buffalo brought DH Canada together with Bell Aerospace Company of Buffalo, New York. Bell had been experimenting for years with an air cushion landing system (ACLS) on smaller aircraft to the point where the system was ready for test on a larger scale. Canadian Forces CC-115 Buffalo 115451 was chosen as the vehicle and a combined U.S./Canada research and development program was organized. Bell built the air cushion trunk, while Pratt & Whitney Canada supplied two ASP-10 air supply systems using ST6 gas turbine engines driving axial fans. DHC did the installation and the test flying for system function and aerodynamic stability. Proving flights were conducted in 1975 by the USAF 4950th Test Wing at Wright Patterson Air Force Base, Ohio. Costs were shared by the USAF and Canada's Department of Industry, Trade and Commerce.

It was a challenging exercise for DHC's experimental test department under technical project manager C.J. "Chris" Austin. First, the two slim turbine engines were installed on the fuselage under the Buffalo wings. Ductwork was attached to a 32- by 14-ft. (10 by 4.3 m) inflatable "doughnut" on the underside of the aircraft. In normal flight the two-way-stretch rubber/nylon composite skirt clung closely to the bottom of the fuselage like a well-fitting girdle. For landing, the air cushion was inflated to about 160 pounds per square foot. Escaping air from over 700 small holes around the ground contact area provided a supporting "lubricant." Bob Fowler did the aerodynamic testing on the regular gear and proved the aircraft's flight stability with the trunk in both positions before turning it over to the USAF.

Unfortunately most de Havilland personnel who had watched the test vehicle take shape were unable to witness the field trials in 1975, in which it was tested on all manner

A preproduction Buffalo lands after a test flight at Downsview. (DH)

of rough terrain by the USAF. The Buffalo, looking more like an ungainly hippo, proved it could traverse pavement, grass, mud and snow – even six-foot-diameter craters. It tracked sideways in a cross-wind and achieved braking through inflatable skids in the trunk. Wingtip floats and skids kept the wings level on ground or water. The tests fulfilled all expectations for performance and controllability within the limits of the program and showed that the ACLS concept was compatible with a STOL high-wing turboprop. For military purposes the bell-bottom Buffalo proved it could handle emergency rescue roles in a variety of terrain, although considerable trunk material development would be required to achieve adequate life. After Buffalo 115451 was restored to Canadian Forces configuration at Downsview, it was no longer the showpiece it had been, but it was still pointed out to visitors as the ACLS Buffalo with the comment, "It used to take off and land on a cushion of air."

The Bell ACLS (Air Cushion Landing System) on a modified Buffalo with the inflatable trunk extended. Note the port compressor turbine under the wing, as well as the stabilizing outriggers. (DH 39423)

Powered Lift Research

A long-term V/STOL research program known as the "augmentor wing" began at Avro Canada in 1960 with theoretical studies into ducted jet flaps and powered lift. Thrust deflection or thrust vectoring, as it is called, was an essential element of the new concept. With the Avro shut-down, augmentor wing project leader Don C. Whittley moved to DHC to continue the work and become program manager in advanced research and technology. In 1965 a combined program began, bringing together the U.S. National Aeronautics and Space Administration (NASA) and the Cana-

dian Department of National Defence. A large-scale model with a wing span of 42 ft. (13 m) was built by DHC for test in a 40 by 80-ft. (12 by 24 m) wind tunnel at NASA's Ames Research Center at Moffett Field, California. Success with these tests warranted a proof-of-concept aircraft.

The U.S. and Canadian governments agreed that NASA and the Canadian Department of Industry, Trade and Commerce would modify a C-8A Buffalo for flight research. DITC contracted with DHC and Roll-Royce of Canada to provide the propulsion system and new engine nacelles. NASA had Boeing of Seattle modify the aircraft, install the wing duct system and do initial flight tests. Two Spey turbofan engines were modified at the Rolls-Royce plant in Montreal to supply an air distribution system for vectoring cold by-pass thrust through the augmentor flap and directing hot propulsive thrust (about 60 per cent of the total) to rotating nozzles (similar to those on the Harrier V/STOL fighter). The concept was called the augmentor wing because the combination of a blown wing and vectored thrust serves to "augment" wing lift and thrust simultaneously.

Wing changes involved reducing the span by 17 ft. (5m) and replacing all original wing structure aft of the rear spar. Here the air distribution ducting was installed, along with augmentor flaps, ailerons and spoilers. Fixed full-span leading edge slats were installed. Little was left of the original wing. When the special engine nacelles, complete with the modified Speys, were shipped from DHC, final assembly took place at Boeing and the Augmentor Wing Buffalo was rolled out and flown initially on May 1, 1972. Boeing pilot Thomas E. Edmonds tested the aircraft for basic airworthiness and flight characteristics before delivering it to Ames. An interesting eight months of flying followed, with a number of U.S. and Canadian test pilots, including DHC's Bob Fowler, participating in the evaluations.

Cost dictated an austere test vehicle in which to test Whittley's concepts. The landing gear did not retract and most of the systems were modified from the original Buffalo. The engines, which had been chosen for their ease of modifi-

The augmentor wing Buffalo in a dramatic takeoff photo, then in flight during NASA trials. In a later version four Spey engines were fitted. (DH)

G/DE HAVILLAND

A photo and diagram illustrating the augmentor wing principle. Air is blown through the ducted augmentor flap, while most of the thrust is obtained from the rotating nozzles. (DH)

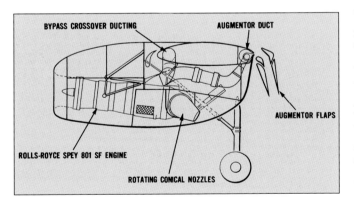

BYPASS CROSSOVER DUCTING   AUGMENTOR DUCT

AUGMENTOR FLAPS

ROLLS-ROYCE SPEY 801 SF ENGINE

ROTATING CONICAL NOZZLES

DHC engineers Jack Uffen, second from left, and Don Whittley, second from right, visit Boeing for discussions on the augmentor wing. (DH)

cation, were noisy and subject to high fuel consumption. The cost-cutting features did not detract in any way from the low-speed performance and handling qualities. In all vital parameters the aircraft met or bettered expectations. The rotating thrust nozzles allowed a steep descent at high power settings. Cross-ducting in the wings combined the cold flow with the hot thrust of the engines to compensate for asymmetric roll and yaw.

The Spey-powered Buffalo regularly performed STOL-type approaches and landings on a 7½-degree glide slope at speeds from 55 to 65 knots (100 to 120 km/h). Takeoff rolls averaged 600 ft. (183 m), and 900 ft. (274 m) to clear a 35-ft. (11 m) obstacle. Using a higher flap setting, these values later were reduced to 300 and 450 ft. (91 and 137 m). When all factors were established, in 1975 the program moved to aerial navigation and automatic terminal guidance. By 1976 flying totalled 250 hours and all areas of certification had been examined.

The joint government contracts ended in 1980, bringing the first stage to a successful conclusion. With over 900 flying hours, the test vehicle was returned to Canada in 1981 by Canadian Forces test pilot Major Larry Dufraimont. It went first to Downsview and then to the Canadian Forces base at Mountainview, Ontario. Here it began a 30-month project-definition exercise sponsored by Ottawa to assess the commercial aspects of a new generation aircraft in either a military or civil configuration. Don Whittley and his team visualized an advanced STOL transport in the Boeing 737 class with fuel efficient, high-bypass engines having a noise level approaching that of the Dash 7. Whittley also pointed out that other applications were possible including a Lockheed C-130 Hercules replacement or a smaller naval support aircraft.

Don Whittley received wide recognition for his work in augmentor technology. In 1973 he received the Canadian Aeronautics and Space Institute McCurdy Award for his contributions. In 1975 he presented the 32nd British Commonwealth Lecture at the Royal Aeronautical Society meeting in London, England.

(Above) The DHC-5 Transporter demonstrates LAPES, where a load on a skid is pulled from the rear ramp by parachute. The Transporter was DHC's attempt to market an increased-all-up-weight civil Buffalo. This effort failed due to a steep price tag and the impractical (for civil purposes) T64 engine. (DH 52213 Terry Shwetz)

Antarctic Action

Service crews from DH Canada have often been called upon to perform outstanding maintenance feats far from home, particularly during the Vietnam War. It happened again in the summer of 1980, but this time the locale was 1,500 miles from the South Pole. It all started with a minor mishap to the touring DHC-5 Transporter, which was on O'Higgins Island in the Chilean section of the Antarctic. The port landing gear had broken through the ice crust, resulting in propeller and engine damage. Replac-

Members of the Transporter recovery team on O'Higgins Island survey the damage to their wind-blown tent before resuming the propeller change. (DH 49354)

ing a propeller was routine, but getting seven and a half tons of supplies and equipment to retrieve the airplane developed into a major expedition. Crawford Byers was despatched to Alaska to get a set of Caribou skis. Doug Fleming prepared a new propeller. Norm Bailey organized the equipment needed for the changeover. Everything was shipped to Chile, then forwarded, first by Chilean Lockheed C-130 Hercules from Punta Arenas to Base Frei, then by Chilean Twin Otters.

The DHC crew built a tent around the engine, but on August 12, raging winds wrecked the tent, curtailing work for three days. When the winds relented, there was a massive snow removal job before the new propeller and

the skis could be fitted. This would be the first time skis had been used on the DHC-5, but they allowed pilot Bill Pullen to ease the aircraft out of the snowdrift, pack their equipment and head north to warmer weather. Fleming and Bailey described it as "just another job" when they got back to Downsview, but confessed to an aversion to ever shovelling snow again.

It took an exceptionally hard landing to make DHC-5 C-GCTC (No. 103) come apart at the Farnborough Air Show in September 1984. No one was injured and the fire was just a brief flash. (Ron Nunney)

(Above) The second Buffalo does an engine run at Downsview in September 1964. Needing a Caribou replacement, the U.S. funded the Buffalo, but when the U.S. Army ceded its fixed-wing fleet to the USAF, support for the Buffalo died. DHC had to find a new market for this specialized product. This proved tough, but customers gradually came forward. As for Buffalo No. 2, it later was N326D with the University of Michigan (operating for the National Center for Atmospheric Research), then N715NA, based with NASA at the Ames Research Center at Moffett Field, California. (Larry Milberry)

(Above) Buffalo 115460 of 424 Squadron (CFB Trenton) at London, Ontario, on June 2, 1991. In January 1996 it went to Avior Technologies of Miami, then was leased to Inter Air of Zimbabwe. (Dave Thompson)

(Right) Canada's Buffalos (designated CC-115 in CF service) worked in search and rescue for three decades. Nos. 413, 424, 440 and 442 squadrons and No. 103 Search and Rescue Unit used them at bases from Comox, B.C., to Trenton, Ontario, St. Hubert, Quebec, Greenwood, Nova Scotia, and Gander, Newfoundland. In 1998 only 442 Squadron in Comox had Buffalos. Of the original 15, only six remained in service. Here 115451, formerly the "Bell-bottom Buffalo," lands at Hamilton in June 1982, wearing a modified United Nations colour scheme. (Dave Thompson)

(Left) Buffalo 115456 of 442 Squadron lands at Abbotsford in August 1986. (Swartz Col.)

231

Buffalo 115451 in for maintenance at Comox in April 1990. (Larry Milberry)

(Below) No. 115457 at the Hamilton International Airshow in June 1996. The Canadian Forces ordered its Buffalos in 1967. They went to Mobile Command at St. Hubert (429 Squadron) in the army tactical support role, but the fleet gradually moved to search and rescue. (Andrew H. Cline)

(Left) The original four Buffalos took on many projects in the U.S. Here N13689 (serial No. 3, ex-63-13689) of the U.S. Department of Commerce visits Downsview in February 1975. (Larry Milberry)

C-GTLW-X was modified for commercial use as the DHC-5 Transporter. It made an international sales tour, but little interest resulted. Here the Transporter was doing certification trials at North Bay in May 1980. (Dave Thompson)

(Left) This Ethiopian Airlines Buffalo served for years in the Horn of Africa. Here it was involved with humanitarian relief in Kenya and Sudan in March 1993. (Larry Milberry)

(Right) FAC064 of the Ecuadorian Air Force posing for the de Havilland photographer before delivery. (DH)

(Below) One of the versions of the augmentor wing Buffalo performs at the 1986 Abbotsford International Airshow. (Kenneth I. Swartz)

CHAPTER NINE

TWIN OTTER & HYDROFOIL

"There is a tide in the affairs of men," said Shakespeare, "which, taken at the flood, leads on to fortune." In similar vein he went on, "We must take the current when it serves, or lose our ventures." No words could more aptly describe the logic behind the DHC-6 Twin Otter. It emerged in what many considered too much haste, but the time was right and taken on the flood of market demand. The DHC-6 was the most significant happening in a decade at Downsview. It was the project that was to see DHC through a long, difficult period. It came at the height of Caribou sales, when DHC was riding the crest of U.S. Army interest in STOL. It bridged two marketing periods: U.S. military sales and the emerging commuter airline business.

The engineers had always visualized an Otter with two engines – the Caribou resulted from one such study. The Otter was large for one engine and its payload on floats was limited. Northern operators were pleased with its cabin volume, but wanted multi-engine safety and needed more payload to stay competitive. The lack of an engine with a suitable power-to-weight ratio was the obstacle to a twin in that weight category, but news of the PT6 started people thinking. Russ Bannock recalled:

The break came in Vietnam, where we had a lot of Otters and Caribous. The company had a very efficient group of technical representatives and field maintenance personnel there in 1963 and I was over on one of my regular trips. I flew from base to base in U.S. Army Otters, for it was the only way we could get around easily. The officers with whom I flew were all high in their praise of the airplane but were unanimous on two points. They talked constantly of two engines in the Otter for greater safety and would have preferred a tricycle undercarriage to combat the ever-present crosswinds.

On the long flight home in a dreary military transport, I couldn't get one Army general's proposals out of my mind. I drew up numerous plans and sketches based on my talks, to present to the engineers when I got back to Downsview. Dick Hiscocks, "Nero" Rowe and Fred Buller were all in agreement. Peter Martin immediately began preparing a set of preliminary designs. I felt sure that I could sell something like this in quantity to the U.S. Army and it was a natu-

ral for commercial bush operations. We were working very closely at the time with Pratt & Whitney on their PT6, for it offered 50 per cent more power for 35 per cent less installed weight. Bob Fowler had a lot of experience with two of them in the STOL research Otter. The results were just what we were looking for.

It was an extremely busy period for us. We had moved into a new type of management under Hawker Siddeley and announced a program to build DC-9 wings at Malton. We had contracted to build four Buffalos, a hydrofoil for the Canadian Navy and we were also into guided missiles. We had just completed installing a turbine engine in the Beaver and here we were planning a new airplane. The interest in a two-engined Otter was completely genuine; we had to get going at that time or we would lose the market.

An important meeting on the subject was convened on July 22, 1963. Attending were C.H. Dickins, R. Bannock, W.T. Heaslip, F.H. Buller, D.L. Buchanan, L. Trotter, R.D. Hiscocks, P. Martin and N.E. Rowe. All aspects were discussed, including the possibility of an all-new design. This was ruled out because time was short. A retracting gear was discussed, but the speed loss for short-haul STOL operations was not worth the design involved. To gain more cabin and baggage space, the Otter fuselage would be extended.

Not the first Twin Otter, but the first Otter with twin engines. Early planning for a twin-engined Otter came during the last stage of the STOL test vehicle which used two PT6s. (DH 15818)

This meant increasing the wingspan. Good STOL performance was deemed essential and a market for 300 aircraft was envisioned.

The design office maintained basic bush plane simplicity. A rugged fixed gear with compression blocks in the main gear and a steerable nosewheel provided a starting point. Basic Otter wingspan was increased by 7 ft. (2.1 m), overall length by 10 ft. (3 m). Fuel capacity was increased, all doors were enlarged and a new tail was designed. U.S. Army interest was high and was maintained through regular progress reports. This urgency led DHC to start five test aircraft. The object was to fly the first as soon as possible and do static testing of structural components as flying progressed. Phil Garratt thought it was a good idea, but came up with the inevitable questions: "What is it

Twin Otter prototype CF-DHC-X nears completion at Downsview, then does an engine run in a scene from the spring of 1965. Note the STOL Otter in the background. (DH 20964, '994)

going to cost?" and "Can you find out by next Friday?" It was one more challenge to the seasoned group at Downsview, which had faced this sort of thing before. The old fire was ignited again! The heads of departments – Bill Houston on pricing, Fred Buller on engineering and Bill Burlison on production – got their people working and came up on time with a figure of $6.5 million for the development program. The subject was thoroughly discussed while Phil Garratt sat listening. He pushed his chair up to the table, looked around the room and raised the deciding question, "Any objections?" The silence in the room dictated the answer, the minutes were recorded, the Twin Otter was on its way.

The prototype and four pre-production aircraft, designated Series I, had 550-shp PT6A-20s and a limiting take-off weight of 11,000 lb. (4,500 kg). By February 1965 final assembly of the prototype was started; a production go-ahead was issued for 10 additional machines. On April 29, 1965, there was a small roll-out ceremony. Sir Roy Dobson, chairman of

the worldwide Hawker Siddeley organization, of which de Havilland was a part, joined with the DHC directors for an official photograph. Bob Fowler, Mick Saunders and Barry Hubbard flew the aircraft for the first time on May 20. The day after, word came from England that Sir Geoffrey de Havilland had died at age 82. In July, George Mickleborough resigned and on the 29th of that month a major Hawker Siddeley management change took place. Phil Garratt stepped down as president. William Benton Boggs, formerly a vice-president with Hawker Siddeley in Montreal, was appointed president and chief executive officer. A graduate of McGill University (B.Eng., Mech.), he had served in WWII as a squadron leader in the aeronautical engineering branch of the RCAF. He was awarded the OBE in 1944. Next he was assistant superintendent of maintenance at Trans-Canada Air Lines, then production manager at Canadair. In 1957 he joined Hawker Siddeley in Montreal, where he rose from plant manager to vice-president.

The first flight of Twin Otter CF-DHC-X over the outskirts of Toronto on May 20, 1965. This aircraft is now in the National Aviation Museum in Ottawa. (DH 21040)

Twin Otter Certified

Department of Transport certification for the Twin Otter came on April 7, 1966. No. 3, CF-SUL-X, was the certification aircraft; Walter Gadzos was the DOT pilot in charge. The type certificate was No. 82. Four days later Dave Fairbanks demonstrated the aircraft to a growing airline in the mid-western U.S., Air Wisconsin. In September he swung through Boston, New York and the far west, demonstrating the Twin Otter all the way to California. The following month he did a four-day sweep to seven U.S. military bases. Once again the Pentagon showed solid interest – it asked for a quotation for 100 Twin Otters. This was hardly

Air Wisconsin inaugurated Twin Otter service on the same day in 1966 as Pilgrim Airlines. Air Wisconsin started in 1965 with a Dove connecting Appleton, Wisconsin with Chicago. Soon a wide region was being served with Twin Otters and Dash 7s. (Benner Col.)

(Left) The one-of-a-kind decal designed to promote the new PT6-Twin Otter partnership. (DH)

in the mail before talk of another competition complicated the issue. Intense lobbying took place in Washington to have the Army rule out the STOL requirement. Suddenly, takeoff limitations were extended to 2,200 ft. (660 m) over a 50-ft. (15 m) obstacle. These guidelines allowed a Beech entry. The finalists in the competition were the Beech King Air and the Twin Otter. The contest narrowed to a battle of price. Although Bannock pressed for a competitive price, he was no longer in control of the project. With Garratt's retirement, Bannock did not have the backing he once enjoyed. A new DHC study resulted in a price considerably higher than Beech's. The matter was closed without the usual fly-off. The Army took the King Air, even though many demonstrations had proved the Twin Otter's performance to Army and Air Force satisfaction.

It did not take a clairvoyant to read the message: the days of large military orders at DHC had come to an end. But the game was not entirely lost. The Twin Otter – which some publications referred to as the ugly duckling – was performing beyond expectations and the price was right for the times. It was up to the sales department to come through. While Dave Fairbanks was demonstrating in North America and Grant Davidson was south of the equator, Buck Buchanan made sure that the Twin Otter got to the 1966 Hanover Air Show. Mick Saunders and Bob Irving were his demo team. Through the efforts of David Price and Laurie Jones of Hawker de Havilland Australia, Trans-Australia Airlines ordered four Twin Otters. This got world sales off to a good start. This good news was followed by a Chilean Air Force order for eight. Sultan Ghazi of Afghanistan was at Hanover and wanted the Twin Otter for his land-locked, mountainous country. Ontario backed its historic interest in DHC by taking delivery of the first Series I as soon as it was certified for floats. Trans-Australia Airlines took serial No. 6, now called the Series 100 (gross takeoff weight: 11,579 lb., 5,257 kg). Weldy Phipps, who was making a name for himself flying small aircraft on oversize tires in the Arctic, ordered No. 12. Max Ward, who had needled DHC about installing two engines in the Otter and who pushed for such a plane on floats, took No. 35 in April 1967.

A New Market

A bulging Twin Otter order book kept the plant busy, but the Pentagon's change of attitude worried Russ Bannock. He had counted on military business for the Twin Otter, but now would have to find new customers if production was to be maintained. While not planned, a new kind of customer suddenly appeared – with 15-19 seats, at a price of just under $300,000, the Series 100 Twin Otter became an attractive money-maker for aspiring U.S. commuter lines.

DHC test pilot Bob Fowler headed Twin Otter float certification. The first flight was from Toronto Harbour on October 1, 1966. Bob Dingle and Ed Wright were the flight test observers. The huge floats were built by Canadian Aircraft Products of Richmond, B.C. After initial trials with CF-DHC-X, CF-SUL-X was used for float certification. Walter Gadzos and Al Baker were the DOT pilots involved. (DH 24967)

The two DHC people most involved with the civil side were Buck Buchanan and George Hurren. Buck held the reins on world marketing; George was in charge throughout Canada, the U.S. and the Caribbean. When asked how de Havilland got into the airline commuter business, Buck's quick reply was, "If you were going to be perfectly honest, you would have to call it luck." To this George added, "Luck and Joe Fugere!"

The story dates to 1965-66 when the Twin Otter went on the world air show circuit. The 1966 Reading Air Show in Pennsylvania was typical. There, U.S. air taxi operators peered through the Twin Otter door and remarked on such a large cabin for a 12,500 lb. (5,625 kg) class airplane. Air taxi services had sprung up all over the U.S., particularly on the California coast and in the busy New York-Boston corridor. Typical in the New York area was Pilgrim Airlines, headed by Joe Fugere, one of the first to size up the Twin Otter's potential as a commuter aircraft. This ex-Navy aviator, who had bought out New London Flying Service in 1962, defied the cynics by calling his expanded service Pilgrim Airlines and selling flights from New London, Connecticut, to New York/Idlewild. It was a struggle but by 1965 his airline needed more capacity. He wanted Twin Otter No. 6, but had to settle for a later place on the line. On November 1, 1966, Pilgrim made its inaugural run with No. 14, from Groton/New London to New York's JFK International. This was the first scheduled Twin Otter service.

Air Wisconsin, which had Twin Otter No. 13, began scheduled flights on the same day and at the same hour, but the difference in time zones shaded the statistics in favour of Pilgrim. Within six months, these airlines had their second Twin Otters, which set a convincing precedent in the burgeoning short-haul market. Preston Welbourne of Air Wisconsin and Joe Fugere of Pilgrim became respected spokesmen for commuter airline affairs. Fugere became the first chairman of the Commuter Airline Association and served three years as a member of the Urban Transportation Advisory Council.

Orders from other fledgling airlines began flowing into DHC's sales department, where juggling priorities in the order book became the outstanding problem of the day. Competing airlines grew up around Boston and Los Ange-

DHC customer support manager Phil Halsey (left) with Joe Fugere. In 1960 Fugere took a stake in Connecticut-based New London Air Service (later Pilgrim Airlines), serving New London, Washington and New York. An airline strike in 1966 brought windfall business to small operators like Pilgrim. Within weeks Fugere had the money to buy his first Twin Otter. Pilgrim grew steadily, but eventually disappeared – Fugere sold to Business Express in 1986. By then the fleet included nine Twin Otters. Fugere used to say that he was the one who convinced DHC that the Twin Otter had a future in the U.S. commuter market. (DH 39860)

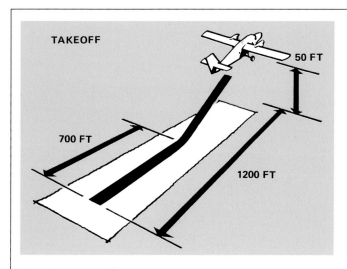

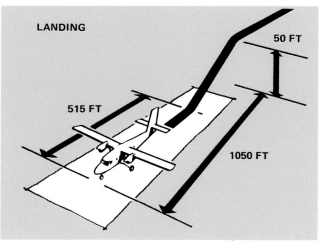

Licensing standards for the Twin Otter were based on an imaginary barrier or screen height of 50 ft. (15 m) for takeoff and landing. The approved takeoff distance was measured from throttle opening to that screen height and the landing distance until the airfraft came to a complete stop. Ground roll was included in the performance criteria.

PERFORMANCE STANDARDS – TWIN OTTER

	STOL	SFAR 23
Takeoff ground roll	213 m (700 ft.)	262 m (850 ft.)
Takeoff to 15 m (50 ft.)	366 m (1,200 ft.)	457 m (1,500 ft.)
Landing roll	157 m (515 ft.)	290 m (950 ft.)
Landing from 15 m (50 ft.)	320 m (1,050 ft.)	457 m (1,500 ft.)

les, all using Twin Otters, and a surprising number of orders came from small airlines in other countries. These squat-looking turbines with distinctive fixed gear were soon operating in the Caribbean, Mexico, Italy and Hawaii. Indonesia started a jungle airline with Twin Otters. Air Alpes in France put a landing strip on the side of a mountain, bringing customers from nearby cities to some of the best ski hills in the world. The exciting touchdown on the edge of a cliff with an uphill run to the ramp became routine, as did departures down the slope and off into space, like going down a mammoth ski jump.

As DHC demonstrated their brand of STOL, the major effort had been toward military customers. There were no special rules governing civil STOL when the Twin Otter be-gan carrying passengers; it was regarded simply as a normal CAR 3 category (criteria for general purpose U.S. civil aircraft). No credit was given for the fact that its ground rolls were shorter than other CAR 3 types or that its approach angle had a built-in steeper gradient. Twin Otter brochures carried two sets of field performance figures, one headed "STOL" and the other "CAR 3." It was sometimes difficult to explain that the airplane designed for a STOL landing distance of 1,050 ft. (320 m), over a 50-ft. (15 m) obstacle to a stop, was certified in CAR 3 at 1,940 ft. (591 m). Later, under U.S. Special Federal Air Regulations No. 23, the landing distance became 1,500 ft. (460 m). If the Twin Otter could talk, one could imagine it saying to the pilot, "What rules are we working under today, Boss? I can give you three choices."

Fifteen per cent of new Twin Otters went to Central and South America, starting with aircraft No. 7 to the Chilean Air Force in September 1966. The largest number went to Argentina, which took 22. Chile took 20, Peru 20, Colombia 15, Mexico 12 and Ecuador 10. Others later went there as used aircraft. Here Aeropostal's six Twin Otters await delivery to Venezuela in April 1977. (DH)

While best-remembered as the airline that inaugurated Dash 7 service, Rocky Mountain Airways, which began in 1968, provided Twin Otter service to places such as Denver, Vail, Aspen, Steamboat Springs and Cheyenne, specializing in the ski trade. (DH)

Most operators carrying commercial passengers were dealing with runways at least 3,000 ft. (900 m) long, well above any short-field limitations, so there was little pressure for STOL.

One small U.S. airline came into being because it could use the Twin Otter's short-field capacity. Houston, Texas, had just opened a new international airport. A group under Jay Seaborn sought to connect the busy Clear Lake/NASA space centre with the new airport and with the old Hobby Airport closer to downtown. They built a 2,500-ft. (750 m) strip opposite the space centre, calling it Clear Lake Metroport. Four Twin Otters were put to work on the shuttle service, flying the 32 miles (51 km) from Clear Lake in 11 minutes and making flights between the two airports in nine minutes. Aircraft were in the air from 6 a.m. until midnight, making 75 flights daily. The short runway concept proved

itself from the beginning, and later, as Metro Airlines, with Twin Otters, they pioneered using short strips in the corners of major airports, away from the big airliners. Metro thus established the first total STOL operation in the U.S.

A STOL Showcase

DH Canada is still proud of the Norwegian operation that took its STOL concept and built an airline around it. Norway's mountainous shores had always posed a transportation problem. Although seaplanes had played an important role in recent years, they had limitations. Widerøe Flyveselskap A/S had pioneered a successful float service on the coast, helping to break the isolation of the scattered communities. Seaplanes showed Norway the advantages of air transportation, at a time when it sought to improve ser-

Executive Airlines had its roots with Joseph C. Whitney. He began in 1960 operating Aero Commanders between Boston and Martha's Vineyard. He added de Havilland Doves and by 1969 ran the largest U.S. commuter airline, the fleet including 12 Twin Otters. Executive folded the same year, a victim of over-enthusiastic expansion, and a refusal by new owners to heed Whitney's advice. This Executive Twin Otter is in a typical feeder line scene – at a major terminal connecting with the trunk carriers. A United Airlines B.727 is beyond. (DH)

Widerøe senior pilots, Eric Langset, K.F. Baastad and Odd Schipberg, take delivery of their first Twin Otter in June 1968. (F.W. Hotson)

vices to remote areas. The Norwegians were studying the subject when Mick Saunders and Bob Irving arrived to demonstrate the Twin Otter. The Norwegians immediately recognized it as the answer to their problem. If communities would build small strips, a specialized air service could be set up, replacing the usual long sea voyages. Health services could be improved and the inhabitants would lose that feeling of isolation. After Widerøe studied the four Norwegian Air Force Twin Otters that arrived in Bodø in 1967, their minds were made up.

While one group began searching for landing sites, the Ministry of Transport and the Directorate of Civil Aviation prepared an operating structure. The government studied Twin Otter runway lengths and came up with a practical length of 2,600 ft. (800 m), which they set as a standard. They even coined their own terminology, calling the system their "short field services." Widerøe, as Norway's oldest independent operator, was asked to handle the new operation in all areas relating to staff and services. It was reconstructed with a wider range of shareholding which included local interests and Norway's other airlines – SAS, Braathens SAFE, and Fred Olsen. A practical plan with national unity as the common goal was evolved, based on a government subsidy.

On June 1, 1968, a group from Widerøe and the Directorate of Civil Aviation reached Downsview to train and take delivery of their first Twin Otter Series 200. By now the airport plan was completed south of Bodø. The first service was begun linking five communities to Trondheim. Each field had a paved landing strip, a control tower and a terminal building. Aids at each place included VASI, DME and a localizer. Citizens groups, unlike their counterparts in North America, encouraged the building of airstrips and the provision of fire fighting services. The DCA was represented at each field and the system was tied to the national airlines for everything from weather information to seat reservations.

Norwegian thoroughness paid off during the inaugural year 1969 when the lone aircraft, LN-LMN, carried 25,000 passengers and 300,000 lb. (135,000 kg) of freight. LMN was in the air 12 hours a day, six days a week. In spite of such utilization, involving 120 landings a week, Widerøe experienced only a single one-hour delay for technical reasons. Flight cancellations for weather occurred only three days in the first year. Those along the route were delighted with the service and the far-sighted Norwegian government planned to extend service north of the Arctic Circle.

Four Twin Otter Series 300s were ordered in 1971 for a new service north of Bodø, linking the isolated Lofoten Islands with communities along the northern tip of Finnmark. The main operations base at Bodø expanded, with a sub-base and hangar at Hammerfest,

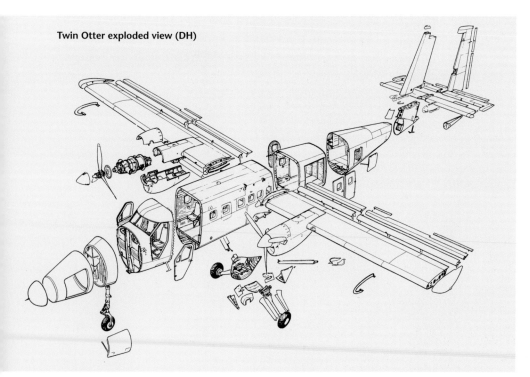

Twin Otter exploded view (DH)

(Left) Series 200 demonstrator CF-YFT at Malton airport near Toronto in July 1971. Note its large water-bombing belly tank (this system didn't reach production). YFT later worked in the Arctic for Bell Canada, but in 1992 went to Indonesia as PK-KVK. On September 30, 1996, it landed hard in a rainstorm. Its wings tore off, but everyone survived. Although often listed as "damaged beyond repair," many such aircraft eventually fly again. (Larry Milberry)

(Right) The 844th and last Twin Otter went to Malaysia Airlines; it remained in service there in 1998. Here it was at Toronto's Pearson Airport, awaiting paint and delivery late in 1989. (Andrew H. Cline)

(Left) Air Alpes Twin Otter F-BSUL at a remote French ski resort in January 1978. SUL was later sold in Iceland. (Swartz Col.)

Twin Otter No. 533 began with Northern Thunderbird Air of British Columbia. A later career was in Colombia, but in 1989 it became 4X-AHZ for Arkia-Israel Inland Airlines. Here it was at Sdedov Airport near Tel Aviv in August 1991. (Kenneth I. Swartz)

The spacious Twin Otter cockpit. Note the variety of DHC types parked in the background. (DH)

Europe's northernmost city. Maintenance was of the highest order, pilot training and operating techniques on a par with the major airlines. Step by step the Norwegian showpiece service grew to 35 airports (20 north of the Arctic Circle), using as many as 14 Twin Otters. The aircraft proved equal to the task and laid the groundwork for the larger Dash 7 and Dash 8.

Canadians in Afghanistan

A study of ancient Afghanistan is one of bloodshed, destruction and poverty which has gone on since the days of Genghis Kahn. There were occasions when the tiny country seemed ready to take its place on the world stage, but each time, the rugged mountains and lack of roads prevented any chance of unity. After WWII, Afghanistan had a King, royal family and parliament. They sought foreign aid and were one of the first signatories of the 1944 Chicago Air Convention that started ICAO. Through this contact they won as-

sistance building airports and the help of Pan American Air Lines in building a national airline, Ariana Afghan. These programs provided an air link to the outside but had little impact on internal transportation, which depended on donkeys, camels and overcrowded buses.

By 1965, Ariana Afghan was making progress with four DC-3s and two DC-6Bs serving nine airports. One member of the Royal Family, HRH Sultan Ghazi, who also headed the Air Authority, was developing a dream of his own for opening up the country. He had attended the 1966 Hanover Air Show and had seen the Twin Otter perform. He matched the Twin Otter's STOL ability with Afghanistan's transportation needs, and again sought outside aid. Would ICAO help in a plan to supply Twin Otters? Canada was also approached for help in acquiring two aircraft on a trial basis, but was very cautious of such a prospect. ICAO headquarters in Montreal was briefed about the request at an early stage and asked that the Twin Otter at the 1966 Farnborough show visit Afghanistan.

ICAO contracted for a Canadian pilot, Fred Hotson, to conduct a fact-finding mission in the country during the summer of 1966.

As soon as Hotson arrived, Sultan Ghazi arranged airline flights with Ariana to the few existing airports. He also set up a 1,400-mile (2,240-km) tour in a four-wheel-drive Kaiser pickup truck, providing a driver and Afghan interpreter. The route via Bamiyan and Chakhcharan turned north at Herat to Mazar-I-Sharif near the Russian border, before turning south again at Kunduz to Kabul. The last section of the road had recently been paved by the Russians, who had also built an extensive tunnel through the Hindu Kush mountains. In later years it was easy to see why the Soviets had been so kind to the Afghans. A special diversion with the DC-6B was arranged for Hotson over the mountain ranges north of Faizabad.

The plan for an eventual operation was based on a donor country (or company – similar to Ariana under PanAm) providing management and training under the ICAO banner until the locals could become self sufficient. Hotson recommended that the aid program be run as a self-contained unit, and have no contact with Afghan Airlines. Thus did ICAO become the overseeing authority for the Twin Otter operation that lay ahead. In the fall of 1966, after the Farnborough Air Show, DHC pilots Tom Appleton and Armand Hollinsworth took a Turbo Beaver and Twin Otter to Afghanistan for a series of local demonstration flights. Sultan Ghazi was able to arrange funding for two Twin Otters and

signed an order at Downsview. By this time Hotson had been hired as a DHC test pilot and was assigned, along with engineer Harry Hunter, to accompany the first Twin Otter, YA-GAS, for training and indoctrination. Bakhtar Afghan Airlines now was under way, but it was all new for the three pilots presented for training. Hunter was given a group of apprentice mechanics graduated from the ICAO school in Beirut, but having no experience in maintenance.

One of the pilots did not make the grade, so a senior captain was seconded from Ariana to take his place. The operation started well as a money maker, taking tourists to the Bamian statues and other historical sites. An Indian captain (Law) was later hired. Routine visits by DHC tech reps Dick Gleasure, George Naida, Harry Hunter and others reported difficulties in maintaining basic standards and tried their best to help. In 1969 the ICAO representative in Kabul, T.R. Nelson, was concerned with the state of maintenance and questioned the ability of the Twin Otter Series 100 to perform on one engine at high altitude airports. He asked DHC for more assistance; Pilot Tony Shrive and tech rep George Kelly were sent over to work on these, and to try improving overall servicability.

By now Sultan Ghazi had gained more financial help, including Canadian, for additional Twin Otter Series 300s, which were delivered in stages. Dave Fairbanks and Bruce Jack delivered one; Mick Saunders took two, remaining for an extended period of pilot training. Bakhtar Afghan ended with three Series 300s, plus the original two Series 100s.

The inhabitants of the central Afghanistan town of Chakhcharan welcome the first Twin Otter to land in their area. (F.W. Hotson)

Unfortunately, accidents occurred, starting with YA-GAT at Bamian on April 18, 1973, when the crew and two passengers died. On March 10, 1983, YA-GAZ crashed into a mountain and on August 8, 1985, YA-GAY crashed at Bamian. The original YA-GAS was sold to Canada for much-needed cash, becoming C-GDQY in 1976.

Afghanistan's efforts to bring a few 20th century benefits to its hard-pressed inhabitants were ultimately thwarted through age-old tribal rivalries. In a complicated coup, the king and his family, including Sultan Ghazi, were forced to flee. In 1979 the Soviets invaded Afghanistan, creating a state of all-out war. What happened to the last Twin Otter is unknown, but the story may surface some day. This well-publicized war of a major nation trying to subdue a smaller neighbour did not end until 1988, when the Soviets admitted defeat and withdrew. This void revived the traditional fueding among rival warlords and the country slipped back another generation. Many of the quaint streets and historic buildings that so many Canadians viewed during the short period of modernization now lie in ruins along with Sultan Ghazi's dream of an internal airline.

Showmanship

Life in Flight Operations at Downsview was never dull nor was the pilot's job description confined to testing airplanes. The flying assignments were many and varied. Pilots were a vital part of the sales team and assignments took them to the far corners of the world. The man who allotted the tasks during the surge of Twin Otter demonstration tours was operations manager Dave Fairbanks, who took such assignments regularly to keep up his proficiency. He had taken part in all the major demonstrations since the days of the

Otter and was internationally recognized as one of the best in the business.

It was late 1973 and a crew change was needed in Peter Adams' Far East sales area. George Northrop had been demonstrating the Twin Otter for a month and was called back for another assignment. There was still another swing to be done through the Middle East following the Japanese aerospace show which was sponsored by the Society of Japanese Aircraft Constructors the second week in October. Fairbanks arrived in Tokyo on the 7th ready for whatever was needed.

The three competing aircraft – Short Skyvan, Britten Norman Islander and Twin Otter – were to perform on the 10th. Asked what sequence he would prefer, Fairbanks said, "Last." The Skyvan went first, and when the pilot of the BN Islander did his routine it consisted of circles and dives on the Twin Otter waiting in the ready area with engines running. If this display was intended to rattle the Twin Otter crew, the BN pilot had underrated Fairbanks.

Dave had his own series of manoeuvres and usually chose last spot on the program so he could improvise as the occasion demanded. The royal box with the dignitaries, including the Crown Prince, was positioned for the best possible view. Fairbanks now knew what he had to do. His short takeoff was followed by a series of dumbbell turns including a fast and slow flypast. On the last climb he feathered both engines and continued in the turns as before. At the correct moment his crewman Bruce Jack returned the propellers to normal and CF-DHA settled in to the shortest of landings at the far end of the runway. Fairbanks then did three more takeoffs and landings on the same runway, ending up in front of the crowd. A slight turn faced the Twin Otter to the box and, with precise manipulation of reverse thrust and

The Twin Otter demonstrator bows to the crowd after completing its demonstration routine. (DH 39547)

brakes, Fairbanks bowed the Twin Otter to the crowd. He had used the manoeuvre before but in Japan it was an instant hit. The crowd applauded and all began bowing in return. Several Twin Otters eventually went to Japan.

A Royal Visitor

With a reputation for slow-flying airplanes that could take off and land in extremely short distances, it was common to welcome interested visitors from foreign countries, particularly dignitaries who were themselves pilots. Prince Bernhard of the Netherlands had been in to fly the Otter with minimum publicity, but when the colourful Mohammed Reza Pahlavi, Shah of Iran, arrived on May 26, 1965, it was a different matter.

The Shah and his entourage were in Toronto on a number of missions including a trip to Downsview for a flight in a company aircraft. In view of the large retinue and the style of the East, the telephone calls in advance of the visit were frequent and detailed. All efforts were made to provide a welcome befitting a world figure and no one was closer to the barrage of phone calls than Garratt's secretary, Enid Koyl. The luncheon would be easy to arrange, for such functions were routine, but one last-minute request posed a new problem.

It was mentioned that the Shah's practice was to take a short nap after lunch and it would be appreciated if the appropriate facilities were provided. There was no "snooze room" at Downsview and there wasn't much time. Mrs. Koyl made a quick trip to a furniture store, bought a couch of the right size and had it delivered to the general manager's office. The couch drew a raised eyebrow and "What's all this?" from Phil Garratt, who agreed that their honoured guest should be invited to take a rest in the office if he so desired.

Mrs. Koyl prepared to do her part and kept an eye on the dining room for her cue. To her dismay the party headed straight for the line of aircraft, where a crowd gathered and photo bulbs flashed. Bob Fowler showed the Shah the Otter and Russ Bannock guided him through the Caribou. Dave Fairbanks took the royal visitor (and his bodyguard) for a flight in the Turbo Beaver and, combining salesmanship with diplomacy, Punch Dickins joined the bodyguard in the back.

Apparently the Shah had shrugged off the invitation for a nap as the temptation of adding another aircraft to his list of conquests was too great. This left the enterprising secretary with another problem: an unused couch that wasn't appropriate in the head office, didn't match anything and nobody wanted. It took considerable sales expertise to dispose of the "surplus material," which ended up in Doug Annan's recreation room.

After a tour of the plant, the Shah of Iran went up in a Turbo Beaver with Dave Fairbanks, Punch Dickins and a bodyguard. He is shown with Phil Garratt and Defence Minister Paul Hellyer. (DH 21119)

(Right) Crown Prince Birendra of Nepal, who later became King, is welcomed to Downsview by president William B. Boggs during a 1968 visit. (DH 29829)

Phil Garratt Retires

Phil Garratt's last year at Downsview was a mixture of pride and frustration. He saw the Twin Otter, which he had launched, start on its successful road to world sales. He heard the success stories of the Buffalo in Vietnam and saw the last of 1,350 aircraft delivered to the U.S. military. It wasn't until after Sir Geoffrey died that a noticable change took place. On July 29, 1965, Hawker Siddeley had brought in W.B. "Bill" Boggs as their president to reorganize Downsview. It all occurred during the confusion of another strike, lasting only five weeks this time.

During the strike, Phil Garratt continued to come down from his cottage to the plant in his Beaver to save trouble at the gate. He brought his neighbour, William Brown, back and forth each day as he had been doing all summer. Brown's duties were to man the picket line while the boss spent his day in the office. This story made the Toronto newspapers and was one more sample of the Garratt approach to employee relations. It did not take Phil long to realize his days were numbered, but he occupied his corner office until the very last. He weathered the storm of being made an advising director and saw his longtime friend and associate, George Mickleborough, retire the day the change took place. The DC-9 wing program had been a burden Phil neither wanted nor approved. It only complicated his tenuous position with the new masters in England. Whenever he was out of town it was his practice to phone his secretary at Hawker Siddeley head office and have her read any special mail. On one such call in mid-November 1965, a letter from Hawker Siddeley in England looked important, so Garratt

T.J. Emmert, chairman of Hawker Siddeley Canada, presents P.C. Garratt with a model of his Beaver at his retirement party March 16, 1966. The new president, W.B. Boggs, sits at the right. (DH)

asked Mrs. Koyl to read it. It was from Sir Arnold Hall, asking him to submit his resignation. There was a pause at Garratt's end of the line and the simple question, "Is that all?" So it was that, on November 22, 1965, the man who always said that he would retire at 90, prepared a short notice for everyone in the plant, announcing his retirement at the age of 71. George Luesby of DHC noted in his engineering diary for this day: "This represents the end of the 'father image' in the company, and is deeply regretted by everyone. He was the stabilizing anchor for the whole organization." In recognition of his years in command, Garratt was allowed a place of honour on the company's board of directors (and an office outside the confines of Downsview) but his days of "biting the bullet" were over.

Additional recognition came to P.C. Garratt as he entered retirement. In 1966 he was named the first winner of the newly-established C.D. Howe Award recognizing leadership in aircraft manufacturing. The same year he was awarded the McKee Trophy, making him the second double winner of the trophy. (T.M. "Pat" Reid, 1942-43, P.C.Garratt, 1951-66.)

The Bombings

North Toronto was wrapped in fog on the morning of September 24, 1968, as Frank Stanley prepared to leave for work. DHC's vice-president of finance had enjoyed a good night's sleep and his mind was occupied with plans for the coming day. As he looked out the window to check the fog,

Max Ward in a replica of his first Fox Moth poses for a photo with Phil Garratt. The occasion was the christening of a new Wardair Boeing 747, "Phil Garratt." (Wardair)

For 37 yearsGeorge Mickleborough played a vital role in the history of de Havilland. Here at his retirement party with Mrs. Mickleborough, George admires the Bob Bradford painting depicting his 1930 trip across Canada selling the Puss Moth. (DH 21205)

Twin Otters take shape on the line at Downsview. (DH)

he remembered he was to take his wife's Corvair to work that morning and it had been parked in the driveway overnight. He had trouble starting the engine, but gave it little thought until it began hesitating at the first stop sign. Stanley thought that there must be water in the gas. The Corvair continued to run, but when he parked along the south wall of head office, he thought, "I'll have to get that car down to the garage tonight."

When Stanley reached the second floor, he was accosted with the question, "How about you? Were you bombed last night?" According to a police officer, a number of small bombs had exploded on the lawns of Hawker Siddeley executives and Larry Clarke's car had run out of gas two blocks from home. "Not me," said Frank, but then he remembered his halting trip along Wilson Avenue. A quick return to his parked car confirmed the worst – when he opened the engine compartment a mess of broken wires and twisted metal confronted him – it was a wonder the engine had run at all!

Stanley returned to his office with the news, "Yes, you can count me in," and joined the police investigation. He returned home with one of the officers and there, on the side of the driveway, was a piece of two-inch cast iron pipe, seven inches long and capped at each end, the remnants of an amateurish schoolboy bomb. When the story hit the *Toronto Star* afternoon edition, it noted that 10 senior officers of

Hawker Siddeley had been subjected to similar bombings at 4 a.m. that morning, but nobody was injured. Some bombs had damaged lawns and shrubs, some broke basement windows, and others had been planted in cars. Hawker Siddeley's list involved the homes of A.A. Bailie, J.H. Ready, Evan Bull, W.D. Walker, D.G. Kettering and W.W. Muir. The de Havilland officials whose homes or cars had been slightly damaged were President W.B. Boggs, Larry Clarke, Paul Davoud, and Russ Bannock, who had resigned the year before to start his own company. After further investigation another three DHC names were added to the list – Phil Garratt, Alex McIntosh and Frank Stanley. Those officers living in apartments, including Ted Emmert, Hawker Siddeley president and chief executive officer, were not bombed.

Metro Detective Kenneth Craven described the bits of pipe as protest bombs intended to frighten. They were composed mainly of ammonia salts and acid, separated by a thin piece of metal. The pipe bombs were cradled in stands made of coat hangers, so the acid would eat through the thin metal and unite with the ammonia. The 14 bombs had exploded over four hours across a wide area of Etobicoke, North York and Toronto. One policeman and a reporter were starting to examine an unexploded bomb when second thoughts caused them to take cover. It exploded harmlessly moments later, leaving a hole in the ground.

This was the period of the early draft dodgers from the U.S. and, according to police, the bombings were a demonstration against the sale of Caribous for use in Vietnam. Police Chief Mackey felt it was the work of students under the direction of a well-trained subversive. Police kept the executives' homes under surveillance for another week. Although a reward of $10,000 was offered, no culprits were apprehended.

A Variety of Customers

It was not the passenger-carrying aspect alone that provoked the sudden interest in the Twin Otter. By the end of 1968 seven air forces and seven oil companies had purchased them. Others were leased in the search for petroleum on four continents. Mineral exploration companies eyed the easy transportation the Twin Otter provided. International Nickel had C-FINB equipped with magnetometer equipment, with so much external rigging that it was dubbed "the flying clothesline."

In 1971 Ontario started a successful commuter service with Twin Otters. Called norOntair, it came under the Ontario Northland Transportation Commission. The mandate was to link small, northern communities. The first two Twin Otters, in their garish orange colour with large mauve and white loons painted on the side, were operated under lease by White River Air Services of Sault Ste. Marie. Initial routes linked Sudbury, Earlton, Timmins and Sault Ste. Marie. norOntair soon gained respect for on-time, efficient service. With more Twin Otters the line expanded to cover all of northern Ontario.

As Twin Otter orders soared, pressure was put on the production department, whose planning had not counted on such demand. Space was leased back in the old north plant, which began to take on the activity of Mosquito days. Twin Otter production grew from three a month to a peak of 10. The best year was 1968, with 102 sales. Everything about the Twin Otter worked in its favour and encouraged new customers. Its size and self-sufficiency made it useful for photography and fire bombing, for ice patrols and remote supply.

Two of the six Alaska Army National Guard Twin Otters in an October 1976 pre-delivery photo near Downsview. After 21 years of service from Fort Richardson, near Anchorage, these aircraft were replaced by larger Short C-23B+ Sherpas, the tails for which were built by de Havilland Canada. (DH)

Many thought that a nosewheel ski on an aircraft this size would be a problem, but soon Twin Otters were on skis in the tough Arctic and Antarctic environments.

With the strike and plant shutdown of 1972, Twin Otter sales dropped to 12 for the year and, in a similar strike of 1975, to 34. In 1976 deliveries rose to 41, including the first two to the U.S. military. It was almost a case of history repeating itself when a request for search and rescue aircraft came from Alaska. Two specially-fitted Twin Otters (designated UV-18A) went to the Alaska Army National Guard for logistical flights to remote villages. They had oversize tires for rough terrain and could switch to skis or floats as required. In presenting the log books to LCol. E.J. Dolan Jr. of the National Guard Bureau, DHC vice-president Doug Annan recounted the long association between the U.S. Army and de Havilland. It was a fitting postscript, one year later, that the U.S. Air Force accepted two UV-18B Twin Otters for paradrop training at the USAF Academy in Colorado Springs.

Float Flights to the Amazon

The Peruvian Air Force was an old DHC customer, having operated Beavers in the upper reaches of the Amazon River for many years. In 1967 Peru ordered its first Twin Otters. Delivering these proved a most interesting venture. Departing Toronto Harbour on floats, the planes covered a route of more than 3,500 miles (5,600 km) to Iquitos, on the Amazon. This was de Havilland's longest delivery flight from Toronto of float-equipped aircraft. Pilot George Northrop and engineer Harold Williams flew the first aircraft, remaining in Iquitos for a period of training and evaluation. Flight operations manager Dave Fairbanks and engineer Ben Cox delivered the remaining aircraft at intervals.

The first Twin Otter got away on November 13, 1967. The crew flight-planned for the first logical stopover, Charleston, S.C., which showed a seaplane base 10 miles (16 km) to the southwest. The first leg was the longest of the trip – more than 800 statute miles (1,280 km). At Charleston, Northrop and Williams found that, although there were customs and fuel services, the place could not accommodate seaplanes. The U.S. Coast Guard came to the rescue, co-ordinating arrangements and countering the many telephone calls that a plane had crashed in the bay.

There were delays in obtaining highway approval for airport refuelling trucks, and finding a road close to the water. Then the Department of Agriculture got into the act – oranges and other edibles were found aboard the aircraft. There was a moan from all concerned when they heard that two more Twin Otters were to follow. By the time the second aircraft arrived, a kindly barge operator had offered his services, greatly easing the confusion.

Next stop was the holiday resort of Nassau which has a seaplane base of sorts in the busy harbour off Bay Street. But many years had passed since the area was used for flying

boats and the pilots again found difficulty in refuelling from a tank truck on the shore. From there the journey was lengthened by the need to fly around Cuba, but a Jamaican Defence Force pilot, George Brown (who had recently taken delivery of a Twin Otter), organized a suitable strip of beach on the edge of the Palisadoes Airport, which could be reached by the regular fuel tender. This worked so well that, by the time the second aircraft arrived, Fairbanks was able to receive airport control instructions and docking directions from a walkie-talkie on the shore.

A choice of two routes lay ahead after Kingston, one down the Pacific coast through Turbo and Buenaventura, the other following the Magdalena River to Palanquero. The inland route was recommended, since turbine fuel was available at the Colombian military base 64 miles (102 km) from Bogotá. The base had a large river and an old floatplane ramp.

From Jamaica, neither the weather reports nor the radio facilities proved reliable. An occasional glimpse of the winding river through the clouds proved the best navigation aid. On the arrival of each aircraft, Palanquero was wide open to receive its Canadian visitors. If the flight through the Colombian mountains required a degree of alertness, it was mild compared with the welcome here. The town and military base were as expected, but the river this time of the year was in flood. The rainy season had been reckoned with, but not the debris floating downstream. Northrop and Fairbanks found moderately clear spots to set down, but had to manoeuvre carefully to avoid floating palm trees, complete with coconuts. The flow was at least 20 knots and required

Peruvian Twin Otter 390 was the 73rd aircraft off the line. Delivered in late 1967, it served in Peru to 1971. In the 1990s it was in Yellowknife with Petro Canada Exploration. (DH)

considerable power from the turbines to hold the aircraft stationary.

Since river height fluctuated during the night, guards were posted to keep the floats secure. This precaution proved timely, for the water had risen five feet by departure time. Fuelling went well the next day, and after another battle with floating debris, they took off on the final hop to Iquitos.

Twin Otter No. 500 was delivered to Metro Airlines of Dallas. This carrier served communities throughout Texas and Oklahoma. (DH)

The mountains surrounding the Colombian capital of Bogotá called for an early climb to 10,000 ft. (3,000 m) and all three flights were conducted between cloud layers at this altitude until the jungles of the Amazon began to show. Mile after mile of trees and winding rivers pointed to the value of seaplanes in country where the only other travel is by slow river boat. The Peruvian Air Force base at Iquitos was a welcome sight for the weary Twin Otter crews as they circled to land. Here the river was wide and inviting, with proper seaplane facilities. From here, the Twin Otters provided many years of vital transportation among the region's widely scattered communities.

Waterfront Activity

Time was when the motorist driving along Toronto's waterfront would see numerous floatplanes bobbing at their buoys, presenting an ever-changing colour spectacle. In the thirties it was the air harbour at the foot of Yonge Street and in later years, the Island Airport ramp. There was always action around the floatplane dock: boats back and forth, planes under tow, the going and coming of aircraft. Times have changed and very seldom does the motorist view much floatplane action in Toronto Harbour. One reason is the fact that there was sometimes too much action: the kind that gives insurance underwriters sleepless nights.

Every year, with regularity, one or more aircraft would sink during the autumn windstorms. Often they were de Havilland types and sometimes they were owned by the company. The Moths with their lower wings were extremely vulnerable for they would literally fly at their buoys during storms and once they dipped a wing in the water would soon turn turtle and slowly sink. Hornet Moth CF-BFK involving the author in 1937 was a case in point, but there were others.

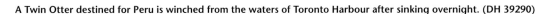

A Twin Otter destined for Peru is winched from the waters of Toronto Harbour after sinking overnight. (DH 39290)

(Right) The Twin Otter was a boon to transportation in mountainous Nepal. Fourteen served through the decades. Jamison is typical of the rugged Himalayan strips that challenged pilots. (George Lothian)

(Below) With 135 and 102 aircraft respectively, the U.S. and Canada were the world's leading Twin Otter users in 1998. This Air BC Twin Otter is seen in a typical Vancouver setting. (Brent Wallace)

The Beavers and Otters, with their metal construction, were a little less costly to salvage under such circumstances but sinkings occurred even into Twin Otter days. On one of these occasions, Operations Manager Dave Fairbanks got a frantic call from the Island that a Twin Otter was sinking and they were having trouble getting it to the ramp. By the time Dave got there the tail and one wing were submerged but clear of the buoy. He was taken out and climbed into the tilting cockpit for a try at starting the still-dry engine. Although the battery was under water, he got the engine started and pointed the aircraft at the ramp. With full power and very little control he managed to get enough of the high float on the ramp to prevent the aircraft from sinking and saved a costly salvage operation.

The next time there was no warning. A Twin Otter, destined for Peru, sank during the night. It had been fully loaded, ready for an early morning takeoff, but at first light only a wing tip and part of an engine remained above the surface. It took a lot of drying out and many man-hours of work before it was serviceable again. Times have indeed changed at the Toronto island Airport, where the talk today is more of short-haul air services. Water operations are minimal. Floatplanes are not stored at the buoy any more (they are hauled up the ramp) and the insurance people rest more easily.

Twin Otter Variations

The Twin Otter was introduced during a period of rapid change in light transport aircraft. From navigation avionics to brakes, everything was new. The Twin Otter kept pace with its competition in the fast-moving commuter business and improved models followed in quick succession. Each was given an identifying number, but the changes came so thick and fast that the product support department issued a bulletin on their respective differences. The prototype and pre-production DHC-6 Series 1s had PT6A-20s and a gross weight limitation of 11,000 lb. (4,950 kg). The first production DHC-6 Series 100s, approved on July 29, 1966, with PT6A-20s and a gross weight of 11,579 lb., (5,211 kg). They differed little from the Series 1. All had the stubby nose and ran from serial number 6 to 115 inclusive. In the Series 200, which started at No. 116, a longer nose was the pronounced change. Together with added space in the rear compartment, this doubled baggage capacity to 126 cu. ft. (4 cu. m). The PT6A-20, with its "toothpick" Hartzell propellers and 550 shp, powered the Series 200 (to No. 230) but Pratt & Whitney Canada were working on a bigger version.

The PT6A-27 (25 per cent more horsepower at five per cent increase in weight) was the next major change for the Twin Otter, boosting speed to 150 knots and allowing a gross takeoff weight of 12,500 lb. (5,625 kg). These aircraft, from No. 231 onward, were the Series 300. Aircraft 130 and 210 were also converted to these specifications during the certification program. The most prominent exterior changes were the "paddle blade" propellers, larger exhaust stacks, and wing fences and vortex generators on the tail surfaces. There were new seating arrangements and cabin refinements, while the pilots had improved instrumentation, including automatic feathering switches.

New emergency exit standards (Special FAR No. 23) were introduced in the U.S. for CAR 3 airplanes. Although the Twin Otter already had five such openings (including the crew doors), DHC built two more under the wings and closed off the one in the roof. Special FAR No. 23 came in about the same time as the Series 300. To meet it, earlier Twin Otter series could be retrofitted with kits supplied by de Havilland. To the casual observer Series 110, 210 and 310 further complicated the numbering – initially for customers in Australia, these met British Airworthiness requirements. French Twin Otters also had special certification which, combined with existing approvals, allowed worldwide coverage outside the Communist countries. One last variant was developed for the Airtransit experimental STOL exercise. This was the Series 300S ("S" for STOL), which met FAR 25.

Twin Otters to China

In April 1978, a Twin Otter went to the People's Republic of China. This crowned a five-year sales effort – one of the most complex in Twin Otter history. China's search for geophysical aircraft had begun in 1973 with a delegation of 10 specialists and an interpreter visiting Downsview. They were headed by the China Geophysical Survey Company and were sponsored by the Canadian Department of Industry, Trade and Commerce. The delegation worked closely with Scintrex Limited of Concord, Ontario, and other suppliers of geophysical equipment. Len Trotter, assistant vice-president of marketing and sales, co-ordinated negotiations through 1974-76. These involved meetings with Canadian and Chinese officials. The sale of four aircraft was announced at the Paris Air Show in 1977. The first two, equipped for photography, rolled out in February 1978 for delivery by DH crews. The third was the most complete geophysical Twin Otter ever to leave Downsview. A fourth machine followed.

The Transglobe Twin Otter at one of its Antarctic stopovers. (DH 50077)

Transglobe Twin Otter

An unusual exploit involving the Antarctic and de Havilland support was the Transglobe Expedition of 1979-82, described by its patron, Prince Charles, as "a suitably mad and splendidly British idea." Headed by Sir Ranulph Twisleton-Sykeham-Fiennes, the adventurers set out to circle the globe via both poles, by foot, ship, Land Rover, snowmobile and sledge. In the Antarctic they duplicated Sir Vivian Fuchs' crossing, supported this time by a Twin Otter. The brilliant red, white and blue aircraft, sponsored by the Chubb group of companies, had seen service earlier in the North Sea oil business with Loganair. It was fitted for Arctic work in Canada and was operated on the expedition by pilot Giles Kershaw and flight engineer Gerry Nicholson, who had been regular visitors to Downsview as crew of the British Antarctic Survey.

HMCS Bras d'Or

Since the invention of the marine screw propeller, engineers have striven to increase the speed of ships in rough seas. In only 60 years, flying has progressed from the Wright Brothers beyond the Concorde to the moon, but ships with displacement hulls have always been limited to a maximum speed by the physics of water. In Cape Breton, N.S., Alexander Graham Bell was one of the first to reduce hull resistance by lifting it out of the water on "hydrofoils." In 1919 his Hydrodome 4 reached a record speed of 61.5 knots on the calm waters of Lake Bras d'Or.

In the 1950s the Canadian Defence Research Board developed hydrofoil craft to explore their behaviour in rough water. Nine years later DRB scientists concluded that a 60-knot, open-ocean, hydrofoil was feasible for anti-submarine warfare. The concept was based on surface-piercing foils for simplicity. The design would provide acceptable ship motions in the foil-borne attack mode and the long-range hull-borne search mode. The concept won the moral and technical support of the British and U.S. navies.

Because of the similarities to aviation, de Havilland Canada entered the hydrofoil field with a three-year feasibility and design study. This was sponsored by the Department of Supply and Services, working closely with DRB researchers and the RCN. Their concept was based on a canard arrangement of surface-piercing foils to provide stability in all conditions. There were commercial hydrofoils in service but these were limited to sheltered waters. Surface-effect ships, such as hovercraft, were being proved in moderate seas, but open-ocean use dictated enormous craft of great complexity to cope with steep waves.

When the hydrofoil study was awarded to DHC, the Engineering Department was occupied with the DHC-5 Buf-falo. Fortunately, some talented engineers were available from the cancelled Avro Arrow program. A 12-man group was formed to assess and develop the hydrofoil. During these studies, craft motions in a random seaway were simulated in Toronto on what was probably the world's largest computer. Simulated motions were checked on the largest of many models, a quarter-scale craft, in the approaches to Halifax Harbour. Other model trials were conducted in Ottawa, Stockholm, New York and London in some of the world's best hydrodynamic facilities. Key design features included a steerable superventilating bow foil of seven tons, hydrofoil sections capable of operating at 60 knots, and super-cavitating propellers capable of absorbing 15,000 horsepower at 1,800 rpm.

In 1963 the Defence Department accepted DHC's findings, awarding it a design and construction contract for the Fast Hydrofoil Escort (FHE 400). This would be a 200-ton anti-submarine warfare (ASW) hydrofoil. The study group of 12 expanded to 150 engineers and technicians during the detail design stage. Phil Halsey was the first program manager during the early phases of prototype construction. Dick Becker became assistant chief designer. Transmission design

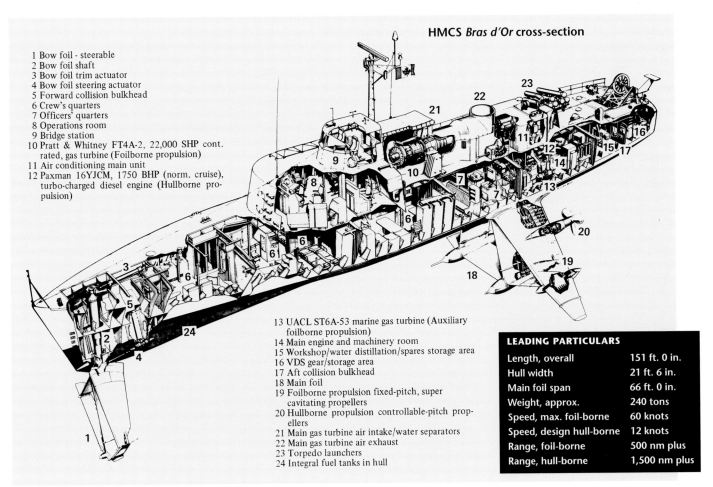

HMCS *Bras d'Or* cross-section

1 Bow foil - steerable
2 Bow foil shaft
3 Bow foil trim actuator
4 Bow foil steering actuator
5 Forward collision bulkhead
6 Crew's quarters
7 Officers' quarters
8 Operations room
9 Bridge station
10 Pratt & Whitney FT4A-2, 22,000 SHP cont. rated, gas turbine (Foilborne propulsion)
11 Air conditioning main unit
12 Paxman 16YJCM, 1750 BHP (norm. cruise), turbo-charged diesel engine (Hullborne propulsion)

13 UACL ST6A-53 marine gas turbine (Auxiliary foilborne propulsion)
14 Main engine and machinery room
15 Workshop/water distillation/spares storage area
16 VDS gear/storage area
17 Aft collision bulkhead
18 Main foil
19 Foilborne propulsion fixed-pitch, super cavitating propellers
20 Hullborne propulsion controllable-pitch propellers
21 Main gas turbine air intake/water separators
22 Main gas turbine air exhaust
23 Torpedo launchers
24 Integral fuel tanks in hull

LEADING PARTICULARS	
Length, overall	151 ft. 0 in.
Hull width	21 ft. 6 in.
Main foil span	66 ft. 0 in.
Weight, approx.	240 tons
Speed, max. foil-borne	60 knots
Speed, design hull-borne	12 knots
Range, foil-borne	500 nm plus
Range, hull-borne	1,500 nm plus

The *Bras d'Or* in drydock at Halifax while in its initial trials period. (DH 29911)

launched from the marine railway and towed down the St. Lawrence River to the Halifax Naval Dockyard, to the toasts, in English and French, of the Marine Industries and de Havilland teams.

After the party, Harry Beffort, who had succeeded Halsey as program manager, returned to other duties at Downsview. Dick Becker became program manager for the sea trials phase and drove the 800 miles (1,280 km) to Halifax with the senior engineering staff and tradesmen to set up shop. There the ship was commissioned HMCS *Bras d'Or*, in recognition of Alexander Graham Bell's pioneering efforts. The RCN crew, under Commander "Tino" Cotaras, had been appointed during the fitting-out phase in Sorel.

and construction were awarded to General Electric in Lynn, Massachusetts, the acknowledged experts in hydrofoil transmissions. A 2,000-bhp engine turned two quiet, controllable-pitch propellers for the hull-borne mode. A 22,000-shp P&W gas turbine drove twin super-cavitating propellers at 1,800 rpm in the foil-borne mode.

Most of the foils and the complex systems were built by DHC, except for the propellers, hydraulic and electrical components, which were subcontracted. The largest item was the welded aluminum hull, built by Marine Industries in Sorel, Quebec. Automatic welding machines were built at Sorel to fabricate the huge skin panels from extrusion and plate. Aircraft type sub-assembly jigs were used for welded frame assemblies. Shipyard skills in handling large components were invaluable in mating the hull to the foils. Company tradesmen and engineers moved to Sorel for the fitting and activating of the various systems.

A serious fire gutted the engine room in 1966, delaying rollout and launch to mid-1968. The cost of repairs used up funds allocated to installation of the fighting equipment (developed by Canadian Westinghouse as prime contractor). A decision was made to defer installation of the integrated navigation and torpedo fire control equipment and the towed sonar until the FHE 400 had been put through its paces in the open ocean. A special floating slave dock was built for the hydrofoil. After weighing (aircraft style) at 273,345 lb. (123,005 kg), the ship was placed on the dock,

The de Havilland crew retained responsibility for testing and maintenance during contractors' trials in calm water. Systems shakedown trials and late delivery of the foil-borne transmission delayed the start of high-speed trials until April 1969, with Commander Gordie Edwards as captain. On July 9, 1969, he "flew" *Bras d'Or* at a record speed of 63 knots, exceeding design speed.

More important were the subsequent rough water trials in North Atlantic winter weather – wind, sleet and 15-ft. waves. The commander of a nearby destroyer signalled that the 200-ton *Bras d'Or* looked more comfortable at 40 knots than his 3,000-ton ship at 18 knots, taking "green ones" over the bow. After a succession of short cruises, Edwards arranged to cut the "Halifax umbilical cord" and took his ship on a triangular course to Bermuda and Norfolk, Virginia, returning to Halifax 14 days later. Several thousand people visited the ship in Bermuda. The Norfolk visitors were senior NATO officers and attachés from a dozen countries. Apart from stress corrosion cracking in the main foil, none of the teething problems was related to the advanced features of this state-of-the-art design. The *Bras d'Or* performed as predicted, and the joint RCN-DRB-DHC trials team worked well together. Regrettably, defence priorities changed in the 1970s. The project was shelved and the *Bras d'Or* was placed on its slave dock on the Dartmouth side of Halifax Harbour. Eventually it was sold for scrap, then towed up the St. Lawrence in June 1983 to the Bernier naval museum at L'Islet–sur-Mer.

(Left) While prototype CF-DHC ended in the National Aviation Museum, most Twin Otters remained in service late in the century. In March 1998 there were 628 still in service. This Series 100, an early company demonstrator, was at Abbotsford in August 1967. Later it was sold to Trans East Airlines in New Hampshire, one of the commuter carriers that boomed with the advent of designs like the Twin Otter. In 1971 it returned to Canada as CF-QHC to fly for Time Air, Harbour Air and Kenn Borek Air. (Terry Waddington)

(Right) C-FQBV originally went to Quebecair in 1968, then worked for Northward Airlines of Edmonton. It is shown still later with Calm Air at Churchill, Manitoba in 1982. (Richard Beaudet)

(Below) Like its single-engine ancestor, the Twin Otter served on wheels, skis or floats. Saskatchewan operator La Ronge Aviation Services purchased CF-WTE new in 1968. Brent Wallace photographed it on floats at Yellowknife in August 1981.

Twin Otter No. 34 (CF-AUS) began in 1967 with Golden West Airlines of California. In 1971 it joined the famous Manitoba bush operator, Lambair. Later it went to Labrador Airways. In 1984 it ended its days in a weather-related accident near Goose Bay. (DH)

(Left) Beginning in 1971, the Canadian Forces took nine Twin Otters for general use, search and rescue, and UN duties. Four remained in service in 1998. No. 13804 of 440 Squadron was over down-town Yellowknife when Henry Tenby photographed it in April 1996.

(Right) An early Twin Otter 100 serving a mineral survey camp on the B.C.-Yukon bor-der in September 1979. STOL design, coupled with large tires, made operations on such rugged strips routine. This Twin Otter later served in Belize with Tropicair. (Kenneth I. Swartz)

(Left) Twin Otter 200s in final assembly at de Havilland in 1968. No. 146 (C-GNTA) is in the colours of Northern Thunderbird Air. In the late 1990s it was with Kenn Borek Air of Calgary. Along with other Borek Twin Otters, it did stints in the Indian Ocean with Maldivian Air Taxi, and in the Antarctic. (Larry Milberry)

CF-YTH spent many seasons in aerial survey, first for Canadian Nickel Air Service of Sudbury (a branch of Inco), then for Survair of Ottawa. Here it was practising landings in Toronto Harbour in July 1972. It flew later with Canadian, U.S. and Colombian operators. In 1995, for example, it was with Kenn Borek Air, but on lease in Cuba as CU-T130. (Larry Milberry)

(Below) When the Ontario government formed norOntair to serve isolated northern communities, it began with Twin Otter 300s. Here C-GGVX gets a wash at Thunder Bay in July 1991. (Larry Milberry)

(Left) Not many airplanes succeeded so well as the Twin Otter at replacing DC-3s. By 1998 few DC-3s were operating in the Arctic. Here Austin Airways Twin Otter C-GDAA sits at Timmins in September 1982 with the company's last DC-3, C-FAAM. DAA later went to Iceland, where it remained in the late 1990s. (Larry Milberry)

(Below) C-FGOG loading at Yellowknife in July 1992. Series 300 No. 348, it had begun in 1972 with Gulf Oil Canada. (Larry Milberry)

(Above) Yellowknife-based C-GKBO at MacKay Lake Lodge, NWT, while on a 1995 lease to Air Tindi. (Larry Milberry)

(Right) C-GNPS, originally with Austin Airways, arrives at Yellowknife after a July 1992 trip. (Larry Milberry)

(Right) Bradley Air Service, one of Canada's leading Twin Otter operators, stationed its fleet throughout the Arctic for many years. CF-NAN is shown in a typical tundra setting near Resolute Bay, NWT, in August 1982. It had a party of tourists out for a day of char fishing. (Richard Beaudet)

(Below) Bradley Twin Otters and a DC-3 at the Arctic outpost of Resolute Bay in the summer of 1980. They were supporting the Polar Continental Shelf scientific research project. (Brent Wallace)

The Ontario government pioneered in fire fighting with Twin Otters. Here one demonstrates at Toronto's 1968 air show, dropping water from specially designed floats. (Right) A modern development was the Wipaire 13000 amphibious 550 U.S.-gal. (2,000 l) water bombing float. With it a Twin Otter can fight fires all day, then, instead of being confined to a water base, return to an airport for servicing. Wipaire-equipped Twin Otter C-FOPI was at Sudbury in September 1997. (Larry Milberry)

(Above) CF-CST was one of the specially-equipped Series 300s involved in the experimental Ottawa-Montreal STOL project of 1973-76. It's shown over Rockcliffe, home of the National Aviation Museum, with the Ottawa River in the background. CST later joined Transport Canada. (DH)

259

The Twin Otter long has been important on the West Coast. This Vancouver scene from February 1981 is typical. In the 1990s Twin Otter service remained brisk between Vancouver and Victoria, with business travellers, government employees and tourists being regular passengers. Here C-GQKN waits as C-GGAW departs. QKN, recently arrived from Surinam Airways, still carried its sunny Caribbean colours. (Kenneth I. Swartz)

(Left) C-GGAW goes into the Middle Arm of the Fraser River at Vancouver International Airport. It had operated in Florida and the Caribbean from 1967, then came to Canada in 1976. Twin Otters often make long over-water flights. These usually end routinely, but the case of N242CA, the 342nd Twin Otter, was different. On April 12, 1997, it ditched 63 nm northeast of Hilo, Hawaii, while ferrying from Oakland, California. The pilot ditched safely and was rescued. (Kenneth I. Swartz)

(Right) West Coast Air took over Air BC's Vancouver-Victoria run in the mid-1990s. Its Twin Otter C-FWCA, with vista windows, was at Vancouver in May 1996. It was formerly a Grand Canyon sight-seeing plane with Las Vegas-based Scenic Airlines. (Jan Stroomenbergh)

(Below) Kenn Borek/Harbour Air Twin Otters at Vancouver Airport in August 1995. These aircraft became famous on the B.C. coast; in the Antarctic, supporting scientific teams and small groups of adventure tourists; and in other faraway regions like Africa and the Indian Ocean. With 23 examples, Kenn Borek Air had one of the world's biggest Twin Otter fleets in 1998. (John Morrison)

(Above) In the 1950s U.S. scheduled air taxis were operating such types as the Beech 18 and Dove. As they matured, they needed new equipment – the Twin Otter was like manna from heaven. With powerful, light PT6s, it carried 19 passengers. It was efficient and, above all, made money. By 1978 Washington was allowing small carriers to operate 12,500 lb. aircraft (Twin Otter category), and big carriers like American to drop unprofitable routes. Local airlines jumped in, making profits with smaller planes. Business boomed, especially in areas like New York, Miami and Los Angeles. Commuter carriers kept Downsview humming. On November 1, 1966, Pilgrim Airlines inaugurated scheduled Twin Otter service in the U.S. with N121PM. Here N124PM waits at New York's JFK Airport in September 1967. (Benner Col.)

(Left) In July 1972 Downtown Airlines inaugurated New York-Philadelphia service, using float-equipped Piper Aztecs. These soon gave way to the Twin Otter. Like many an upstart operation, this scheme soon failed, victim of the competition – highways and railways. In 1975 N200DA, shown in Manhattan, moved to Ptarmigan Airways of Yellowknife as C-GARW. (Benner Col.)

(Right) Texas-based Rio Airways, started by F.E. "Pete" Howe in 1972, began servicing places like Killeen, Temple and Waco that had been dropped by larger airlines. Beech 99s were replaced in 1979 by Twin Otters. Dash 7s and Metroliners followed. But Rio was shortlived. As Killeen prospered, bigger carriers returned, encouraged by deregulation. This squeezed Rio's market share, and the recession of the early 1980s didn't help. Rio folded in 1987. N46A, photographed in September 1981, migrated to Colombia, where it was lost in a crash in July 1991. (Benner Col.)

(Below) A Twin Otter of Scenic Airlines at Las Vegas in March 1992. Beyond is N414H, the company's 1920s-vintage Ford Trimotor. (Kenneth I. Swartz)

(Left) N999PG was delivered in 1980 in aero survey configuration. In 1988 it joined the Australian Geographic Society as VH-SWH, and later was with Air Seychelles in the Indian Ocean. Gary Vincent photographed it at Toronto in January 1983.

(Right) This corporate Twin Otter 300 was delivered to Esso in 1970. It later became 5A-DKE in Libya. (DH)

(Left) Beginning with aircraft No. 73 in December 1967 and finishing with No. 689 in May 1980, there were 20 Twin Otters for Peru. This example was doing float trials in Toronto Harbour on July 21, 1971. (Larry Milberry)

(Right) ACES took Colombia's first Twin Otter. This one was delivered in November 1977. In 1998, 18 Twin Otters were on Colombia's register, ACES with 10 being the biggest operator. (Swartz Col.)

(Above) Since early Norseman and Beaver days, the remote South Atlantic Falkland Islands favoured Canadian products. Twin Otter VP-FAO was delivered to the British Antarctic Survey there in October 1968. It's seen with Turbo Beaver VP-FAM clearing customs at Toronto on March 12, 1971, after ferrying back to Canada. Soon it was sold in France. It later went to Air Djibouti, then to the U.S. (Larry Milberry)

(Above) Twin Otter FAC932 of the Chilean Air Force during Antarctic operations at General Bernardo O'Higgins camp in July 1980. The Chileans were helping to recover a DHC Buffalo stranded in the snow. (David C. MacKenzie)

Africa naturally took to the Twin Otter, its first operator being East Africa Airways of Kenya. Shown is 5H-MNR in February 1971. It later returned to Canada as C-FGQH. (Peter Keating)

(Below) Afghanistan Twin Otters YA-GAY and YA-GAT at Kabul with two Yak-40s. Of the five machines that went to Afghanistan, three eventually crashed in the inhospitable terrain. YA-GAS returned to Canada as C-GDQY. (Dick Gleasure)

(Left) A Twin Otter ready at Downsview for delivery to China in February 1978. In 1998 this example was re-registered B-3501 with China Flying Dragon Aviation of Harbin. (Dick Gleasure)

(Right) Twin Otters also made themselves at home "down under." Since aircraft No. 6 was delivered to Trans-Australian Airlines in July 1966, 40 Twin Otters went to Australia, six to New Zealand. TAA's VH-TGW is seen at Brisbane in November 1971. It later served with Talair in Papua New Guinea. (Peter Keating)

(Right) Wherever there is mountainous terrain, from British Columbia to Switzerland to Nepal, the Twin Otter has proven invaluable. Here HB-LID of the Swiss Air Force lands at Bern in April 1985. (Anton Heumann)

Norway had a commitment to DHC since early post-WWII years. First came the Otter – 15 served. Then, 29 Twin Otters were purchased, the first delivered in July 1967. Widerøe was the main Norwegian user of the Otter and Twin Otter, and later of the Dash 7 and Dash 8. Ken Swartz photographed this Twin Otter beside an EH101 helicopter at Farnborough, England, in September 1990. LN-BMH, with Widerøes since 1979, was evaluating four-blade propellers, designed to make a quieter Twin Otter.

CHAPTER TEN

AIRLINE STOL

In the early days of commercial aviation, when flying was still much "by the seat of the pants," there often were arguments over which was the best Canadian bushplane. Some had more horsepower, while others had larger wings; all would lift off sooner or later, given a long enough run. Design concepts of the day generally remained the same, as the engineers compromised between speed and payload, but WWII was to change that. Technology advanced in a hurry to the benefit of the entire industry. The airlines profited immensely from this after the war and the benefits spilled into general aviation.

Canadian bush operators who opened the north immediately after the war had to do so with whatever prewar equipment they could find. The Beaver brought a welcomed change, but some old attitudes lingered: pilots were pleased with how de Havilland's new bushplane got out of a small lake, but most gave credit to its powerful Wasp engine on a relatively small airframe, than to aerodynamic innovation. Oldtimers still felt that the secret of a steep takeoff was to gain lots of speed while still on the runway and that it was compromising safety to operate any aircraft at low speeds.

Through early experience, the U.S. military readily accepted the Beaver's low-speed qualities as a design feature, and not due to power alone – the wing/flap combination and airfoil had much to do with the equation. The Otter, when it arrived, only emphasized the point, for it had even more aerodynamic advancements. Other companies also were designing aircraft to take off and land in short distances, but they were doing it in different ways. All such aircraft were lumped in the new STOL category. The term STOL was not completely descriptive, but did differentiate from the helicopter term VTOL – vertical take off and landing. (Vertical clearly means straight up and down, but in the case of STOL the question often was asked, "How short is short?") DHC's advanced flap design had been refined and improved through each successive model until it became a company trademark. The moving of control surfaces through large angles provided a high level of control with no unorthodox handling characteristics. No new operating techniques were forced on a transitioning pilot with de Havilland STOL and the nose-down attitude with the use of flap even improved the view of the runway.

Metro 66

The U.S. forces ordered the Beaver, Otter and Caribou after competitive demonstrations. It was beginning to look as though a similar show would be needed to convince civil aviation. Up to now, U.S. military pilots were almost alone in pioneering the art of STOL. A few forward thinkers and airways planners in the U.S. were also studying short field techniques and could see a practical application for one major concern – congested air traffic at major airports. The leader in this crusade was Oscar Bakke, Eastern Regional Director of the Federal Aviation Agency. His view was that air traffic generated by commuter airlines and intercity short-haul operations soon would have to be separated from trunk-line operations. STOL was a possible answer, but Bakke's promotions and traffic seminars received only lukewarm attention. He realized that STOL was not clearly understood and that a full-scale demonstration was needed to sell the concept. He picked New York City as the site for his showpiece – Metro 66 was staged to demonstrate aerial support in a disaster-relief situation but, at the same time, to show the feasibility of full-scale passenger operations. Bakke's object was to prove that, with all regular forms of transportation disrupted, STOL and VTOL aircraft could give air access to New York's centre, providing logistic support in a major emergency.

Two hundred representatives of the U.S., New York State and City of New York governments gathered in downtown Manhattan on September 5-6, 1966, to review one of the most momentous exercises in the deployment of STOL utility aircraft. All manufacturers of STOL and VTOL equipment were invited, but de Havilland provided the largest contingent. George Neal flew the Turbo Beaver, Mick Saunders the Twin Otter and Dave Fairbanks the Buffalo. Joe Fugere from nearby New London took part with his new Twin Otter in Pilgrim Airways colours.

Landing sites included three VTOL areas and four for both STOL and VTOL aircraft. Of the STOL strips, Pier No. 26, on the Hudson River, was the shortest, with 900 ft. (275 m) of runway. It was also where most attention was centred, as it was the type of STOLport Bakke visualized for commercial use. Most of the passenger movements were from this location. Sixty-four missions were flown into Pier 26, during which 300 passengers arrived from six local staging sites – Teterboro, Linden, Flushing, John F. Kennedy and two military airports. This impressive performance was concentrated into a $3\frac{1}{2}$-hour period on the first day.

South Street opposite Roosevelt Drive was Mick Saunders' area of operation with the Twin Otter. (DH 25495)

The cast of this show comprised Helio Stallions and Couriers, Fairchild-Hiller Turbo Porters, a Turbo Beaver and the star performer, the Twin Otter, the largest of the STOLS to use the pier. It delivered 70 passengers in five missions. Governors Island, a mile off the southern tip of Manhattan Island, provided the biggest landing area – four baseball diamonds in a row on the East River with a 1,900-ft. (580 m) grass area. This was the site of the most spectacular demonstration and the most substantial cargo operation. Dave Fairbanks and Norm Paterson landed the Buffalo with a 6,000-lb. (2,700 kg), 80-piece field hospital, which subsequently was transferred to a Sikorsky S-64 Skycrane to be slung to Bellevue Hospital in Manhattan.

The largest of the STOL aircraft in Metro 66 was the Buffalo, with Dave Fairbanks and Norm Paterson in charge. They are shown landing and taking off from the East River Park. (DH 25663, '25490)

Consternation was caused by the Buffalo landing in the East River Park. Some residents, seeing such a large aircraft disappearing in a cloud of dust on the baseball diamond, called radio stations to report a crash. But the Buffalo came to a full stop somewhere around second base of the third diamond and took off again, using only half the space available. The only dangerous aspect was several near-collisions among rubber-necking motorists on the adjoining express-way. Just to prove that the landing was routine, Dave Fairbanks took the Buffalo in a second time, which movie cameras recorded for posterity.

The next day saw most STOL activity concentrated on a 1,200-ft. (365 m) strip on South Street, opposite Roosevelt Drive, where turbulence caused by tall buildings demanded considerable pilot skill. There were 17 scheduled landings and takeoffs. The Twin Otter again was the largest aircraft using the strip, delivering two loads of 14 passengers each. During the exercise, more than 40 aircraft, including six STOL types and six VTOLs, performed 440 takeoffs and landings at eight different Manhattan sites. In 220 missions, 765 passengers and tons of cargo were delivered. When the results were examined, it was apparent that Metro 66 had achieved its objective. Operations were conducted without incident to aircraft, property or personnel. It also was noted that the passengers and cargo carried were only a fraction of what could be transported in a real emergency. The exercise opened the eyes of a lot of people to the potential of STOL airports.

The exercise did not provide the immediate results Bakke sought, and a surge of community opposition eventually ended his pioneering. Only years later was the use of sepa-rated approach patterns and stub runways realized – in the same area where his vision had sown the seed. It did not take long for New York streets and parks to get back to normal af-ter Metro 66, but the memory of the successful STOL dem-onstration made a distinct impression on the minds of trans-portation planners. As air traffic grew in areas like New York and Washington, the thinking turned to special routings and STOL airstrips. In October 1967 the U.S. Civil Aeronautics Board summoned 16 airlines, nine cities and two federal government departments to an investigation of air traffic along the Washington-Boston corridor. The purpose was to explore the use of STOL-VTOL beyond main terminals, us-ing new routes and landing strips. A companion study was begun in Canada by the Department of Transport to link Ottawa, Montreal and Toronto.

At Downsview it was business as usual with the emphasis in 1967 shifting from engineering to sales. The usual liaison with the U.S. military was maintained, but new customers would have to be found for the Buffalo and Twin Otter. These export sales started with an order for 12, then 12 more, Buffalos for Brazil. Beaver and Otter production ended in 1967 with deliveries of 19 and three respectively. Nine Caribou were exported in 1967, while Turbo Beaver

deliveries grew to 13. Other items of interest that summer were the July 21 "rollout" ceremony of the hydrofoil *Bras d'Or* at Sorel and the sale on October 10 of the Special Prod-ucts Division, as SPAR, to a group of employees under Larry Clarke. In 1967 Bill Burlison retired for health reasons, end-ing a long career with DHC. On December 5 that year an-other major change in top management occurred when Russ Bannock resigned to start his own sales and consulting busi-ness in Toronto.

A Downtown Airliner

By 1968 the hearings on the Northeast corridor study by the U.S. Civil Aeronautics Board were in full swing. They were looking into the feasibility of downtown air service along the Washington-Boston corridor. DHC participated and two airlines began serious studies. Eastern Airlines' ap-proach was a series of shuttle runs without passengers be-tween Washington and New York using France's four-engine, 52-passenger Breguet 941. It had made a favourable impression at the Paris Air Show and McDonnell Douglas were interested in building it in the U.S. as the MD188E. Eastern demonstrated the Breguet in Washington at the end of August and did six weeks of trial runs, using a newly-built 1,095-ft. (334 m) STOL strip at La Guardia Airport. Ameri-can Airlines had a concept based on Metro 66. Mindful of the Buffalo demonstration, they looked at de Havilland's plans for a civil version of the Buffalo. The exercise on the New York pier led American to study the floating STOLport idea. They chose a site in the Chelsea section of the Hudson River. Artists' concept drawings were hardly dry when a citi-zens' group for the "preservation of Chelsea" went into action. They caused such a clamour that American lost interest.

Studies at de Havilland into converting the military Buf-falo soon shifted to a new STOL passenger aircraft twice the size of the Twin Otter and more in keeping with the "Corri-dor concept." The project won enthusiastic backing from president Boggs and by 1967 had moved from the prelimi-nary stage to a full-scale product allocation. The project that eventually became the DHC-7 emerged in January 1968 as DH Project 35, but design configuration was to change many times. As first proposed, the aircraft was a T-tailed transport of 26,500 lb. (12,000 kg) gross weight to carry 39 passengers 200 miles (320 km). The original model showed a novel fixed "grasshopper" undercarriage, and a high wing with four 780-hp PT6A-30 engines. Planning moved to the product development stage with the financial aid of the De-partment of Industry, Trade and Commerce. Preliminary

A model of the DHP35 proposal that led to the Dash 7. It was to carry 38 passengers and had a fixed undercarriage. The dimensions approximated the later Dash 8. (DH 30683)

specifications were reviewed in the light of the latest CAB rulings. Worldwide market studies began in late 1968, based on the concept of improved interurban and regional air transport. This led to revised specifications, with an increase to 48 passengers and a gross weight of 38,000 lb. (17,250 kg). Throughout the program the performance target was built around 2,000-ft. (600 m) runway limitations and a low noise level.

Wind tunnel testing took place at the National Aeronautical Establishment in 1969, and a full-scale engineering mock-up was built. Design engineering finalized the basic lines, the wing structure and the intricate flap geometry. Thousands of drawings emanated from the enlarged drafting department and undercarriage design reverted to a conventional wide-track, retractable format. An engineering go-ahead was given early in the year and a search was made for a manufacturing partner. Early discussions were with Saab in Sweden, who were contemplating a similar project. They opted out and negotiations were conducted with Messerschmitt-Bölkow-Blohm in Germany. No agreement was concluded.

In-house Complications

Even though planning went forward, all was not well in the boardroom at Downsview. Although an extensive sales tour began in September 1969, word came in December from Hawker Siddeley in England to shelve the project. Though de Havilland Canada had been self-sufficient for so many years, it was still British-owned. The de Havilland organization long since had been swallowed by giant Hawker Siddeley, run by astute businessmen whose first responsibility was to their shareholders. Hawker Siddeley had the competing HS748 and a new short-haul project, the bigger, pure-jet HS146.

Continued successes through the years at Downsview had put a distinctive stamp on DH Canada, but they were now muddying the waters of the parent pool. Hawker

Siddeley's logo at Downsview had become the symbol of an absentee landlord. Constant directives came from England suggesting that they were not interested in a short-haul transport, but neither the president nor the Canadian government seemed to pay attention. As interest in an all-Canadian STOL transport and national STOL policy grew at Downsview, British interest waned. Hawker Siddeley had changed DHC from being a small aircraft maker by shutting down Turbo Beaver production. It was not ready to invest in a STOL airliner. For the first time in 42 years a major difference of opinion had arisen between the parent and its Canadian branch. The situation was also beginning to strain the good relations that always had existed between DHC and Ottawa.

All this made life difficult for Bill Boggs, who was trying to build up his company, while he was receiving every encouragement from the Canadian government to launch a new product. The British directors, unable to sway Ottawa, asked Boggs to leave, and sought a new man to manage the only portion of their empire still bearing the single name de Havilland. The official date of Boggs' resignation was May 1, 1970. Bernhard B. Bundesman took over as president.

Bundesman, began his aviation career with Douglas Aircraft in 1934. He was associated with Bell Aircraft in WWII. In early 1951 he joined Lockheed in Georgia and worked his way up to chief salesman on the Jetstar, Lockheed's early entry into the business jet market. "Bundy" was well liked in corporate aviation. When the Hawker Siddeley Group began marketing the D.H.125 in the U.S., he was appointed president of Hawker Siddeley International Limited at La Guardia. Bundy, an American, moved as a stranger in troubled times to the Canadian branch to carry out their directions, which could only be described as "winding down" the company.

The Canadian government stepped in on July 23, 1970 with the announcement that DHC-7 funding would con-

The HS748 was an important factor in Hawker Siddeley's opposition to the Dash 7. About 350 HS748s were built. (DH)

Airtransit's DHC-6S fleet lined up at Downsview before delivery. The buildings in the distance, the centre of wartime Mosquito production, were later the focus of RCAF activity and in the 1990s housed various enterprises, including an aviation museum. (DH)

tinue until September 30, 1971. This saved jobs and kept thousands of engineering man-hours intact. Other changes brought D.N. "Doug" Kendall to the board of directors along with Bill Heaslip, vice-president engineering, and Buck Buchanan, vice-president sales.

In 1970, according to chief designer Fred Buller, the STOL concept took its greatest step forward. Close liaison with the Federal Aviation Administration brought the right meeting of minds to produce a clear definition of STOL. DHC acted as a catalyst at these meetings to bring decisions about runway size, approach angle, height over the threshold and many other details hammered out in friendly consultation. By September 1971 the FAA had finalized its decision into Part 298 of the regulations. Other projects at Downsview kept everyone busy, but there was a feeling of uncertainty in middle management. The Twin Otter Series 300, with improved performance and gross weight, was selling well; even Caribou sales, with U.S. orders filled, were 295 and climbing. By the end of 1970 the 24 Brazilian Buffalos had been delivered and a new order of 16 had come from Peru. This was commendable, but everyone knew that the future hung on decisions being made in engineering. All their eggs were in one basket with the DHC-7 and the political climate was unsure. The company's stature and record were carrying government support for now, but how long would it last?

There were few DHC-7 milestones in 1971. Government help was renewed as a Flight Development Project, while full-scale market studies were enlarged. A similar FDP go-ahead for the PT6A-50 engine was given to Pratt & Whitney Canada in 1972, lending support to an all-Canadian engine/airframe combination. Another positive step, announced on March 30, was a joint marketing agreement between DHC and Boeing of Seattle. This came at a crucial point in DHC history, for it marked the company's full entry into the air-

line market. DHC in no way competed with Boeing, but there was much to be gained from the expertise of this prestigious manufacturer of big jets. Most of 1972 was complicated by the longest strike in de Havilland Canada history, lasting eight months. Major sales were lost, but promised deliveries were completed by supervisory personnel. On the brighter side, the year ended with an announcement on October 16 by the Minister of Industry, Trade and Commerce that two pre-production DHC-7s would be built for test and type certification. No production decision was taken.

Airtransit

Nineteen seventy-three was another year of ups and downs, with the bad news first. Early in April, the U.S. CAB was forced to terminate plans for a Northeast Corridor STOL project, due mainly to strong community opposition outside the major airports. The use of these locations away from the major hubs was part of the CAB's main strategy in eliminating traffic congestion. Termination of the plan was a major blow for all who had worked on the project. By this time, preparations for a Canadian government STOL demonstration linking Montreal and Ottawa were on the way. It began to look as though Canada must back its years of STOL experience with its own demonstration of interurban transportation. Six special Twin Otters were delivered by mid-year and work began on two STOLports, one in the old Montreal Expo 67 parking lot, the other on the main runway of historic Rockcliffe airport. Called Airtransit, the experiment was to demonstrate a system concept involving the latest in navigation aids, special air traffic control, STOLport management, government regulations and, above all, an aircraft capable of landing on a 2,000-ft. (600 m) runway. The six Twin Otters were modified as the Series 300S to provide the most complete STOL package available. They included technical refinements to improve short takeoff and landing and additional safety features associated with transport category airplanes (under FAR Part 25). These were the most sophisticated Twin Otters ever to leave the line at Downsview. Every item had to duplicate the Dash 7 as closely as possible. Pilots of standard Twin Otters eyed with envy the features in the 300S that could make their work easier: high capacity brakes, anti-skid braking, wing spoilers, propeller de-icing, electrical and hydraulic improvements, emergency brakes, propeller auto-feather time delay, and improved engine fire protection.

The key to precise navigation and schedule reliability was sophisticated new avionics. The units chosen were off-the-shelf items from leading manufacturers. The detailed selection of navigation aids, including the ground approach method, was the result of lengthy evaluation by the Department of Transport. The Twin Otter 300S had the usual avionics for air transport category IFR operation, plus dual Collins 109 flight directors. Each had the latest Litton Industries area navigation system, providing pre-planned, card operated automation. Perhaps the most sophisticated feature was the CO-SCAN microwave landing system, quite new in Canada, from Cutler Hammer's AIL Division. With this type of guidance the aircraft could select the most appropriate path to the runway and avoid locations on the ground that presented obstructions or were sensitive to noise. By combining area navigation with microwave instrument landing systems, and by using a new low-level air routing, the Twin Otters could fly from the runway at Montreal on a pre-determined route to the runway in Ottawa while remaining clear of the standard air traffic patterns.

There were delays in starting the experiment, caused by everything from strikes to shortages of steel. History even repeated itself – just as the Ontario Department of Lands and Forests had once built hangar doors too small for their Beavers, Airtransit duplicated the feat in 1973. This time the doors did not have sufficient clearance for the high Twin Otter tail. The slip-up was corrected, and by mid-summer the service was ready to begin.

The two-year, $25.5-million project was handled as a subsidiary of Air Canada, with Gary G. Vogan as president. Walk-in terminals were built. The newly hired pilots practised back and forth between Ottawa and Montreal for weeks before taking fare-paying passengers. The interiors of the Twin Otters were furnished in comfortable style with only 11 seats, instead of the usual 19. This would not be economic but, in the case of seating, the object was to duplicate as closely as possible the DHC-7. When service finally began on July 24, 1974, it was an immediate hit with the briefcase

trade in both cities. Flight time was 46 minutes, which, with minibus time at both ends, brought downtown-to-downtown time to 1 hour, 25 minutes. This compared favourably with regular airline time of 2 hours and the automobile time of 2 hours, 39 minutes. An innovation was a one-way fare of $20, including ground transportation.

At first, 16 daily flights were scheduled, but the response was so encouraging that there soon were 30. There were the inevitable rush hours and slow weekends, but the load factor for the first year was an acceptable 58.2 per cent. The experiment provided a wealth of data, but, while all eyes were on the project, probably the least concerned were the passengers. They were happy getting the kind of service they wanted. The critics looked mostly at the costs and scoffed at the limited number of seats. The planners held to their vision of a complete STOL package and did their advance thinking in terms of a 48-passenger DHC-7. The newspapers had a heyday reporting both sides. When the project ended on April 30, 1976, it had met all objectives. It had proven that STOL could operate in the same sky as the major carriers in a complex area like Montreal and do it on a round-the-clock basis. For the forward thinkers, the demonstration was an ideal showcase – a concept pioneered in Canada with Canadian-manufactured aircraft and engines, ready for export.

The Dash 7

In May of 1973 the first run of the PT6A-50 was completed by P&WC in Montreal. Preparations were made to install it on the nose of a Vickers Viscount for air testing. Since its introduction into service in 1964, the PT6 had become the world's most popular and thoroughly proven small turbine engine. As propulsion requirements changed, so models grew in size, even though the basic concept remained. The PT6A-50 was planned around the DHC-7. Engine manufacture had reached the point where airframe designers could make some specifications of their own: the PT6A-50 was an example, for it had a special reduction gearbox to accommodate low-speed, low-noise propellers. Because of increased gearbox diameter and large propeller manoeuvre loads, a twin exhaust port was also incorporated. These exhausts were directed over the wing to discharge noise and emissions away from the aircraft. A host of other improvements included simplified power management and propeller control systems.

The first de Havilland Canada design had been designated DHC-1, and Phil Garratt named it the Chipmunk. Thereafter, new types were also given the names of animals – DHC-2 Beaver, DHC-3 Otter, DHC-4 Caribou, DHC-5 Buffalo. The DHC-6 Twin Otter was easy to name, but not

The ex-TCA Vickers Viscount fitted as a PT6A-50 test bed by Pratt & Whitney. (P&W Canada)

the DHC-7. Through all the early discussions, the four-engined STOL airliner was referred to simply as the '7 or the Dash 7. The name "Dash" stuck and was made official on October 1, 1973. Marketing accelerated from early 1973 and a worldwide sales program began on May 22, 1974. Sales efforts were consolidated under one department, with Boeing stalwart Joe Andrews in charge. Regional teams were formed and the whole effort was co-ordinated with the Boeing world sales organization. Since this arrangement was made in 1972, much sales engineering and marketing expertise had been exchanged. Promoting a new airliner in a sceptical market was a challenge for both companies, and DHC profited immensely from the arrangement, which continued into 1981.

Government Ownership

The most traumatic period in the history of de Havilland Canada was the transition from a thriving private enterprise organization through the amalgamation process to a government-owned establishment. In the end, the Hawker Siddeley years combined with the changing times to upset the orderly development of the previous 30 years. It was known that early in the Dash 7 period, Hawker Siddeley were willing (if not anxious) to sell DHC. A joint offer by Air Canada and Canadian International Comstock was made through Ottawa. Another feeler was extended by Douglas Aircraft, but the only commitment resulted when Ottawa underwrote the first two Dash 7s for $75 million. Under this agreement, Ottawa held an option to buy DHC, which was valid until June 28, 1974.

As that day neared, Clive Baxter in his Ottawa column in the *Financial Post* speculated that the government would pick up the option and mentioned a study on Canada's aircraft manufacturing future being conducted by the Department of Industry, Trade and Commerce. The story came out in the *Globe and Mail* on May 28, 1974, when aviation reporter Ken Romain outlined the government's move to take over aircraft manufacturing in Canada:

The government announced it will exercise its option to purchase de Havilland Aircraft of Canada Ltd., Toronto, at an estimated cost of $38 million, and will seek an option to purchase Canadair Ltd. of Cartierville, near Montreal, at a cost of $32 million.

Ottawa plans to offer them for sale as a package to Canadian interests, stating it only plans to operate them on an interim basis.

The announcement of the government's intentions was made by Industry, Trade and Commerce Minister Alastair Gillespie. The option to purchase de Havilland was negotiated two years ago and was to expire on June 28.

Mr. Gillespie said control of de Havilland will be transferred to the government within 30 days of the effective date of the notice.

A new board of directors consisting of Canadian businessmen and senior company officials will be appointed to assume control on an interim and trusteeship basis.

After all the rumours and speculation, the transition of ownership on May 27, 1974, went well. Three new directors – Dr. J. Herbert Smith, R.M. Barford and J.G. Grandy – were appointed to the board, but the operating management was unchanged. President Bundesman was asked to continue on an interim basis and it was Dr. Smith's responsibility as chairman to guide the company into a new era. Current programs at Downsview continued, while Ottawa negotiated with Canadair. There was an October 15 deadline with General Dynamics of St. Louis, owner of the Montreal company, for a top price of $38 million.

When that sale was concluded, enquiries were invited for an all-Canadian buyer and even a joint ownership. Seven proposals were made by various Canadian companies as a "package deal", but few details emerged. The aviation press was critical of any suggestion that the companies merge. Nothing came of the proposals that ended on Alastair Gillespie's desk and he calmed the waters with the statement that the government would continue an "interim operation" until a suitable purchaser could be found in each case. Negotiations still were under way when word came that Phil Garratt had died in Toronto. He had been off the board since April 6, 1971, and had received further honours in his final years. He received the prestigious Canada Medal in 1971 and was inducted into Canada's Aviation Hall of Fame in 1973. The memorial service, held five days later, was described by his friend, columnist Bruce West, in the *Globe and Mail*, November 21, 1974:

Last Thursday I went up to Christ Church, Deer Park, to attend a memorial service for Phil Garratt, who died a week ago at the age of 80. The big church was packed to the doors, with a crowd containing an impressive cross-section of the whole Canadian aviation industry, pilots, air engineers, company executives. They came to honour the memory of this big, friendly man because he, perhaps more than any other individual in this country, had personified the hopes, the struggles and the amazing successes of the aviation industry in Canada for more than half a century.

An era had certainly ended with the death of Garratt, but a new one was beginning under government ownership. The fact that there were no solid Dash 7 orders was drawing unfavourable comment in the press. Nothing came of the private offers to purchase de Havilland or Canadair and it was apparent that both would have to be operated as crown corporations for some time. The economic climate was poor with only 2,600 employees at DHC and 2,700 at Canadair.

As far as DHC was concerned, Twin Otter sales were steady, the Buffalo was being upgraded and two Dash 7s were well into their certification program. Russ Bannock rejoined the company as director of sales on July 11 in time to witness the regular strike, which lasted for four months. Bundy Bundesman retired as president on January 6, 1976, and was replaced by Bannock. Dr. J. Herbert Smith remained as chairman of the board. John A. Timmins joined as director of sales, and the early Dash 7 sales team was absorbed into the overall marketing group. Joe Andrews and most of the former team left the company, but Mike Kilburn, one of the originals from D.H. sales in England, remained at Downsview. It was time for the company to settle down and adjust to all the changes.

With de Havilland Canadian-owned and a major government investment involved, there was less doubt about the future of the Dash 7. The program had gained considerable momentum by the end of 1974. The first PT6A-50 was delivered in September, followed by the DHC directors' approval on November 26 of a production launch for 25 aircraft. By now the first pre-production aircraft was on its wheels and ready to move. By Christmas of 1974 it went into the paint shop for a colour scheme similar to Airtransit's. The Dash 7 made its public debut on February 5, 1975, when the Honourable Alastair Gillespie, Minister

of Industry, Trade and Commerce, unveiled the "Quiet STOL Airliner" to 600 guests. It was a colourful, dramatic affair as a curtain was drawn and floodlights revealed the glistening aircraft.

One of those attending had more than the average interest – flight operations manager Dave Fairbanks. In his war days and his commercial flying career, he had won a reputation as a brilliant demonstration pilot. His Caribou world flights, his Farnborough demos and the Buffalo STOL landings in New York were just a few of his accomplishments. He had been scheduled to go to Ethiopia that week to promote an Otter sale, but had bowed out because of a medical appointment. He had been working closely with the Dash 7 design team and was taking part in cockpit layout discussions. He was looking forward to this new aircraft. He stood at the door as the crowd gathered for the ceremony, greeting friends and acting the part of company host. He circulated during the rollout and joined the crowd for the cocktail party that followed.

Another of Fairbanks' specialties was playing the piano, although he never performed professionally. He was prevailed upon this evening to sit down and go through his lively routines, completely by ear. To those who knew him, his showmanship at the keyboard matched his flair in the cockpit. When Fairbanks reached home that night there was a message from his doctor, who had been trying all evening to contact him. The message read, "Report immediately to the hospital." His tests indicated that he had suffered a recent heart attack. Fifteen days later S/L David C. Fairbanks, DFC and two bars, war ace and world flyer, was dead at the age of 52.

Dave Fairbanks was one of the stalwarts in DHC's flight operations department. (DH)

The Dash 7 Flies

Other dates will be added to the chronology of the Dash 7, but none more important than the first flight on the cold, bright afternoon of March 27, 1975. Test pilots Bob Fowler and Mick Saunders were on board with flight engineers Jock Aitken and Bob Dingle. The onlookers were almost all employees who were used to STOL and expected a short takeoff. What they had come to witness was the extremely quiet noise level. As Dash 7 C-GNBX-X climbed for its 2 hour, 20 minute test flight, the main noise came from the Twin Otter flying photographic chase with flight operations manager George Neal and chief photographer Ron

(Left) After its career as a test and demo plane, in 1988 the Dash 7 prototype went to the National Aviation Museum. (DH 47241)

(Below) DHC president Bernhard Bundesman joins Dash 7 pilots Bob Fowler and Mick Saunders after a successful first flight. (DH)

Nunney aboard. Test flying began immediately and the second prototype joined the program on June 26.

By the fall of 1976 the Dash 7s had accumulated 1,000 hours and the "Ranger" reconnaissance version had been announced at the Farnborough Air Show. Another big day was May 2, 1977, when Department of Transport Chief of Airworthiness, Ken Owen, presented the Dash 7 type approval certificate to project engineer G. Ron Jackson in a ceremony at Downsview. A month later the first production aircraft rolled out at an employee family day gathering. In June, C-GNBX-X made its international debut at the 32nd Paris Airshow. It performed from June 1 to 12, introducing thousands to quiet STOL. It left immediately after the show to tour France, Turkey, Greece, Yugoslavia, Norway, Sweden, Denmark and England. In England it concentrated on the small feeder-line runs and headed for an important demonstration to Scotland's North Sea oil installations. Twin Otters were already operating there and Loganair's chief pilot, Ken Foster, accompanied DHC pilot Tom Appleton on a four-airport tour. Bad weather complicated the day's flying with fog, rain and hail, putting the crew and aircraft to the test and showing off the Dash 7 to even greater advantage. Two important demonstrations were completed in Iceland and Greenland on the return flight to Downsview, where C-GNBX-X arrived on July 25. During its 55 days away, it flew over 160 hours, completed 200 flights in 11 countries and carried nearly 4,000 passengers. A look at the press reports when the flight was finished revealed that the Dash 7 was, as hoped, being regarded not merely as another turbo-prop replacement, but with its quiet operation and short runway performance, as a new concept in short-haul transportation.

The Proving Ground

For every new aircraft there is much selling to be done, even though the company product record has been good. DHC's experience lay mainly in military STOL, but their latest product was in the most sophisticated form, a 50 passenger pressurized aircraft designed specifically for short-haul airlines and conforming to the most stringent civil regulations. The first sales drive revealed a wait-and-see attitude among the carriers. The argument often heard was, "Who needs the extra cost of STOL – we always have lots of runway."

The company's sales effort was two-fold. It had to promote STOL, along with the hardware capable of small field operations and the use of secondary runways. The aircraft had to meet the test of round-the-clock operations, including dispatch reliability (the percentage of scheduled flights completed without a mechanical delay exceeding five minutes). Yet the order book was slow in filling as the Dash 7 approached certification. A convincing display would be needed from those early airplanes. Gone were the experimental exercises of Metro 66 and Airtransit, the meetings on regulation and instrumentation. The airline world would be watching the first customers.

It was not by luck alone the first Dash 7 operators were ideally suited to demonstrate the aircraft. Rocky Mountain Airways had pioneered with six Twin Otters using the microwave landing system and short runways in the mountain resorts around Denver. With minimum effort they projected

Rocky Mountain's first Dash 7 served from 1978 until the airline joined Continental Express in 1990. Then, A6-ALM, Dash 7 No. 9, went to Emirates Air Service in Dubai in July 1978. (DH)

the Dash 7 into identical route structures, descent patterns and runways. Spantax Airlines of Spain, with a distinctive short-haul operation, was the second operator. Wardair, which had set a new standard in northern transportation with the Twin Otter, took on a broader range of activity with its first cargo/passenger Dash 7. The ninth Dash 7 went to the oil fields of the Middle East with Emirates Air Service, a specialist service requiring short hauls and coping with a variety of runway conditions. The question of how such a big aircraft could pay its way in each environment was on everybody's mind, but improved economics emerged in all cases.

Rocky Mountain president Gordon Autry had watched Dash 7 certification during 1975-76. All the advance figures told him it was ideal for his competitive Denver-Aspen resort run. He secured the first delivery position. As soon as possible, the demonstration aircraft went to Denver to verify his calculations. Autry took delivery of Dash 7 No. 4 in a January 18, 1978, ceremony and inaugurated Dash 7 service on February 3.

To Rocky Mountain, dispatch reliability was a challenge. The route, the Talar microwave landing system and the steep approaches to short runways had all been proven. Now it was time to see how reliable the first aircraft would be. Autry made the point in his first report to de Havilland that, although he had to introduce the Dash 7 in his busiest month, he was able to start with a dispatch reliability of 98.5 per cent – including all the variables of the learning curve. By October 1978 Rocky Mountain reached 100 per cent dispatch reliability while operating 9.9 hours a day, seven days a week on short stage lengths. It was exhilarating news for

the DHC engineers who had been working tirelessly with that goal in mind, but they were quick to credit the outstanding work of Autry and his director of maintenance, Dennis Wells. In its first year, the aircraft made 4,250 flights with an average flight time of 40 minutes. After the first seven weeks, Rocky Mountain ordered a second Dash 7 and took an option on a third. In December 1979 they became the first airline with two Dash 7 aircraft in revenue service. Their successful pioneering in short-haul air transport won Rocky Mountain the *Air Transport World* "Commuter Airline of the Year" award.

To the North with Wardair

With the Dash 7, Wardair Canada updated the old term "bush flying." C-GXVF (Serial No. 7) was the first Dash 7 in Canadian service. The circumstances could not have been more appropriate. The aircraft was named after one of Wardair's pioneer pilots, Don Braun. He had done much to establish the Otter and Twin Otter in the north. Max Ward accepted the aircraft at Downsview on May 23, 1978, with Mrs. Braun performing the christening. It went north to work from Yellowknife and, after training and certification, flew its first revenue flight on June 20. The company's target for a profitable northern operation was 200 hours per month, so the two crews under northern operations manager, Dave Watson, had a formidable challenge.

The first revenue flight, to a number of Alberta airfields, carried an advance party planning the royal visit in July. The next, on the 23rd, was a charter taking foreign diplomats on tour through the high Arctic. On July 31, the royal tour began with Queen Elizabeth, the Duke of Edinburgh and Prince Andrew. Dave Watson was captain on the flight, which involved ceremonial stopovers at Peace River, St. Paul, Lloydminster, Vegreville and Namao. With the glamour events over, it was time to begin cargo operations and start the Dash 7 living up to the Twin Otter reputation. The inaugural exercise was ideal for such a test, as it involved an all-freight contract from Yellowknife to the Echo Lake copper and zinc mine on Great Bear Lake. The contract involved flying general freight in and returning with containers of mineral concentrate. The unpaved airstrip was 3,000 ft. (900 m) long, or DC-3 length. The Dash 7 was soon going in and out with maximum payloads of 12,000 lb. (5,450 kg) (nearly double a DC-3 load) and making 10 round trips a day. The operation went off without a hitch.

In the summer of 1979 there was a contract to fly to the North Pole for the Department of Energy, Mines and Resources. Such an exercise would have warranted headlines in bygone years, but in 1979, for Wardair

Canada and the Dash 7, it was routine. The Earth Sciences Division of DEM&R was placing 50 Canadian, U.S. and Norwegian scientists as close to the Pole as possible. They were to spend two months working on a series of projects named Lorex 79 and were to be serviced by Canadian Forces Hercules doing LAPES (Low Altitude Parachute Extraction System, formerly called LOLEX). Dr. Hans Weber was in charge; he went north in March on a Bradley Air Service Twin Otter to prepare a site. They found a patch of level ice about 800 by 60 metres, just right for the Dash 7, and prepared to set up camp. It was Wardair's job to bring in the base camp.

The Dash 7, with two crews under Dave Watson, arrived at CFB Alert on Ellesmere Island, and began operations during the period of 24 hours of daylight. They remained 11 days, flying 19 round trips of $2^{1}/_{2}$ hours each from Alert to the polar ice strip, with routine 25 minute turn-arounds. On the final trip the crew positioned directly over the Pole and,

Maxwell W. Ward, a long-time friend of de Havilland, helped prove the Otter and Twin Otter in the north. Here Max takes delivery of the first Dash 7 with a cargo door. This was the first civil Dash 7 operated in Canada. It's seen with a flying replica of Max's original Fox Moth. (DH 46458, '46460)

just for the record, did the first round-the-world Dash 7 flight before returning to Yellowknife. Once again the "Don Braun" came through with no snags.

In four different parts of the world and in a wide variety of uses, the Dash 7 established itself in a matter of months. The air transportation community had been watching and the flow of orders began. Rocky Mountain's convincing display, and deregulation of the industry in the U.S. brought back an earlier de Havilland customer, Air Wisconsin. The Canadian Forces bought two for Europe.

Fifty Years in Canada: The Good News First

The company began its second half-century on a wave of acclaim for the Dash 7. The Canadian press, which previously had leaned heavily on the lack of pre-production orders, were now calling the growing sales a "turnaround." Everything was reported under headlines about "taxpayers' dollars" when DHC was taken over by Ottawa. The news now emphasized the employment the Dash 7 would generate and the value of export sales to Canada's economy.

Reporters began to emphasize how 55 man-years were needed to build just one Dash 7 and how five of the first six planes ordered were bringing in export dollars. Even the controversy over whether Toronto Island Airport should be

The 50-year emblem flew on the company flag throughout 1978 and was used on all stationery and publications.

used for intercity STOL took on a new light when Bob Fowler demonstrated the Dash 7 at that historic terminal. After touchdown, he turn-offed at the first intersection. On continued passenger flights the Dash 7 routinely used less than half of the 4,000 ft. (1,200 m) runway. Even more convincing was the low noise level – less than the snarling single-engine floatplanes using Toronto Harbour. Howard Tinney, who led the Boeing group assisting DHC with sales, called the Dash 7 "the only game in town."

With Twin Otter deliveries nearing 600 by January 1978, and Buffalo sales steady, de Havilland's standing in the popularity polls improved. The anniversary year looked promising. The plant took on a festive appearance, with flags and gold 50-year stickers everywhere. Bob McIntyre

A Dash 7 lands at a typical Rocky Mountain STOLport. (DH)

The Dash 7 prototype over Toronto Island Airport. The concentrated central business district in the background was the market coveted by those envisioning TIA as ideal for STOL airliners. (DH)

and his anniversary committee had been meeting for months; their program emphasized an impressive first half-century. A family day was planned and a booklet on the company history produced. The actual date of DHC beginning its second half-century went unnoticed during blustery March, the ceremony being reserved for a warmer time of the year.

In February 1928, British de Havilland Moths had been shipped to Canada. In February 1978, the process was reversed when a Twin Otter was delivered to Britain to begin scheduled operations for Brymon Airways of Plymouth. This took place 50 years to the month after Bob Loader arrived in Canada with his crate of two little Cirrus Moths. On April 1, Herbert Smith retired as chairman of the board and was replaced by Douglas Kendall, who had been a director since 1970.

On June 24, the 50-year celebration took place. The gates were opened that afternoon to 10,000 people as employees took their families on a tour of the factory, viewed displays and watched an air show. Lucky draws were held for Twin Otter rides, while thousands of hot dogs and gallons of soft drinks were consumed. A highlight of the afternoon was the handover of Twin Otter No. 600 from the production line

to Aero Mech of Clarksburg, West Virginia, part of the Allegheny Commuter network. Two original DHC employees, Frank Warren and George Mickleborough, were introduced to the crowd by Russ Bannock.

Passages

de Havilland Canada's 50th anniversary brought with it one of life's mathematical factors – retirement. Long-service employees had always enjoyed recognition with a retirement party. Now, many who had played a major role in the formative years were passing the responsibility to younger hands. Even before the 50-year mark the names of George Mickleborough, Frank and Ab Warren, George Blanchard and John Slaughter were on the retirement list. Buck Buchannan, George Hurren, Geoff Priestly and Len Trotter took reluctant leave of the sales organization they worked so hard to build and Harry Beffort retired from the thankless job of union negotiations. In October 1979 Dick Hiscocks retired and the office of vice- president engineering went to M.C.W. "Mike" Davy. In December, Fred Buller retired as chief designer and was replaced by John Thompson. Buller

Air Wisconsin, formed in 1965 under Preston H. Wilborne, was a classic case of a commuter line linking an out-of-the-way market (Appleton, Wisconsin) with a major hub (Chicago). Growth led from a nine-seat Dove to Twin Otters, then to the Dash 7. The Dash 7 generated so much business that the 100-seat BAe146 was added. In 1986 Air Wisconsin became a United Express partner. (DH)

(Right) Brymon Airways was one of many operators that flew a number of de Havilland types. They were the earliest operator of the Twin Otter in England, taking delivery of their first aircraft in DHC's 50th year. (DH 39924)

(Below) Commuters then and now. A restored 1930s-vintage D.H.84 Dragon and a Brymon Dash 7. (DH)

The Dash 7 proved ideal for Hawaiian Airlines short-haul flights on the much-travelled island routes. N919HA, dubbed "Kaunakakei," served from 1981 to 1992. (DH)

278

Having begun in 1977, the Dash 7 remained busy in the commuter role 20 years later. Most, however, had been replaced by the Dash 8 and Canadair Regional Jet and were working in other roles. This Pan Am Express Dash 7 was at Washington National Airport on September 2, 1991. It had been with Ransome Airlines until Pan Am absorbed that carrier in 1986. (George W. Hamlin)

and Hiscocks had become a formidable team in design engineering since the Chipmunk/Beaver days. Alex Watson, engineering manager, prepared for retirement in January 1980. Test and demonstration pilot Don Rogers left in February. DH England veteran Phil Halsey retired in June 1982. This trend continues, of course, but when that post-war group departed, it was the end of a special era.

A New President

With the 50th anniversary over, a complicated six months lay ahead. The presidency changed hands again when Russ Bannock returned to his aircraft sales business on July 14. A new chief executive officer moved in, and the company magazine, *High Lift*, introduced John Sandford to the DHC family and their customers:

John W. Sandford was appointed president of The de Havilland Aircraft of Canada Limited on July 14. The appointment was something of a 'homecoming' for Mr. Sandford who began his career in North America when he emigrated from England to join Avro Canada in 1957 – just two years before cancellation of the much-discussed Arrow program. Like some of his contemporaries at Downsview, Sandford made his first acquaintance with aviation in Britain as an apprentice with Westland Aircraft. From there he went on to take a masters degree in aeronautical engineering at the Cranfield Institute of Technology.

After cancellation of the Arrow, John joined North American Rockwell in the United States and went on to establish an outstanding reputation in the U.S. aerospace industry. As director of engineering for advanced launch systems, Sandford took part in development of the Saturn rocket boosters that took men to the moon . He

Honouring long-service employees is a tradition at de Havilland. In 1981 several new 40-year members were rounded up for a photograph. From the left: Howard Hall, Alex Saychuck, Jack Watson, John VanDuesen, Ken Bell, Stanley Shield, Ken Walker, Charlie Smith, Bill Bozanin and Phil Halsey. Absent were John Aitken, Bill Duck, Bob Prout, Crawford Byers and Bob Innis. (DH)

279

was also responsible for the winning proposal to NASA for the design, development and production of the shuttle vehicle system. At his own request John transferred to Rockwell's General Aviation Division, which brought him back to Canada in 1975, as president of Canadian Admiral Corporation.

Sandford had a busy month settling into his new job, for this was the year for union negotiations. Once again, as in former years, bargaining broke down and picket lines formed. It was not the best of welcomes for the new president, but he took the situation in stride and began an intense communications program to let everyone know what was going on. During the strike, DHC kept up its reputation at the year's Farnborough Air Show. The non-union staff at home pitched in to cope with pending aircraft and spare parts deliveries.

A trend in the airline industry at the time of deregulation proved advantageous to de Havilland: as they dropped less productive routes, the trunk airlines began associating themselves more closely with the commuters. Co-operation with the major lines was eagerly sought by the smaller operators, who gained the use of booking services and terminal facilities in exchange for the transfer of passengers – the true definition of a feeder-line. The introduction of the Dash 7 with its quiet, short-field capability provided a new dimension to this hub-and-spoke concept.

The Dash 7 proved just right for this unexpected swing in market conditions, even though STOL was not a prime concern. A contributing factor was a change in U.S. regulations permitting commuter airlines, previously restricted to 30 seats, to use up to 56-seat aircraft. The fact that the Dash 7 could use any Twin Otter runway gave it a distinct advantage over the competition in certain areas. Everyone agreed it was the quietest airliner in the business and talk began, once again, about using reliever runways at major airports. Not only did U.S. orders come in, but the long world-wide sales promotion began to pay, with orders from Norway, Austria and England. The strike was settled in November. President Sandford now had an announcement of such importance that a full-fledged press conference was called.

Expansion Again

Coinciding with this conference, the employees received possibly the best news they had heard in a decade – there were new orders and options for the Dash 7 and a multi-million dollar plant expansion was imminent. The Dash 7 production rate would go from one to two a month, the Twin Otter from four to five. Sandford's announcement vindicated the once-criticized Dash 7. Orders stood at 32, including 13 for U.S. commuters. The plant expansion involved an assembly area, a small-parts manufacturing area and 65,000 sq. ft. (6,000 sq. m) of hangar storage. New subcontract work was announced along with the prospect of 300-400 new jobs at Downsview. John Sandford announced that sales for the fiscal year ending May 30 totalled $125 million, with a profit of $2 million, and that more than 85 per cent of production was exported. DHC's first half-century had closed on a sound footing. Industry Minister Jack

A unique role for the Dash 7 was flying ice patrol for Environment Canada. The only such aircraft is distinguishable by its side-looking radar and observation bubble. (DH)

John Sandford assumed the presidency of de Havilland Canada on July 14, 1978. (Below) At a press conference in 1981 to announce a series of orders for the Dash 7 plus a plant expansion, increased production and more jobs, Sandford addresses the media, while Industry Minister Jack Horner waits to congratulate the company. (DH 46710, '46949-3)

Airworthiness – An Explanation

Through all the years that de Havilland Canada sold products from the parent company the original airworthiness certification was completed in England. It was recognized by Canadian authorities, and DHC's responsibility was to maintain the airworthiness specifications laid down. Even the certificate for the post-WWII D.H. 83C Fox Moth was an extension of the original British Airworthiness certification. It was not until Chipmunk, Beaver and Otter days that DHC became involved with its own certification procedures, but these were relatively simple to begin. The Chipmunk and Beaver were certified to conform with British Civil Air Regulations (BCAR) and the Otter with International Civil Aviation Organization (ICAO) requirements. U.S. FAA rules were also accepted as standard in Canada, and were spelled out in what was then called the FAA Civil Air Regulations (CAR for short). de Havilland types fell into the category of "normal Utility and acrobatic category airplanes" and thus complied with Section 3 of the Regulations or CAR3.

When the Caribou was designed it was a different matter. Although it was primarily a military design, it would need airworthiness standards to comply with "transport category airplanes," which came under regulations section 4b or CAR 4b. When the Buffalo came along, the target was also for full transport category certification and it went to the 4b standard in Subsection SR 422, the turbine category covering differences in airplane performance. Some time after the

Horner injected his contribution to the conference, stating that Ottawa had no plans of returning the plant to the private sector. All these details were reported by an eager press.

The buoyant feeling at Downsview that came with $100 million in new sales continued into 1979. Conditions were similar to 1929, when a large backlog of orders fuelled the desire to expand. Like 1929, it was a year of decision – management was faced with extending the life of existing products, while solving problems of space and equipment. The advanced design group was asked to explore the growth potential of the product line, while Maurice Crawford took over details of the plant expansion. The main decision for management was a little more difficult – a new aircraft design that would see the company through the next decade.

Time Air was Canada's premier Dash 7 operator. Here three of its aircraft await despatch from Calgary in 1983. (Robin Brass)

The impressive journal published at the British head office often featured products of the Canadian company, the Beaver and Caribou being shown here. (Hotson Col.)

Twin Otter was certified, U.S. regulations were completely overhauled and called FARs (Federal Air Regulations) from then on. The old CAR3 became FAR Part 23 and CAR 4b became FAR Part 25.

A new requirement was introduced in 1969 for the light twin CAR3/FAR23 types carrying more than 10 occupants. It was a mandatory upgrading of CAR3 and involved additional features such as auto-feathering propellers, improved electrical circuitry, additional emergency exits, etc. Thus the Twin Otter with its original CAR3, now conformed to Special FAR Part 23, British ARB and French DGAC airworthiness approval, along with a number of other countries recognizing any of the above.

The Dash 7 received full airline certification under FAR Part 25, but as there was no category for STOL, a special condition was applied for the Dash 7 alone, to allow a steeper approach and shorter landing. In the case of the Dash 8, it remains a standard FAR 25 airplane, together with FAR 36 governing noise standards, and SFAR 27 covering such things as fuel venting and exhaust emissions.

The Stub Runway Technique

The Separate Access Landing System or SALS, was developed along with the STOL concept to let aircraft with this capability use the ends of idle runways. It was developed by DHC to blend the capabilities of the Dash 7 with the three-dimensional advantages of radio navigation, permitting operators discreet access to busy airports. The DHC system allowed complete separation of commuter and jet traffic and was based on the Airtransit trial.

Two U.S. airlines in the eastern corridor, Henson Aviation of Salisbury, Maryland, and Ransome Airlines of Philadelphia, began working with the FAA in 1982 to evaluate SALS. During the Airtransit experiment only one short runway was used at each end of the route. But SALS allowed aircraft to land on a stub or secondary reliever runway. It represented savings in fuel for the operator over the year and improved service for passengers. Developments in technology have superseded this system.

Communications

Employee communications was one of Geoffrey de Havilland's policies that went back to his first company. It started with the *Airco Rag* during the years with the Aircraft Manufacturing Company in WWI and later the de

de Havilland *high lift* Vol. 3, No. 3

de Havilland *high lift* Vol. 3, No. 6

November/December, 1979

High Lift covered DHC products and activities worldwide in the 1970s and 1980s. The Bombardier Aerospace **Globe** promoted the company's products in the late 1990s.

Havilland *Enterprise.* The in-house *Enterprise* became so sought-after by the aviation fraternity that the *de Havilland Gazette* emerged as a sales promotion medium. It became a high quality publication with glossy paper, excellent photographs and accurate technical articles. On the back page the work of noted aviation cartoonists provided a touch of English humour. The *Gazette* was suspended during the slump in the 1930s, but Martin Sharp took over as editor in 1937 and brought it back to life until another curtailment during WWII. Sharp revived it once more during the era of the DH Comet and Canadian bushplanes, when it reached its highest level. The *Gazette* merged into Hawker Siddeley in 1960 and ended one year later.

The Canadian scene was covered in the early issues of the *Gazette* with photos and stories as far back as 1928. During the war years at Downsview the policy of in-house communications continued with the *de Havilland Mosquito* and surviving copies are now collectors' items. Various news sheets followed during the fifties and sixties with Fred de Jersey and Ernest Ball creating lively publications such as the *Progress Report* and *High Lift,* which was first published in 1976, Allan Austin and John Davy being editors. *High Lift* was discontinued in 1989. In 1978 another publication, *Downsviews,* appeared, edited by Murray Baker, John Davy and Pam Taraday successively. In 1988 *Downsviews* became *Just Plane Facts.* Vince Santoro (1988), then Bill Perry (1992) were the first two editors. In March 1997, *Just Plane Facts* merged with the Bombardier Aerospace *Globe.*

(Above) The first Dash 7 is revealed to a packed hangar at Downsview in February 1975. The new airliner first flew on March 27 as C-GNBX-X. (Larry Milberry)

(Right) NBX at the 1986 Abbotsford International Airshow. When its flying days were over, it was donated to the National Aviation Museum. (Kenneth I. Swartz)

(Left) Development of the PT6A-50 for the Dash 7 involved this five-engine Viscount. CF-TID-X served P&WC from 1972-89, when it was replaced by a Boeing 720. Here it was visiting Downsview for the Dash 7 rollout from its base at St. Hubert. (Larry Milberry)

(Right) Wardair was the first Canadian airline with Dash 7s. Its first, C-GXVF, is seen at Edmonton in July 1978. It was later joined by C-GXVG. These aircraft, short-lived at Wardair, were at work in the late 1990s with other companies. (John Kimberley)

(Above) Time Air of Lethbridge served Calgary, Edmonton, Vancouver and intermediate communities like Kelowna. Here C-GTAD was at Abbotsford in August 1980. In 1998 it was N8041D with Paradise Airlines of Fort Lauderdale.
(Kenneth I. Swartz)

(Right) C-GCFR, operated by Bradley Air Service for Environment Canada, specialized in ice patrol. Here it was in First Air's Carp, Ontario, hangar in December 1997, getting routine maintenance. In the late 1990s the Dash 7 still had a traditional role in Canada, often serving northern regions like Labrador.
(Andy Graham)

(Below) Two Dash 7 aircraft (designated CC-132 by the Canadian Forces) served at Lahr, Germany. They flew passenger-freight skeds and special VIP services, until replaced by the Dash 8. Here 132001 was at Lahr in March 1987. Later it flew with Arkia as 4X-AHI. (Larry Milberry)

Since 1978 Rocky Mountain Airlines, Air Wisconsin, Golden West Airlines, Henson Airlines, Ransome Airlines and others also flew the Dash 7. This trend helped satisfy the burgeoning commuter market, built up in previous years by the Twin Otter. Several Dash 7 operators eventually failed. Others merged in code-sharing arrangements with bigger carriers. Ransome took eight new Dash 7 aircraft, including N171RA (No.16), seen in 1980 in Allegheny colours at Washington National Airport. It later served Trans World Express. (Andy Clancy)

Golden West, pleased with years of profitable Twin Otter operations, added its first Dash 7 in 1980. N701GW (No. 21) was photographed at Santa Barbara, California, in July 1981. Later it flew for Arkia-Israel Inland Airlines as 4X-AHK. With 12 examples, Arkia had more of this type in 1998 than any other airline. (Below) US Air Express Dash 7 N905HA (No. 70) was at Washington National Airport on November 18, 1990. (John Kimberley, George W. Hamlin)

(Above) In March 1980 Tyrolean Airways took the 22nd Dash 7, then added four more. Success with them sold Tyrolean on DH/ Bombardier products. Its fleet in 1998 included a Dash 7, 22 Dash 8 and eight CRJ aircraft, with four of the Dash 8-400 on order. (Anton Heumann)

(Left) Brymon Airways of Plymouth was another European airline that favoured the Dash 7. Brymon only phased out its last in the late 1990s. G-BRYC (No. 54) was photographed in August 1984. In 1996 DH took it back on trade for a Dash 8, re-registering it C-FYXV. (Anton Heumann)

C-GGXS, the 64th Dash 7, climbs away from Pearson International Airport on December 17, 1994. It began with Arkia in 1981, then served Toronto-based City Express. In 1998 it was in the colours of charter carrier Trans Capital, of Toronto. (Andrew H. Cline)

287

A good deal of attention had always been given to future products at DHC. Two proposals (called DHPs) during the Bundesman years had been for executive aircraft. Two others were turbine engine conversions for the Caribou and Otter. A 50-passenger turbofan had been considered in 1970, as well as a turbine-engine Otter replacement, DHP 56, having a long, square fuselage (its profile was similar to the later Cessna Caravan.) While DHP 35 developed into the Dash 7, DHP 58 of 1978 was a twin turboprop, 30-passenger commuter. With DHC's sudden pre-eminence in the regional airline field, it seemed logical to continue by exploring DHP 58. Sales studies showed a distinct gap between the $2 million and $5 million commuter airliner, somewhere between the Twin Otter and Dash 7.

While Brian Eggleston and his advanced design group were creating a technical outline called the Dash X, Bob McIntyre, Ron Jackson, John Shaw, John Glaser and others headed across North America gathering airline reactions.

CHAPTER ELEVEN

THE DASH 8

The DHP 58 was the twin-engine, 30-passenger proposal represented by this model, called the Dash X. Formal announcement came on May 30, 1980, when it was named the Dash 8. (DH 47327)

Their reports were favourable; the timing for such a product was considered sound. The new short-haul airliner would be in the 20-40 passenger bracket and retain some commonality with the Dash 7. In this way, the engineering talent of past years would be preserved and DHC's hard-won, short-haul technology expanded. Everyone knew that the competition would be strong in a market where other nations were already at work.

President Sandford summed up the situation in "The Changes Ahead," a paper delivered for the annual meeting of the Canadian Aeronautics and Space Institute in Ottawa on May 3, 1979. He reviewed the plans for existing products, including a civil version of the Buffalo called the Transporter. He described a family of aircraft options in the regional transport field similar to the well-known Boeing line of big jets. He pointed to the growth potential of the Dash 7, which could be expanded to the 70-passenger class and provide a choice of four aircraft in the airline category. He called it a "step up or sell up" approach and the key would be the Dash X, soon to appear as the 36 passenger Dash 8.

The May announcement was followed by another presentation at Paris in June, where the three current DHC types, sporting matching paint schemes, put on an imposing display. The latest Buffalo had been converted to the civil role with a new name, the Transporter. Back at Downsview the ramps and taxiways were a mass of colour with aircraft for every corner of the globe in the testing, training or delivery stage. Signs of new construction were everywhere. The parking lots were crowded, new ones were planned, and staggered working hours were implemented. For the rest of the year there was steady progress, but a new Progressive Conservative government under Joe Clark had taken over in Ottawa, with all the uncertainties of changing cabinet ministers and policy reversals. The PC's Sinclair Stephens had long been a critic of everything that took place at Downsview – he was once quoted as saying that, given the opportunity, he would have the DH plant torn down and paved over as a parking lot. With these attitudes at the ministerial level, it was reasonable to expect the worst in the hazardous world of government ownership. The ever-vigilant newspapers reported talk of privatizing all government-owned aircraft manufacturing in Canada. Sandford cautioned that any new owner should be a "buyer of quality." "There are many people who can buy us," he said, "but few who can afford us. We have to order the material for the Dash 7 two years before we sell it. There is a great deal of front-end investment before the plane goes out the door."

Boom Times

On December 13, 1979, the Conservatives were toppled in Ottawa and talk of selling the company faded into the turmoil of parliamentary business. The year had produced 16 Dash 7 sales and had seen the delivery of 52 Twin Otters and eight Buffalos. Other statistics as the Christmas holidays approached placed sales at $247 million and staff at 4,600. For three years running, life at DHC had been positive and rewarding. No one could blame the board of directors and management committee for feeling optimistic about the coming Dash 8.

When the Aviation and Space Writers Association visited de Havilland Canada on May 30, 1980, there was another important announcement. Formal commitments had been received from purchasers for 55 Dash 8s, representing a sales value of $400 million. It was a heady period, for never in company history had so many orders been received for an aircraft that was still only in the mockup stage. The Dash 8 was off to a better start than the Dash 7. Coupled with these announcements was word from Ottawa that a second site was planned to meet expansion. This was treated with the respect such Ottawa directives receive, but it was hard to explain the idea outside the realm of politics. As John Sandford outlined, there were 12 locations under consideration and a decision would come in July. This started a scurrying by numerous Ontario municipalities and howls from Mayor Mel Lastman of North York (which included Downsview) at the thought of losing any DHC jobs.

As it turned out, this coast-to-coast search for a new plant site began while the Progressive Conserva-

tives were in power and talking of selling DHC to private enterprise. Expansion at Downsview required a small section of land at the south end, owned by the Department of National Defence, who operated the dwindling air force base at the north side. The DND refused to sell under the circumstances and started this wasteful game of politics (the DND base eventually closed in 1995). The expansion controversy was resolved early in 1981 with the decision to remain at Downsview. Evidently 65 Canadian municipalities had made strong applications, particularly Peterborough and Windsor. The controversy was a useless waste of time and money, hinging on the need for a simple 100 acres (40 hectares). When this property eventually was made available, the most prudent line of action was to remain as one unit at Downsview. It did not take long to re-plan the hangars and office space. It was to total 669,000 sq. ft. (60,210 sq. m) and cost $75 million.

An encouraging announcement in December 1980 noted four Dash 7 aircraft sold to Atlantic Southeast Airlines of Atlanta. Air Wisconsin ordered a tenth Dash 7, making it the largest U.S. regional operator with this type. An optimistic start to the new year was reflected in a January 1981 article by Ron Lowman in the *Toronto Star*. He had interviewed Dawson Ransome, head of Ransome Airlines, which operated under the Allegheny banner in the competitive Philadelphia-Washington-New York circuit. Ransome had three Dash 7 aircraft and was in Toronto ordering three more. The article, headed "U.S. Boss Loves Our Dash 7," went on to explain that Ransome's enthusiasm was such that he would

To speed the pre-test period of the Dash 8, an instrumented engine test rig was built for the new-technology PW120 engine. By the time the aircraft flew, most of the parameters for the electronic engine and propeller controls were in place, requiring only in-flight data. (DH 52363 Charles Bryant)

have loved to take on something as interesting as the proposed Toronto-Ottawa-Montreal STOL service. He talked about the aircraft's tight turn capability, which was impressing U.S. controllers and made for less complicated arrivals and departures. "The short-haul business is booming," said Ransome, who explained that he was trying to replace his French Nord 262s with the Dash 7.

Taking the Gamble

The go-ahead for full-scale Dash 8 development came in September 1980. Market forecasts showing that over 70 per cent of production would be for scheduled airlines had much to do with the final configuration. The Dash 8 design specification included certification under FAR 25 requirements for operation from a 3,000-ft. (900 m) runway at sea level and ISA +15° Celsius (59°F) conditions. This would allow the new airplane to operate economically at crowded hub airports on short, independent stub runways, using the procedures developed by some U.S. Dash 7 operators.

The Dash 8 was simply described by DHC as "a multi-purpose regional transport airplane optimized for regional operations yet adaptable to anything from unpaved runways to corporate flying and the military." Low-speed controllability in the approach mode would continue to be a distinct feature, while the minimum-drag airframe would provide quick climb to altitude and higher cruise speeds. Needing an engine with maximum fuel efficiency, the 2,000-shp P&WC PW120 engine was selected.

The Pratt & Whitney PW 120 advanced technology engine and Hamilton Standard 14SF propeller in the test rig. (DH 51886)

Douglas N. Kendall had a distinguished wartime career at the leading edge of photo interpretation. Later he founded Photographic Survey Corporation of Toronto and Kenting Aviation on behalf of the British Hunting Group. He joined the DHC board of directors in 1970 and became chairman in 1978. (DH 4669 Terry Wildman)

A Change in the Weather

The company's annual report in May of 1981 showed sales for the previous year of $347 million and provided optimism throughout the summer. Everyone thought the once-dreaded fuel crisis was under control, even if prices remained high. The U.S. had welcomed back the Iran hostages and the new Reagan administration was forcing interest rates upwards, when the August air traffic controllers' strike dealt the teetering airline industry a blow. Perhaps the parties involved misread the times, for the strike started a dramatic chain of events that reached right back to aircraft production – including de Havilland Canada.

Commuter airlines, with their quick, frequent services were the first to suffer, particularly those that had invested heavily in new equipment. By the fourth week of the strike, the losses for San Fransisco-based Golden Gate Airlines reached $40,000 a day and they were forced to suspend services indefinitely. The trunk airlines were also suffering; United Airlines laid off 2,100 staff within days. A cold wind blew into Downsview when Golden Gate folded on April 22, 1983, for they operated nine Dash 7 aircraft and had ordered five more. Their closing made things very difficult for de Havilland by thrusting their aircraft onto a softening market, causing a reshuffling of the delivery list. Another blow (for the same reason) was a slump in Twin Otter sales. So many orders were cancelled in one short period that monthly production was chopped from six to three, with 214 workers laid off. The news got worse when President Reagan fired the striking controllers and even more confusion hit the U.S. industry. The business that Dawson Ransome said was booming in January was now in disarray. Cutbacks continued throughout the industry and 450 more layoffs were announced at de Havilland during October.

Since aircraft manufacturing was a major employer, it drew a lot of editorial comment. In a *Financial Post* interview, John Sandford placed 20 per cent of the blame on the controllers' strike, 40 percent on predatory financing (nations competing by supporting their products with unrealistically favourable financing), 20 per cent on high interest rates, and 20 per cent on a general economic decline. Long before the onslaught of these effects, the wooden mock-up of the Dash 8 had been built in the experimental hangar. In 1982 came the metal mock-up, while the jigs and fixtures were being prepared and sub-contractors organized. On December 1, at the Airline Association convention in San Francisco, Sandford announced the Dash 8 roll-out for April 1983. Following type certification, the first Dash 8 would be delivered to Ontario's regional airline, norOntair. The action moved to Bay 8 where the eighth such drama in the company's history began to unfold – preparing a new aircraft for its first flight.

Despite the drop in Dash 7 and Twin Otter sales, interest in the Dash 8 remained high. Excitement built as the test aircraft came together over the winter of 1982-83. As a finishing touch to its paint job, the registration C-GDNK was applied, honouring the retiring chairman of the board, Douglas N. Kendall, who had served since 1970. When the time

came to unveil the Dash 8, the event developed into a twofold presentation. A private in-house ceremony for the employees and their families was held on April 16, 1983, with the Honourable Pierre Elliot Trudeau attending. The visit by Canada's Prime Minister demonstrated his interest in the industry and recognized the people who had worked so hard to make the new airplane a reality.

The official roll-out ceremonies on April 19 were described by *The Canadian Aircraft Operator*:

It was pure theatre. Looking on were 1,600 guests representing customers, suppliers and good friends of de Havilland from all over the world. The big production bay was blackened out. The curtain withdrew dramatically to reveal 411 Reserve Squadron's band marching out playing a jaunty rendition of "Those Magnificent Men and their Flying Machines," while behind the band a tug-towed Dash 8 emerged from the shadows in a silhouette created by brilliant backlighting. As it came to a full stop before the applauding audience, the house lights were brought up to reveal the aircraft in all its gleaming splendour, its pristine white finish offset by a tapered nose-to-tail yellow/orange/red/ burgundy speed line.

The first Dash 8 Series 100 was presented to the public at a colourful rollout on April 19, 1983. When the curtains were drawn, C-GDNK followed the 411 Reserve Squadron band playing a jaunty rendition of "Those Magnificent Men and Their Flying Machines." (DH 42454-21 Tony Honeywood)

Former president William Boggs (left) chats with author Fred Hotson at the Dash 8 rollout. Boggs was called out of retirement in January 1985 to resume the presidency. He played a major roll in the transfer of de Havilland from government control to Boeing. (DH 52465 Tony Honeywood)

The Dash 8 Flies

On June 20, the Dash 8 flew – still ahead of a schedule set three and a half years earlier. Pilots Bob Fowler and Mick Saunders were at the controls, with Don Brand and Geoff Pyne at the engineering stations. Two chase aircraft followed, a Buffalo for photography and a Dash 7 with President Sandford and Douglas Kendall on board. "Delta November Kilo" flew a triangular course over Peterborough and Lake Scugog, completing a series of prescribed manoeuvres. It also performed several optional tests and landed after 90 minutes with Fowler's comment, "A lovely test, the best we have ever done." When asked how the first flight compared with that of the Dash 7, Fowler was quick to point out the difference in the design specifications of the two airplanes. "We were able to predict much more in advance with this aircraft." He added, "The engine controls were calibrated ahead of time in the test rig and worked perfectly. The flight controls felt so good after our skips down the runway that we knew we were in for a good ride."

The euphoria of the first flight was brief. Intensive testing began immediately under J.P "Jack" Uffen, director of De-

The first Dash 8 poses over the Downsview plant at the start of its certification program. Orders for the new plane were growing fast, but the days of government ownership were coming to an end. (DH 52797 Charles Bryant)

John Sandford welcomes the test crew back from the first flight of the Dash 8: Mick Saunders, Bob Fowler, Sandford, Don Brand, Geoff Pyne and Ron Jackson. (DH 52682 Tony Honeywood)

the Dash 7 stopped completely. The assembly bays and service ramps grew quiet, even though the test hangars were busy. Empty desks reflected a dwindling office staff and spaces began to show in the once-full parking lots. The press went into high gear the moment cost overruns began to show at DHC and Canadair. Stories about the national challenge to Canadian technology, manpower and world competition were lost in the shuffle. Everything, once again, was reported in tax dollars. Even before the rollout, John Sandford had written a letter to the *Toronto Star* countering an unfavourable article that called de Havilland a money-losing company. The letter received no headlines and it wasn't the last time the term "money-losing company" was used by the press:

I can only say that the company has made a profit in each year since 1974 when it was acquired by the Crown. Since acquisition, total profit is approximately $16 million. At this point, like so many aerospace companies throughout the world, we are suffering the effects of a world economy in recession. In spite of that, as recently as May of this year, we announced record sales. Since the Crown acquired de Havilland eight years ago the company has recorded about $1.6 billion in sales of aircraft and services – $1.4 billion of this has been in the highly competitive export market. In this same period we generated 32,000 person-years of work for de Havilland employees, and almost 20,000 person-years of work have been generated within our suppliers' factories across the country. About 900 Canadian suppliers participate with de Havilland in building the best aircraft to fly in the world today.

velopment Engineering. It was to be a long program. The second pre-production Dash 8 began flying on October 26. By November 15 the first two machines had logged 120 flying hours. In the end, five aircraft would log 1,670 hours over 14 months. The availability of state-of-the-art test improvements added efficiency and speed to the FAR Part 25 certification. Engineering Test Flight, under W.M. "Wally" Gibson, was an efficient unit with a blend of experienced leaders, like Ron Jackson, as well as new specialists. When Uffen retired in 1984, R.G. "Dick" Batch took over. Other important figures in the program were D.R. "Roy" Madill in Technical Design; senior aerodynamicist, T.R. "Tom" Nettleton, who earlier had worked on the Dash 7; and Maurice Rose'Meyer and Jock Aitken.

Deliveries begin

By the time the Dash 8 flew, there were 53 confirmed sales and 60 options. In other times that would have been an excellent start, but enthusiasm was dampened by the announcement of a $265.2 million loss during the seven-month period ending December 31, 1982. A week earlier a similar loss at Canadair was reported at $1.4 billion. This cast a dark cloud over Canada's aerospace industry – the thunder and lightning were to follow in due course. The airline upheaval in the United States put so many Twin Otter and Dash 7 aircraft on the market that new sales in that segment almost dried up. All DHC production was cut back;

A bright spot at DHC was the delivery of the first Dash 8 to norOntair on October 23, 1984. Ontario Premier William Davis attended the ceremony and watched Sandford hand over the log books to Northern Affairs Minister Leo Bernier. The first Dash 8 airline flight occurred on December 19, when the norOntair aircraft completed a scheduled run from Sault Ste. Marie to Kapuskasing. That same day, another handover ceremony saw the first Dash 8 delivered to a U.S. operator – Eastern Metro Express took possession of their first of eight aircraft.

Management CDIC Style

From the day de Havilland Canada and Canadair entered the public domain, they fell under control of the Canadian Development Investment Corporation (CDIC), responsible to the Minister of Industrial Expansion. Preserving Canada's aerospace industry was the reason Ottawa purchased these major companies. It had the genuine intention to move both into the private sector when the time was right. DHC continued in a favourable financial position even though the Dash 7 had been a slow starter. Canadair was well into its Challenger program on the same basis, but was running an even greater deficit due to performance shortfalls.

The downturn in the North American economy wasn't making life easy for Joel Bell, the CDIC boss, who was caught with two expensive, high profile development programs. The media were in full cry at the amount of government assistance and instant experts of every political hue emerged. Back in the short-lived Tory regime of 1981, when talks of privatization were raised, John Sandford had made the remark, "It takes a great deal of front-end investment before the plane goes out the door." This applied even more, now that a recession was in the equation. Break-even for the Dash 8 was set around 300 machines, so front-end investment was bound to be high.

With all the howls from the media, Bell made a move that was never completely understood by the aviation fraternity. In the latter part of September, the press was informed that John Sandford would become vice-chairman to see the Dash 8 program into airline service. An interim president would be announced later. Sandford was an ideal choice to market the Dash 8, now that it was flying, but why the shift? After all, it was his pet project from the beginning. Bell's master plan also included Sandford heading a program bringing de Havilland and Canadair closer together – but

The handover of the first production Dash 8 to norOntair on October 23, 1984, was attended by guests, suppliers, customers and employees. John Sandford presented the log books to Northern Affairs minister Leo Bernier. (Right) Ontario's retiring premier, William Davis, joined the Ontario government group after the ceremony. From left: Wilfred Spooner of the ONTC, Bernier, Davis and John Sandford. (DH)

this never got off the ground. Timing was critical for this plan – an election was coming and the Liberals were down in the opinion polls. There were worried looks in both Downsview and Ottawa. The position of president remained open until August, when it was announced that D. Brian Long, a senior advisor at CDIC, would fill the role on an interim basis. It was difficult for an outsider to follow the script in this unfolding drama. About the same time an announcement was made that the Dash 8 had cracked the military market with an order for six from Canada's Department of National Defence: two transports and four trainers. Two others went to the Department of Transport for airways calibration. It was a nice order to talk about at the coming Farnborough Air Show.

Farnborough 1984

If ever there was a political watershed for de Havilland Canada, it was the Farnborough show of 1984. Every second year, when the producers of aircraft and supporting hardware met in England, it was the custom of the participants to boast

City Express commuters over the Toronto waterfront. This airline's first two Dash 8 aircraft made 10 flights a day between Toronto Island and Montreal. Its Dash 7 fleet flew Toronto-Ottawa eight times daily. (DH 54901 Tony Honeywood)

1 Weather radar
2 Glideslope antenna
3 VOR antennas
4 Weather radar receiver/transmitter
5 Transformer/rectifier unit
6 Electrical contactor box - DC
7 28 VDC, 40 amp/hr Nicad battery
8 28 VDC, 13 amp/hr Nicad auxiliary battery
9 Ground crew interphone
10 External DC power receptacle
11 Forward retracting, steerable nosewheel
12 Access panel to rudder pedals and control cables
13 Access panel to aileron quadrant and flight control cables, pulleys and rods
14 Electrically-operated windshield wipers
15 Static ports, one each side
16 Pitot head for Captain's instruments, left side and First Officer's instruments, right side
17 Rudder pedals
18 Captain's control column
19 First Officer's control column
20 Flight controls in underfloor area
21 Center console - engine & propeller levers, flap lever, gust lock lever and elevator trim handwheels, etc.
22 Captain's and First Officer's instrument and glareshield panels.
23 Overhead console - DC system and control, ice protection, windshield heat, fuel control, battery, exterior and panel lighting, AC system and control, air conditioning, etc.
24 Captain's seat
25 First Officer's seat
26 Nosewheel steering control
27 Captain's chart case stowage
28 Circuit breaker panels - both sides
29 Emergency hydraulic handpump handle
30 Emergency nose landing gear release and handpump system
31 Flight compartment crew escape hatch - inward opening, removable
32 Control pulleys and cables - flaps, ailerons, engine controls
33 Control pulleys and cables - gust lock, engine controls, brakes
34 Flight compartment/cabin door - with integral forward observer's seat
35 Toilet - externally serviced
36 Toilet compartment folding door
37 Main electrical distribution panels - accessible through toilet compartment wall
38 Buffet unit - hot beverage containers, soft drinks and liquor stowage, etc.
39 Aisle service trolley - optional
40 Wardrobe compartment with cabin attendant's switch panel above.
41 Avionics compartment
42 Cabin attendant's folding seat with interphone
43 VHF No. 1 antenna, VHF No. 2 antenna on fuselage underside
44 Passenger emergency exit - Type II, floor level
45 Eighteen pairs of forward facing passenger seats - 36 seat configuration
46 Airstair door - manually operated, counter balanced
47 Airstair door external release handle
48 Airstair door internal release handle
49 Seat rails
50 Air conditioning air outlets

51 Emergency exits - Type III
52 Emergency exit internal release handle
53 Emergency exit external release handle
54 Front spar frame - wing/fuselage attachment
55 Wing/fuselage attachment points - front spar
56 Rear spar frame - wing/fuselage attachment
57 Wing/fuselage attachment points - rear spar
58 Engine control pulleys and cables
59 Wing front spar
60 Wing rear spar
61 Aileron splitter quadrant and gust lock
62 Aileron/spoiler and disconnect clutch
63 Flight spoiler control cables
64 Power control unit - flap drive
65 Flap line primary drive shaft, driven from power control unit, - a secondary flexible drive provides power to the flap screwjacks should the primary drive shaft fail

66 Flap screwjack - non-reversible, two per each inboard flap section
67 Flap screwjack - non-reversible, two per each outboard flap section
68 Flap drive transfer gearbox - transfers power to flexible drive should the primary drive shaft fail, - includes flap position sensor
69 Inboard flap section - constant chord, supported by cantilever rollers located in tracks mounted on the fuselage side and inboard side of nacelle
70 Outboard flap section - tapered, supported by rollers in tracks mounted on the outboard side of the nacelle and at wing stations YW261.0 and YW369.0
71 Flap track No. 4 roller carriage mounting at YW261.0
72 Flap track No. 5 roller carriage mounting at YW369.0
73 Left aileron
74 Right aileron
75 Aileron hinges
76 Aileron spring tab - left aileron
77 Aileron spring/trim tab - right aileron
78 Aileron output quadrant and control rod
79 Aileron spring tab operating lever
80 Roll spoilers - outboard, operate in conjunction with ailerons at air speeds below 200 knots. At speeds in excess of 200 knots, ailerons operate alone
81 Outboard spoiler actuator - hydraulic, No. 2 system

Roll spoilers - inboard, operate in conjunction with ailerons and outboard roll spoilers at air speeds below 130 knots

Inboard spoiler actuator - hydraulic, No. 1 system

Ground spoilers - outboard

Outboard ground spoiler actuator - hydraulic, No. 2 system

Ground spoilers - inboard, operate with outboard ground spoilers to provide wing lift dumping on landing. Operation is automatic through sequenced switches on the engine power levers and main landing gears

Inboard ground spoiler actuator - hydraulic, No. 2 system

Left and right elevators

Elevator horn mass balance

Elevator trim tabs

Elevator trim tab mechanism

Elevator spring tabs

Elevator spring tab mechanism

Elevator trim tab actuator - non-reversible

Elevator control input mechanism

Elevator control push rod

Elevator control quadrant

Fore rudder

Trailing rudder

DASH 8
DE HAVILLAND CANADA

107 Deicing lines - horizontal stabilizer
108 Deicing lines
109 Deicing distributor valves and water separator
110 Pressure regulators - rudder hydraulics
111 Emergency location transmitter antenna
112 Emergency location transmitter
113 Flight data recorder
114 Cockpit voice recorder
115 Primary/secondary heat exchanger - air conditioning
116 Air cycle machine - supplies cooling air to air conditioning system
117 Air circulating/mixing unit
118 Rear pressure bulkhead
119 Baggage compartment rear bulkhead
120 Baggage restraint nets and posts - optional
121 Baggage restraints - cargo door
122 Baggage compartment door - inward opening, rolls upward on tracks to clear baggage door opening
123 Baggage compartment door tracks and rollers
124 Access panel to rear baggage compartment

Trailing rudder gearing push rod - upper

Trailing rudder gearing push rod - lower

Rudder actuator - hydraulic, No. 1 and No. 2 systems

Rudder control quadrant

Fore rudder hinges - four places

Trailing rudder hinges - three places

Horizontal stabilizer deicing boots - pneumatic

125 Pipe lines in dorsal fin - one bleed air to air conditioning system, two deicing to horizontal stabilizer deicing and four hydraulic to rudder hydraulic actuators, etc.

126 Engine/nacelle fire extinguishers
127 Deicing lines - pneumatic
128 Wing leading edge deicing boots - pneumatic
129 Deicing isolate valve
130 Deicing distribution valves
131 Deicing water separator
132 No. 2 hydraulic power system ground service panel on nacelle right wall. No. 1 hydraulic power system ground service panel is installed in left engine nacelle.

Hydraulic power is provided by two engine-driven hydraulic pumps, delivered to the systems at 3000 psi.

133 No. 2 hydraulic system reservoir
134 Hydraulic ground pressure connector
135 Pressure refuel/defuel fuel filler
136 Fuel master shut-off valve
137 Refuel/defuel lines
138 Fuel tanks, integral - one each wing. Total usable fuel, 5790 lb. (850 U.S. gallons). Optional 8200 lb. long range capacity available.
139 Fuel surge bay
140 Fuel collector bay - containing fuel high pressure ejector pump and electrical auxiliary pump
141 Magnastick fuel quantity backup indicating system - operable from ground
142 Capacitance probe - fuel contents, 6 per tank
143 Fuel vent and fuel pressure relief valves and fuel low pressure ejector pump
144 Fuel vent lines
145 Access panels to fuel tank
146 Access panel to fuel tank end rib
147 Overwing fuel filler - each wing
148 Landing lights - two each wing
149 Wing stall bar
150 Lift transducer - left wing only
151 Wing position lights
152 Tail position light - lower
153 Tail position light - upper
154 Anti-collision light - upper
155 Static discharge wicks
156 H.F. antenna
157 Rearward retracting main landing gear
158 Main landing gear drag strut
159 Main landing gear support structure
160 Main landing gear doors
161 Engine firewall
162 Engine nacelle lower cowling - hinged
163 Engine air intake - deiced
164 Engine nacelle top front cowling
165 Engine yoke support structure
166 Engine mount yoke
167 Engine access panels
168 Engine nacelle side cowlings - hinged
169 Engine nacelle rear side panels - hinged
170 Engine mounting support structure - aft
171 Pratt & Whitney PW120, 2000 SHP, free-turbine powerplant
172 Propeller reduction gearbox
173 Hamilton Standard 14SF, fully-feathering, constant speed, propeller - electrically deiced
174 Propeller pitch control mechanism
175 28 VDC starter/generator - one each engine
176 115/200 VAC generator - one each engine
177 Engine air exhaust ducting
178 Speed decreaser gearbox cooling air intake
179 Wing inspection light - each nacelle
180 Access panel to tail cone
181 Space provision for optional APU
182 Taxi light

N. MERRIN

of their latest sales. The company had more than the DND sale to discuss. Others were a confirmed Dash 8 sale to an old customer, Tyrolean Airways of Innsbruck; one to North Africa; and two to the Far East. Twin Otter sales had revived, with orders from China and Ethiopian Airlines. This seemed encouraging, but a pall hung over the Canadian chalet atop Farnborough's famous hill. It was election week in Canada and a trend for change was indicated. The mood of the Canadian contingent was not improved when the attending Buffalo broke up in an overzealous STOL demonstration landing. If nothing else, it confirmed the structural integrity of the aircraft, for the three occupants crawled out unhurt. News came from home during the flurry of this unfortunate accident that the Progressive Conservatives had won an overwhelming victory. From that moment, a new era began unfolding at de Havilland Canada.

The Rocky Road to Change

While campaigning for election, Michael Wilson, the eventual finance minister, promoted a plan to merge de Havilland and Canadair as a first step toward privatization. This idea, similar to one that Joel Bell had promoted, received wide editorial support. It did not take long for the PCs to settle into their new role on Parliament Hill and allot portfolios. Gone were the great plans of a consolidated aerospace effort. The new Minister of Regional Industrial Expansion, Sinclair Stephens, quickly returned to a pledge he had made during his lean years in opposition. He put de Havilland and 54 other crown corporations up for sale.

The Liberal incumbents at CDIC soon left the scene. Joel Bell departed in October 1984, Paul Machlin Marshall (president and CEO of Westmin Resources) taking his place. In January 1985, Bill Boggs came out of retirement to become president of DHC, the role he had vacated in 1970. It was a supreme challenge for the veteran Boggs, who had headed Canada Systems Group during the intervening years. For the next two years de Havilland would suffer comments like "money losing," "debt ridden" and the old favourite, "awash in red ink." Even Peter C. Newman in his colourful prose called de Havilland "Ottawa's perpetual problem child." Hugh Whittington, however, editorialized in the magazine *Canadian Aviation* that governments usually got behind their aerospace industries in good times and bad and that, in spite of heavy expenditures, de Havilland was "on the brink of a profitable future." Even the harshest critics praised the Dash 8. Few reported the record of self-sufficiency that DHC had achieved over 50 years, or that the "problem child" was holding its own long after Ottawa res-

cued it from Hawker Siddeley in 1974. The costs of bringing the Dash 8 to life outweighed sales income in the latter half of 1982 and 1983. A good year of $204 million in 1984 eased the loss to $40 million, but the decline continued into 1985.

During March, in spite of these discouraging figures, a short 15 day strike took place. Negotiations hinged on job security should the company change hands – which was beginning to look quite likely. Some Twin Otter and Buffalo sales were recorded during the next month, when John Sandford announced he was leaving for a position as vice-president of Fairchild Industries Inc. Plans for a stretched Dash 8, already under way, were announced to the press in May. It did not bring Sandford any joy to remember that he had lost a sale of six aircraft in 1984 for lack of a government commitment to an eventual Dash 8 stretch.

The Bidding and Choosing

The "For Sale" sign at de Havilland did not bring an immediate response. A lot of specialized items had to be considered that only experts fully understood. According to Paul Marshall, there were a number of interesting nibbles. That was all he would divulge, but by the spring of 1985 he identified seven interested companies. At one time it looked like British Aerospace might be interested in buying back the company, but that did not last. In June the Boeing Commercial Airplane Company of Seattle indicated its interest, and by August, Marshall had narrowed the list to four or five. By November 1985, bidding for DHC and Canadair began to heat up. Marshall announced that Boeing was interested only in de Havilland. A consortium headed by entrepreneur Justus Dornier proposed buying both companies. Boeing was a long-time friend of de Havilland and already was established in Canada. The Dornier proposal (to operate each concern in its respective location under the umbrella of a single holding company) was one that had been broached before but was never taken seriously. While Boeing remained a leading contender, Amsterdam-based Fokker BV joined Versatile Corporation of Vancouver and unidentified backers in filing an application under the name of Rimgate Holdings Ltd. Boeing soon became the front runner for, as Marshall put it, "their offer was superior."

A New Owner

At 3:30 p.m. on December 2, 1985, the Hon. Robert de Cotret, President of the Treasury Board of Canada, announced that the federal government had reached an agreement for the purchase of de Havilland Canada by Boeing. At the same moment, Bill Boggs was informing more than

4,000 employees at a special meeting called in Bay 7. The simultaneous announcements ended weeks of speculation and rumours about the future. Boggs joined Richard Albrecht, chairman of Boeing of Canada, and Paul Marshall of CDIC in a meeting with supervisory staff and, later, with a gathering of newsmen in the sales mockup area. Public reaction was swift and varied. Opposition parties in the House of Commons called the sale a "giveaway", but financial analysts called it a "good deal" for all.

Negotiations continued for the rest of the month amid speculation that it might be possible to cancel the deal. Sinclair Stephens was in hospital at the time and pressed for a December 31 closing date. Opposition in parliament was so great that a delay in signing was granted to allow for a committee of investigation. Everyone pressed for details of the purchase and the following list was issued to the employees by the combined heads, Boggs, Albrecht and Marshall. The story was now up front for everyone to see:

PRICE: The total purchase price is $155 million, consisting of a $90 million down payment and promissory notes totalling $65 million over 15 years. The notes carry no interest but will be adjusted to reflect inflation. This $65 million will be forgiven if Boeing invests $325 million for Canadian goods and services unrelated to the operation of de Havilland or Boeing in Canada.

Projects such as the just-launched Dash 8 series, for example, or modifications and improvements to the line, will not be eligible for this debt relief.

ROYALTY PAYMENTS: Boeing is to pay a royalty of $275,000 for every Dash 7 sold beyond number 122 (108 had been sold to that date). A royalty of $225,000 for every Dash 8 or derivative beyond aircraft number 400. All on-going development costs are to be paid by Boeing.

ADDITIONAL INVESTMENTS: Boeing has announced plans to invest $115 million in product development and upgrading facilities at Downsview. They have just announced the launch of the Dash 8 series 300 and also will be picking up all future losses of the company.

SALES FINANCING: de Havilland will continue to be eligible for EDP and EDC support, as in the past. In addition, Boeing has given up substantial tax benefits except those tax benefits to support sales financing for Canadian purchases of de Havilland products.

DIPP GRANTS: Certain product development costs may be shared by Ottawa on a project-by-project basis, providing that eligibility requirements are met under the Defence Industries Productivity Program. These grants can cover up to 50 per cent of the development costs but are expected to be repaid from products sold. DIPP grants are now available to all other companies manufacturing in Canada, and will be reinstated for de Havilland under the new ownership.

LAND VALUE: Land speculation has been eliminated as an issue in this agreement. Under the terms of the letter of intent, if any of the lands acquired by Boeing become surplus to further requirements, the government may repurchase those lands at a price stipulated in the agreement.

(Below) The sign-over of company assets from Canadian government control to the new owner, Boeing. From the left: Paul Machlin Marshall, head of CDIC; Sinclair Stephens, Minister of Regional Industrial Expansion; Richard Albrecht, chairman of Boeing of Canada; and Bill Boggs, president of de Havilland Canada. (Right) Boggs announced the purchase to DHC employees at the same time the news was released in Ottawa. (DH 55721, '55466-3 Charles Bryant)

An early view of the Dash 8 production line. (DH 55456 Charles Bryant)

On January 31, 1985, the formal signing took place and Boeing became owner of The de Havilland Aircraft of Canada Limited in its 58th year. The two proud names in aviation would now be working as one, but each would retain its product identity and family heritage. The Downsview complex would now be known as "The de Havilland Aircraft Company of Canada, A Division of Boeing of Canada."

Customer Support

Customer Support began at de Havilland with the sale of the first Moths. The company built an excellent reputation for parts supply in those early days; even field support was available. Specialists were pulled from the shop floor whenever a need arose and would find themselves with a train ticket and a little bit of cash as they packed their tool boxes. Service manager Bill Calder ruled supreme on matters of service in the thirties and his Scottish approach to expense accounts set new standards in frugality. Don Murray spent a winter "on assignment" with Quebec Airways Rapides on the lower St. Lawrence and was loaned as service engineer with the *Globe and Mail* "Flying Newsroom." It was common practice to have maintenance engineers from the major customers such as Canadian Airways or Consolidated Mining & Smelting working with factory staff for a week or two be-

fore delivery of a new aircraft. On emergency calls Walter Rinaldo usually got the engine assignments, while Frank Warren or Harry Proctor specialized in airframe problems. If woodworking was involved, the call would be either George Blanchard or John Slaughter.

During the war, technical support changed to a military system, complete with resident inspectors. When Canadian Mosquitos began arriving in England, Earl Ferguson went over as squadron liaison, replaced later by George Smith. A typical support feature late in the program was a hand-picked group of four who were dispersed to the Ferry Command staging routes when Mossies began having delivery problems. Bruce Glassford was assigned to Belém, Brazil, Jerry Irvine to Nassau, Bahamas, Eddie Jack to Natal, Brazil and Bill Duck to Rabat-Salé, Morocco. They became part of No. 45 Group, RAF Transport Command, and wore the standard blue civilian uniform.

The postwar system continued much as before, under service manager Calder but there was rapid growth in overhaul and a sudden need for roving maintenance specialists. When the call came for a Beaver technical representative in Korea, Bruce Best, chief engineer at the Toronto Flying Club, accepted the posting. The arrival of the Otter and Caribou expanded the load. Wherever the U.S. Army was in action a DHC tech rep was there. Their collective experi-

The first Dash 8 for the Canadian Forces was delivered in April 1987 for service with 412 Detachment, CFB Lahr, West Germany. There it took over from the Dash 7. (DH 56530 Tony Honeywood)

ences would fill a book. Early members such as Mackenzie Brown, Crawford Byers, Bruce Jack, Bill Kavanaugh, Bob Irving, Dick Gleasure and Jacques Loriaux were always on the move. Most did Vietnam assignments, usually up to a year at a time. Some returned for a second posting. John Aitken went to India and South America, Henry Jones to Australia and Bob Irving had a special assignment to Kenya. When the RCAF bought two Comets, Harry Hunter arrived from England as the resident technical expert in Ottawa. When that mission ended, he joined the DHC tech reps in their travels. A fully organized service school was needed to train customer personnel on a large scale. Mack Brown spent three years on a mobile training unit in the U.S. and four years instructing in the school at Downsview. Pilots from flight test instructed at the factory or on location. The need for operations manuals expanded overnight, requiring an enlarged technical publications department.

Bill Calder Retires

By the time Bill Calder retired at the end of the Caribou period, his army of tech reps was travelling the world. Bill Kavanaugh took

A typical Caribou delivery to the Cameroons combining the sales department and customer support. Shown with two African representatives are: Mick Saunders, pilot; Mal Aplin, sales; customer; Len Trotter, sales; customer; Buck Buchanan, sales; and Mack Brown, tech rep. (DH)

over field service, with Bob Irving assisting. When the Twin Otter entered the commuter airline industry, the main support thrust changed from a military to an airline focus. By 1968 it was clear that the varying disciplines of support should be under one responsibility at the vice-president level. F.A. "Ted" Johnson became vice-president, Product Support, bringing all associated services under manager Phil Halsey. Phil came to Canada in charge of the Comet program and accepted Phil Garratt's offer to join DHC in January 1955. The plan united Bill Kavanaugh's Field Service Department with Technical Support under Ian Gilchrist, Technical Publications Department under Lief Gustafson,

Havilland Inc. of Chicago, under a former U.S. resident and Caribou tech rep, Ben Cox. On the technical side, most representatives circulated throughout the system, with regular visits back to head office. Ken Tilley concentrated on Twin Otters in South America while Tom Quan became the Buffalo specialist in Peru.

The Twin Otter brought another period of vital support in classroom training for air and ground crews – plus the delivery of aircraft. When the question of Twin Otter deliveries arose, Dave Fairbanks accepted the role as part of flight test duties. The U.S. military usually picked up their Otters and Caribous, but a new service grew with the Twin Otter

A Horizon Dash 8-100 is de-iced at Vancouver before departing for Seattle. N818PH was the 58th Dash 8 off the line. (Jan Stroomenbergh)

along with the Spare Parts Department headed first by M.C "Max" Fumerton, then by Frank Cochran. During Punch Dickins' reign, spares depots were established close to points of action, to shorten delivery time. In the Canadian west, for instance, Norm Davis established a depot in the Edmonton area; Charlie Smith managed a similar service in Vancouver. The plan quickly expanded to Australia under Denis Morgan, and New Zealand under Jacko Lorenze. Business in Africa called for a base in Nairobi, managed by long-time tech rep and electrical specialist, Jacques Loriaux. This served the purpose but, as improvements in communications and shipping led to a 24-hour parts service direct from head office, the depots slowly were phased out. One of the last to go was de

sales to foreign lands. The common practice for these long-range deliveries was to install nine standard fuel drums in tandem, lashed to the floor. The usual delivery crew consisted of a pilot and a service representative, plus all the immunization records and pills that go with world travel. Those were the glory days of flight test, with lots of grinding flying hours to world glamour spots, and the excitement that comes from customs hassles in strange countries. Delivery pilots included Fairbanks, Mick Saunders, Tom Appleton, Don Rogers, Army Hollinsworth, Doug Givens, George Northrop, Bob Wilhelm and Bill Pullen. Tech reps who saw most of the ferry work were: Mack Brown, Dick Gleasure, Bruce Jack, Harry Hunter, George Naida, John

In ferrying Twin Otters long distances, a series of interconnected 45-gallon drums, fixed to the cabin floor, provided the fuel required. (DH)

Aitken and Bob Irving. The same applied to demonstration tours when a tech rep from Bill Kavanaugh's group was always included on the team. It was about this time that the name of the department changed from Product Support to the more-appropriate Customer Support.

When Dave Fairbanks died suddenly in 1975, one of his last wishes was that his ashes be spread at a certain latitude and longitude over the Atlantic. George Northrop and Dick Gleasure were charged with the solemn duty on their upcoming delivery to Lina Congo in Brazzaville. Several company support people gathered by the Downsview ramp to

give Dave his final send-off, but the Twin Otter twice ran into mechanical problems approaching the Atlantic. This forced a return to Toronto. When the aircraft finally left on the trip, Gleasure was on holiday and George Naida attended to the ritual of dropping the ashes at the assigned coordinates – somewhere south of Iceland.

FlightSafety Training

With the Dash 7 and Dash 8, the delivery of aircraft switched from company to contract crews. In the fall of 1985, de Havilland signed with FlightSafety International for a 25,000 sq. ft. (2,250 sq. m) state-of-the-art training centre to be built next to the cafeteria. Classroom and flight simulator facilities for all current de Havilland Canada types were made available to corporate, military and airline customers to speed aircraft into service. With the Dash 8-400 on the horizon, by mid-September 1997, a 2,200 sq. ft. (2,044 sq. m) area was added. Next came two new simulators, seven classrooms for Computer Based Training (CBT), a conference room and three avionics training rooms.

In the days when product support functions were consolidated in one department, vice-president Ted Johnson formed a new overhaul and repair division called Aero Services. Bert Ellis moved from the technical support wing to be manager and a surprising number of contracts emerged in connection with customer operations. This unit became an effective arm of customer assistance for 10 years. Ellis could point to annual profits of $3 million, but his department, along with Twin Otter and Dash 7 production, fell to the axe during Boeing's period of radical adjustment.

C-GTCO of Air Atlantic, the 119th Dash 8-100, at Toronto Markham Airport in October 1992. (Kenneth I. Swartz)

(Right) On October 23, 1984, C-GJCB of norOntair became the first Dash 8 delivered. A month later it was joined by C-GPYD. JCB is seen being de-iced at Thunder Bay in February 1992. Its registration honoured James C. Bell, one of Austin Airways' veteran pilots. PYD honoured Paul Y. Davoud, an RCAF wartime pilot and postwar figure in the plan to install modern airstrips across Northern Ontario. When norOntair ceased operations in 1996, JCB and PYD were sold in Papua New Guinea. (Larry Milberry)

City Express was close behind norOntair with the Dash 8, taking delivery of No. 5 in September 1985. Here it was at Toronto Island Airport in May 1990. Unable to survive on the highly competitive Toronto-Montreal-Ottawa triangle, City Express folded in 1990. (Kenneth I. Swartz)

The Dash 8, considered the finest of the turboprop commuters, was welcomed by Canada's growing regional carriers. With traffic increasing through the 1980s, they needed replacements for smaller or older types like the Beech 99, Twin Otter, DC-3 and BAe748. Air BC was the first major regional with the Dash 8. Its first (C-GGOM, No. 3) was delivered in December 1985. Here C-FACD boards passengers at Vancouver for Campbell River and Comox on April 4, 1990. (Larry Milberry)

Air Ontario started building a Dash 8 fleet in 1987. By 1998 it had 17 Dash 8-100 and six -300 aircraft. Here Dash 8-100 C-GJMI "City of Montreal" turns around at North Bay on August 3, 1997. With Air Ontario, the Dash 8 was ideal, linking North Bay, Windsor, London and other centres with Toronto. (Andrew H. Cline)

(Right) Quebec-based Air Alliance took its first Dash 8 in March 1988. While Air BC, Air Ontario and Canadian Regional had mixed fleets of the 37-seat Dash 8-100 and 50-seat -300, Air Alliance and Air Nova viewed the -100 as best for their markets. C-FVON is seen at Ottawa in April 1997. (Andy Graham)

(Below) C-FGRM "City of Thunder Bay" runs up at Toronto City Centre Airport in an award-winning photo by de Havilland's Tony Honeywood. Delivered in March 1990, this was the 199th Dash 8. (DH 94-0192-4)

(Above) A Canadian Regional Airlines Dash 8-300 during a turn-around at Vancouver on July 31, 1993. The 174th Dash 8, it was delivered to Time Air in October 1989. Time Air later joined the CRA family. (Larry Milberry)

(Right) Transport Canada and the Canadian Coast Guard operate the Dash 8-100, the former mainly in calibrating airport navigation equipment, the latter on pollution and ice patrol. Here the Coast Guard's C-GCFJ lands at Ottawa in January 1997. (Andy Graham)

(Left) The Canadian Forces ordered six Dash 8 aircraft – two for general transport duties, four for training navigators. One of the trainers, easily recognized by its bulbous nose packed with electronics, is seen at Winnipeg in June 1990. (Andrew H. Cline)

(Below) The Dash 8-200 was developed for "hot and high" operations. The same size as the -100, it has more powerful engines to suit hot desert or mountain environments. Here Series 200 demonstrator C-GGOM gleams at Toronto's Pearson International Airport in September 1992. (Dave Thompson)

Dash 8-100 No. 215 nears completion at Downsview in April 1990. It became EI-CBJ with the Irish leasing company GPA Jetprop. (Kenneth I. Swartz)

The Dash 8 competed well with the ATR42, Brasilia and Saab 340. Here a Dash 8-100 boards at Panama City, Florida for Atlanta in October 1986. Formed in 1969, Metro Express was one of many regionals to blossom in the turboprop era. In 1984 it entered a code-sharing agreement with Eastern Airlines. It began with 19-seat Jetstreams, but business took off, quadrupling after only a year. Eastern Metro Express was the first U.S. airline with this type. (Larry Milberry)

(Left) A US Air Express Dash 8-100 taxis at Washington National Airport on November 18, 1990. US Air Express arose in the 1980s as an amalgamation of airlines, including Henson, Piedmont, Suburban and Allegheny Commuter. In 1998 this Maryland-based commuter airline had more than 50 Dash 8 commuters. (George W. Hamlin)

(Right) Horizon Air of Seattle accepted its first Dash 8 in December 1985. Here N816PH (No. 54, "The Great Tri-Cities") lands at Vancouver. In 1998 Horizon had 23 Dash 8-100 aircraft, but also had the Dash 8-200 on order. (Larry Milberry)

(Left) Various specialized Dash 8 aircraft have been delivered – the Canadian navigation trainers, coastal patrol versions for Australia, the E-9, etc. Two E-9s have operated since 1986 from Tyndall Air Force Base in Florida. Flown on behalf of the USAF by LTV Aerospace, their job is controlling Gulf of Mexico airspace used as an air weapons range by the USAF. Here E-9 N801AP was at Tyndall in October 1992. Its side-looking radar is its most prominent modification. (Larry Milberry)

(Right) Many European airlines fly the Dash 8. The first was Tyrolean, which accepted OE-HLR, the 10th Dash 8-100, in May 1985. Here OE-LLN was on departure from Frankfurt in April 1990. For 1998 Tyrolean's fleet included seven Dash 8-100, 15 -300, eight CRJ and a Dash 7 aircraft. Four of the Dash 8-400 were on order. (Anton Heumann)

(Above) Lufthansa CityLine used the Dash 8 widely, creating new business by pairing many communities. Success at this led CityLine to replace the Dash 8 with the Bombardier Regional Jet, the first of which was accepted in January 1993. The move to regional jets was a trend in the late 1990s, but turboprops remained the backbone of the regional airlines. Here a CityLine Dash 8-300 taxis at Lugano, Switzerland, in October 1992. (Anton Heumann)

In 1998 Ryuku Air Commuter of Okinawa operated four Twin Otter and three Dash 8-100 aircraft on local and inter-island service. Here JA8973 was at home base in December 1997. (Kenji Ikegami)

When the Boeing Commercial Airplane Company of Seattle, Washington, purchased de Havilland in 1986, it was no stranger to Canada. William Edward Boeing had flown into Vancouver in 1919 on the first international mail flight. Ten years later he returned to establish Boeing Aircraft of Canada Ltd. Through the 1930s, it built U.S. designs: the C-204 flying boat and the 40H mail plane. It also developed a Canadian flying boat, the Totem, which did not reach production. The Depression reduced the company to repair and overhaul status, but by 1937 a new plant was established at Vancouver's Sea Island Airport. Under licence, it turned out 19 Blackburn Sharks for the RCAF.

CHAPTER TWELVE

THE BOEING YEARS

Boeing reached its peak during WWII, using the original building and expanding to a number of small plants at Victoria, Chilliwack and Nelson. Total manufacturing space during the war was 878,479 sq ft (80,000 sq m) and employment reached 10,315. The company built 307 Consolidated Catalina flying boats and Canso amphibians, along with various parts for the Anson, tailplanes for the Mosquito and wing spars for the Norseman. There was also a major overhaul shop. All operations ceased after the war and the Sea Island factory was sold to Canadian Pacific Airlines. The company reappeared in 1960 as Boeing of Canada Ltd., with a helicopter overhaul factory (formerly Vertol Aircraft Ltd.) at Arnprior, Ontario. A Winnipeg Division was formed in 1971 to make high strength-to-weight, fibre-composite plastic components, many of which were used in the Dash 7 and Dash 8. A smaller company, Boeing Computer Services, Canada Ltd., had offices in Vancouver, Calgary and Toronto. Later, Boeing had a close association with the much-modified STOL Buffalo, building its intricate blown wing. It also joined DHC in Dash 7 worldwide sales, being particularly helpful in market analysis. When the two companies merged, Boeing had 1,000 employees in Canada which, with the staff at Downsview, brought the total to 5,500.

A reasonable calm prevailed after the agreement was signed, for increased deliveries and new sales were beginning to tell a favourable story. The *Financial Post* said: "The deci-

sion of the federal government to sell de Havilland Aircraft was a sound one. The sale to the Boeing Company could be a good deal for de Havilland and the country. Instead of hand-wringing, a little clapping would be in order." These sentiments were echoed by John Sandford, by then president of Fairchild Republic, who said: "Boeing is the best thing that could have happened to de Havilland. Who is best suited to manage the company, the cabinet of Canada or the board of Boeing?"

The Dash 7 market revived in 1984 with sales to New Guinea, Egypt and a Dash 7-R ice reconnaissance model to Environment Canada. A rush of orders through the last six months of 1985 brought steady deliveries into the next year. Dash 8 sales received a boost when three Canadian carriers ordered 46, worth $410 million. This boosted sales and options to 144. By June, DHC employed 4,800 and the parking lots were full again. Export deliveries broadened to New Zealand and Papua New Guinea, with Taiwan showing interest. In two years, the Dash 8 had gained 30 per cent of the world market share in its class. Interest was growing for the stretched 300 Series, with 23 firm orders and 15 options.

A boost for the 20-year-old Twin Otter and its supporters came in 1985 with the *Esso Air World* annual survey of turbine aircraft. The numbers from Aviation Data Service of Wichita, Kansas, reported 488 Twin Otters in airline service, well ahead of the Fokker/Fairchild F-27. In spite of the downturn in the economy, 30 new Twin Otters were delivered between January 1983 and October 1986, as were eight Buffalos and 17 Dash 7 aircraft. After the CDIC years, these were good numbers. Meanwhile, Canadair, still unsure of its future (Industry Minister Sinclair Stephens was anxious to sell it), was enjoying success with Challenger sales. Suddenly, on August 16, 1986, word came that Canadair had been purchased by Bombardier Inc. of Montreal.

October 1986 was a milestone for the de Havilland team, as it recorded the 7,000th aircraft manufactured at Downsview. The customer was Horizon Air and the aircraft was the fifth Dash 8 in their order of 10. The occasion also served as an official opening of Bay 9, which, since 1982, had sat dor-

DHC employees shared in company history on October 3, 1986, when Dash 8 No. 50, became part of the growing Horizon Air fleet. It was the 7,000th aircraft manufactured at Downsview. The Horizon Air Dash 8 fleet had grown to 35 by 1998. (DH 56360-29 Tony Honeywood)

mant with a dirt floor. Horizon president Milt Kuolt took delivery of the airplane and gave a spirited motivational message to DHC's employees.

Ron Woodard Joins

For the first year under Boeing, Bill Boggs and Richard Albrecht continued to run DHC in their respective roles. At the end of January 1987, Boeing appointed Ron Woodard as president. Boggs, who had proven the ideal leader during the difficult transition from crown corporation to private ownership, remained as a member of the board. In 1988 he was awarded the Order of Canada.

Ron Woodard came to Downsview with 20 years experience in aerospace. Previously he had been vice-president and general manager of Boeing's Materiel Division. He had been program manager on 707 tankers outside the U.S., and had taken part in Boeing foreign sales. He arrived in time for the rollout of the Series 300 on March 22, and its first flight two months later. These were all landmarks in a company history now nearing 60 years, but Ron Woodard could not get rising costs out of his mind.

During the controversy surrounding the de Havilland sale, one commentator remarked that Boeing was buying an opportunity to spend money. It did not take long for the sequence to begin. On Woodard's first visit to Downsview in

August 1986, he found a group of workers playing ball on the apron in front of the hangar. They were refusing to work on the grounds of inadequate ventilation in the plastic shops. Safety inspectors backed their complaint, and Woodard had to agree that the shops did not meet Boeing standards. A report noted that the new owner was also spending $20 million on computerized numerical control equipment, automatic riveting machines, increased capacity for making composites, and computerized manufacturing. Combined with the planning for the next Dash 8, costs were mounting far beyond estimates. These, however, were not problems for the average worker on the shop floor, where a sense of well-being prevailed. Some objected to the introduction into such a small company of Seattle shop procedures, but that was to be expected.

Ron B. Woodard became president of the Boeing Canada de Havilland Division in 1987. In 1998 he was head of Boeing Commercial Aircraft Group in Seattle. (DH)

(Above) The experimental Dash 8 showing the 11.5 feet (3.5 m) added to the fuselage to make it a Series 300. The patches in front of and behind the wing are the fuselage plugs. (DH)

(Below) The Dash 8 Series 300 at its dazzling rollout before an audience of employees, suppliers and customers on March 22, 1987. (DH Ron Nunney)

The first flight of C-GDNK in its stretched version took place on May 15, 1987, with pilots Wally Warner and Bob Fowler and flight test engineers Dave Monteith and Joe Fasken. (DH 57286-5)

The year 1987 started well. Bill Boggs was called to Ottawa on January 22 for a unique presentation in the parliament buildings by then-Prime Minister Brian Mulroney. The Canadian Engineering Centennial Board recognized the DHC-2 Beaver as one of the top 10 achievements in Canadian engineering in the past century. This was a singular honour, considering that the board had dealt with some 110 submissions in reaching a decision. The trophy was designed in marble and plastic with a suitable scroll. A year later the Historic Sites and Monuments Board of Canada presented de Havilland with a bronze plaque honouring the Beaver for its contribution to Canada's north. The words were cast in bronze and dedicated during the 60th anniversary. The monument sits beside the employee entrance in the front of the building, the inscription reading:

The "Beaver" was developed in 1946 at Downsview under P.C. Garratt of de Havilland Canada for flying in the Canadian north. The single engine, high wing monoplane, built for bush work, achieved world-wide civil and military sales. Used in some 60 countries from the Arctic to the Antarctic, it served in the Korean and Vietnam wars. It was noted for its simplicity, ruggedness and short take-off and landing ability. Over half of the 1,692 produced from 1947 to 1968 were sold to the U.S. armed forces. Designed and built without government aid, the "Beaver" was an ideal workhorse of the air.

Just 16 months after Boeing began spending heavily on improvements, unionized workers went on strike for the 10th time since 1954. The new owners sought concessions on everything from job classifications, to scheduling, seniority and grievance procedures. They were obviously trying to put the labour picture on a par with the parent organization in Seattle, but union leader Bob White called it "arrogant Americanism." The strike lasted 10 weeks, while customers watched anxiously and deliveries slipped badly. When the directors read press comments by the union leaders and listened to the chants of "Yankee Go Home," they knew they had more than a monetary problem on their hands. By now Boeing had become disenchanted with the purchase that so many had said was a give-away. Those in Seattle who had been against the purchase were beginning to say "I told you so."

The monument that pays tribute to the worldwide success of the de Havilland Beaver. (DH 98-1896-6 Guy Levesque)

Selling STOL

Before the Dash 7, de Havilland's image had hinged on STOL, which had been so successful with world military organizations; but the practice of steeper approach gradients remained outside the public transportation realm. There were no regulations covering shorter field requirements, yet an entire department at de Havilland had been dedicated to planning commercial STOL. Bob McIntyre, director of market development, had spearheaded a series of promotions arranging countrywide flight demonstrations to back his glossy brochures.

The government-financed Airtransit experiment had proven the viability of commercial STOL, but without a 50-passenger aircraft it had little impact. Endless negotiations and studies were carried out on the possibility of a Toronto-Ottawa-Montreal system using the Toronto Island Airport,

An artist's impression of the LDDC STOLport with a Dash 7 on approach, and (inset) a Dash 7 takes off in a typical LDDC setting. (DH)

but the opposition was tough. While talks inched closer to approvals, a small Peterborough airline, Otonabee Airlines, using Saunders ST-27s (PT6-powered Herons), won a licence to run sked flights into TIA. Soon Ottawa and Montreal were added, with convenient shuttle buses at each base. Service was on a small scale until a more experienced airline man, Victor Pappalardo, saw the potential. He bought Otonabee from owner Joe Csumrik, and changed its name to City Express. He put a couple of quiet, brightly coloured Dash 7s into service, and watched the traffic grow. Fares were low and a series of innovations brought prompt passenger approval. The timing coincided with deregulation in Canada – City Express became a showcase of private enterprise in the short-haul field.

The London Docks STOLport

By the 1970s, the Thames Upper Docks, lying within six miles of Trafalgar Square, were the focal point of a giant revitalization plan. In time, the British government created the London Docklands Development Corporation (LDDC), giving new life to the entire Thames estuary. An airport, based on the de Havilland STOL concept, was discussed, but it wasn't until the Dash 7 entered British service in 1982 that such a plan was taken seriously. Steeper-than-average trial landings were conducted on a disused wharf by Brymon Airways, convincing the construction firm of John

Mowlem and Co. to plan a full STOL service. The usual hue and cry from the environmentalists was directed at LDDC, followed by a public enquiry and an inspector's report. There were more delays as the Greater London County Council fought the project in court. General permission was given in May 1985; by 1986 detailed planning permission had been won. A month later, John Mowlem and Co. had demolished the empty warehouses, and by the end of the year a runway was in place on the wharf between King George V and Royal Albert Docks. The delay enabled the Environment Ministry to establish noise and runway restrictions, while the Civil Aviation Authority evaluated the technical aspects of instrument landings off a $7^1/_2°$ glideslope. New life dawned for the Royal Docks when the Queen officially opened the London City Airport, as it was called, on November 5, 1987. Unfortunately, Bob McIntyre, the great promoter of this concept, did not live to see the fulfillment of either his Toronto or London dreams – he had died on September 23, 1985.

Production line workers pause to record the last Twin Otter built. Serial No. 844 was sold to Etty Aerospace, which in turn sold it in Malaysia. (DH 59294-11)

Visitors

There always were dignitaries anxious to visit de Havilland. Norway's King Olaf V was in Canada late in 1987, anxious to learn more of the aircraft that had become so important in his country. After a reception and plant tour, president Woodard presented the King with a scale replica of the historic Canadian schooner *Bluenose II* . The following month came Prime Minister Branco Mikulic of Yugoslavia, whose country manufactured emergency exit doors for the Dash 8. In 1972 a Chinese delegation had arrived to study the Twin Otter. Negotiations continued for the next five years, till many thought that China's interests had died. "Don't worry," said Buck Buchanan, "they will be back; it just takes time." He was right – 13 Twin Otters eventually operated in mainland China. The DHC-China relationship continued into the Dash 8 period with visits from Taiwan. This led to the purchase of two Dash 8-100 aircraft for Great China Airlines of Taipei. By 1998 it was operating 12 Dash 8-300 aircraft and had become the launch customer for the Dash 8-Q400 in the area.

Demise of the Twin Otter

The Twin Otter inevitably fell victim to expansion in the very industry it had helped establish. With its fixed undercarriage and slow speed, it now was an "ugly duckling."

STOL had become passé on most interurban runs. While the Twin Otter was still a welcome sight in developing countries and in Canada's north, its future in production looked bleak. Sales department attention now focused on the Dash 8-300.

Expectations for Twin Otter production in 1963 had been for 300 aircraft, yet more than 800 had been built by 1987. Twin Otter manufacturing methods, however, were outmoded, and more upgrades were not feasible. Head office was solidly behind the Dash 8 – no more STOL bush designs. The new owners were big airplane people and the Twin Otter was in the way. Even the truly STOL Dash 7, which Boeing's Howard Tinney had once described as "the only show in town," was not in future plans. By the time of the April 22 rollout for the Dash 8-300, Twin Otter and Dash 7 activity had almost died and there were rumours of shutting down the lines.

The people who now knew most about the Twin Otter market were outsiders dealing in resale. They didn't like the thought of cancelling the Twin Otter. One of these companies was Etty Aerospace, headed by Don Etty, a one-time foreman on the Twin Otter line and later a member of the sales team. He had sound financial backing and the co-operation of all who knew him in the plant. When he saw a possible closing, he came up with a proposal – if de Havilland would re-open production for another six aircraft, he would buy them. The plan won a reluctant blessing from management, even though it was an opportunity to tidy up the company spares inventory. Once Etty's six were completed, the jigs and fixtures were put out to pasture.

Upswing, Downfall

The mood was justifiably upbeat throughout the summer of 1988, with growing Dash 8 sales and options. A full-time study began within sales and engineering regarding a new model (initially called the Dash X) to fill the 64-70 seat gap in the short-haul market. It soon became the Dash 8 Series 400. A major decision concerned the type of engine for the new model's increased specifications. The GE 38, the Rolls-Royce RB.550 and the Pratt & Whitney Canada PW300/4 were contenders. By February 1988 pressure had mounted for a board decision to start production, but there was hesitation. Plant improvement expenditures kept growing, leading to another operational deficit. By February 1989, president Woodard announced an indefinite delay in a production start, although engineering would continue. It would be another five years before the subject of a Dash 8-400 was revived.

60 Years of Age

The 60th anniversary of de Havilland Canada was marked on June 4, 1988, with a huge family picnic in the factory compound for 10,000 employees, retirees and special guests. The company's products were available for inspection, along with rides for the kids and plenty to eat. *Canadian Aviation* published a special DHC edition, which everyone received. The guest of honour, Olivia de Havilland, was a legend in her own right. The famous Hollywood actress (and two-time Oscar winner) had a career spanning 50 years. She charmed everyone as she moved around the exhibits to the delight of photographers. She captivated a crowd with her recollections of Sir Geoffrey de Havilland and his son, Geoffrey Jr.

By July 1988 the long-awaited order came to shut down Twin Otter, then Dash 7 production. Some were surprised that the Dash 7 was included, for by now it was a proven specialist in its role; but circumstances and timing forced it out of the running. True STOL came at an extra cost, and most of the world's customers did not need those spectacular approach gradients. The Dash 8, though still a normal category aircraft, profited from the Dash 7's STOL engineering and was now the popular choice. Coinciding with the cancellations, Dean Thornton, head of Boeing's Commercial Aircraft Division in Seattle, visited Downsview for a talk with the supervisors. While being interviewed by the press, he freely admitted that Boeing's de Havilland Division was

Honoured guest at the 60th anniversary celebration was the legendary movie star Olivia de Havilland. Here she meets four of the early employees beside a Tiger Moth: Russ Borrett, George Blanchard, Ab Warren and Frank Warren. (DH 58486-16)

(Left) In October 1988, test and development Dash 7 C-GNBX was presented to the National Aviation Museum. Tom Appleton made the handover to former NAM director Robert W. Bradford. (DH 59093)

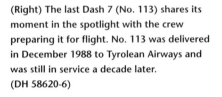

(Right) The last Dash 7 (No. 113) shares its moment in the spotlight with the crew preparing it for flight. No. 113 was delivered in December 1988 to Tyrolean Airways and was still in service a decade later. (DH 58620-6)

AIRCRAFT 113
The Last
DASH 7

a "nightmare." Rumours that Boeing was unhappy did not help sales, even though the Dash 8 remained popular. In the back rooms of the airline business it was common knowledge that the Boeing-de Havilland marriage was on the rocks.

On October 26, 1988, the Dash 7 prototype C-GNBX made its final STOL landing at Rockcliffe. There, on behalf of Boeing Canada Ltd., de Havilland Division, it was formally presented to the National Aviation Museum by Tom Appleton, vice-president of marketing and sales. NBX had been in constant use since its inaugural flight, during the first flush of airline enthusiasm for STOL. It had borne the brunt of all the preliminary testing and three world tour demonstrations. Former museum director Bob Bradford rode on that final flight from Downsview and accepted the plane on behalf of the NAM.

In 1989, Bruce Gissing became chairman and president of Boeing Canada. With a bachelor's degree in business administration and a master's from the University of Denver, he had joined Boeing in 1965 in the Materiel Division, rising through the ranks to be senior vice-president of the Boeing Commercial Airplane Co. He now became involved in the growing problems at Downsview .

A noteworthy date in August 1989 was the retirement of Myrtle Magill from the president's front office. She had served six presidents. The role as "The Boss's Secretary" at de Havilland dates to 1928 and the first day the company opened its Bay Street office in downtown Toronto. With the problems of a flying field and a workshop over, Bob Loader established a corporate headquarters in what was then called the Stirling Tower. The prestige was great, but the office small – a table and three chairs. The secretary was Mrs. E. Coates and her name shows up as one of the first provisional directors of the company. When the plant moved to Downsview, offices were provided above the shops with a balcony overlooking the assembly floor. The Depression years curtailed all office help until 1935 when Anne O'Neil became secretary to P.C. Garratt. She remained with him until he moved the head office downtown to the Bank of Commerce Building late in WWII. A notice in an issue of *The Mosquito* shows her changing her name to Mrs. Donahue. The next woman to guide the destiny of head office and Phil Garratt was Enid Coyle, wife of Dr. Leon F.

Coyle, the company medical consultant for 34 years. Mrs. Coyle had served as secretary to the wartime interim manager, Grant Glassco, and became Garratt's secretary in 1950. Her next 15 years were never dull. One of her last duties was to read the boss a Hawker Siddeley message over the phone, asking him to step down as president.

The next president, W.B. Boggs, moved from Montreal and brought his own secretary. When he was replaced by Bernhard Bundesman in 1970, Myrtle Magill moved to the secretary's desk and began her successful career training six presidents. Myrtle had been a de Havilland employee since 1954, first with John Garratt, then with Bob Imrie. As secretary to Bernhard Bundesman, she saw the Hawker Siddeley years change to government ownership, when Russ Bannock returned as president. The next transition involved John Sandford and a new office with a much better view of the flying field. This was followed by a short period when Brian Long of CDIC occupied the presidential chair. It began to look as if Myrtle had the only stable job on the de Havilland flight deck. Her services again were required when Bill Boggs returned to oversee the sale by the Canadian government. While the political battles

W. Daniel Heidt joined de Havilland in October 1989 as executive vice-president, adding general manager to his responsibilities in 1990. He became president in April 1991. (DH)

raged outside the main office, Myrtle, in her efficient way, returned the company to commercial status under the Boeing banner. It was business as usual at the front desk – outside the office of Ron B. Woodard this time. Her many friends gathered for a retirement party hosted by Woodard some time later. A complementary letter from former president John Sandford was read. He and Woodard agreed that "Myrtle brought a presence and level of dedication to the Office of President that was invaluable."

In November of 1989 Daniel Heidt, who had begun his career with Lockheed, became vice-president to Ron Woodard. Most recently he had been with Textron Inc. (Lycoming Division), and had been a president of Fairchild-Swearingen. He was entering the scene at a difficult time, but was destined to fill an important role in the events ahead. The company had a disappointing year in 1989, although the Dash 8-300 was doing well in the market with 104 sales and options. It was a blow to engineering when work on the Series 400 was put on hold in February, but there were reasons, such as rising plant improvement costs, even for such basic items as the steam generating system. The boiler at DHC was 35 years old and it was Boeing's lot to replace it with a larger, more efficient unit. The new one produced twice the steam, using either gas or oil, but was expensive.

For Sale Again

Even though the plant publication *Just Plane Facts* put on a brave front, telling of the latest achievements, overall funding was causing concern to government and company alike. Serious negotiations with Ottawa, due to higher-than-expected modernization costs, netted Boeing a $161 million relief, but problems continued. The paint shop, built in Otter and Caribou days, brought justifiable worker complaints about health hazards. Boeing realized that the shop was inadequate and added it to the list of renovations only a month after replacing the boiler. By July 1990, the decision was made: Boeing placed the de Havilland Division up for sale, even though Dash 8 orders had topped 350 and the em-

Myrtle Magill, "the secretary who trained six presidents," at her desk during the Boeing years. By the time of her retirement she had served presidents Bundesman, Bannock, Sandford, Long, Boggs and Woodard. Messages of congratulations were read at her retirement party, held in the president's office. (DH 59093 Tony Honeywood)

A promotional cutaway by Gary Aldred of the 50-passenger Dash 8-300. (DH)

ployee count stood at about 5,500. By now, Ron Woodard had departed for Seattle. Ken Laver moved up to vice-president finance, joining chairman Gissing and president Heidt (who had taken over from Woodard) in the problems ahead.

Competitors

A serious interest developed from the industrial conglomerate Selenia-Eslag SpA., formed by Aerospatiale of France and Aeritalia SpA of Italy, a prime contractor of Airbus Industrie. Aerospatiale and Aeritalia jointly owned Avions de Transport Regional, builders at Toulouse of the ATR42 and ATR72 commuter airliners – direct competitors of the Dash 8. Negotiations brought concern about an offshore competitor being interested in such an acquisition and what might happen if the sale went through. These were difficult days at Downsview, starting with the layoff of 300 workers.

To an average person with only newspaper reports to go on, the future of Canada's aviation industry looked bleak. The spending spree was at an end. Losses in developing the Dash 8-300 and modernizing the plant reportedly were over $400 million for Boeing's five year tenure. No profit had resulted in any of those years. Boeing had been a good cor-

porate citizen; everyone admitted to the improvements throughout the plant. They were handling negotiations, but Ottawa was watching closely. The developing scenario had all the earmarks of a disaster.

That ATR was a competitor and held the lead in commuter sales, raised eyebrows. ATR seemed to want a production base in North America, where half the world's commuter planes were sold. Their representative openly criticized Downsview for making too many of their own parts. This may have been true, but it led many to reason that Downsview would become a place only to assemble parts made elsewhere. ATR claimed that the Dash 8 would still be produced, which did not reassure the skeptics. When a reporter asked an Aerospatiale representative which aircraft would get top billing, the answer was, "It will be up to the airlines to place orders." As the unanswered questions mounted, Ontario Premier Bob Rae set up a working group to study the situation on behalf of provincial interests.

The federal Progressive Conservatives had been backed into a corner by a demand for substantial Canadian government support in the event of a sale. Negotiations were becoming serious enough that Ottawa considered a veto. Aerospatiale was given 30 days to come up with a better offer. The case died completely, however, when the European Community's competition watchdog cancelled the deal on the grounds that it would give ATR a monopoly. At the time they led with a 30 per cent market share. With the Dash 8's 20 per cent, this would have been detrimental to the industry.

Of major importance was the opening of the new paint shop in Bay 7. When completed in December 1990, it was state-of-the-art in every way. It totalled 27,000 sq ft (2,508 sq m) with two independent areas, one for complete aircraft, another for sub-assemblies. A central office provided controls and visual monitoring for both. Everything from downdraft air flow to vented floor drains had safety in mind. Even the sprayers were the new electrostatic type to save paint. The facility opened on January 8, 1991 amid persistent rumours of an uncertain future.

Bombardier Mentioned

The furor surrounding a second sale of de Havilland in six years brought an editorial cry for a truly Canadian solution – naming Bombardier of Montreal as the logical buyer. The enterprising transportation manufacturer had turned Canadair around since buying it in 1986. Then it moved worldwide, acquiring Short Brothers PLC in Northern Ireland (1989) and Learjet in the U.S. (1990). Bombardier chairman Laurent Beaudoin and his board had been watching the Downsview drama and knew where they would stand on a purchase. The new paint shop was on line and other valuable improvements had been made by Boeing. The Bombardier brass were familiar with the halls of power in Ottawa and were well-acquainted with de Havilland's turbulent labour history. It was still a major move, but there was no hurry, now that Aerospatiale was out of the pic-

ture. Beaudoin now won support from a new source – the Ontario government under the New Democratic Party and its premier, Bob Rae.

The last months of 1991 were taken up with four-way negotiations among two governments, Bombardier and Boeing. This brought them together at one table on January 22, 1992, for the signing of a formal purchase agreement before an appreciative crowd of 3,700 employees. The chairman of Boeing Canada, Bruce Gissing, de Havilland president, Dan Heidt, Canadian Auto Workers representative Jim O'Neil, Premier Bob Rae, his industry minister, Ed Philip, federal trade minister Michael Wilson, and Bombardier's Laurent Beaudoin were present for the occasion.

Dash 8 sales had dropped steadily from 104 in 1989 to 44 in 1990, then 32 in 1991. More layoffs were in progress. Bombardier was certainly in a strong bargaining position, but buying an organization with deteriorating sales and dwindling manpower called for caution. Besides financial discussions, the overriding factor was the compatibility of de Havilland's product line with Canadair's. There had never been a close relationship between the two companies; each had gone its own way over the years. Together they could make a formidable team in Canada's largest manufacturing centres; and Canadian aerospace, with its thousands of suppliers across the country, could work with a fully-integrated manufacturing industry for the first time, something former governments had talked about, but never achieved.

Smiles and a mutual handshake after the signing of the Bombardier agreement to purchase de Havilland. From the left, Bruce Gissing, chairman, Boeing Canada; Laurent Beaudoin, chairman and chief executive officer, Bombardier Inc.; Bob Rae, premier of Ontario; and Ed Philip, industry minister for the Province of Ontario. (DH)

The best-selling Dash 8-300. This 50-passenger airliner links smaller centres with major ones, where connections with other airlines are made. It also provides high-frequency commuter service between major cities. Shown are examples in British, Canadian and Belgian markings. (Ruben Husberg, Andrew H. Cline, Georges Van Belleghem)

(Above) A Brymon-British Airways Dash 8-300 at Gatwick in 1997. This fleet serves many U.K. and continental cities. (Ruben Husberg)

(Right) Series 300 C-FJFM of Canadian Regional Airlines was the 240th Dash 8. It's seen landing at Vancouver on July 31, 1993. Typical services for CRA's Dash 8 fleet include Vancouver-Victoria and Vancouver-Calgary. (Larry Milberry)

(Below) A Chinese Dash 8-300 taxis at Downsview in January 1990. Zhejiang Airlines is a local carrier based in Hangzhaou. In 1998 it operated the Dash 8 (three) and Airbus A320 (three). (Kenneth I. Swartz)

The Toronto *Globe and Mail* put Bombardier's purchase of de Havilland into perspective, noting that the Montreal-based industrial company "could now fly with the captains of the world aerospace industry–a remarkable feat for a company that got its start making snowmobiles." Meetings between the two companies and governments took place early in the New Year, so that by January 13, 1992 the financial arrangements were approved.

The March 9, 1992, final signing made Bombardier the majority shareholder of de Havilland with a 51 per cent interest and an option to buy Ontario's interest between February 1, 1996 and December 31, 1997. In addition, Boeing agreed to leave its top executives in place at de Havilland during the transition, including the incumbent president Dan Heidt. After the confusion and tension of the previous year, there was relief for everyone.

Laurent Beaudoin summarized his reasons for acquiring de Havilland: "Industry experts and financial analysts concur in pointing out what we have known all along: our regional aircraft–the de Havilland Dash 8 and the Canadair Regional Jet–complement each other. Thanks to that ... we will be in a favourable position to offer a broader range of products to the growing regional market. Because this is a business we understand, and a business that requires staying power, long-term commitment as well as a sound mix of

CHAPTER THIRTEEN

BOMBARDIER AEROSPACE

technology, engineering and marketing drive, we will be able to help each other. After all, attending to niche markets on the international scene is Bombardier's game and the main source of its business."

For nearly five years the Dash 8 was de Havilland's only product, so the company was vulnerable to the slightest ripple in the economy. Bombardier, however, had demonstrated its success with troubled companies; no one doubted its ability to do the same at de Havilland. Media coverage was favourable and experts lauded the transaction as good for all concerned. Robert E. Brown, president and chief operating officer of Bombardier Aerospace Group, complimented Boeing's five years of ownership, adding: "The biggest changes to come are strategic rather than operational."

Bombardier Inc.

In the 1930s Joseph-Armand Bombardier had considerable success with tracked vehicles he had designed to travel over the snow in rural Quebec. He began producing and marketing the vehicles in 1937 and, before the limitations of the war effort interrupted his plans, built a factory capable of producing 200 vehicles a year, as well as developing a larger, more powerful model. From 1942 to 1946, more than 1,900 Bombardier military models were produced for the armed forces, mostly under licence by other companies.

Laurent Beaudoin was born in Laurier Station, Quebec, in 1938. He earned a Bachelor of Arts degree at Ste-Anne College in Nova Scotia and his Master of Commerce at the University of Sherbrooke. After two years as an accountant in private practice, he joined Bombardier Inc., rising to be chairman and chief executive officer in 1979. He is the chief architect of the company's dramatic expansion from a manufacturer of snowmobiles to a major builder of railway and rapid transit rolling stock and one of the world's largest aircraft makers.

Born in England, Robert Brown earned his B.Sc. degree at the Royal Military College in Kingston, Ontario. He spent four years in the Canadian Forces, including a tour in Germany. Later he attended the Harvard Business School. He entered the public service in 1971, holding senior positions with the departments of Industry Trade and Commerce and of Regional Industrial Expansion. He joined Bombardier in 1987 as vice-president, corporate development, becoming president of Canadair in 1989, and of Bombardier Aerospace Group in 1992.

Joseph-Armand Bombardier's product line expanded after the war, particularly with light-tracked vehicles for the forest industry, and a new model designed for use by individuals, the Ski-Doo. First intended for use by surveyors, game wardens, prospectors and others who had to get around in snowbound regions, the Ski-Doo's popularity took off when the machines were adopted by outdoor enthusiasts for recreational use. Starting from 225 units in the 1959-60 season, production peaked at 210,000 in 1971-72, when the North American market amounted to 495,000 snowmobiles. At the time, Bombardier commanded more than 40 per cent of a market contested by more than 100 manufacturers.

In 1970 Bombardier took over Löhnerwerke GmbH of Austria and its affiliate, Rotax-Werk AG, manufacturer of engines for the Ski-Doo (and, later, for Bombardier's recreational watercraft). This was the Bombardier's first foreign acquisition, and the new company became Bombardier-Rotax GmbH.

Bombardier was well established by 1964 when the founder died at the early age of 57. His oldest son, Germain, took over as president with his brother-in-law, Laurent Beaudoin, as general manager. When Germain Bombardier was unable to continue due to failing health, Beaudoin became president in 1966.

While snowmobiles had delivered outstanding prosperity for Bombardier, by the early 1970s growth was slowing, largely due to saturation of demand. The energy crisis of the fall of 1973 dealt a blow to the snowmobile industry and sales plunged, declining to about 315,000 units by 1974-75. To protect its hard-won industry leadership position, the company added new recreational product lines, and diversified its operations into counter-cyclical new markets where it could apply its manufacturing and production management expertise.

Although the energy crisis had battered snowmobile sales, it boosted the mass transit industry. In early 1974 the City of Montreal announced an expansion of the local sub-

Before returning to Boeing in 1992, Jim Schwalm (left) spent three years at de Havilland, including four months as president. Ken Laver (right) was the last of the Boeing transition team to leave de Havilland. He had risen through the ranks of Boeing Canada before moving to Downsview as vice-president of manufacturing, vice-president of finance, then president in 1992. (DH)

way system and Bombardier seized the opportunity, winning the Montreal Urban Transit Commission contract worth $117.8 million for the production of 423 subway cars over four years.

Bombardier also added a licensing agreement from two French firms and introduced rubber-tired technology to the Montreal line. Such experience led to expansion through the purchase of other locomotive companies in the area, and some important international mass transit contracts. Bombardier's stature was fully established in 1982 (the year the first Dash 8 flew), with a contract–valued, ultimately, at more than $1 billion–to build 825 steel-wheeled subway cars for the New York Metropolitan Transportation Authority. Laurent Beaudoin later described this as "the big step forward that showed our diversification was working."

Bombardier also supplied rail cars to Amtrak and monorail cars to Walt Disney World in Florida. In Europe, Bombardier also became involved in rail transportation, acquiring leading rolling stock companies in Belgium, France and Britain. In 1989 Bombardier was the only North American member of the consortium selected to provide rail equipment for the development of the Eurotunnel rail system linking England and France.

Bombardier's activities through the 1970s and '80s had established its reputation for assessing new markets, for knowing how and when to buy companies to enter those markets, and for knowing how to restore troubled companies to profitability. This led Bombardier to consider further diversification into aerospace, through Montreal-based Canadair, a Crown Corporation with a long track record. Like de Havilland, Canadair had been owned by a foreign corporation experiencing its own challenges and which was not much concerned with its distant subsidiary's needs or proposed new programs. Rather than see the company decline further–with the accompanying loss of highly skilled personnel–Ottawa stepped in and acquired Canadair in January 1976.

While government ownership prevented the loss of de

Havilland and Canadair, both companies remained chronically undercapitalized, and neither could grow or even remain current in modern manufacturing infrastructure. Government ownership was necessary to ensure their survival, but most observers also recognized that it was no long-term solution. Bombardier's purchase of Canadair, effective December 23, 1986, and its subsequent turnaround, became one of the great business stories of the decade and the foundation of Bombardier's second great diversification thrust. Its general strategy was to compete in carefully selected niche markets where it could achieve and maintain leadership. In addition, it offered a complete range of products in any market in which it competed.

In the following six years, Bombardier acquired additional aerospace assets. Short Brothers PLC of Belfast, Northern Ireland, was purchased in 1989. This strengthened the company's

The Canadair CL-215 water bomber was introduced to de Havilland when five arrived from Montreal for conversion to turbine power. (Above) The first CL-215T is shown ready for delivery to Spain on February 26, 1993. Then (below), a Cl-215T at work on a fire. (DH)

design and manufacturing capability, with particular expertise in advanced composite materials, and gave Bombardier a foothold in European aerospace.

Learjet was acquired in 1990, extending the company's business aircraft line from Canadair's wide body Challenger, through a range of mid-size and light business jets. With Learjet, Bombardier's U.S. presence grew. This also provided Bombardier with a flight test base having consistently better flying weather than northeastern North America.

The final element in this emerging picture was de Havilland, which was acquired in 1992 from Boeing in co-operation with the Province of Ontario. In addition to gaining a substantially renovated manufacturing facility, adding the

Dash 8 turboprop airliner family (then comprising the 37-passenger Series 100 and 50-passenger Series 300) complemented Bombardier's Canadair Regional Jet airliner.

Leadership Overlap

When Boeing had acquired de Havilland in early 1986, Bill Boggs remained as president until January 1987 to manage the transition to private sector ownership. Then Ron Woodard arrived from Seattle to assume the presidency. In November 1989 Dan Heidt became vice-president of de Havilland, then president in March 1991, succeeding Ron Woodard. Heidt served through an unsettled year that ended with negotiations for the Bombardier sale, continuing until August 1992. Then Jim Schwalm—who had spent most of his career in manufacturing at Boeing Helicopters and with McDonnell Douglas Helicopter Co.—took over briefly in 1992.

Ken Laver was the last of the transition presidents between Boeing and Bombardier. His career had begun with Canada's Department of Supply and Services. In 1981 he joined Boeing Canada's Arnprior Division as business director, rising to vice-president and general manager by 1983. Three years later he moved to de Havilland as vice-president of manufacturing. Ken Laver became vice-president of finance in 1990 and president in December 1992.

A New Life

Bombardier soon found an opportunity to express confidence in its new acquisition. On February 26, 1992, just 35 days after the signing, the company announced the launch of the Dash 8-200. This model was the company's response to a survey of operators serving high-elevation airports or flying in hotter-than-average conditions. Fitting de-rated PW123 engines to the Series 100 improved performance under "hot-and-high" conditions, while incorporating the Series 300's propellers, nacelles, instrumentation, and the Series 300A's auto-feathering feature, assured Dash 8 family commonality. The Series 200 received type approval on March 9, 1995.

In spite of the good news that the plant was now in Canadian hands, the bad news leading up to negotiations had been a reduction in staff. Bombardier's answer to the latter was to use vacant hangar space and look within the organization for work. Canadair had a pending CL-215 water bomber upgrading program for 13 Spanish aircraft. With help from Downsview, the program could be accelerated and five conversions done in Toronto.

This program replaced the water bomber's piston engines with more powerful turboprops, the wings and fin were strengthened, and small fins were added to improve stability. New avionics and electrics also were incorporated and the aircraft was designated CL-215T. Later models, even more capable than the CL-215T, were designated CL-415, with components such as engine nacelles manufactured at Downsview. Something else Bombardier must have been watching during Boeing's final year was the

Pierre Lortie became president of Bombardier's Regional Aircraft Division when Robert Wohl retired. He took part in an unprecedented upswing in sales. In March 1998 Lortie was named to head a new unit – Bombardier International, designed to market company products in greater depth beyond North America and Europe.

new Downsview paint shop. Bombardier tested it by sending the first customer Canadair Regional Jet (s/n 7004) for painting in Lufthansa CityLine colours.

A New Approach to Marketing

By 1992 there were other activities within Bombardier's growing world, including a major reorganization for many Downsview activities. A new organization, known as Bombardier Regional Aircraft Division (BRAD), combined marketing, sales, contracts, customer support and life-cycle management functions for the full regional aircraft product line—that is, both de Havilland Dash 8 turboprop and Canadair Regional Jet airliners—in a single entity based at Downsview. BRAD brought a more consistent focus on the needs of regional airline customers, who increasingly operated both turboprop and jet equipment. Engineering, manufacturing and aircraft operations remained part of the de Havilland organization.

Robert Wohl became BRAD's first president, responsible to Robert E. Brown, president of Bombardier Aerospace, North America. The new division included many names from the former DH marketing team: Tom Appleton, executive vice-president, John Howarth, vice-president, the Americas, and John Giraudy, vice-president International Sales. Larry Dugan became vice-president customer support, and Paul Francoeur, vice-president contracts. In August 1993 Robert Wohl retired and was succeeded as president of BRAD by Pierre Lortie. Born in Giffard, Quebec, Lortie was a graduate of Laval University in Quebec and Belgium's Louvain University. He received a business administration degree from the University of Chicago and a doctorate in civil law from Bishop's University in Quebec. He became chief executive officer of the Montreal Stock Exchange and later president of Provigo Inc. In 1989 Lortie chaired the Royal Commission on electoral reform and the following year joined Bombardier as president of Bombardier Capital.

The 1992 Farnborough Air Show provided the first opportunity for Bombardier to present its family of regional aircraft to the international market. The Canadair Regional Jet, recently certified by Transport Canada, appeared in the flight program each day, along with the Dash 8. As well as promoting the new Dash 8 Series 200 at

Building the Learjet 45 wing was a key Bombardier project for Downsview. Here the first wing is being prepared for shipping to Wichita. (DH 940165)

Farnborough, the company announced a new noise suppression system for Dash 8 aircraft, and introduced a wider choice of Pratt & Whitney engines, providing the whole Dash 8 family with improved payload, speed and takeoff distances.

The Learjet 45

Through the early 1980s, while de Havilland was building the first Dash 8, Bill Lear's classy business jets were riding high, capturing more than half the market. Later, however, competition from the Cessna Citation, affected sales so badly that Learjet's owner, Denver's Gates Corp., wanted out of aerospace. Five years later Integrated Resources Inc.

G.R. "Ron" Jackson proudly displays the J.A.D. McCurdy Award he won in 1995 after a lifetime career with de Havilland. He joined DH Engineering in 1953 during the Otter program, after graduating from the University of Toronto. He rose quickly to the post of assistant chief designer, then product manager of the Dash 7 in 1976. He became vice-president of production development in 1987 and retired in 1994, during the successful launch of the Series 200 Dash 8.

took over in a reconstruction bid, but this failed in spite of numerous improvements to the product line. Learjet's market share sank to 15 per cent. Something had to be done.

Brian Barents, in charge of Learjet, sought a partner to share the load. Bombardier purchased the troubled business for $60 million. On January 14, in the midst of the Learjet negotiations, it was announced that Germain Bombardier, eldest son of founder Armand Bombardier, had died.

During negotiations, Brian Barents and Laurent Beaudoin agreed that Learjet's practice of updating earlier models had run its course. Bombardier soon committed to invest in product development to ensure Learjet's future. In this case, the new product was the Learjet 45, a new, small business jet for the 21st century. The Learjet 45 would be an all-new design that would establish new standards of performance, reliability and comfort in a light jet. Following the purchase, Bombardier also continued development on two derivative aircraft already under way, the Learjet 31A enhanced light jet and the mid-size Learjet 60. After a successful introduction at the fall meeting of the National Business Aircraft Association, the formal program go-ahead for the Learjet 45 came in February 1993.

Using a technique it first employed on the Canadair Regional Jet airliner and now standard across the aerospace operation, Bombardier divided Learjet 45 responsibilities and work among different members of its team. While Learjet would retain responsibility for final assembly and

The Learjet 45 made its inaugural flight on October 7, 1995, with pilots Pete Reynolds and Jim Dwyer. (DH A204)

flight testing, as well as overall program direction, much of the detail design and manufacturing went elsewhere. Short Brothers PLC in Belfast would build the fuselage and empennage, while looking after "iron bird" static and fatigue testing. A de Havilland team undertook detailed design of the Lear 45 wing, along with plans to manufacture it at Downsview under project manager Mike Ioannou.

A new-concept, all-aluminum wing assembly jig was built at Downsview, and the first metal was cut in August 1993 (a second Learjet 45 wing assembly jig was added in 1998). The first wing was completed at Downsview by September 27, 1994 and turned over to Learjet vice-president André Brais. De Havilland president Ken Laver hosted a handover ceremony for project workers, with Ontario Premier Bob Rae attending. As the employees built further wings, they followed the stages of assembly in Wichita with great interest. Rollout of the first Learjet 45 aircraft came in September 1995, and first flight a month later.

Subcontracts

Outside contracts had not been a major activity at de Havilland for many years, but 1993 brought two that broadened manufacturing capabilities. The first, in March, was for Lockheed Marietta of Georgia. Lockheed was faced with a rush order of P-3C Orion maritime patrol aircraft for Korea. The contract called for eight shipsets of stub wings and aft body sections. Seventy-five employees under Wally Cormack set up a work area in Bay 9 and shipped the first components to Lockheed on May 31.

The subcontract for eight sets of Lockheed P-3C Orion stub wings helped build the work force at Downsview. Here the first shipset, attached to its fuselage section, is ready for delivery to Lockheed. (DH)

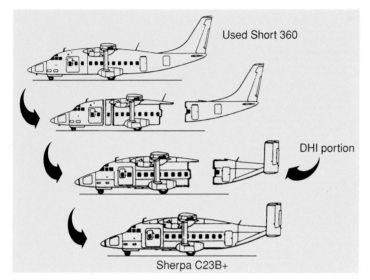

Used Short 360

DHI portion

Sherpa C23B+

In the subcontract with Shorts, the aft section of the SD-360 was removed (left) and replaced with a tail unit manufactured by de Havilland. (Below) A finished rear section is loaded for shipment to the West Virginia Air Center for final assembly. (DH 94-02321-8)

The other subcontract involved a modification program for Short Bros. C-23B+ Sherpa transports (based on the SD-360 airliner) used by the U.S. Air Force and Air National Guard, beginning in October 1993. Components built by de Havilland included a new tail and a hydraulically operated rear ramp. These were shipped to the Shorts-operated West Virginia Air Center at Bridgeport, West Virginia, where the aircraft were completed. The former flight test building at Downsview was cleared for this work, which later moved to Bay 10, then to the North Plant. Twenty-eight sets were ordered, representing the first direct collaboration with Shorts.

Turbulence

Even with improving conditions at Downsview, lingering effects of the 1990s recession affected Dash 8 production. A significant challenge arose when a valued customer cancelled several near-term orders. Ken Laver and his management team considered a wide range of strategies to prevent layoffs and regain stability, including rescheduling, production line planning and renegotiating customer contracts. In mid-April 1993 Laver called for a line shutdown affecting 2,000 employees from July 5 to September 3, followed by a return to a production rate of two Dash 8 aircraft per month. Subcontract and design continued throughout the period.

As part of the Bombardier purchase, a relieved union had offered a one-year extension of the existing labour contract. That concession ended in mid-1994 and the possibility of a strike loomed. Employees speculated that a repeat of 1990 might be achieved, when the company averted a walkout for the first time in two decades. The mood throughout the plant was upbeat, but Bombardier was behind schedule on

planned transition expenditures. The company sought a three-year extension to the wage freeze, and elimination of a cost-of-living allowance. These were normal topics for discussion with the union, but the company's business philosophy now included global manufacturing and international partners. Bombardier felt these partners should be allowed to continue work on their contracted assignments in the plant. The company also wanted to add versatility to the work force and amalgamate job categories through employee training.

Gaston Hébert became president of de Havilland on February 1, 1995. He came from the mass transport division, where he had headed Bombardier's Eurotunnel consortium. In April of 1996, he returned to Montreal as Group Executive, Vice-President operations.

These requests brought opposition from union leaders. A strike was called for the 1,900 workers of Locals 112 and 673, who walked out on June 23. The usual newspaper headlines resulted, but much must be said for the work on both sides of the bargaining table over the following few days. Ratification of a new agreement came on June 30, with the vote strongly in favour, and the workers were back at their jobs on July 4.

A New President

Bombardier's Gaston Hébert replaced Ken Laver, the last of Boeing's management team, on February 1,

1995. His arrival coincided with the first flight of the Dash 8-200 in January, and its certification in March.

Hébert was born in 1947 in Quebec City. By 1969 he had earned a Bachelor of Science degree in engineering from Laval University. His first position was with General Electric in Toronto, where he spent 10 years in engineering and manufacturing. He joined Bombardier's Mass Transit Division in 1979, becoming vice-president of Engineering Research and Development. He spent three years in Europe heading a Bombardier consortium designing, building and commissioning the Eurotunnel shuttle trains.

One pleasant assignment for the new president was a February 22 trip to Washington, D.C., accompanied by three retirees from the Dash 8 engineering team. Their purpose was to accept *Air Transport World* magazine's Technology Achievement Award on behalf of de Havilland employees. The retirees, who had been involved in the early days of the Dash 7 and Dash 8, were Mike Davy, former vice-president of engineering; Dick Batch, former engineering director, and Bob Fowler, former chief engineering test pilot through both programs. This award, previously presented to Boeing, Douglas and Aérospatiale, confirmed Bombardier's coming of age among large aircraft manufacturers.

Horizon Head-Up

A September breakthrough in 1994 added the Dash 8 to the list of aircraft capable of takeoffs and landings in marginal visibility. The equipment used was the Hughes-Flight Dynamics Inc. HGS 2000 head-up guidance system, a combination of avionics and optics displaying final approach information on a transparent screen at the pilot's eye level through the windshield. The Dash 8 thus became the first regional turboprop certified by the U.S. Federal Aviation Administration for category IIIA approaches.

The project was completed in collaboration with Horizon Air of Portland, Oregon, permitting landings with 50-foot (15-m) decision height and 700-foot (213-m) runway visual range. This gave the operator a distinct advantage over the competition with fewer flight delays or cancellations. The system proved advantageous at the fog-plagued airports in Horizon's system and became available to other Dash 8 operators.

In a similar move, Lufthansa CityLine was the first regional airline in Germany approved for the head-up, category IIIA landings in their Canadair Regional Jets. The early adoption of this leading-edge technology by Bombardier customers indicated the growing maturity of the regional airline industry and was a sign that—like their main-

line counterparts—regional airlines can employ high technology to deliver important customer benefits.

A Double-Header Delivery

On April 19, 1995, four thousand de Havilland and BRAD employees gathered in Bay 7 to witness delivery of the first Dash 8 Series 200 aircraft, as well as the delivery of Dash 8 number 400.

British Petroleum Exploration Colombia was an ideal customer for the Series 200, for it had hot temperatures and mountains to deal with in its South American petroleum operations. Phil Mead, operations manager of BPX, accepted the aircraft, complimented the Downsview workforce and described the role of aircraft transporting employees between the Bogotá base and oil field operations, 150 kilometres away.

At the same event the 400th Dash 8 to leave the production line was delivered to longtime customer Tyrolean Airways—12 years to the day from the first Dash 8 rollout. In accepting for Tyrolean, managing director Fritz Feitl noted, "Of all the Dash 8 aircraft built, about one in 20 have been delivered to Tyrolean."

Unhappy news arrived on August 3, 1995—Punch Dickins died in Toronto at age 96. His illustrious career had begun in the skies of the First World War, where he was credited with downing seven enemy aircraft. He was instrumental in the development of early flying in Canada's far north

The Technical Information Centre is one of the departments housed in a renovated office complex at Downsview. It opened on May 21, 1996, under supervisor librarian Cathy Parsons and librarian Barbara Chiaramonte. The original library was established in 1954 under Dennis Newman. In 1960 it became the Standards & Engineering Library. The TIC holds information on all de Havilland aircraft, plus the latest aviation trade magazines. By early 1997 it had an on-line database system and Internet links. Here, in the TIC, are John Galizia, director of airworthiness and engineering methods; Cathy Parsons, TIC supervisor; and Carl Gerard, vice-president of engineering. (DH)

The Global Express rollout, showing the aircraft draped with the flags of the participating countries. To the left is the orchestra, choir and rows of employees in white. (DH 080664-13)

and joined de Havilland in 1947 as director of sales during the Beaver program. He remained a de Havilland director until May 1967, retiring at the height of the Twin Otter era.

The Global Express

The June 1992 issue of de Havilland's newsletter *Just Plane Facts* carried the announcement of a grand new project—the Bombardier Global Express ultra-long-range business jet. The Global Express had been introduced with a full-scale cabin mockup at the National Business Aircraft Association convention the year before.

This aircraft was designed to appeal to major corporations and governments in response to the increasing globalization of business and international affairs by compressing time and distance with high-speed travel and great range.

The program was to be an undertaking of truly global proportions, and involve de Havilland as a participant. The aircraft would have a new wing, powerful new engines, and a large, luxurious cabin, which could be configured to include a boardroom and fully equipped office. The Global Express would take eight passengers and a four-person crew more than 7,400 miles (12,000 kilometres), sufficient to link major city pairs such as New York–Tokyo, nonstop, in either direction.

Bombardier's responsibility-and-work-sharing approach was expanded to encompass nine risk-sharing partners from six countries and the Global Express program received formal approval in December 1993. De Havilland would build the Global Express rear fuselage, engine pylons and vertical stabilizer, and do final assembly. The nose section would come from Canadair. Program management, marketing and customer support would be overseen by a new Bombardier organization. Shorts would provide the forward fuselage, horizontal stabilizer and body fairings, while certification flight testing would to be done at the Bombardier Flight Test Center in Wichita.

International partners included BMW Rolls-Royce, of Germany for the engines and Mitsubishi Heavy Industries, of Japan, for the wing and mid-fuselage. From France came flight control systems by Sextant Avionique and environmental systems from Liebherr-Aerospace-Toulouse SA. From the U.S. came fuel systems by Parker Aerospace, avionics by Honeywell and the auxiliary power unit and environmental controls by Allied Signal Aerospace. The electrical system was to be developed by Britain's Lucas Aerospace, while the landing gear was to be developed and produced by Messier-Dowty International (now Messier-Bugatti) of Canada.

By 1996 Global Express components began arriving at Downsview. Excitement built for months in Bay 9, where the first aircraft grew daily. The bay took on an international atmosphere, with workers from each country involved on the shop floor. As rollout day approached, preparations for a suitable introduction of the aircraft grew alongside the pressure to maintain the first aircraft's production schedule. New aircraft launchings are noted for their glamour, but Bombardier decided this one should be uniquely memora-

Two views of the first flight of Bombardier Global Express No. 9001 from Downsview on October 13, 1996. Pete Reynolds and Ron Haughton were at the controls. Then, pilots Haughton and Reynolds flank John Holding, vice-president engineering, who rode in the chase plane. (DH)

ble. Arrangements for the celebration were superb, bringing together a gathering of world customers, employees, suppliers, industry leaders and politicians.

On the morning of August 26, 1997, under partial cloud, a lineup of business jets and limousines at Downsview set the scene as 2,000 guests made their way to a huge tent in front of Bay 7. They walked the red carpet into a darkened flight test hangar, taking their places in theatre-style tiered seating. The subdued lighting and wall-to-wall screen gave all the drama of

Global Express wings and centre fuselage, in protective wrappings, make their way to Downsview from Japan. Until May 1998 they went from Mitsubishi Heavy Industries by ship to Kansai Airport, the closest airport large enough for the Antonov AN-124 freighter. After a stop in Vancouver for fuel, the aircraft continued to Toronto's Lester B. Pearson International Airport. From there the components were trucked (left) to Downsview. Since May 1998 the components have travelled by sea and rail to the Downsview spur line (below). Similar shipments of Dash 8 Series 400 fuselages, which began with the Antonov, were also changed over to the sea-rail route. (DH)

to the world of business flight. The audience immediately gave the new aircraft a well-deserved standing ovation, and VIPs came forward for their personal inspection, followed by the crowd of eager visitors. It was a moment in history for Downsview and a unique celebration of world technology in harmony. Former business pilots marvelled in envy at the progress since the days of flying glamorized DC-3s and Lodestars.

With Pete Reynolds, Bombardier's vice-president, flight test, at the controls, Global Express 9001 made its first flight on October 13, 1996. Reynolds was accompanied by engineering test pilot Ron Haughton, while John Holding, group vice-president, engineering, flew in the Challenger chase plane. The flight went so well that additional parameters were explored before landing after 2:46 hours. Two weeks later 9001 was on its way to the Bombardier Flight Test Center in Wichita and 9002 moved to the front of the hangar. By January 6, it too was turned over to engineering and later joined 9001 in Wichita, where four aircraft would complete an 18-month, 2,000-hour flight-test program.

a Hollywood opening night extravaganza. The stage was small and the speeches brief. Laurent Beaudoin, chairman of Bombardier Inc., Robert Brown, president and chief operating officer of Bombardier Aerospace, and John Lawson, president of Canadair Business Aircraft represented the hosts. The guests of honour were Canada's prime minister, Jean Chrétien, and Ontario premier Mike Harris.

At the signal for the show to begin, an audiovisual presentation eased the crowd into a mood of expectation. Then the curtain rose to the music of a 45-piece orchestra, accompanied by a 300-voice choir. The musical score "The Power of Global Vision" was written for the occasion by René Dupéré and directed by Wayne Strongman. Draped in the foreground was the outline of a jet transport under a white sheet, accented by the partners' splendid national flags. In the background, 700 employees dressed in white and representing the skills that brought it all together stood shoulder to shoulder on five levels of scaffolding.

The highlight came as the new aircraft's navigation lights began to flash, its windows lit up, and the cover was slowly withdrawn. Here in the floodlights was the latest contribution

Business and Real Estate

The first four years of Bombardier control quickly passed. Progress at Downsview had been so significant that the Province of Ontario wanted to negotiate a new agreement. The Canadian Auto Workers Union supported this concept, and the discussions remained on track through closing, at the end of January 1997. Bombardier would purchase Ontario's minority interest over a 15-year period, thus obtaining title to the Downsview establishment while retaining a financial partnership with the Province of Ontario.

Years earlier, when de Havilland was easing itself out of the former Avro buildings at Malton, the spare parts department was the last to leave because of its ideal location—

(Above) An overall view of Downsview in 1997. The growth of this complex is best appreciated by referring to earlier aerials on pages 30, 69, 93, 108, 162 and 196. Note the parking lots, which seem to be ever-expanding. FlightSafety Canada's training complex is to the right of the cafeteria. The north plant remains intact, while the Canada Lands Company decides what to do with the area. (DH A0272)

Ground-breaking for the new spares facility at 1900 Derry Road West, Mississauga, took place on February 6, 1997, with Pierre Lortie and Mississauga mayor Hazel McCallion officiating. The warehouse of 84,000 sq ft (7,800 sq m) opened for business in September 1997. (DH 97-1639E-2, '97-1302A-15)

The Global Express production line in mid-1998, with aircraft 9010 to 9014 nearing completion. The Global Express completed its Transport Canada certification on August 4, 1998. At that time 80 firm orders were reported. (BA 98-2048G-4)

plenty of space and close to airline shipping. When the building was taken over as a trade show centre, spares moved to Downsview for a few years, but this was not entirely satisfactory. The situation came to a head when the spares area at Downsview was needed for wing production and a satellite cafeteria. Temporary space was leased on Bath Road. In 1990 Bombardier Real Estate Ltd. had been created to deal with space problems such as this. In 1996, it contracted for a new warehouse and administration headquarters to be built on Derry Road West, close to Toronto's international airport. The February 1997 sod breaking, headed by Pierre Lortie and Mississauga Mayor Hazel McCallion, was followed by the opening on September 3. The new facility housed a large spares inventory and 128 employees ready to provide 24 hour, 7-days-a-week service.

Aircraft spares played just one important role in the increasingly vital function of continuing customer support. Bombardier Regional Aircraft Division's senior management recognized that customers faced competitive pressure to keep their aircraft in profitable service, with a high standard of dispatch reliability and on-time schedule completion—customers couldn't afford delayed departures or cancelled flights due to inadequate reliability or missing parts.

The established de Havilland support functions were expanded to meet the growing demand. BRAD managers soon recognized that reliability and cost-effective maintenance and spares support were just as important to customers as aircraft performance and price. In addition, the rapid growth of the de Havilland Dash 8 and Canadair Regional Jet fleets had to be supported with increased resources from Bombardier. By the end of 1998, the combined total of Bombardier regional aircraft delivered to 48 countries had reached 790, with a sales backlog of 314. Added to these growing product support responsibilities were more than 2,000 out-of-production Dash 7, Twin Otter, Buffalo, Caribou, Otter and Beaver aircraft still in service around the world.

Accordingly, BRAD undertook a major program to expand and enhance its customer support, with significant investments in people, training, systems and spare parts, under Paul Francoeur vice-president, customer support (now called Airline Services). To capture the new spirit of professionalism, excellence, and the importance of individual initiative in continuing customer support, the department launched many of its new programs and services under the ProFormance banner.

Eight worldwide spares distribution centres were established in Montreal, Toronto, Detroit, Sydney, Paris, Amsterdam, Kuala Lumpur and Singapore. Additional initiatives included training, maintenance planning, service readiness, technical publications, field services and supplier liaison. The payoff has been repeated top scores in *Professional Pilot* magazine's annual customer support surveys.

Bombardier's continuing rapid development and introduction of new products—including regional, business and amphibious aircraft—also placed a growing strain on flight test facilities and other real estate-intensive activities. In February 1997 Bombardier announced the expansion of the Flight Test Center in Wichita, adding a 54,000-square foot (4,180-square metre) experimental test flight hangar (to accommodate three large Bombardier aircraft simultaneously) plus a 53,000-square foot (4,924 square-metre) office and workshop area.

In September that year Bombardier bought the aircraft completion business of Innotech Aviation Ltd. of Dorval. Quebec. Innotech, in corporate aviation sales in Canada since 1955, had been doing Challenger interiors since 1979. Bombardier also planned a new completions facility for Dorval Airport, concentrating on the Global Express and Challenger jets. This $50-million dollar structure of 415,000 square feet (38,550 square metres), staffed by 270 employees, opened for the first aircraft on December 24, 1997, the end of a busy real estate year.

The Dash 8 Q400

For years the idea of a larger regional turboprop aircraft had been debated and discussed by airlines and manufacturers alike, particularly de Havilland and, later, by BRAD, as a logical extension of the Dash 8 product family. In BRAD's

A Dash 8-400 quarter-scale test model in the NRC wind tunnel in Ottawa. The model measured 26.75 feet (8 m) in length. Back at Downsview, the engineering group supervised a set of five high- and low-speed parameters for the program. (DH)

view, such an aircraft would accommodate 70 to 74 passengers and cruise at a near-jet speed of 350 knots. Approval to launch the Dash 8 Series 400 was finally given and the public announcement was made at the Paris Air Show in June 1995. Employees in Canada learned of the launch decision from Pierre Lortie and Gaston Hébert (presidents of BRAD and de Havilland, respectively), through a special video presentation which was delivered directly to their homes. That Bombardier was already designing a 70-passenger jet, the CRJ-700, was no deterrent. With two new aircraft the company now could offer a complete family of regional turboprop and jet airliners, seating from 37 to 74 passengers.

The Paris announcement noted that manufacture of Series 400 components would start in March 1996. Rollout was set for November 1997, with certification in the first quarter of 1999. A base price of US$17.4 million was quoted. The new aircraft would carry the same common type rating as its predecessors with only minor crew training and maintenance differences.

In comparison to the Series 300, cabin length of the Series 400 is 22.2 feet (6.75 metres) longer. More powerful (4,830 shp) Pratt & Whitney Canada PW150A engines driving six-bladed propellers were to be used. The propellers were to be eight inches (20.3 cm) farther from the fuselage than in the Series 300 to help reduce interior noise.

Noise and Vibration Suppression System

Turboprop manufacturers have long sought an answer to interior cabin noise due to propeller synchronisation and vibration. Added to these was the need to overcome the fluctuations of air pressure from spinning propellers close to the fuselage. A collaboration program between Bombardier and Ultra Electronics, of Cambridge, England, on the subject of cabin noise resulted in what is now called the Noise and Vibration Suppression System (NVS)

This system begins with a series of small microphones concealed in the wall panels that pick up noise at various points in the cabin and relay the information to a central microprocessor, along with inputs of propeller rpm and cabin pressure differential. The resulting signals from the microprocessor are sent to active Tuned Vibration Absorbers (TVAs) attached throughout the fuselage framework to initiate out-of-phase counter vibrations. The latest in engine mount technology was also included in the entire Dash 8 series of aircraft to cut vibrations at source. The resulting balance of dampened vibrations throughout all points in the cabin reduces the overall noise level to that of a comparable-size jet aircraft.

The system will be installed on all Dash 8 aircraft leaving the production line in Downsview and identified by a "Q." Previous Dash 8 models may be updated to "Q" standard with a modification kit. Airline and passenger response to

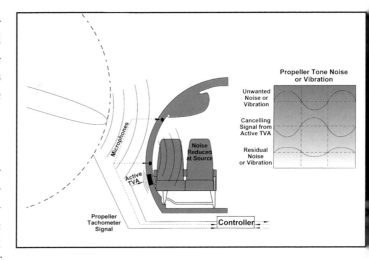

The Noise and Vibration Suppression System is shown with the microphones, the controller/microprocessor and the active Tuned Vibration Absorbers. They all play a role (as described left) in reducing the overall cabin noise level.

the improvements delivered by NVS was positive and the entire Dash 8 product family was re-branded "Q" (for quiet) in time for the 1998 Farnborough Air Show, complete with a new-look livery.

Even before the Dash 8 Q400 announcement at Paris in June 1995, work was under way on three continents among several risk-sharing participants and, by October, Mitsubishi Heavy Industries of Nagoya, Japan, was beginning the fuselage and tail sections. Short Brothers of Northern Ireland began building engine cowlings, and de Havilland was cutting metal for the wings. Pratt & Whitney Canada of Longueuil reported a test cell run for the new engine/propeller combination in December, followed by a successful air test on a Boeing 720 test bed in January. The propellers, a new six-bladed design by Dowty Aerospace Propellers of Gloucester, England, were 13.5 feet (4.1 metres) in diameter, having carbon spars with a polyurethane foam core, and an outer layer of carbon/glass fibre with nickel leading edge-protectors.

In April 1997 Bombardier Aerospace employees on both continents were proud to hear that Bombardier Inc. had been named "Canada's Most Respected Corporation" for the second year running. This annual survey, conducted by The *Globe and Mail* "Report on Business" magazine, involved 380 CEOs grading Canadian companies for their performance in: long term investment value, innovation, human resource management, corporate social responsibility and financial performance.

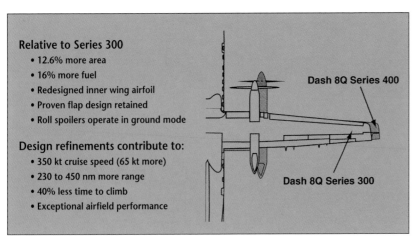

Relative to Series 300
- 12.6% more area
- 16% more fuel
- Redesigned inner wing airfoil
- Proven flap design retained
- Roll spoilers operate in ground mode

Design refinements contribute to:
- 350 kt cruise speed (65 kt more)
- 230 to 450 nm more range
- 40% less time to climb
- Exceptional airfield performance

Dash 8Q Series 400

Dash 8Q Series 300

A comparison between the Series Q400 and the Series Q300 wings showing the increased propeller/fuselage clearance of the Q400.

The "500 and one" ceremony of November 22, 1998, began with the turnover of the 500th Dash 8Q to Horizon Airlines. It's shown with the employees prior to the event. At this time, Horizon was serving 37 cities in California, Idaho, Montana, Oregon, Washington, British Columbia and Alberta. (DH)

The Series 400 fuselage takes the same route as the Global Express wing from Japan – to Toronto aboard an Antonov AN-124. The first is shown being unloaded at Lester B. Pearson International Airport. (DH)

Further recognition came for Bombardier Aerospace in August 1998, with the prestigious International Council of Aeronautical Sciences -Von Karmen Award for international co-operation in aeronautics, presented for the successful international, risk-sharing partnership approach to the development of the Bombardier Global Express business aircraft.

In-house Training

Before Ken Laver left as president, he was to see the Bombardier Manufacturing System (BMS) launched at Downsview and participate in a training program that stressed interaction and teamwork. This was a company-wide effort to have common elements of manufacturing used across the Bombardier Aerospace Group, including Montreal, de Havilland in Toronto, Learjet in Wichita and Shorts in Belfast. The system focused on implementing the same set of optimized manufacturing practices in each organization, so that the flow of parts through production areas would occur in the shortest, most efficient time. The shop floors at Downsview were reorganized to incorporate the new system and provide a brighter working environment. Meanwhile, head office was renovated with the same objectives in mind.

The employees' entrance was simplified and a bright, new lobby was added to welcome visitors.

The introduction of the Six Sigma approach to quality and cost control throughout the Bombardier Aerospace organization was another advance. Six Sigma is a statistical measurement of quality achieved when control over a process is improved to the point that defects are reduced to less than four per million operations. The Six Sigma approach to quality, developed by Dr. Mikel J. Harry, founder of Six Sigma Academy, was implemented by Motorola, General Electric and other large manufacturers, where outstanding improvements in all areas resulted. At Bombardier, educational material was developed in conjunction with Dr. Harry. Responsibilities were defined for everyone, including senior management, through all stages of implementation,

In November 1997 the Dash 8-400 was unveiled at de Havilland. At this gala event, all present were invited to autograph the unpainted prototype. First delivery was to be in 1999 to Great China Airlines of Taiwan. (Right) Bombardier's Robert Brown and Pierre Lortie add their signatures. (Larry Milberry, DH)

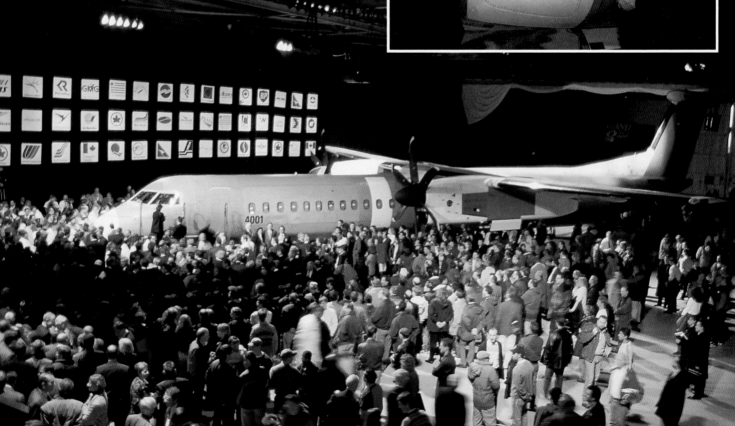

The first flight of the "Jackson 'Jock' Aitken," named after the popular member of the propulsion section of flight test crew, who had died suddenly in June 1997. Wally Warner, Barry Hubbard, Angelo Susi and David Monteith crewed C-FJJA on this occasion. The aircraft was airborne for three hours. (DH)

whether the projects involve modified work practices, improved communications or a general attack on lost time and material. Bombardier introduced Six Sigma training in March 1997; within a year significant financial benefits were evident in a many areas.

Launching the Q400

The rollout for the long awaited Dash 8 Q400 took place November 22, 1997, with the catchy title "500 and One Good Reasons to Celebrate." The "500" referred to the delivery of the 500th Dash 8 to Horizon Air. Horizon gave even more impact to the occasion by signing for an additional 10 Series 200 aircraft, moments before the ceremony began. George Bagley and Glenn Johnson of Horizon accepted the ceremonial key from Pierre Lortie. At this time Horizon served 37 cities in California, Idaho, Montana, Oregon, Washington, British Columbia and Alberta. Next on the program was a preview of the latest, largest and fastest Dash 8, the much-discussed and once-postponed Series 400.

Still in green primer paint, it was an impressive sight. Employees and guests were given markers and invited to autograph this new member of the Dash 8 family.

For 10 years the Series 400 had been a favourite topic with both the engineering and sales departments at de Havilland—now it was fact. Unforeseen delays, however, plagued the first flight, giving test engineers cause to recall the answer veteran Jock Aitken always used at such times, "It will be ready when it's ready!" Finally, with a lot of overtime and hard work, the first 400 was ready. Jock had died of a sudden heart attack on June 9 while in the midst of the program he was enjoying so completely. He had been in de Havilland test engineering for 34 years as a propulsion expert, had flown with Bob Fowler on the first flight of the Turbo Beaver, and had manned one of the stations on the Dash 7 inaugural flight. Everyone in Flight Test regretted that Jock would miss the thrill of that coming first flight. "Not necessarily," said one. "Let's name the aircraft after Jock and he'll be a part of them all."

The new look of the latest Dash 8 demonstration aircraft accents the Q for quiet feature that is now standard on all models. The profile of the newest family member, the Q400, is easily recognizable by its length and the bullet fairing on top of the tail section. (Bombardier)

Aircraft No. 4001, registered C-FJJA in Jock's memory, taxied out on a bright Saturday morning, January 31, 1998. The name of Jackson "Jock" Aitken was stencilled below the cockpit window. Captain Wally Warner and first officer Barry Hubbard were at the controls, with Angelo Susi and David Monteith at the flight test engineer stations. They backtracked to the end of Runway 15, then turned into a moderate crosswind. Takeoff looked like that of any other Dash 8—except for the green primer paint, the long fuselage and perhaps a shorter ground roll. From their east parking lot vantage point, retired test pilots Bob Fowler and George Neal (with a few first flights of their own to remember) watched with a mixture of pride and envy.

A short climb over the field and the Q400 was off to the Peterborough-Lake Scugog area for a prearranged program with ground control. All the test items went so well that the original flight plan was expanded to two hours. Warner and Hubbard took an additional hour to get the feel of the controls—and give photographer Rick Radell and video operator Alain Girard, keeping pace in the chase plane, a chance to document the event. One more pass over the runway at Downsview and they landed to the cheers of the attending crowd. Warner's comment to the waiting reporters gave the answer everyone wanted to hear: "This is a delightful airplane to fly, just like a Dash 8." Once the initial tests were completed, the "Jock Aitken" flew to the Bombardier Aero-

The Photographic Services Department in 1988 crowded together for an experiment of their own. Back row, from the left, Terry Schwetz, Ron Nunney, manager, Gail George, secretary, Tony Honeywood and Charles Bryant. Front from left, Guy Levesque and Larry Boccioletti. (DH)

George Carere completes the installation of a brushed aluminum motif in the lobby of the new reception area in 1996. With him are those who planned the interior: Helen Trudelle, plant engineering, Julie Hanson, assistant to the president, and Donna Rodrigues, receptionist. (DH)

space Center in Wichita, where it would be joined by three other Q400s in the flight test certification program. The order book at the time of the flight stood at 31 firm and 32 options from six airlines in five countries.

Chipmunk, Beaver and Otter Events

On June 26, 1997, two DHC-1 Chipmunks landed at Downsview to be met by a group of light-plane enthusiasts and historians. The aircraft bore Royal Air Force markings and were on "Northern Venture," a nostalgia trip around the world, sponsored by a number of British organizations. The "Chippie", an RAF primary trainer since 1949, was now being phased out. The two aircraft had departed London on May 20 and had already crossed Russia, the Bering Strait, Alaska and northern Canada. The crews were accorded an official company welcome at Downsview by vice-president and general manager Steve Cavanaugh. Each tour member received a special Chip-

munk coin from the Royal Canadian Mint's aircraft series.

Another celebration of de Havilland's past took place in Victoria, B.C., on the weekend of October 17-19, 1997. "50 Years of a Great Canadian Masterpiece" honoured the DHC-2 Beaver. This trade show and seminar was the brainchild of former Beaver pilot Jack Schofield, now editor of the *West Coast Aviator*. The weekend was sponsored by Bombardier Aerospace and Viking Air Limited—headquarters for Bombardier/de Havilland-approved Beaver and Turbo Bea-

To commemorate the end of the Chipmunk's service in the RAF, a pair of these trainers left London City Airport, England on May 20, 1997 to circumnavigate the globe. This was known as Exercise Northern Venture. On June 26 the Chipmunks were welcomed on a courtesy visit to Downsview. (Kenneth I. Swartz)

The Bombardier Aerospace "Ride for the Heart" cycling team of 1998 after winning the Heart and Stoke Foundation's corporate challenge for the fifth year in a row. Their 1998 total on the June 7 ride was a record-breaking $59,000. On the extreme right is captain Byron Warren, who turned responsibilities for the 1999 ride to Bill Perry, on the extreme left. (Bombardier Aerospace)

Tom Whitfield, present chairman of the de Havilland Employees Sports Club, has been on the DHESC executive for 25 years. The club began in 1957 and all sport activities, whether golf, baseball, soccer, hockey or the children's Christmas party, come under the club's direction. Flight training is another club activity with a Cessna 172 and 150. In 1980, a corner of the cafeteria was organized as a headquarters and sales outlet for company-related items. A membership fee of 50 cents per week is collected through the payroll system for the present 2,100 participants. All business is conducted during lunch breaks and after working hours. Other active organizations in the company through the years include the DH Management Association, the Retirees Association and, of course, the record breaking "Ride for the Heart" cycling team. (Bombardier Aerospace)

ver spares, and Twin Otter wing replacement centre. Each booth displayed its own specialty in supporting de Havilland bushplanes—a growing industry in the West. There were overhaulers for piston and turbine Beavers, and specialists in welding, sheet metal, paint, avionics, upholstery and other specialties. Large "Alaska" doors, cabin extensions, advanced floats, special wingtips, wing vortex generators and even a complete new-concept wing were among the products available for Beaver operators.

Fifteen thousand people gathered on May 30, 1998, to take part in the annual family day and celebrate de Havilland's 70th anniversary—a beautiful day, amusements for the kids, shop tours, the Toronto police motorcycle ride and plenty to eat. (Bombardier Aerospace)

Turbine conversions of the Otter drew much attention. The two organizations holding the lead in this regard are Kenmore of Seattle and Vazar of Bellingham, Washington. Airtech Canada of Peterborough, Ontario, was promoting its 1,000 hp Polish PZL radial engine. Fifteen had been completed for Canadian bush operators. Schofield and his committee provided a feast of new ideas for Beaver owners and operators or just plain Beaver buffs. Five hundred people crowded the hall for the Saturday night banquet.

Mick Saunders and Bill Loverseed

Longtime members of the company were shocked on September 3, 1998, by the sudden death of retired test pilots A.W. "Mick" Saunders (72) and R.E.W "Bill" Loverseed (66) in England. They were involved in worldwide ferry duties and were on a routine test flight of a Dash 7 at the time of the accident. The aircraft, registered in the Cayman Islands, had been stored for several months on the Island of Guernsey.

Saunders, who was a Typhoon pilot during WWII, had joined de Havilland flight test in 1958. He was highly respected for his professionalism in the cockpit, a pleasant personality and a wide range of experience. He had teamed with company pilot Bob Fowler on the first flights of the Buffalo, Twin Otter, Dash 7 and Dash 8. He was director of flight operations from 1983 until his retirement in 1988.

Bill Loverseed spent most of his career in the RAF, was a member of the "Red Arrows" display team for a number of years and leader in 1971. He served in the de Havilland flight test department from 1975 to 1984.

70 Years On

As de Havilland moved toward its 71st year, a new corporate identity was launched to promote the Bombardier name in international markets. This new identity unites all aerospace branches under the Bombardier Aerospace banner. The sprocket symbol in the logo, tracing company history to the snowmobile, remained, but in modified form, giving more emphasis to the Bombardier name and the core businesses: aerospace, recreational products, transportation, services and capital.

A new division, Bombardier International, headed by Pierre Lortie, was created in May 1998 to increase the company's presence in new markets outside Europe and North America. The new president of Bombardier Aerospace Regional Aircraft was Robert Gillespie. His career had begun with the Canadian government, where he was Assistant Deputy Minister, Materiel with the Department of National Defence. He joined Bombardier Aerospace in 1992 as vice-

president strategic planning and business development, where he launched Bombardier's fractional ownership program in North America—Business Jet*Solutions*.

Fractional ownership has since become the fastest growing segment in U.S. corporate aviation. Under this plan a customer can purchase as little as 1/16th ownership in a business aircraft. A certain number of annual hours is established in the contract at a monthly charge along with a fee for hours flown. With Gillespie moving to Toronto, Dennis Keith, who had been with him on the fractional ownership development, became president of Business Jet*Solutions*.

Other Changes

A new organization chart came into effect in Toronto in November 1997, with Alain Dugas as de Havilland's vice-president and general manager of operations. Dugas received a Bachelor of Science degree from Laval University and managed the manufacturing practice of DMR Group, a Canadian consulting firm, before joining Bombardier in 1986. He held several senior management positions in Montreal before moving to Toronto.

On Wednesday, April 1, 1998, de Havilland Canada's first employee, Frank Warren, passed away 70 years to the day from his first employment. Like others of the period he had worked on all plant projects and began the war in charge of Tiger Moth construction. He retired in 1975 and was inducted into the de Havilland Hall of Fame in September 1993.

In May 1998 a major move was made in the Amphibious Aircraft Division, headed by Tom Appleton, to assemble the Canadair CL-415 at the former Canadian Forces complex at North Bay, Ontario. This was done to free up floor space in Montreal for the upcoming CRJ-700. The move to North Bay was to create some 50 new jobs in that city. The 1998-99 fiscal year was brought major sales success to the CL-415 program, with orders for nine aircraft for Ontario and 10 for Greece, with options on five more.

On July 31, 1998 word came from the Bombardier Flight Test Center in Wichita that the Bombardier Global Express had received certification from Transport Canada. Basic price for a Global Express was noted as US$37.5 million; 80 firm orders had been received, and the assembly line at Downsview was in full swing. U.S. certification was received from the Federal Aviation Administration in mid-November, and European Joint Aviation Authorities' certification soon afterwards.

21st Century Products

In keeping with forward planning within Bombardier Aerospace, two major new designs were announced in 1998, one

With the departure of Pierre Lortie for Bombardier International in April 1998, Robert Gillespie (left) was appointed president of Bombardier Aerospace, Regional Aircraft. He joined Bombardier Aerospace in 1992 and in 1995 became president of Business Jet*Solutions* in Dallas. Alain Dugas (right) became vice-president and general manager–operations at de Havilland in the fall of 1997. He joined Bombardier in 1986 and held several management positions before coming to de Havilland. (Bombardier Aerospace)

An artist's computer rendering of the Bombardier Continental business jet, conceived as a new machine with superior performance for light and mid-size bizjet operators, a replacement for aging aircraft and a new offering in the fractional ownership market. (Bombardier Aerospace)

at the top of the regional transportation market, the BRJ-X, and the other a unique entry in the mid-size business jet field.

At the 1998 Farnborough Air Show, Bombardier announced the launch of a new, 90-passenger class regional jet airliner to be known as the BRJ-X. This aircraft is aimed at a market expected to reach 2,500 aircraft in the 90- to 110-seat category over the next two decades. As it had with the announcement of the original Canadair Regional Jet airliner in 1989, Bombardier again signalled that it was prepared to pioneer the creation of a completely new category of aircraft to anticipate its customers' needs. The BRJ-X is scheduled to enter service in 2003.

The Bombardier Continental was introduced at the NBAA convention of 1998 by Laurent Beaudoin, Robert Brown and Michael Graff, Bombardier's president of business aircraft. It was the result of a two-year market study and designed with inputs from a wide range of customers. The specifications were built around an intercontinental range with eight passengers, capable of Mach 0.8 speed and to sell for under $15 million U.S.

As with previous designs, risk-sharing partners and suppliers would be used and the first partner announced was Allied Signal of Phoenix, which will supply the AS907 engines. At press time it was announced that Rockwell Collins of Cedar Rapids, Iowa, would be responsible for the design and supply of the Pro Line 21 avionics systems. The Bombardier Continental received strong early support and is projected to fly in the first quarter of 2001 with type certification in 2002.

Looking Ahead

For one who learned his trade on the shop floor of de Havilland 60 years ago and has maintained a close relationship with the company ever since, there is a tendency to review its history with a critical eye and a sentimental heart. After many years of mixed fortunes, de Havilland now finds itself an integral part of the world's third largest civil aircraft manufacturer, and that must be a matter of pride for all concerned.

Through the decades, the company's focus has constantly evolved, from a branch-plant manufacturer of wooden biplanes in the 1920s and '30s, through the production of trainers and Mosquito bombers and fighters during the war. Following the war, de Havilland found its first great commercial success with a line of homegrown short takeoff and landing (STOL) utility aircraft for use in Canada's north and around the world. In fact, it was the success of the DHC-6 Twin Otter with small airlines in the United States that stimulated the move to de Havilland's current product line—regional airliners. The change to serving airlines began during the Dash 7 era and was irreversible even before the Dash 8 flew. Although the company was careful to ensure the widest customer appeal for the Dash 8 and stress its exceptional short field performance, they were quick to point out it was not a STOL airplane by either design or certification.

While the company's product line evolved, so did its ownership, with the Downsview facility changing hands three times over the past 25 years. The first change arose due to the combined effects of a shrinking aerospace industry in Britain and conflict with the parent company's product development plans, forcing the federal government to intervene to save the company and its jobs. And no review of de Havilland should short-change Boeing's contribution. The outcome may not have been what either side sought when the Seattle-based giant acquired the company, but it left Downsview a better place than when it arrived. Boeing's efforts were based on high standards and good corporate citizenship.

The 1992 entry of Bombardier was not to prove "more of the same." For the first time in its history, de Havilland is now on a sound corporate footing, owned by Canadian corporation with a continuing interest in aerospace. Since acquiring DHC, Bombardier has invested in people, systems and equipment, facilities and training to enable de Havilland to compete and succeed.

Within a few years, Bombardier has launched and delivered the Dash 8 Series 200 and, at the time of writing, the Dash 8 Series Q400 was only a few months away from certification and the start of deliveries. The Dash 8 order book has surpassed the 563 mark established by only two previous de Havilland Canada designs (the Beaver and the Twin Otter), and further plans are under consideration to enhance the product line's appeal well into the future. In addition, de Havilland has completed subcontract assignments for other members of the Bombardier aerospace team and for outside customers. Other Downsview activity has expanded to include the design and manufacture of the wings for the Learjet 45 and final assembly of the Bombardier Global Express ultra long range business aircraft. De Havilland now finds itself involved with a modern product line and diversified operations, certainly the most promising beginning yet.

The year 1998 ended with an unprecedented wave of sales in both rail and aerospace lines for Bombardier Inc.

GLOBAL EXPRESS PARTNERS AND MAJOR SUPPLIERS

Aft fuselage	de Havilland
Mid fuselage	Mitsubishi
Forward fuselage	Short Brothers
Vertical stabilizer	de Havilland
Horizontal stabilizer	Short Brothers
Cockpit	Canadair
Wing	Mitsubishi
Wing devices (flaps/slats)	Sundstrand
Landing Gear	Messier-Dowty International
Powerplant	BMW Rolls Royce
Hydraulics	Parker Bertea Aerospace
Electrical power generation	Lucas
Flight controls	Sextant Avionique
Avionics	Honeywell
Fuel System	Parker Bertea Aerospace
Air management system	Liebherr Aerospace Toulouse
Auxiliary power unit	AlliedSignal Aerospace
Static fatigue tests	Canadair
Body fairings	Short Brothers
Final assembly	de Havilland

This obvious vote of confidence by both industries came at a time of top management reorganization as the corporation prepares for the future.

On December 8, Chairman Laurent Beaudoin announced that he would be succeeded by Robert Brown, Bombardier Aerospace's president and COO. Brown was to become president and CEO of Bombardier Inc., with Beaudoin remaining as executive chairman and president of the executive committee, concentrating on the long-term orientation of the corporation.

Michael Graff, president of Bombardier Aerospace Business Aircraft, was to replace Brown as president and COO of Bombardier Aerospace. These changes took place on February 1, 1999. Along with Pierre Lortie in the new position as head of Bombardier International, and Robert Gillespie, president of Bombardier Aerospace Regional Aircraft, the changes put in place a strong, stable management team to face the 21st century.

Q400 PARTNERS AND MAJOR SUPPLIERS

de Havilland Inc. (Canada) Wing and nose section

Mitsubishi Heavy Industries (Japan) Fuselage, tail and empennage

Aerazur (France) Ice and rain protection

Sundstrand (U.S.A.) APU (optional)

Pratt & Whitney (Canada) Engines

Microtecnica (Italy) Flap system

C & D (U.S.A.) Interior

Allied Signal Aerospace (Canada) Electrical system

Sextant Avionique (France) Avionics

Parker Aerospace (U.S.A.) Fuel system

Menasco Aerospace Ltd. (Canada) Landing gear

FSI (Canada) Flight simulator

Abex (U.S.A.) Hydraulics

Dowty Aerospace Gloucester Ltd. (England) Propellers

Short Brothers (Northern Ireland) Nacelles

Parker Aerospace (U.S.A.) Flight controls	Liebherr (France) Cabin pressure control system	Walter Kidde (U.S.A.) Fire protection & detection	Sierracin (U.S.A.) Windshield
Hamilton Standard (U.S.A.) Environmental control & pneumatic systems	Ratier-Figeac (France) Pilot's control pedestal	Puritan Bennett (U.S.A.) Crew oxygen	Eaton (U.S.A.) Caution & warning panel

Michael Graff, president of Bombardier Aerospace. During the senior management changes of Febuary 1, 1999, when Bob Brown became president and CEO of Bombardier Inc., Michael Graff replaced him as president and COO of Bombardier Aerospace. Graff had joined Bombardier in 1996 from a consulting career in the aerospace and automotive field to become president of Business Aircraft. (Bombardier)

© S. SNIDER '96

A DE HAVILLAND COLOUR GALLERY

(Facing page) Stephen Snider, *Hot Off the Line: The Wooden Wonder*, acrylics, 19 x 28 inches. A newly built Mosquito is test flown near the Downsview plant about 1944. The painting was done for Artflight '96, the National Aviation Museum's annual aviation art show. That year's theme was "Pushing the Envelope." What could be a more fitting subject than the Mosquito!

(Below) These DHC-1 Chipmunks were consecutive on the production line when built for the RCAF in 1956. Forty years later they were together at the North Bay Heritage Festival and Airshow in August 1996. Hank Dielwart of North Bay was flying RCAF-041. Steve Oliver of Arvada, Colorado, was in N260DC – "The Pepsi Skydancer." Andy Cline took the photo from a Cessna 172 piloted by Chris Charland.

(Below) In May 1989, Ralph Leonardo took this view of the Fox Moth that Max Ward donated to the National Aviation Museum at Rockcliffe. It had just been delivered by DHC test pilot George Neal.

(Below) Jerome Labbé flies Slate Falls Airways Beaver C-FDIN near Sioux Lookout on June 19, 1999. He's in formation with Cessna Citation N57MC flown by Randy Brooks of the Kansas City company Massman Construction. (Richard Hulina)

Alaska is home to so many DHC aircraft that it attracts bushplane fans every summer, one of them being Norwegian oil-rig worker Ruben Husberg, who took these two photos. Alaska's rugged Beavers and Otters are ideal for the local terrain, lakes and rivers, and coast. N98EL is typical of many Beavers flown by Alaska tour operators. No. 1416, it originally was USAF L-20 58-7022. (Below) Regal Air of Anchorage is one of Alaska's many DHC operators. In 1998 its fleet included Beaver N9878R and two single-engine Cessnas. N9878R started as L-20 56-398, the 1,135th Beaver. (Ruben Husberg)

(Left) Otter C-GOFF spent its first years with the RCAF, went next to the OPAS, then joined Ignace Airways. Andy Graham caught it in action at home base on July 20, 1995.

(Right) Kachemak Air's Otter at Homer, Alaska, on May 30, 1992. It had begun in 1955 with Taxi Aero de Santander in Colombia. Later it came to Yellowknife to Bob Engle's Northwest Territorial Airways (CF-NTR), then moved to Homer in 1970. (Ruben Husberg)

(Left) This spiffy-looking, DHC-built Tracker visited Downsview on August 20, 1987, to commemorate the 30th anniversary of RCN/CF Tracker service. (Kenneth I. Swartz)

(Left) LN-BNT was one of many Twin Otters used in Norway. The 628th of its type, it was delivered to Widerøe in June 1979. It was shot at Bergen on November 6, 1989. Later it served in Germany as D-IFLY. (Ruben Husberg)

(Below) A wonderful view of Air BC's Twin Otter C-GJAW with a Vancouver backdrop. It had started its career in Mexico in 1970, then came to B.C. in 1978. (Lenn Bayliss)

(Right) Swiss Twin Otter HB-LRT at Laàyoune, Western Sahara, on UN duty, May 1993. Delivered to Air Portugal in 1980, LRT later was in Denmark with Satair, then Farner Air Transport of Basel in 1992. The Twin Otter proved well-suited on the short, dusty Western Sahara strips, where temperatures often reached 40°C. (Kenneth I. Swartz)

(Right) For this early 1970s view of Caribou CF-UYM, the de Havilland photographer used Toronto's new Aeroquay as a backdrop. UYM, Caribou No. 250, served briefly as a company demonstrator, then was sold in the U.S. The Aeroquay was slated for demolition in the early 2000s. (DH)

(Right) Another of Howard Levy's great air-to-air photos of the Pen Turbo Aviation multi-role DHC-4T Caribou. Improved STOL performance, lower long-term costs, turbine reliability, increased payload, single-point refuelling, modern avionics and a new interior were some of its features, compared to the basic Caribou. New roles being marketed for the Turbo Caribou included waterbomber (1,228-U.S. gal., 4,650 liters) and oil slick sprayer.

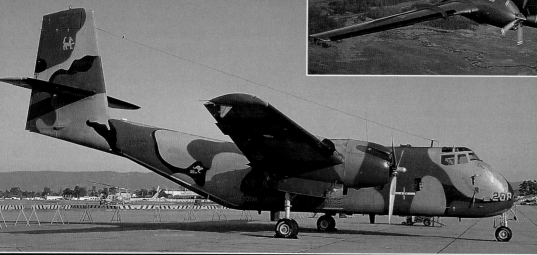

(Left) An RAAF Caribou in a unique camouflage scheme. In 1997-98 Australia's Caribous were busy with drought relief in Papua-New Guinea. (Lenn Bayliss)

(Right) The DHC-5 Trans-porter makes a STOL ap-proach during training at North Bay on May 30, 1980. (Dave Thompson)

LN-WFG, one of nine Norwegian Dash 7s, was at Sola, Norway, in May 1985. Later, it flew in Egypt with National Aviation. (Ruben Husberg)

(Left) Dash 7 No. 54 went to Brymon Airways of Plymouth, England, in August 1981, initially christened "City of London." Brymon's Dash 7s served commuter destinations, including London STOLport, but also supported North Sea oil operations. (Andy Clancey)

A City Express Dash 7, cargo door agape, turns around at Dorval on November 9, 1988, while an Air Ontario Dash 8-100 waits. This Dash 7 began as Wardair's "Don Braun." Most recently it was in the U.S. as N273EP. (Kenneth I. Swartz)

(Right) A Contactair Dash 8-100 at Copenhagen on June 3, 1988. It later flew with Lufthansa CityLine, but in 1993 was sold to Eastern Australia Airlines as VH-TQN. (Ruben Husberg)

(Right) Dash 8-100 V2-LCZ of the Caribbean operator LIAT on February 11, 1992. This was the 48th Dash 8. (Michael Magnusson)

(Left) This Air Maldives Series 100 was at Field Aviation in Calgary for painting in November 1996. (Kenneth I. Swartz)

(Left) A United Express Dash 8-200 taxis at Denver's new airport on January 28, 1997. (Kenneth I. Swartz)

(Below) Widerøe Dash 8-300 LN-WFH at Stavanger on April 11, 1997. (Ruben Husberg)

GLOSSARY

AC Air Canada

A/C Air commodore

ADC Aircraft Disposal Co., also Airdisco

AFB Air force base

AIAC Aerospace Industries Association of Canada

A/M Air marshal

Airco Aircraft Manufacturing Co.

ATR Avions de Transport Regional

A/V/M Air vice marshal

BAGNA Bombardier Aerospace Group North America

BARA Bombardier Aerospace Regional Aircraft

BES Bombardier Engineering System

bhp Brake horse power

BMP Bombardier Manufacturing Process

BRAD Bombardier Regional Aircraft Division

CAB Civil Aeronautics Board

CAF Canadian Armed Forces

CAHS Canadian Aviation Historical Society

CAR Civil Air Regulations

CASI Canadian Aeronautics and Space Institute

CATIA Computer Aided Three Dimension Interactive Application

CBAA Canadian Business Aircraft Association

CDIC Canadian Development Investment Corporation

CF Canadian Forces

CFB Canadian Forces Base

CL Canadair Limited

Cmdr Commander

compass swing Pointing an aircraft to known magnetic headings on the ground to apply compensating deviation adjustments to the compass.

DH de Havilland

DHC de Havilland Canada

DHP de Havilland Proposal

DIPP Defence Industry Productivity Program

DITC Department of Industry, Trade & Commerce

DME Distance measuring equipment

DRB Defence Research Board

EDC Export Development Corporation

FAR Federal Air Regulations

F/L Flight lieutenant

F/O Flying officer

FSgt Flight sergeant

glassy water A condition when the water surface is dead calm, making it difficult for a pilot to judge height

G/C Group captain

hp Horsepower

HQ Headquarters

ICAO International Civil Aviation Organization

IRAN Inspect and Repair as Necessary

JFK John F. Kennedy International Airport

LAPES Low altitude parachute extraction system

LCol Lieutenant colonel

Lofting Laying out shop working drawings in full scale.

MAP Ministry of Aircraft Production

MHI Mitsubishi Heavy Industries

monocoque Fuselage construction that relies on the outer shell to carry part of the structural loads.

NACA National Advisory Committee on Aeronautics

NAE National Aeronautical Establishment

NASA National Aeronautics and Space Administration

NVS Noise and Vibration Suppression system

NYC New York City

OBE Order of the British Empire

OPAS Ontario Provincial Air Service

P&W Pratt & Whitney

P&WC Pratt & Whitney Canada

P/O Pilot officer

RAF Royal Air Force

RAFTC Royal Air Force Transport Command

RCAF Royal Canadian Air Force

RCNVR Royal Canadian Navy Volunteer Reserve

RFC Royal Flying Corps

RCN Royal Canadian Navy

RNoAF Royal Norwegian Air Force

SALS Separate Access Landing System

Sgt Sergeant

shp Shaft horsepower

S/L Squadron leader

SPAR Special Products and Applied Research

STEM Storable Extendable Tubular Member

STOL Short takeoff and landing

TC Transport Canada

TTC Toronto Transit Commission

UN United Nations

VTOL Vertical takeoff and landing

W/C Wing commander

WTO World Trade Organization

WWI World War I

WWII World War II

APPENDICES

Recognition at de Havilland

Two C.D. Howe Award winners: P.C Garratt, 1966 (left) and Laurent Beaudoin, 1995.

Trans-Canada McKee Trophy

Endowed by Capt. J.D. McKee, to the Canadian whose achievements were the most outstanding during the year in the promotion of aviation.

W. M. Archibald	1935
P.Y. Davoud	1985
C.H. Dickins	1928
D.C. Fairbanks	1976
R.H. Fowler	1974
P.C. Garratt	1951, 1996
R.T. Heaslip	1956
G.A. Neal	1989
D.H. Rogers	1983

J.A.D. McCurdy Award

Introduced in 1954 to commemorate the many engineering contributions made by John A.D. McCurdy, for outstanding achievement in the science of engineering relating to aeronautics and space research.

F.H. Buller	1971
M.C.W. Davy	1988
B. Eggleston	1998
R.D. Hiscocks	1954
G.R. Jackson	1995
J. Thompson	1991
J.P. Uffen	1982
D.C. Whittley	1973

C.D. Howe Award

Established by the CASI in honour of the Right Honourable C.D. Howe in achievement, planning and policy-making related to aeronautical and space activities.

L. Beaudoin	1995
P.C. Garratt	1966

F.H. (Casey) Baldwin Award

Commemorates this early Canadian pilot, for the best article published in the CASI Journal in the preceding year.

B. Eggleston	1977
L.K. John & G.A. Terwissen	1982
D.C. Whittley	1968

Order of Canada

L. Beaudoin	1991
W.B. Boggs	1988
R.W. Bradford	1990
C.H. Dickins	1968
R.H. Fowler	1975

Canada's Aviation Hall of Fame

Documents, preserves and publicizes those persons whose contributions to aviation have been a benefit to the nation.

W.M. Archibald	1973
L. Beaudoin	1998
R.W. Bradford	1995
F.H. Buller	1998
C.H. Dickins	1973
R.H. Fowler	1979
P.C. Garratt	1973
R.T. Heaslip	1973
R.D. Hiscocks	1997
F.W. Hotson	1997
G.A. Neal	1994
D.H. Rogers	1997
F. Russell	1993

Romeo Vachon Award

Introduced in 1969 by the CASI in memory of the early Quebec pilot, for initiative and practical skills in solving problems related to aviation in Canada.

P.H. Bootsma	1987

Gordon R. McGregor Trophy

In memory of former Air Canada president, awarded by the RCAF Association for outstanding contribution to Air Transport.

W. Warner	1989

The de Havilland Canada Hall of Fame

To recognize outstanding achievements by de Havilland employees whose long-term association with the company and unselfish contributions have been a major benefit to de Havilland Canada and the world of aviation.

Members (to December 1998)

Russell Bannock
George Blanchard
Russ Borrett
Fred Buller

Bill Burlison
Bill Calder
Lee Capreol
Clenell "Punch" Dickins
Sir Geoffrey de Havilland
Phil Garratt
Dick Hiscocks
Fred Hotson
Robert Loader
Betty McNichol (Potts)
George Mickleborough
Lee Murray

George Neal
Geoffrey O'Brian
Harry Proctor
Arthur Robins
Bill Rouse
Charles Smith
Francis St. Barbe
Frank Trethewey
Ab Warren
Frank Warren

Three-views of de Havilland Canada Aircraft

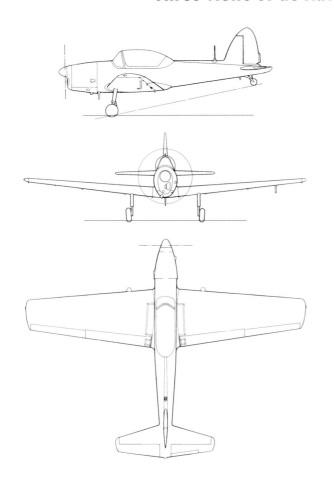

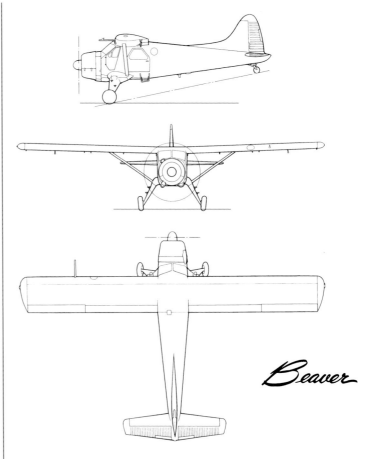

Beaver

DHC-1 CHIPMUNK

Powerplant   Gipsy Major 1C reciprocating BHP 140;
Propeller   Fixed pitch wood or metal

External Dimensions

Wing span	34 ft. 4 in.	10.4 m
Length overall	25 ft. 5 in.	7.75 m
Height over tail	7 ft. 0 in.	2.13 m
Tailpane span	11 ft. 11 in.	3.63 m
Wheel track	8 ft. 11 in.	2.7 m
Wheel base	17 ft. 20 in.	5.5 m
Wing area	172.5 sq. ft.	16.03 sq. m
Horizontal tail	31 sq. ft.	2.88 sq. m
Vertical tail	12.7 sq. ft.	1.18 sq. m

Weights

Basic	1,184 lb.	537 kg
Max. takeoff	1,930 lb.	875 kg
Max. landing	1,930 lb.	895 kg

Performance

Max. speed S/L	140 mph	225 km/h
Max. cruise (5000 ft.)	124 mph	200 km/h
Stalling speed	52 mph	83 km/h
Rate of climb S/L	900 ft./min.	4.57 m/sec
Climb speed	80 mph	128 km/h
Glide speed	70 mph	110 km/h
Service ceiling	17,200 ft.	5,200 m
Takeoff to 50 ft.	870 ft.	265 m
Landing over 50 ft.	930 ft.	284 m
Range	485 mi	295 km

DHC-2 BEAVER

Powerplant   P&W R985 Wasp Junior; BHP 450,
Propeller   Hamilton Standard C/S, 2-bladed.

Exertnal Dimensions

Wing span	48 ft. 0 in.	14.6 m
Length overall	30 ft. 4 in.	9.2 m
Height over tail	9 ft. 0 in.	2.17 m
Tailplane span	15 ft. 10 in.	4.83 m
Wheel track	10 ft. 2 in.	3.1 m
Wheel base	22 ft. 9 in.	6.94 m
Wing area	250 sq. ft.	23 sq. m
Horizontal tail	100 sq. ft.	9.3 sq. m
Vertical tail	110 sq. ft.	10.2 sq. m

Weights

Basic	3,000 lb.	1,360 kg
Max. takeoff	5,100 lb.	2,313 kg
Max. landing	5,100 lb.	2,313 kg
Max. payload (470 mi) 1,350 lb.	612 kg	

Performance

Max. cruise S/L	135 mph	217 km/h
Stalling speed	60 mph	97 km/h
Rate of climb S/L	1,020 ft./min.	518 m/min.
Service ceiling	18,000 ft.	5,490 m
Takeoff run	560 ft.	170 m
Takeoff run to 50 ft.	1,015 ft.	310 m
Landing run	500 ft.	152 m
Landing run from 50 ft.	1,000 ft.	305 m
Payload (470 mi)	1,350 lb.	612 kg
Range max payload	483 sm	177 nm

Internal Dimensions

Cabin length	9 ft. 0 in.	2.7 m
Dabin width	4 ft. 0 in.	1.22 m
Height	4 ft. 3 in.	1.3 m
Floor area	31.5 sq. ft.	2.9 cu. m

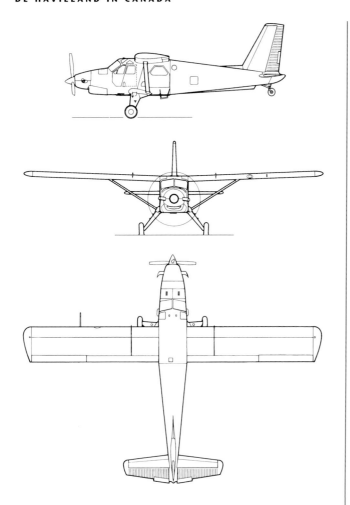

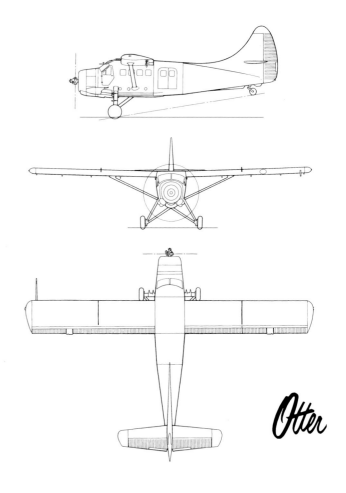

Otter

DHC-2 TURBO BEAVER 9 (Landplane)

Powerplant   P&W PT6A-20 (turboprop); SHP 550
Propeller   Hartzell, 3-bladed, full feather and reverse.

External Dimensions

Wing span	48 ft. 0 in.	14.64 m
Length overall	35 ft. 3 in.	10.75 m
Height over tail	11 ft. 0 in.	3.35 m
Tailplane span	15 ft. 10 in.	4.82 m
Wheel track	10 ft. 2 in.	3.10 m
Wheel base	22 ft. 9 in.	6.94 m
Wing area	250 sq. ft.	23.23 sq. m
Horizontal tail area	32.5 sq. ft.	3 sq. m
Vertical tail area	48.4 sq. ft.	4.5 sq. m

Weights

Basic	2,760 lb.	1,252 kg
Max. takeoff	5.370 lb.	2,435 kg
Max. landing	5,100 lb.	2,313 kg

Performance (landplane)

Max. cruise S/L	157 mph	252 km/h
Stalling speed	60 mph	97 km/h
Rage of climb S/L	1,185 ft./min.	361 m/min.
Service ceiling	20,500 ft.	6,250 m
Takeoff run	510 ft.	155 m
Takeoff run to 50 ft.	920 ft.	280 m
Landing run	380 ft.	116 m
Land run from 50 ft..	870 ft.	265 m
Range	260 mi	418 km

Internal Dimensions

Cabin length	11 ft. 6 in.	3.50 m
Cabin width	4 ft. 0 in.	1.22 m
Height	4 ft. 3 in.	1.30 m
Floor area	40.5 sq. ft.	3.76 sq. m
Volume	141 cu. ft.	5.0 cu. m

DHC-3 OTTER (Landplane)

Powerplant   P&W R1340 Wasp S1H1 reciprocating, BHP 600
Propeller   Hamilton Standard hydromatic, 3-bladed.

External Dimensions

Wing span	58 ft. 0 in.	17.68 m
Length overall	41 ft. 10 in.	12.80 m
Height over tail	12 ft. 7 in.	3.83 m
Tailplane span	21 ft. 2 in.	6.46 m
Wheel track	11 ft. 2 in.	3.42 m
Wheel base	27 ft. 10 in.	8.49 m
Wing area	375 sq. ft.	34.84 sq. m
Horizontal tail area	60 sq. ft.	5.57 sq. m
Vertical tail area	85 sq. ft.	7.89 sq. m

Weights

Basic	4,431 lb.	2,010 kg
Max. takeoff	8,000lb	3,629 kg
Max. landing	8,000 lb.	3.629 kg

Performance (landplane)

Max. cruise S/L	132 mph	212 km/h
Stalling speed	58 mph	93 km/h
Rage of climb	850 ft./min.	259 m/min.
Service ceiling	18,500 ft.	5,730 m
Takeoff run	630 ft.	192 m
Landing run from 50 ft.	880 ft.	268 m
Range (at 2,100 lb.. 953 kg)	875 mi	1,410 km

Internal Dimensions

Cabin length	16 ft. 5 in.	5.0 m
Cabin width	5 ft. 2 in.	2.58 m
Height	4 ft. 11 in.	1.50 m
Floor area	79 sq. ft.	7.34 sq. m
Volume	345 cu. ft.	9.77 cu. m

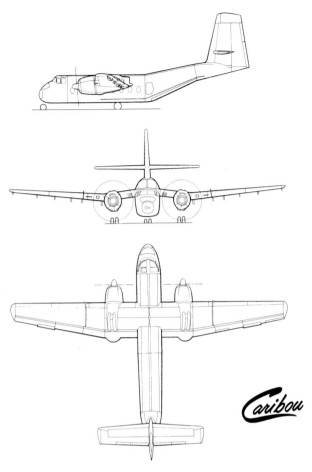

Caribou

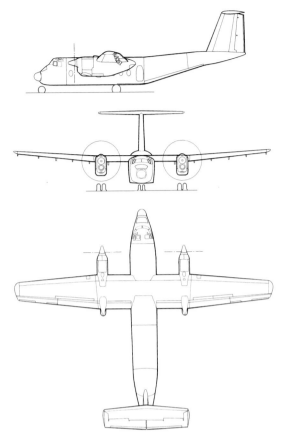

DHC-4 Caribou

Powerplant 2 x P&W R-2000 7M2 reciprocating, BHP 1450
Propellers Hamilton Standard, 3-bladed, full feathering and reverse.

External Dimensions

Wing span	95 ft. 7.5 in.	29.15 m
Length overall	72 ft. 7 in.	22.12 m
Height over tail	31 ft. 9 in.	9.67 m
Tailplane span	36 ft. 0 in.	10.97 m
Wheel track	23 ft. 1.5 in.	7.05 m
Wheel base	25 ft. 8 in.	8.08 m
Wing area	912 sq. ft.	84.7 sq. m
Horizontal tail area	230 sq. ft.	32.4 sq. m
Vertical tail area	211 sq. ft.	20 sq. m

Weights

Basic	17,620 lb.	7,997 kg
Max. takeoff	28,500 lb.	12,928 kg
Max. landing	28.500 lb.	12,928 kg
Max. payload	5,417 lb.	2,457 kg
Zero fuel weight	27,000 lb.	13,247 kg

Performance

Max. cruise (7,500 ft.)	180 mph	291 km/h
Stalling speed	68 mph	109 km/h
Rate of climb (2 eng)	1,355 fpm	6.9 m/sec
Rate of climb (1 eng)	235 fmp	1.2 m/sec
Service ceiling (2 eng)	24,800 ft.	7,559 m
Service ceiling (1eng)	8.800 ft.	2,682 m
Takeoff length	3,355 ft.	1,023 m
Landing length	2,960 ft.	902 m
Payload 600 nm	6,916 lb.	3,137 kg
Range	1,210 nm	2,242 km

Internal Dimensions

Cabin length	28 ft. 9 in.	8.76 m
Cabin width	87 in.	221 cm
Height	75 in.	190 .5 cm
Floor area	176 sq. ft.	16 sq. m
Volume	1,150 cu. ft.	107 sq. m
Cabin doors, 2 x	4 ft. 7 in. x 2 ft. 6 in.	1.4 x 0.76 m
Rear door	6 ft. 2 in. x 6 ft. 1.5 in.	1.90 m x 1.86 m

DHC-5D BUFFALO

Powerplant 2 x GE CT64-820-4 turboprop, 3,133 shaft horsepower
Propellers Hamilton Standard 63E60-25, 3-bladed, feathering & reverse.

External Dimensions

Wing span	96 ft. 0 in.	29.26 m
Length overall	79 ft. 0 in.	24 m
Height over tail	28 ft. 8 in.	8.76m
Tailplane span	32 ft. 0in.	10 m
Wheel track	30 ft. 6 in.	9.3m
Wheel base	27 ft. 0 in.	87.8m
Wing area (total)	945 sq. ft.	87.8 sq. m
Horizontal tail	152 sq. ft.	14 sq. m
Vertical tail	233 sq. ft.	22 sq. m

Weights

Basic O.W.E	25,052 lb	11,362 kg
Maximum takeoff	49,200 lb.	22,316 kg
Maximum landing	46,900 lb.	21,273 kg
Maximum payload	18,000 lb.	8,164 kg
Zero fuel weight	43,500 lb.	19,731 kg

Performance

Maximum cruise (10,000 ft.)	261 mph	420 km/h
Stalling speed	82 mph	130 km/h
Rate of climb, S/L 2 engines	1820 ft./min.	555 m/min.
Rate of climb, S/L one engine	370 ft./min.	113 m/min.
Service ceiling, 2 engines	25,000 ft.	7,620 m
Service ceiling, 1 engine	13,900 ft.	4,235 m
Takeoff run	2,300 ft.	701m
Takeoff to 50 ft.	2,875 ft.	7,010 m
Landing run	850 ft.	259 m
Landing from 50 ft.	2,010 ft.	613 m
Payload/range		
690 mi (1,110 km)	18,000 lb.	8,165 kg
1150 mi (1,851 km)	15,000 lb.	6,804 kg
2,000 mi (3,218 km)	12,000 lb.	5,443 kg

Internal Dimensions

Cabin length	31 ft. 5 in.	9.6 m
Cabin width	8 ft. 9 in.	2.7 m
Max height	6 ft. 10 in.	2.08 m
Floor area	243.5 sq. ft.	22.63 sq. m
Rear loading	20 ft. 9 in. x 7 ft. 8 in.	6.3 m x 2.3 m

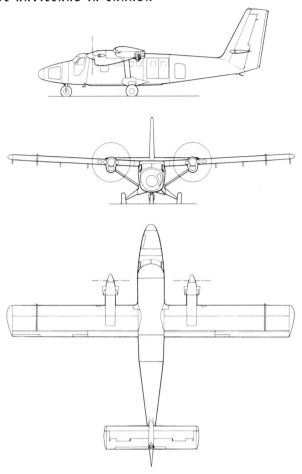

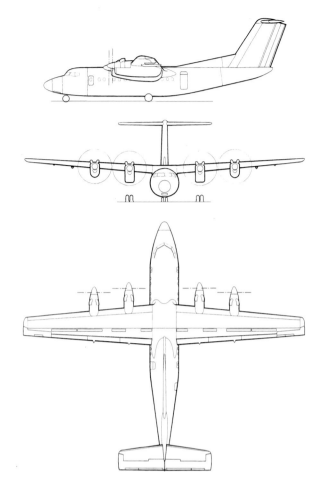

DHC-6 TWIN OTTER (Series 300 Landplane)

Propulsion   2 x P&W PT6A-27 (turboprop), 620 SHP
Propellers   Hartzell, 3-bladed, full-feathering, reverse.

External Dimensions

Wing span	65 ft. 0 in.	19.81 m
Length overall	51 ft. 9 in.	15.77 m
Height over tail	19 ft. 6 in.	5.94 m
Tailplane span	20 ft. 8 9 in.	6.30 m
Wheel track	12 ft. 2 in.	3.71 m
Wheelbase	14 ft. 10.5 in.	4.53 m
Wing area (total)	420 sq. ft.	39 sq. m
Flap area	112.2 sq. ft.	10.42 sq. m
Tailplane area	100 sq. ft.	9.29 sq. m
Elevator area	35 sq. ft.	3.25 sq. m

Weight

Basic operational	7,407 lb.	3,320 kg
Max. takeoff	12,500 lb.	5,670 kg
Max. landing	12,300 lb.	5,579 kg

Performance (landplane)

Max. speed (sea level)	196 mph	315 km/h
Max. cruise (10,000 ft.)	210 mph	337 km/h
Stalling speed	67 mph	107 km/h
Rate of climb (2 eng,)	1,600 ft./min.	488 m/min.
Service ceiling (2 eng.)	26,700 ft.	8,140 m
Takeoff run	860 ft.	262 m
Takeoff dist.50 ft. (SFAR23)	1,500 ft.	457 m
Landing run	950 ft.	33 m
Landing from 50 ft. (SFAR23)	1,500 ft.	457 m
Accelerated-stop (SFAR23)	2,280 ft.	695 m
Range max. payload	830 miles	1,328 km

Internal Dimensions, 20 passengers

Cabin length	18 ft. 6 in.	5.64 m
Max. Width	5 ft. 3.5 in.	1.61 m
Max. Height	4 ft. 11 in.	1.50 m
Floor area	80.2 sq. ft.	7.45 sq. m
Volume	384 cu. ft.	10.87 cu. m
Cabin door (L)	4 ft. 2 in. x 2 ft. 6 in.	1.27 m x .76 m
Total baggage area	126 cu. ft.	3.57 cu. m

DHC-7 DASH 7-100

Powerplants   4 x P&W PT6A-50 turboprop;
Propellers   4 x Hamilton Standard, 4 bladed, full feathering & reverse.

External Dimensions

Wing span	93 ft.	28.35 m
Length overall	80 ft. 8 in.	24.58 m
Height over tail	26 ft. 2 in.	7.98 m
Tailplane span	31 ft.	9.45 m
Wheel track	23 ft. 6 in.	7.16 m
Wheel base	27 ft. 6 in.	8.38 m
Wing area (total)	860 sq. ft.	70.90 sq. m
Horizontal tail area	170 sq. ft.	15.79 sq. m
Vertical tail area	217 sq. ft.	20.16 sq. m

Weights

Basic	27,700 lb.	12,542 kg
Maximum takeoff	44,000 lb.	19,958 kg
Maximum landing	42,000 lb.	19,051 kg
Maximum payload	11,300 lb.	5,148 kg
Zero fuel weight	39,000 lb.	17,690 kg

Performance

Maximum cruise (15,000 ft.)	281 mph	452 km/h
Stalling speed	76 mph	122 km/h
Rate of climb 4 eng.	1,310 ft./min.	399 m/min.
Rate of climb 3 eng.	760 ft./min.	231 m/min.
Service ceiling 4 eng.	22,200 ft.	6,770 m
Takeoff field length	2,260 ft.	770 m
Land. Field length	1,950 ft.	665 m
Payload (800 miles)	9,400 lb.	4,264 kg
Range (1335 miles)	6,400 lb.	2,903 kg

Internal Dimensions 50 passengers

Cabin length	39 ft. 6 in.	12.04 m
Cabin width	8 ft. 6 in.	2.6 m
Max. height	6 ft. 4 in.	2 m
Floor area	246.7 sq. ft.	23 sq. m
Volume	1910 cu. ft.	54 cu. m
Cabin door (LH)	5 ft. 10 in.	1.78 m
	x 2 ft. 6 in.	x .76 m
Baggage area	240 cu. ft.	6.80 cu. m

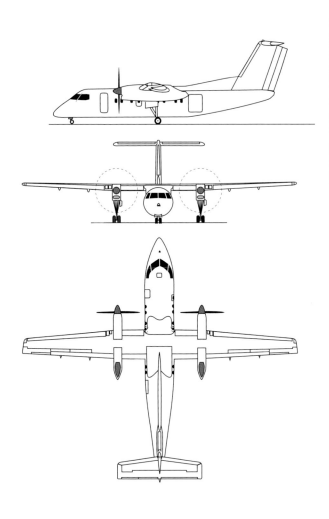

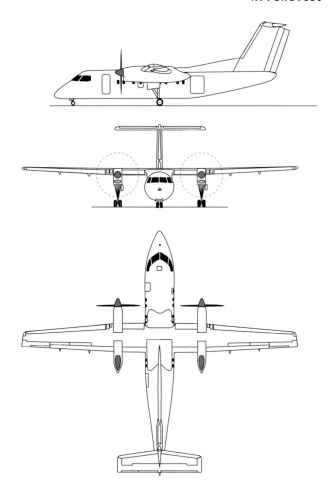

DHC-8 Series-100

Powerplants   2 x P&W PW120A turboprop engines
Propellers   Hamilton Standard 14SF-7, 4-bladed 13 ft. (3.96m)

External Dimensions

Wing span	85 ft. 0 in.	25.92 m
Length overall	73 ft. 0 in.	22.25 m
Height over tail	24 ft. 7 in.	7.49 m
Tailplane span	26 ft. 0 in.	7.93 m
Wheel track	25 ft. 10 in.	7.87 m
Wheel base	26 ft. 1 in.	7.95 m
Wing area	585 sq. ft.	54.3 sq. m
Horizontal tail area	150 sq. ft.	13.9 sq. m
Vertical tail area	152 sq. ft.	14.1 sq. m

Weights

Max. takeoff	34,500 lb.	15,649 kg
Max. landing	33,900 lb.	15,377 kg
Zero fuel weight	31,000 lb.	14,061 kg
Operational wt empty	22,600 lb.	10,251 kg

Performance ISA

Max. cruise (15,000 ft.) TAS	305 mph	491 km/h
Stalling speed	83 mph	133 km/h
Rate of climb (2 eng)	2,070 ft./min.	630 m/min.
Rate of climb (1 eng)	530 ft./min.	460 m/min.
Service ceiling (2eng)	25,000 ft.	7,620 m
Service ceiling (1eng)	16,000 ft.	4,876 m
T/O field length	2,750 ft.	838 m
Land field length	2,870 ft.	875 m

Cabin Data – 37 passengers

Length	30 ft.	9.1 m
Width	8 ft. 2 in.	2.5 m
Height	6 ft. 4.5 in.	1.04 m

DHC-8 DASH 8-200

Powerplants   2 x Pratt & Whitney 123 B turboprop engines driving
Propellers   Hamilton Standard 14SF-23, 4-bladed, 13 ft. (3.96 m)

External Dimensions

Wing span	8.5 ft. 0 in.	25.91 m
Length overall	73 ft. 0 in.	22.25 m
Height over tail	24 ft. 7 in.	7.49 m
Tailplane span	26 ft. 0 in.	7.93 m
Wheel track	25 ft. 10 in.	7.87 m
Wheel base	26 ft. 1 in.	7.95 m
Wing area	585 sq. ft.	54.3 sq. m
Horizontal tail area	150 sq. ft.	13.9 sq. m
Vertical tail area	152 sq. ft.	14.1 sq. m

Weights

Max. takeoff	36,300 lb.	16,466 kg
Max. landing	33,900 lb.	15,377 kg
Max. zero fuel	32,000 lb.	14,515 kg
Operational empty	22,930 lb.	10,401 kg

Performance (Gross Weight & ISA)

Max. cruise (15,000 ft.) TAS	305 mph	491 km/h
Rate of climb (2 eng)	1,560 ft./min.	475 m/min.
Rate of climb (1 eng)	450 ft./min.	137 m/min.
Service ceiling (2 eng)	25,000 ft.	7,620 m
Service ceiling (1 eng)	15,000 ft.	4,575 m
Takeoff field length	3,090 ft.	042 m
Landing field length	2,980 ft.	908 m
Range	944 miles	1,519 km

Cabin Data (37 Passengers)

Length	30 ft.	9.1 m
Width	8 ft. 2 in.	2.5 m
Height	6 ft. 4.5 in.	1.94 m

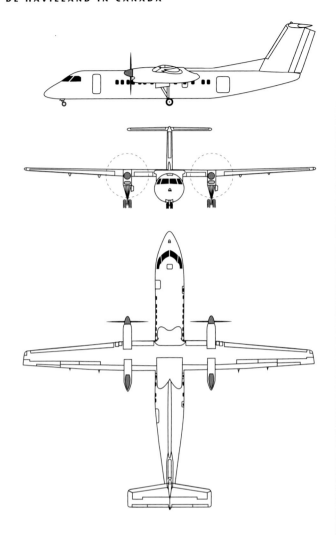

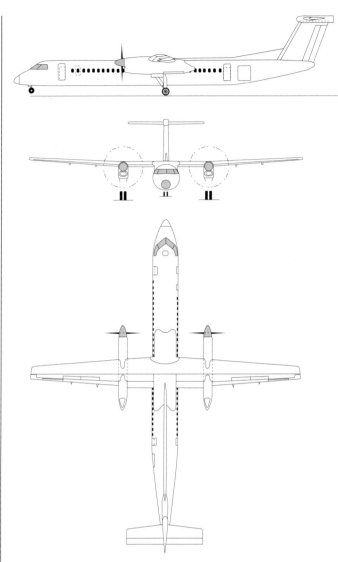

DHC-8; DASH 8-300

Powerplants   2 x Pratt & Whitney PW123 series turboprop engines
Propellers   Hamilton Standard 14SF-23, 4-bladed, 13 ft. (3.96 m) diameter

External Dimensions

Wing span	90 ft. o in.	27.43 m
Length overall	84 ft. 3 in.	25.68 m
Height over tail	24 ft. 7 in.	7.49 m
Tailplane span	26 ft. 0 in.	7.93 m
Wheel track	25 ft. 10 in.	7.87 m
Wheel base	32 ft. 10 in.	10.01 m
Wing area	605 sq. ft.	56.1 sq. m
Horizontal tail area	150sq. ft.	13.9 sq. m
Vertical tail area	152 sq. ft.	14.1 sq. m

Weights

Max. takeoff	41,000 lb.	18,640 kg
Max. landing	40,000 lb.	18,140 kg
Max. zero fuel	37,200 lb.	16,870 kg
Operational empty	25,814 lb.	11,709 kg
Max. payload	11,386 lb.	5,165 kg

Performance ISA – Gross Weight

Max. cruise (15,000 ft.) TAS	330 mph	532 km/h
Rate of climb (2 eng)	1,800 fy/min.	549 m/min.
Rage of climb (1 eng)	450 ft./min.	137 m/min.
Service ceiling (2 eng)	25,000 ft.	7,620 m
Service ceiling (1 eng)	13,500 ft.	4,115 m
Takeoff field length	3,035 ft.	925 m
Landing field length	3,250 ft.	991 m
Range	955 miles	1,538 km

Cabin Data – 50 to 56 pass

Length	41 ft. 6 in.	12.6 m
Width	8 ft. 2 in.	2.5 m
Height	6 ft. 4.5 in.	1.94 m

DHC-8 Dash-8 400

Powerplants   2 x Pratt & Whitney PW150A, 4830 shp turboprop engines
Propellers   Dowty R408, 6-bladed, 13 ft. 6 in. (4.11 m) diameter

External Dimensions

Wing span	93 ft. 3 in.	28.42 m
Length overall	107 ft. 9 in.	32.83 m
Height over tail	25 ft. 5 in.	8.34 m
Tailplane span	30 ft. 5 in.	9.27 m
Wheel track	28 ft. 10 in.	8.8 m
Wheel base	45 ft. 9 in.	13.94 m
Wing area	679 sq. ft.	63.8 sq. m
Horizontal tail area	180 sq. ft.	16.72 sq. m
Vertical tail area	152 sq. ft.	14.1 sq. m

Weight

Max. takeoff	60,250 lb.	27,329 kg
Max. landing	59,750 lb.	27,102 kg
Max. zero fuel	53,750 lb.	24,381 kg
Operat. wt. empty	36,458 lb.	16,537 kg
Max. payload	27,292 lb.	7,844 kg

Performance (ISA – Gross Weight)

Max. cruise (15,000 ft.) TAS	403 mph	649 km/h
Takeoff field length	4,050 ft.	1,235 m
Landing field length	4,215 ft.	1,285 m
Range	1,296 nm	2,401 km

Cabin Data

Length	61 ft. 8 in.	18.8 m
Height	6 ft. 5 in.	1.95 m
Width	98 in.	2.49 m

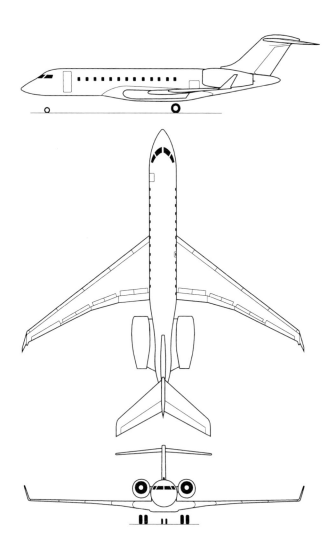

Bombardier Global Express

Powerplants   2 x BMW Rolls-Royce, BR710-48-C2 turbofans, takeoff rating
14,750 lb. (66,1 kN) thrust at ISA +20°C

Crew 2-4, passengers 8-19

External Dimensions

Wing span	94 ft. 0 in.	28.6 m
Length overall	99 ft. 5 in.	30.3 m
Height overall	24 ft. 10 in.	7.57 m
Tailplane span	31 ft. 9 in.	9.68 m
Wheel track	13 ft. 8 in.	4.17 m
Wheel base	41 ft. 11 in.	12.78 m
Wing area (basic)	1,022 sq. ft.	94.94 m
Fuselage max dia.	8 ft. 10 in.	2.68 m

Weight

Basic operational	48,800 lb.	22,135 kg
Maximum takeoff	93,500 lb.	42,411 kg
Maximum landing	78,600 lb.	35,652 kg
Zero fuel weight	56,000 lb.	25,401 kg
Max fuel weight	43,350 lb.	19,663 kg
Max payload	7,200 lb.	3.266 kg

Performance

Maximum cruise	Mach 0.88, 581 mph	935 km/h
Normal cruise	Mach 0.85, 562 mph	904 km/h
Long-range cruise	Mach 0.80, 528 mph	850 km/h
Max. op. altitude	51,000 ft.	15,545 m
Range	7,480 sm, 6,500 nm	12,038 km

Cabin data

Length	48 ft. 4 in.	14.74 m
Height	6ft. 3 in.	1.91 m
Width (centre line)	8 ft. 2 in.	2.49 m
Floor area	335 sq. ft.	31.12 sq m
Volume	2,140 cu ft.	60.60 cu m

Company Logos Through the Years

The DH logo that began with the parent company in England flourished in Canada. The original was designed by Leonard Bridgeman, editor of *Jane's All the World's Aircraft*. He was reputed to have received a gold watch for his efforts.

The original design by Leonard Bridgeman which also formed a decal used on Moth interplane struts.

Another combination of the familiar DH seen on wheel hub covers of the early Moth series.

The original Moth logo was combined with a maple leaf and used extensively during the pre-war period.

The wartime logo using the Mosquito as the aircraft symbol.

The last DH Canada logo saw wide use even after the company moved to government hands.

A modified version of the original as used during the Beaver and Otter period.

When de Havilland became a subsidiary of the Boeing Company, new distinctive letter styles were used.

Bombardier ownership brought a new logo with the famous sprocket symbol reflecting the company's snowmobile history.

The worldwide expansion of Bombardier called for a new logo reflecting a united front in their growing involvement in aerospace.

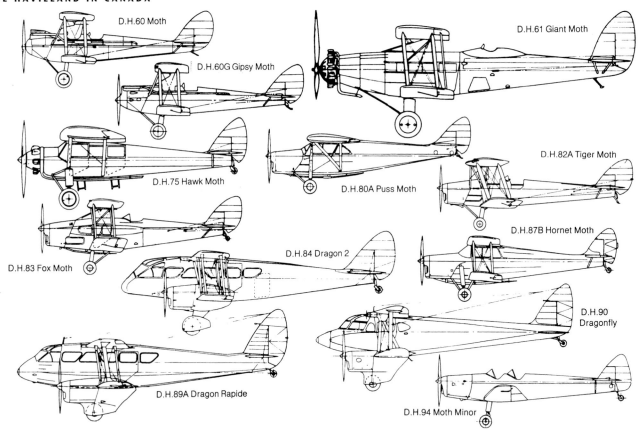

D.H.60 Moth

D.H.61 Giant Moth

D.H.60G Gipsy Moth

D.H.82A Tiger Moth

D.H.75 Hawk Moth

D.H.80A Puss Moth

D.H.87B Hornet Moth

D.H.83 Fox Moth

D.H.84 Dragon 2

D.H.90 Dragonfly

D.H.89A Dragon Rapide

D.H.94 Moth Minor

DH England Designs Imported to Canada before World War II

Designation	Name	First Imported	Engine	BHP	Gross Wt. lb.	Total
D.H.4	D.H.Four	1917	R-R Eagle VIII	325	3500	12
D.H.9A	D.H.NineA	1920	Liberty 12	400	5000	12
D.H.60 & 60X	Cirrus Moth	1926	ADC Cirrus I, II & III	85 & 90	1550	100
D.H.60	Genet Moth	1928	A-S Genet	75	1550	2
D.H.60G	Gipsy Moth	1928	D.H. Gipsy I	100	1750	15
D.H.60M	Gipsy Moth	1934	D.H. Gipsy I & II	100 & 120	1750	202
D.H.60T(spl)	Tiger Moth	1931	D.H. Gipsy III	120	1750	1
D.H.61	Giant Moth	1928	Bristol Jupiter	465	7000	3
D.H.75	Hawk Moth	1930	A-S Lynx	247	3500	3
D.H.80A	Puss Moth	1930	D.H. Gipsy III	120	2050	34
D.H.82A	Tiger Moth	1935	D.H. Gipsy Major	130	1825	5
D.H.83	Fox Moth	1933	D.H. Gipsy Major	130	2100	8
D.H.84	Dragon	1933	D.H. Gipsy Major	130 x 2	4500	3
D.H.87A	Hornet Moth	1935	D.H. Gipsy Major	130	1950	2
D.H.87B	Hornet Moth	1936	D.H. Gipsy Major	130	1950	8
D.H.89	Dragon Rapide	1935	D.H. Gipsy Six	205 x 2	5550	16
D.H.90	Dragonfly	1936	D.H. Gipsy Major	130 x 2	4000	8
D.H.94	Moth Minor	1939	D.H. Gipsy Minor	90	1550	1

Aircraft Produced by DH Canada under Licence

Designation	Name	Engine	Horsepower	Years	Production Military	Civil	Total
D.H.82A (Can)	Tiger Moth	Gipsy Major I	130 bhp	1938-39	25	3	28
D.H.82C1 & 3	Tiger Moth	Gipsy Major IC*	142 bhp	1940-42	1384	–	1384
D.H.82C2 & 4	Menasco Moth	Pirate D4	125 bhp	1940-41	136	–	136
D.H.83C	Fox Moth	Gipsy Major IC	142 bhp	1945-47	–	53	53
D.H.98	Mosquito	Packard Merlin 67	2 x 1705 bhp	1942-45	1133	–	1133
Avro 652	Anson II	Jacobs L6MB	2 x 330 bhp	1941-43	375	–	375
Grumman CS2F-1 & 2	Tracker	Wright R1820-82	2 x 1525 bhp	1955-57	100	–	100

* The Gipsy Major, series I, originally developed 130 hp at 2,350 rpm, with a 5.25:1 compression ratio. It was improved for the D.H.82C Tigers in Canada with the use of leaded fuel, aluminum cylinder heads and dome-forged pistons and called the IC. This new version had a 6:1 compression ratio and developed 142 hp at 2,350 rpm. The Major IC was used in the postwar Fox Moth and the early Chipmunk before changing to the Gipsy Major 10 of 145 bhp at 2,550 rpm.

DH Canada Designs Manufactured in Canada to December 31, 1998

Designation	Name	Engine	Horsepower	Years	Delivered		
					Military	Civil	Total
DHC-1	Chipmunk	Gipsy Major 1C & 10	142 & 145 bhp	1946-56	153	64	217*
DHC-2 Mk.I	Beaver	P&W R-985	450 bhp	1947-67	1098	533	1631
DHC-2 Mk.II	Leonides Beaver	Alvis Leonides 502/4	570 bhp	1953	–	1	1
DHC-2 Mk.III	Turbo Beaver	P&W PT6A-6	550 shp	1963-68	–	60	60
DHC-3	Otter	P&W R-1340 (geared)	600 bhp	1951-67	335	131	466
DHC-4	Caribou	P&W R-2000-7M2	2 x 1450 bhp	1958-73	293	14	307
DHC-5	Buffalo	GE T-64	2 x 3133 shp	1964-88	121	–	121
DHC-6 (100)	Twin Otter	P&W PT6A-20	2 x 579 shp	1965-68	15	99	114
DHC-6 (200)	Twin Otter	P&W PT6A-20	2 x 579 shp	1968-69	10	105	115
DHC-6 (300)	Twin Otter	P&W PT6A-27	2 x 620 shp	1969-88	38	577	615
DHC-7 (100)	Dash 7	P&W PT6A-50	4 x 1020 shp	1975-88	2	111	113
DHC-8 (100)	Dash 8-100A	PW 120A	2 x 2000 shp	1983-	10	286	296
DHC-8 (200)	Dash 8-200A	PW 123C	2 x 2150 shp	1995-	–	70	70
DHC-8 (300)	Dash 8-300A	PW 123B	2 x 2380 shp	1990-	–	145	145
DHC-8 (400)	Dash 8-400	PW 150A	2 x 4830 shp	1997-	–	–	–

* 1014 manufactured in England and 60 manufactured in Portugal.

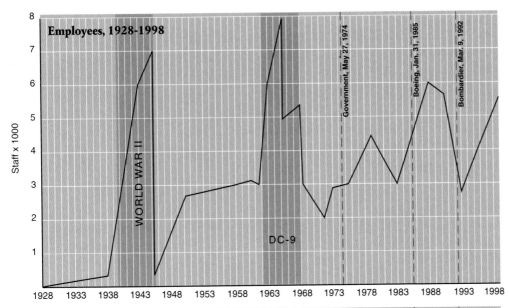

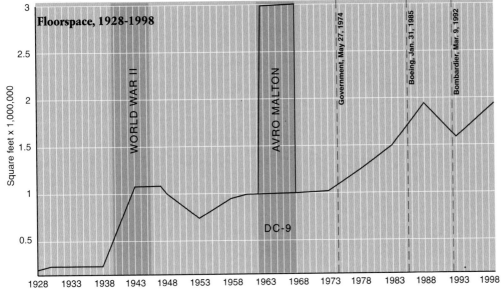

Some Aircraft Selling Prices

These are approximate prices in Canadian funds that applied when the aircraft were first offered on the market.

D.H.60M Moth	$4,450
D.H.80A Puss Moth	$6,850
D.H.82A Tiger Moth	$6,000
D.H.83 Fox Moth	$5,350
D.H.84 Dragon	$15,400

(DM&S traded in a Dragon on a Rapide in 1937 for $11,500)

D.H.87B Hornet Moth	$4,500
D.H.89 Rapide	$23,000
D.H.90 Dragonfly	$13,500
D.H.94 Moth Minor	$3,200
D.H.83C Fox Moth	$10,500
DHC-1 Chipmunk	$10,500
DHC-2 Beaver	$27,000
DHC-3 Otter	$80,000
DHC-4 Caribou	$425,000
DHC-5 Buffalo	$1,550,000
DHC-6 Twin Otter	$248,000
DHC-7 Dash 7	$1,700,000
DHC-8 Dash 8	$4,350,000

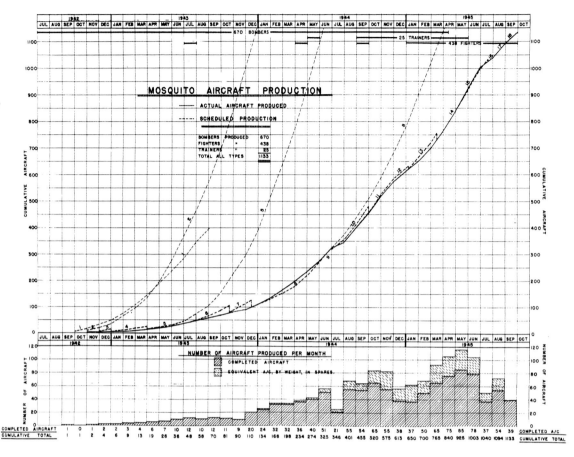

A wartime record of the much-discussed Mosquito production at de Havilland.

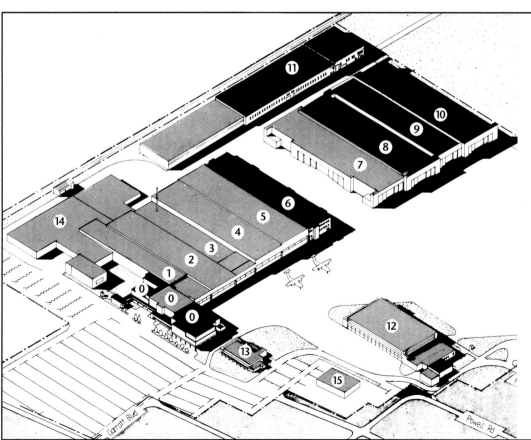

Plant enlargements in 1982 included four new bays, office expansion and a new section (11) for production machinery. The additions at that time are shown in black. Improvements since then include renovation of the office buildings (0) and the main cafeteria (13). A major addition was the Flight Safety Training building (15) behind the cafeteria with an enlargement in 1997.

0. Administration
1. Machine shop
2. Machine shop and press shop
3. Subassembly
4. Component assembly
5. Dash 8 final assembly
6. Engines, propellers and electrical
7. Flight test and paint shop
8. Global Express mod line
9. Global Express assembly
10. Dash 8–400 assembly
11. Lear 45 wings and CL415 nacelles
12. Engineering test division
13. Main cafeteria
14. Superstore
15. FlightSafety training

DH Canada Production Highlights to December 31, 1998

Type	Test Flight (Canadian)	Crew	First Delivery	Total Production	Chief Customer	Remarks
DH.82 A&C Tiger Moth	Dec. 21, 1937	P.C. Garratt	Jan. 18, 1938	1548*	RCAF	136 with Menasco D4 engines
Avro Anson Mk. II	Sept. 21, 1941	R. Spradbrow	Oct. 24, 1941	375	RCAF	Jacobs L-6MB engine
D.H.98 Mosquito	Sept. 23, 1942	R. Spradbrow, F. Burrell	Dec. 30, 1942	1133	RAF/RCAF	9 variants in Canada
D.H.83C Fox Moth	Dec. 9, 1945	G. Turner	Jan. 12, 1946	53	36 Canadian sales	One assembled by Leavens Bros. from spares
DHC-1 Chipmunk	May 22, 1946	P. Fillingham	Jan. 23, 1947	217 in Canada**	RCAF	First DHC design manufactured under licence
DHC-2Mk.I Beaver	Aug. 16, 1947	R. Bannock	Apr. 26, 1948	1631	U.S. Army & Air Force	Civil orders to 62 countries
DHC-3 Otter	Dec. 12, 1951	G. Neal	Nov. 6, 1952	466	200 to U.S. Army & Navy	Used as test bed for 2 PT6A engines
DHC-2 Mk. II Beaver	Mar. 10, 1953	G. Neal	June 13, 1953	1	DH England	Alvis Leonides engine. No further production
Grumman CS2F-1 Tracker	May 31, 1956	G. Neal, A. Verrico	Oct. 12, 1956	100	RCN	Last delivery Oct 27. 1960
DHC-4 Caribou	July 30, 1958	G. Neal, D. Fairbanks, H. Brinkman	Sept. 5, 1959	307	165 to U.S. Army	Test bed for GE T64 engine
DHC-2 Mk.III Turbo Beaver	Dec. 31, 1963	R. Fowler, J. Aitken	Jan. 25, 1965	60	Ontario Ministry of Natural Resources	Production ended June 1968
DHC-5 Buffalo	Apr. 9, 1964	R. Fowler, A. Saunders, R. Dingle	Apr. 22, 1965	121	Brazil Air Force	Production ended 1988
DHC-6 Twin Otter	May 20,1965	R. Fowler, A. Saunders, B. Hubbard	July 18, 1966	844	Short-haul airlines	Production ended 1988
DHC-7 Dash 7	Mar. 27, 1975	R. Fowler, A. Saunders, R. Dingle, J. Aitken	Nov. 21, 1977	113	Short-haul airlines	Production ended 1988
DHC-8 Series 100	June 20, 1983	R. Fowler, A. Saunders, D. Brand, G. Pyne	Oct. 23, 1984	296	Short-haul airlines	In production
DHC-8 Series 200	Jan.31,1995	W. Warner, B. Hubbard, R. MacKenzie, D. Monteith	April 19, 1995	70	Short-haul airlines	In production
DHC-8 Series 300	May 15, 1987	W. Warner, R. Fowler, D. Monteith, J. Fasken	Feb. 27, 1989	145	Short-haul airlines	In production
DHC-8 Series 400	Jan. 31, 1998	W. Warner, B. Hubbard, A. Susi, D. Monteith	–	–	Short-haul airlines	In production
Bombardier Global Express	Oct. 13, 1997	P. Reynolds, R Haughton	–	–	Corporate flight	In production

*   200 fuselages for DH England
** Manufactured under licence: 1014 in England, 60 in Portugal

Dash 8 Family of Aircraft

Series	Model	Weight lb.	Weight kg	Max. Passengers	Engines	MTOP (SHP)	Notes
100	101	33,000	14,970	40	PW120	2,000	No longer in production or in service (converted to Model 102)
	102	34,500	15,650	40	PW120A	2,000	
	103	34,500	15,650	40	PW121	2,150	
	106	36,300	16,466	40	PW121	2,150	
200	201	36,300	16,466	40	PW123C	2,150	
	202	36,300	16,466	40	PW123D	2,150	PW123C thermodynamic limits are identical to PW123
300	301	41,100	18,640	56	PW123	2,380	No longer in production
	311	43,000	19,500	56	PW123	2,380	
	314	43,000	19,500	56	PW123B	2,500	
	315	43,000	19,500	56	PW123E	2,380	PW123E has 5.5% greater MTOP thermodynamic limit than PW123
400	401	62,500	28,350	70	PW150A	5,070	Series 400 certification planned for early 1999
	402	62,500	28,350	78	PW150A	5,070	

De Havilland Canada Directors (to Boeing Purchase)

The original incorporation, March 5, 1928, was a temporary charter that allowed work to begin immediately while preparing capitalization and directors. The permanent charter was established one year later and the original surrendered on August 5, 1929.

The company was incorporated under section 118 of the Ontario Companies Act March 13, 1929, when the first board meeting was held. Authorized share capital included 25,000 Class "A" and 5,000 Class "B" shares plus 5,000 cumulative redeemable preference shares at $100 per share. The parent company main-tained control with 700 preference, along with 12,996 class "A" and 5,000 class "B" shares. Other holders of Class "A" were: W.R.P. Parker, 2,699; R.A. Loader, 449: V.S. Bennett, 200; J.H. Black, 499: and W. Zimmerman, 8,140. A brokerage company, K.F. McLaren and Company Limited, took 2,300 of the preference shares on the first day they were offered. There were minority shareholders at DHC until the Canadian government took over the company in 1974.

Directors elected from the first meeting of the board, March 13, 1929, to the beginning of the Boeing period.

Name	Elected–Retired
Provisional	
A. J. Thompson	
R.A. Loader*	
L.E. Blackwell	
K.D. Haywood	
W. Zimmerman	
G.J. Mickleborough	
Electa Coates	
Gertrude V. Lyons	
W.R.P. Parker	1929–1934
J.H. Black	1929–1934
Sir G. de Havilland	1929–1965
F.E.N. St. Barbe	1929–1966
C.C. Walker	1929–1936
F.L. Trethewey	1930–1939
L.E. Backwell	1930–1933
A.S. Butler	1930–1950
L.C.L. Murray*	1933–1937
A.H.K. Russell	1934–1937
W.M. Archibald	1934–1949
R.A. Laidlaw	1934–1945
G.S. O'Brian	1935–1939
G. J. Mickleborough	1936–1940
P.C. Garratt*	1936–1971
C.W.F. Burns	1937–1941
J. Grant Glassco	1940–1941
C.C. Walker	1940–1952
B.L. Smith	1940–1945
J.D. Woods	1940–1945
L.C.L. Murray	1942–1945
G.J. Mickleborough	1945–1965
W.D. Hunter	1945–1961
H.R. Smyth	1946–1949
C.H. Dickins	1947–1967
W.E. Nixon	1950–1959
R.E. Bishop	1950–1951
R. Bannock	1950–1968
W.W. Parry	1950–1966
D.G. Simpson	1952–1954
A.S. Kennedy	1954–1964
Sir A.F. Burke	1959–1963
F.A. Stanley	1961–1970
T.J. Emmert	1962–1968
N.E. Rowe	1962–1966
Dr. O.M. Solandt	1963–1966
Sir A. Hall	1964–1966
W.B. Boggs*	1965–1970
D.B. Annan	1965–1970
Sir R. Dobson	1966–1967
A.A. Bailie	1966–1968
A. J. MacIntosh, QC	1966–1974
A.S. Kennedy	1968–1974
Sir H. Broadhurst	1968–1974
B.B. Bundesman*	1970–1976
D.N. Kendall	1970–1985
D.L. Buchanan	1970–1975
W.T. Heaslip	1970–1976
S.B. Kerr	1971–1976
F.A. Johnson	1974–1976
R.M. Barford	1974–1976
J.F. Grandy	1974–1976
Dr. J.H. Smith	1974–1978
R. Bannock*	1975–1978
O.G. Stoner	1975–1976
T.M. Burns	1976–1977
J.A. Timmins	1976–1976
D.G.A. McLean	1976–1980
P. Genest	1976–1985
J.S. McLoughlan	1976–1985
G.F. Osbaldeston	1977–1979
A.M. Guérin	1978–1981
J.W. Sandford*	1978–1984
H.W. Grant	1978–1981
G.M. Pierce	1978–1980
M.A. Cohen	1979–1980
J.S. Lyons	1979–1982
R.M. Barford	1980–1983
J.E. Carstairs	1980–1985
S.N.Filer	1980–1984
R. Garneau	1980–1984
W.R. Teschke	1981–1982
B.J. Danson	1981–1984
G.R. Ritchie	1982–1983
J.I. Bell	1983–1986
J.C. Baillie	1984–1985
N.E. Halaby	1984–1986
G.H.G. Layt	1984–1985
J.E. Johnson	1984–1986
K.A. Miller	1984–1986
D.U. Pekarsky	1984–1986
I. Howart	1984–1986
A. Sarlos	1984–1986
R.G. Touche	1984–1986
J.F. Atkins	1984–1986
W.B. Boggs *	1985–1986

* Either general manager or president depending on the period.

BIBLIOGRAPHY

"A Brief Review of de Havilland Military Aeroplanes,"
C. Martin Sharp, *Aerospace*, June/July 1977.

ACAR International: Airline and Commercial Aircraft Report,
Sand Point, Idaho.

Air Pictorial, London, England.

Airborne, Toronto.

Aircraft and Airport, Toronto.

"American Mosquitos," Dana Bell, in *Flight Plan*, International
Plastic Modelers Society, Vol.3, No.2.

Aviation Quarterly, Ottawa

Bishop, Edward, *The Wooden Wonder: The Story of the De
Havilland Mosquito*, London, Max Parish, 1959.

Bombardier Aerospace Globe, Montreal

CAHS Journal, Toronto, Canadian Aviation Historical Society.

Canadian Air Review

Canadian Aircraft Operator, Mississauga, Ontario.

Canadian Aviation, Toronto.

"Chinese Air Force Mosquito Register," M.L. "Mac" McIntyre,
in the *CAHS Journal*, Vol.17, No.2, 1979.

Clarkson, R.M., *The First De Havilland Memorial Lecture*, Royal
Aeronautical Society, 1967.

Davies, R.E.G. and Quastler, I.E., *Commuter Airlines of the
United States*, Washington, D.C., Smithsonian Institution
Press, 1995.

de Havilland, Sir Geoffrey, *Sky Fever*, London, Hamish
Hamilton, 1961.

De Havilland, The Changes Ahead, John Sandford, de Havilland
Canada, 1979.

Design and Development of Weapons, M.M. Postan, D. Hay and
J.K. Scott, London, H.M. Stationery Office, 1995.

Downsviews, Downsview, Ontario.

Ellis, Bert, *You STOL My Heart Away*, Toronto, de Havilland
Canada, 1993.

Ellis, Frank, *Canada's Flying Heritage*, Toronto, University of
Toronto Press, 1954.

Ellis, John R., *The Canadian Civil Aircraft Register, 1920-1945*,
Toronto, Canadian Aviation Historical Society.

Forty Year Bulletin, Association of Polish Engineers in Canada,
1981.

Fuller, G.A., Griffin, J.A., Molson, K.M., *125 Years of Canadian
Aeronautics: A Chronology 1840-1965*, Toronto, Canadian
Aviation Historical Society, 1983.

Griffin, J.A., *Canadian Military Aircraft, Serials and Photographs,
1920-1968*, Ottawa, Queen's Printer, 1969.

Hall, H. Duncan, *History of the Second World War – North American Supply*, London, H.M. Stationery Office, 1955.

Hayes, Karl E., *De Havilland Canada DHC-3 Otter*, Dublin,
Irish Air Letter, 1982.

High Lift, Downsview, Ontario

Holliday, Joe, *Mosquito*, Toronto, Doubleday, 1970.

Hunting, Sir Percy, *The Group and I*, London, 1968.

Jackson, A.J., *De Havilland Aircraft since 1909*, London, Putnam,
1978.

Jane's All the World's Aircraft, 1976-77, London, Jane's Publishing
Co.

Juptner, Joseph P., *U.S. Civil Aircraft Series*, Blue Ridge Summit,
Pennsylvania, TAB Aero, 1981.

Just Plane Facts, Downsview, Ontario

Milberry, Larry, *The Avro CF-100*, Toronto, CANAV Books,
1981.

Milberry, Larry, *Aviation in Canada*, Toronto, McGraw-Hill
Ryerson, 1979.

Milberry, Larry, *Air Transport in Canada*, Toronto, CANAV
Books, 1997.

Molson, K.M., *Pioneering in Canadian Air Transport*, Winnipeg,
James Richardson and Sons, Ltd., 1974.

Molson, K.M., *Canada's National Aviation Museum: Its History
and Collections*, Ottawa, National Aviation Museum, 1988.

Molson, K.M. and Taylor, H.A., *Canadian Aircraft since 1909*,
Stittsville, Ontario, Canada's Wings, 1982.

"Mosquitos Over the Yangtse," George Stewart, *CAHS Journal*,
Vol.17, No.2, 1979.

Pickler, Ron and Milberry, Larry, *Canadair: The First 50 Years*,
Toronto, CANAV Books, 1995.

Propliner, Redlynch, England.

Regional Update, Downsview, Ontario

Sharp, C. Martin, *D.H., An Outline of De Havilland History*,
London, Faber and Faber, 1960.

Sharp, C. Martin and Bowyer, J.F., *Mosquito*, London, Faber
and Faber, 1971.

STOL Operation in the City Centre, Oscar Bakke, Washington,
FAA, 1965.

Sullivan, Kenneth H., and Milberry, Larry, *Power: The Pratt &
Whitney Canada Story*, Toronto, CANAV Books, 1989.

Sutherland, Alice Gibson, *Canada's Aviation Pioneers: 50 Years
of McKee Trophy Winners*, Toronto, McGraw-Hill Ryerson,
1978.

"The Augmentor Wing, Powered-Lift STOL, A Proven Concept," Donald C. Whittley, *Interavia*, Vol.29, No.2, 1974.

The De Havilland Gazette, Hatfield, England.

"The De Havilland D.H.90 Dragonfly," C. Don Long, in the
CAHS Journal, Vol.7, No.4, 1969.

West Coast Aviator, Sidney, British Columbia

West, Bruce, *The Firebirds: How Bush Flying Won Its Wings*,
Toronto, Queen's Printer for Ontario, 1974.

Westflight: The Canadian Airline Journal, Richmond, B.C.

Wings, Calgary.

Wixted, Edward P., *The Last Flight of Bert Hinkler*, New York,
Vantage Press, 1992.

Q400 No. 4006 during pre-delivery test flying at Downsview in September 1999. It was destined for Uni-Air of Taiwan. By this time Q400 orders totalled 57 firm with 66 options. (Bombardier)

INDEX

Frank Ryder from Louisiana makes his grand finale in a modified Super
Chipmunk at the Hamilton International Airshow on June 19, 1994.
Many Chipmunks are still in regular use and are favourites at air shows
around the world. (Dave Thompson)